Gardening Indoors
the Indoor Gardener's Bible

**All-New
Completely
Revised**

by
George Van Patten

For volume wholesale orders please Contact:

Green Air Products   1-800-669-2113
          or
Bloomington Wholesale   1-800-316-1306

Big thanks to Roger Thayer who painstakingly edited this book. His addition and attention to details helped make this book the absolute best possible.

I would also like to express my sincere thanks to all of the wonderful gardeners that helped to make this book a reality. Many individuals, garden center employees and owners contributed information, photos and drawings. Thank you all for your help in making the Fourth Edition of *Gardening Indoors: The Indoor Gardener's Bible* the best book possible.

Special thanks to Tom Alexander and *Growing Edge Magazine* for supplying us with information and many drawings and photographs.

Published by Van Patten Publishing
Author: G. F. Van Patten
Editors: Roger Thayer, J. Chris Thompson, E. Cervantes
Book Designer: J. Chris Thompson
Photographs by: G. F. Van Patten, J. Chris Thompson, Mike Yocina, Tom Alexander, *Growing Edge Magazine* and Nature's Control
Illustrations by: J. Chris Thompson and E. Van Patten
Copyright 2002, George F. Van Patten
First Printing
9 8 7 6 5 4 3 2 1
ISBN: 1-878823-31-0

This book is written for the purpose of supplying gardening information to the public. It is sold with the agreement that it does not offer any guarantee of plant growth or well-being. Readers of this book are responsible for all plants cultivated. You are encouraged to read any and all information available about indoor gardening and gardening in general to develop a complete background on the subjects, so you can tailor this information to your individual needs. This book should be used as a general guide to gardening indoors and not the ultimate source.

The author and Van Patten Publishing have tried, to the best of their ability, to describe all of the most current methods to garden successfully indoors. However, there may be some mistakes in the text that the author and publisher were unable to detect. This book contains current information up to the date of publication.

Neither publisher nor the author endorses any products or brand names that are mentioned or pictured in the text. Products are pictured or mentioned for illustration only.

NOTE: The cover is a montage of photographs taken by J. Chris Thompson in the Netherlands. The inset photo is of television personality, Mike Yocina.

Special thanks to the following companies that provided photos and artwork for the Fourth Edition of *Gardening Indoors*. We could not have produced this fine book without your help.

Canada
  Arista Wholesale Garden Supply, Delta, BC
  B & B Hydroponics, Ottawa, ON
  Brite-Lite, Laval, PQ
  EPI Products, North York, ON
  Grower's Choice, Langly, BC
  Homegrown Hydroponics, Toronto, ON
  Hydroculture Guy Dionne, Montreal, PQ
  Rambridge Distribution, Calgary, AB
  Sure Growth Distribution, Delta, BC
  Sweet Hydroponics, Renfrew, ON

Europe
  Floriade, Amsterdam, Netherlands
  Gavita Lighting, Norway

United States
  A.J. Hamilton & Associates, Denver, CO
  Alternative Garden Supply, Chicago, IL
  American Agriculture, Portland, OR
  American Hydroponics, Arcata, CA
  Eco Enterprises, Seattle, WA
  Everybody's Garden Center, Portland, OR
  Green Air Products, Gresham, OR
  Green Thumb Hydroponics, Underhill, VT
  Harvest Moon Hydroponics, Cheektowaga, NY
  Hydrofarm, Petaluma, CA
  Nature's Control, Medford, OR
  Sunlight Supply, Vancouver, WA
  Urban Flora, Portland, OR
  Worm's Way, Bloomington, IN

If you have any color photos of hydroponic and indoor gardens for the next edition of this book in 2003, please contact us at vanpatten@gardeningindoors.com. We would love to see the photos and possibly include them in our updated edition.

Sincerely yours,

George F. Van Patten

George F. Van Patten

Table of Contents

Gardening Indoors

This book will give you a simple, complete, description of basic and advanced indoor gardening techniques gardeners from North America, Europe, United Kingdom, Australia and New Zealand employ to grow garden-fresh produce and ornamentals year-round. High Intensity Discharge (HID) lamps make the indoor art and science of growing plants expand all over the world. Since the 1980s, when indoor gardeners discovered HID lighting, they have used them as a "substitute sun."

Gardeners must consider many different factors when contemplating an indoor garden. Even more important, indoor horticulturists must monitor and control environmental factors, plus understand the needs of different plants to grow a great garden. This book leads indoor gardeners through the entire indoor gardening process, step-by-step. You will find the answers to virtually all your important indoor garden questions in the following pages.

Icons with text are included to help you remember important points.

Rules of Thumb are given for a quick, easy reference. They are an easy-to-remember guide. They are based on tried and true practices that work for gardeners all over the world.

Super Size Secrets tell you how to get the absolute most from your efforts.

Technical Stuff is information that is beyond basics. Learning this information provides background and depth on the subject.

Warning! tells you to be cautious and keep from committing common errors.

A garden and Checklist in the back of the book lend additional organization for all indoor horticulturists.

Three excellent magazines, *Growing Edge* (USA), *Practical Hydroponics & Greenhouses* (Australia), *Maximum Yield* (Canada), and *Future Grow* (UK), all cover up-to-date developments in indoor gardening, greenhouse growing and hydroponics. These magazines are excellent reading material for the indoor gardener. Several other books, *The Best of the Growing Edge, The Best of the Growing Edge II* and the *Best of Practical Hydroponics and Greenhouses,* are compendiums of back articles in the respective magazines and worth their weight in gold. See advertisements in the back of the book.

Free Garden Information on the Internet!

www.gardeningindoors.com

is packed with current information on indoor growing.
It has pages and pages of up-to-date indoor gardening information.

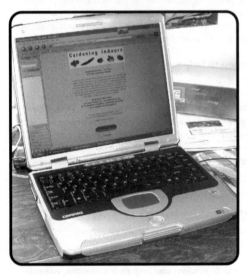

On the Internet, millions of gardeners all over the world share information simultaneously. Please surf the Internet to keep up with current information on indoor gardening. Some of my favorite web sites are:

Check out www.gardeningindoors.com for updated information on indoor growing, links and the newest information available.

www.lightingsciences.com - Light measuring
www.naturescontrol.com - Beneficial insect information
www.eharvest.com - The Canadian agriculture search engine
www.garden.com - Which is laden with garden information
www.hydroponics.com - Excellent Canadian site on hydroponic growing
www.hydromall.com - Wonderful Canadian site updated regularly
www.greenair.com - Outstanding site about plant sciences and hydroponics
www.alternativegarden.com - Hydroponics and indoor/greenhouse information

Internet information is also packed with problems. All gardeners and "authorities" have the same status on the internet and can post "facts" to their site or news group. Many times these unverified poorly researched "facts" are not true. Always play the devil's advocate and ask yourself if the information you are reading makes sense. If it sounds too good to be true, it probably is. Many times I have surfed through page after page of information before I could find something worth retaining. Information is free on Internet sites and too often sales oriented. Writers in news groups are not paid and often uninformed. However, the news groups do provide an excellent forum for discussion and sharing grow stories.

Indoor Gardening

The key to successful gardening is to understand how a plant produces food and grows. Plants have the same requirements for growth regardless of whether they are cultivated indoors or outdoors. Plants need six simple things to grow and flourish: light, air, water, nutrients, a growing medium and heat to manufacture food and to grow. Without any one of these essentials, the plant will die. Of course, the light must be of the proper spectrum and intensity, air must be warm and rich in carbon dioxide, water must be abundant and the growing medium must be warm and contain the proper levels of nutrients. When all these needs are met consistently, at the proper levels, optimum growth results.

Many flowers and vegetables are normally grown as annual plants, completing their life cycle in one year. A seed planted in the spring will grow strong and tall through the summer and flower in the fall, producing more seeds. The annual cycle starts all over again with the new seeds. Marigolds, zinnias, tomatoes and lettuce are just a few examples of plants grown as annuals.

Biennials are plants that normally complete their life cycle in two years. They bloom the year after seeds are planted and die after flowering and producing seed the second year. Examples of biennials include delphiniums, foxglove, parsley, Brussels sprouts and beets. If some biennials are planted early enough in the growing season, they are fooled into believing that two years have passed; will bloom and go to seed the same year.

Perennial plants live for more than two years. Many of the most common houseplants are leafy perennials that are valued more for their lush and interesting foliage than for their flowers. Examples of indoor foliage plants include fiddle leaf and Benjamin figs, false aralea, sansiveria, pothos, philodendrons and peperomias.

Flowering perennials that grow well indoors generally have interesting foliage, but may be a little more difficult to cultivate than indoor foliage plants. Examples of common flowering indoor plants include Christmas cactus, African violets, hoya and many varieties of orchids.

Except for a few exceptions, plants all start their life from seed. Some seeds are very small such as the lettuce, tomato or celery seed while others are quite large such as pumpkin, corn or nut tree seeds. Many plants will reproduce by cuttings or pieces of their roots such as potatoes. We will not deal with many types of propagation in this book, since the subject can become so complex. We'll only look at starting seeds and taking cuttings, the propagation methods most common when gardening indoors. See "Starting Cuttings" for more information.

Seeds are magic. Inside each seed are the complete genetic instructions for a lifetime. Plant breeding has blossomed in the past 50 years. In the last 20 years we have seen an dynamic increase in the amount of seeds that are available to the home gardener. Many small seed companies have started, providing seed from domestic breeders as well as Japanese and European breeders. Many of the seed varieties are acclimated to different geographic areas or specifically designed to grow indoors and in greenhouses. Before these seed companies, the only seeds available commercially to home gardeners were the same seeds that domestic farmers grew. Many companies offer vegetable, flower and exotic seeds. Check with advertisers in the back of the book or in garden magazines.

The seed has an outside coating to protect the embryo plant and a supply of stored food within. Given favorable conditions, including moisture, heat and air, a healthy seed will usually germinate. The seed's coating splits, a rootlet grows downward and a sprout with seed leaves pushes upward in search of light. A seedling is born!

The single root from the seed grows down and branches out similar to the way the stem branches out above ground. Tiny rootlets draw in water and nutrients (mineral elements needed for life). Roots also serve to anchor a plant in the

Roots grow through elongation. Tiny root hairs draw in nutrients and water.

ground. As the plant matures, the roots take on specialized functions. The center and old, mature portions contain a water transport system and also store food. The tips of the roots produce elongating cells that continue to push farther and farther into the soil in quest of more water and food. The single-celled root hairs are the parts of the root that actually absorb water and nutrients, but must be in the presence of oxygen. Without water and oxygen these frail root hairs dry up and die. They are very delicate and may easily be damaged by light, air or careless hands if moved or exposed. Extreme care must be exercised during transplanting to ensure success.

Like the roots, the stem grows through elongation, also producing new buds along the stem. The central or terminal bud carries growth upward; side or lateral buds turn into branches or leaves. The stem functions by transmitting water and nutrients from the delicate root hairs to the growing buds leaves and flowers. Sugars and starches manufactured in the leaves are distributed through the plant via the stem. This fluid flow takes place near the surface of the stem. If the stem is bound too tightly by string or other tie-downs, it will cut the flow of life-giving fluids, thereby strangling and killing the plant. The stem also supports the plant with stiff cellulose, located in the inner walls. Outdoors, rain and wind push a plant around, causing production of much stiff cellulose to keep the plant supported upright. Indoors, with no natural wind or rain present, stiff cellulose is minimal and plants may need to be staked up, especially during flowering.

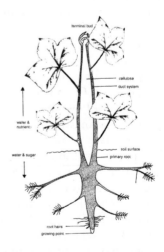

Once the leaves expand, they start to manufacture food. Chlorophyll, the substance that gives plants their green color, converts carbon dioxide (CO_2) from the air and water, which contains nutrients plus light

Plants draw in water and nutrients through the roots to manufacture food and grow.

energy into carbohydrates and oxygen. This process is called photosynthesis. It requires water drawn up from the roots through the stem into the leaves where it encounters carbon dioxide. Tiny pores located on the underside of the leaf, called stomata funnel carbon dioxide into contact with the water. In order for photosynthesis to occur, the leaf's interior tissue must be kept moist. The stomata open and close to regulate the flow of moisture, preventing dehydration. Plant leaves are also protected from drying out by an outer skin. The stomata also permit the outflow of water vapor and oxygen. The stomata are very important to the plant's well-being and must be kept clean at all times to promote vigorous growth. Dirty, clogged stomata breathe about as well as you would with a plastic bag over your head!

Flowers and vegetables flower when conditions are right. Flowering is triggered by different stimulus in different plants. One of the main variables that triggers flowering is the length of nighttime or dark hours plants receive. Short-day plants will flower when daylight diminishes and nights grow longer. Plants in this category include poinsettias, Christmas cactus and chrysanthemums. In the fall, the days become shorter and plants are signaled that the annual life cycle is coming to an end. The plant's functions change. Leafy growth slows and flowers start to form.

The majority of long-day plants bloom according to chronological age. That is, when they are two or three months old they start to bloom. Flowers such as marigolds, petunias, pansies, cosmos, California poppies, zinnias etc., will continue to bloom once flowering starts. Long-day vegetables will set blossoms that soon drop when fruit forms in the wake of the flower. Many common vegetables such as tomatoes, peppers, egg plants, squash etc., fall into this category. Vegetables grown for their roots (carrots, potatoes, onions) generally bloom before the final underground produce is ripe. Leaf crops such as lettuce, spinach, parsley etc., are very productive indoors. The bulk of these crops are consumed and little concern about maturity is needed.

Blooming is triggered in other plants by temperature. Cilantro (coriander), for example, will flower if the temperature climbs above 85 degrees F. for a few days.

Many plants are hermaphroditic, bearing plants or flowers with both male and female parts.

Some plants have both male and female flowers. When both female and male flowers are in bloom, pollen from the male flower lands on the female flower, thereby fertilizing it. The male dies after producing and shedding as much pollen as possible. Seeds form and grow within the female flowers. As the seeds are maturing, the female plant slowly dies. The mature seeds then fall to the ground and germinate naturally or are collected for planting the next spring.

Indoor vs. Outdoor Gardening

Gardening indoors is very different from outdoor cultivation, even though all plants have standard requirements for growth. The critical factors of the outdoor environment must be totally recreated indoors, if a plant is to grow well. Outdoors, a gardener can expend a minimum of effort and Mother Nature will control many of the growth-influencing factors. Indoors, the horticulturist assumes the cherished role of Mother Nature. The horticulturist is able to wield control over many factors influencing growth. Since few people have ever played Mother Nature before, they usually do not fathom the scope of the job. We must realize that Mother Nature constantly provides the many things plants require to grow. The indoor gardener must manufacture the most important elements of the outdoor environment. This requires a general knowledge of the environment about to be created as well as specific guidelines to follow.

Outdoor cultivation is normally limited to one growing season. However, two or more growing seasons are possible in semitropical and tropical climates. Outdoors, light can be inadequate, especially if it is midwinter, and you live in a city or an apartment or both. Outdoor air is usually fresh, but can become uncontrollably humid, arid, cold or windy. Water and nutrients are usually easy to supply, but acid salts or alkaline conditions could keep the nutrients unavailable to the plants.

With indoor horticulture, light, air, temperature, humidity, ventilation, carbon dioxide, soil, water and nutrients may be precisely controlled to yield a perfect environment for plant growth.

Not long ago with fluorescent tubes, this was not true. An inexpensive, easy-to-manage artificial light source, providing adequate intensity, was the main factor that limited growing many varieties of plants indoors.

Technological breakthroughs and scientific research have shed bright light on indoor horticulture, by producing the metal halide and high pressure (HP) sodium, High Intensity Discharge (HID) lamps. Now a reasonably priced artificial light source, providing the color spectrum and intensity necessary to grow any plant imaginable, is on the market. With the HID lamp, a gardener can totally control the indoor environment. The high pressure sodium lamp can be used in conjunction with a halide or in a greenhouse to augment the sun. Conversion bulbs that burn an HP sodium arc tube in a metal halide system are also available. The HP sodium emits a light spectrum similar to the autumn or harvest sun, providing the intense yellows oranges and reds necessary for forming large flowers. When an HP sodium lamp is used, flowers grow 20 to 100 percent larger than if only a single metal halide were used. By using a timer, a regular day-night schedule (photoperiod) can be set up. The HID, with a timer, may be even better than the sun! Exact control can be exercised over the hours of light per day. This control of day length lets the horticulturist create his or her own seasons. Spring and summer and fall are recreated over and over, winter is forgotten and virtually nonexistent to the indoor horticulturist!

In climates where the season is "long" (eight or nine months) a much larger selection of flowers and vegetables can be cultivated. Gardeners living in northern climates can grow tomatoes in containers outdoors until the weather cools, then move them under the halide in the basement for a complete winter crop.

Halides are also used very effectively to get an early start on annuals and vegetables. Since HIDs are so bright, the little plantlets get a very strong start in life. This strong, early start is carried on throughout life.

Flowers and vegetables can also be grown in a greenhouse. The HP sodium lamp works extremely well to provide supplemental light to natural sunlight. Young seedlings get an early start with more hours of light per day. Fruit and flowers that mature late can be forced to produce sooner. All of the extra hours of intense light will make them think it is midsummer!

Outdoors, seeds are normally sown in the spring, mature and bear fruit and flowers in the summer.

Indoors, all growth factors may be individually controlled to give the plant exactly what it needs to promote any stage of growth.

The air outdoors is usually fresh and contains 0.03 to 0.04 percent carbon dioxide. Ventilation is usually adequate, but the wind sometimes howls, burning leaves or even blowing plants over. Humidity and temperature are almost impossible to control.

Indoors, air may easily be controlled to promote growth and create an unfriendly environment for bugs and fungus. The carbon dioxide content may be enriched to double or triple plant growth. An open door and forced-air ventilation system will provide circulation and ventilation necessary to keep air fresh. Raise humidity by misting the air with water or letting water evaporate from a bucket. Lower humidity by drying the air with heat from the HID system, heater, furnace or dehumidifier. Circulation, ventilation, humidity and temperature regulation are also fundamental to insect and fungus control. Cuttings root much faster in a warm, humid indoor environment. Temperature is easy to keep constant. Usually heat from the HID system provides ample heat for the garden room. An indoor garden will flourish between 70 and 75⁰ F (21 and 24⁰ C), but most cuttings root best at 80 to 85⁰ F (27 to 30⁰ C). Air temperature may be raised with extra heat and lowered by means of an exhaust fan attached to a thermostat, if outside air is cooler.

Outdoor soil may vary greatly. It could be too acidic or alkaline, have toxic qualities, drain poorly, be full of harmful insects, fungus and bad microorganisms.

Indoor growing mediums can be purchased from a nursery in the form of potting soil or soilless mix. These growing mediums are generally certified free of fungus, insects

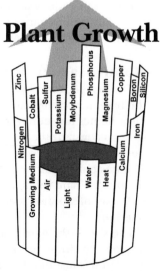

A plant will only grow as fast as the last available factor will allow.

and weeds. The mediums normally have the proper acid-to-alkaline or pH balance. Potting soils usually contain complete, balanced nutrients, while soilless mixes may or may not be fortified with nutrients. Nutrient levels may easily be checked in these growing mediums. Nutrients may then be added or leached (washed) out of containers, providing total soil control. The moisture content of the growing medium can be precisely monitored with a moisture meter and controlled. Potting soil and soilless mixes are blended to retain water evenly, provide good aeration (oxygen to the roots) and consistent root growth.

Outdoors, insects and fungi are usually kept in check by Mother Nature. Indoors, the gardener must take over in Mother Nature's absence. Keep the insects out of the garden room by simple sanitary precautions. It is easy to wash your hands, use clean tools and sweep the floor regularly. If insects and fungus do get started, they are easy to control in an enclosed room, since the gardener controls the factors that inhibit their well-being. Organic or chemical sprays are used in conjunction with humidity, ventilation and temperature regulation to control the pests.

In summary, indoor gardening can be far superior to outdoor cultivation for many gardeners, especially in northern climates. It provides exacting control of all growth-inducing factors. The indoor garden yields vine ripened produce, beautiful fragrant flowers and exotic plants the year round!

About Garden Rooms

The best location for a garden room is an unused corner of the basement. The basement is probably the best room in most homes for indoor gardens, since the temperature is easy to keep constant the year round. Humidity that would destroy the rest of the house can be easily managed in the plant room. The unsightly pots, soil and flats do not have to be shared with the public. The room is well insulated by concrete walls and soil. Basements also remain cool, which helps prevent heat build up.

The size of the garden room and the light intensity required by plants grown determine the wattage of lamp used. A 400-watt lamp is just fine for smaller rooms, spaces from 10 to 40 square feet of floor space. A 1000-watt bulb should be

Two Level Grow Room

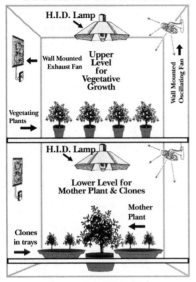

employed for a garden room of 40 to 100 square feet.

The garden room can easily be sectioned off in the basement or spare room. You can frame in quick 2 x 4 walls, screwing them to the floor and ceiling and cover the inside of the room with Visqueen, insulate the space between and cover the outside with plywood or sheet rock. If too difficult to construct a wall, set up a simple room with an Expand-A-Rail, a simple device to partition walls, available from Eco Enterprises, Tel. 1-800-426-6937.

The drawings show several common garden room floor plans. As the drawings of rooms demonstrate, there are several basic approaches to garden room production. The climate you create in the garden room depends on the plants that are grown.

A second method is very similar to the first, but utilizes two rooms. The first room is a nursery for vegetative growth rooting cuttings and growing seedlings. The nursery can also be used to start plants for the outdoor garden. Since plants are small, the room is about a third to half the size of the flowering or production room. The flowering room is harvested and the maturing vegetative crop is moved into the flowering room.

Light Mover System
with three lights constantly moving in a circle

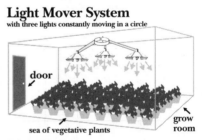

Light Rail System
with one light constantly moving back and forth

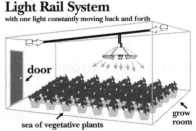

A third method provides a perpetual crop. Lettuce and leaf crops are some of the best choices for this type of garden. Several seeds are sown, or clones are taken each day or two. An equal same amount of plants are moved from the vegetative room to the flowering room. Of course the harvest is essentially perpetual!

Drawings of greenhouses:

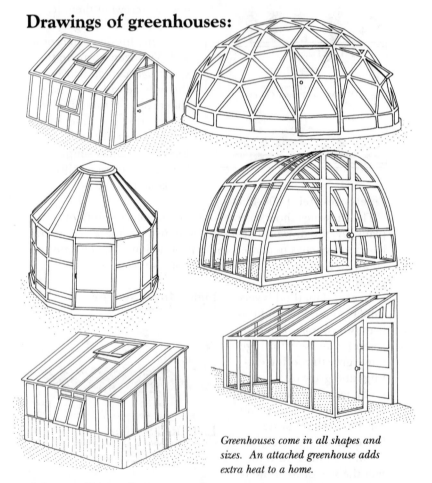

Greenhouses come in all shapes and sizes. An attached greenhouse adds extra heat to a home.

About Greenhouses

Greenhouses or growing environments using natural and artificial lighting are very productive. The same principles can be applied to both the indoor garden room and the greenhouse;

however, the heat and light intensity might be substantially different.

When combined with natural sunlight, artificial light is most optimally used during non-daylight hours. Greenhouse gardeners turn the HID lights on when sunlight diminishes and off when sunlight strengthens.

Turn the HID on when the daylight intensity is less than two times the intensity of the HID. Measure this point with a light meter. Most plants need at least 6 hours of darkness to perform properly.

Turn the HID off when the daylight intensity is greater than two times the intensity of the HID.

 Turn the HID "on" in the greenhouse at sunset and "off" at sunrise.

Supplementary lighting has greatest effect when applied to the youngest plants. It is least expensive to light plants when they are small. Smaller wattage lamps can also be used. This should be considered when budgets are concerned.

One greenhouse is double-glazed on the south, east and west walls and insulated with a reflective interior on the north side.

Developed in England, this cool-weather structure is called the Northern Light Greenhouse. Available from Gardeners Supply, 128 Intervale Road, Burlington, VT 05401.

Setting Up The Garden Room

Before any plants are introduced, the garden room should be set up. Construction requires space and planning. There are a few things that need to be accomplished before the room is ready for plants.

Step One: Choose an out-of-the-way space with little or no traffic. A dark corner in the basement is perfect. Make sure the room is the right size. A 1000-watt HID, properly set up, will efficiently illuminate up to a 10-by-10-foot room if a "light mover" is used. The ceiling should be at least 5 feet high. Remember, plants are set up about one foot off the ground in containers and the lamp needs about a foot of space to hang from the ceiling. This leaves only three feet of space for plants to grow. However, if forced to grow in an area with a low 4-foot ceiling, much can be done to compensate for the loss of height, including bending and pruning.

Step Two: Enclose the room, if it's not already enclosed. Remove everything not having to do with the garden. Furniture, and especially drapes or curtains, harbor many a fine fungi. Having the room totally enclosed will permit easy, precise control of everything and everyone that enters and exits, and who and what goes on inside. For most gardeners, enclosing the garden room is simply a matter of tacking up some sheet rock in the basement or attic and painting it flat white or reflective Mylar. Now is the best time to install a smoke detector.

Step Three: See "Setting Up the Vent Fan." Constant circulation and a supply of fresh air are essential. There should be at least one fresh-air vent in a 10-by-10-foot room, preferably two. The fresh air vent may be an open door, window or heat vent. Most gardeners have found that a small exhaust fan, vented outdoors, pulling new fresh air through an open door will create an ideal air flow. A small oscillating fan works well for circulation. When installing such a fan, make sure it is not set in a fixed position, blowing too hard on tender plants. It could cause windburn or in the case if young seedlings and clones, dry them out. If the room contains a heat vent, it may be opened to supply extra heat or air circulation. Ideally leaves should flutter slightly to ensure fresh air around the garden.

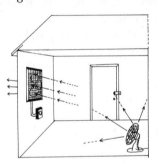

An extraction (vent) fan and a circulation fan are necessary in all garden rooms.

Step Four: The larger your garden gets, the more water it will need. A 10-by-10-foot garden may need as much as 30 gallons a week. You may carry water in, one container at a time. One gallon of water weighs 8 pounds. It is much easier to install a hose with an on/off valve or install a hose bib in the room. A 3 to 4-foot watering wand can be attached to the hose on/off valve. The wand will save many broken branches when watering in dense foliage. Hook the hose up to a hot and cold water source, so the water temperature can be regulated easily to between 65 and 75 degrees.

Step Five: Cover walls, ceiling, floor, everything, with a highly reflective material such as flat white paint. The more reflection, the more light energy that is available to plants. Good reflective light will allow effective coverage of a 1000-watt HID lamp to increase from 36 square feet, with no reflective material, to a maximum of 100 square feet, just by putting $10 to $20 worth of paint on the walls.

Step Six: A concrete floor or a smooth surface that can be swept and washed down is ideal. A floor drain is also very handy. In garden rooms with carpet or wood floors, a large, white, painter's drop cloth or thick white Visqueen plastic, will save floors from moisture drainage. A tray can also be placed beneath each container for added protection and convenience.

Step Seven: Mount a hook, strong enough to support 30 pounds, in the center of the growing area to be serviced by the lamp. Attach an adjustable chain or cord and pulley between the ceiling hook and the lamp fixture. The adjustable cord makes it easy to keep the lamp at the proper distance from the growing plants and up out of the way when maintaining them.

You will be working under the HID lamp. Make sure it is mounted firmly from the ceiling.

CAUTION! *A hot HID may break if touched by a few drops of cold water. Be very careful and make sure to move the HID out of the way when servicing the garden. If the outer bulb or shell should break, do not look at the inner arc tube. Turn off the lamp immediately. Do not look at the arc tube which produces dangerous and blinding UV light.*

Step Eight: There are some tools an indoor gardener must have and a few extra tools that make indoor horticulture much more precise and cost-effective. The extra tools help the horticulturist play Mother Nature and make the garden so efficient that they pay for themselves quickly. Purchase all the tools or hunt them up around the house before the plants are moved into the room. If the tools are available when needed, chances are they will be used. A good example is a hygrometer. If plants show signs of slow, sickly growth due to high humidity, most gardeners will not notice the exact cause right away. They will wait and guess, wait and guess, and maybe figure it out before a fungus attacks and the plant dies. When a hygrometer is installed before the plants are in the garden room, the horticulturist will know from the start when the humidity is too high and causing sickly growth. The majority of long-day plants bloom according to chronological age. That is, when they are two or three months old they start to bloom. Flowers such as marigolds, petunias, pansies, cosmos, California poppies, zinnias etc., will continue to bloom once flowering starts. Long-day vegetables will set blossoms that soon drop when fruit forms in the wake of lower light levels. Many common vegetables such as tomatoes, peppers, egg plants, squash etc., fall into this category. Vegetables grown for their roots (carrots, potatoes, onions) generally bloom before the final underground produce is ripe.

Step Nine: Read and complete "Setting Up the HID Lamp" at the end of Chapter Two.

CLOSET POTTING "SHED"

PLASTIC DROP CLOTH

Step Ten: Move the seedlings or rooted clones into the room. Huddle them closely together under the lamp. Make sure the HID is not so close to the small plants that it burns their leaves. Usually seedlings require a small lamp to be at least 24 inches away. Give seedlings between 200 and 500 foot-candles of light. You may need to cover them with a shade cloth to achieve the proper lighting.

An indoor garden tool shed is a great place to store garden tools and supplies.

Light, Lamps and Electricity

Until the 1980s, light was the limiting factor to grow medium and high-light plants indoors. Until that time, only a few dedicated gardeners, mainly African violet and orchid gardeners who used fluorescent lamps, grew indoors. By understanding how plants use light, indoor gardeners can use High Intensity Discharge (HID) lamp technology to grow spectacular flowers, nutritious vegetables and perennials indoors. We are learning more about the way plants use light every day, and the subject can become very complex. I do my best to spare the complexities and present information in terms the layperson can understand.

Light, Spectrum and Photoperiod

A plant combines light energy with carbon dioxide (CO_2) and water and nutrients to form carbohydrates, releasing oxygen as a by-product. This process is called photosynthesis. Without light, a plant's leaves soon yellow, and eventually the plant dies. Without water a plant cannot produce carbohydrates, and it starts breaking down chlorophyll to cannibalize the molecule for its carbon. With the proper spectrum and intensity of light, photosynthesis is accelerated and growth is rapid.

PAR and Light Spectrum

Outdoors, the sun usually supplies more than enough light for rapid plant growth. The sun also supplies much light plants do not use. Plants need and use only certain portions of the light spectrum. The most important colors in the spectrum for maximum chlorophyll production and photosynthetic response are in the blue and red range. Ironically plants appear green because they reflect green and use very little green light!

This main portion of light used by plants is between 400 and 700 nanometers. This region is called the Photosynthetically Active Radiation (PAR) zone. But some scientists still disagree as to the exact PAR zone and make their calculations based on

350 to 750 nanometers. PAR watts measured with this scale will be a little higher.

One nanometer (nm) = 0.000000001 meter or one billionth of a meter. Light is measured in wavelengths; the wavelengths are measured in nanometers.

 Technical Stuff: PAR watts, developed by photobiologists, are a truly impartial measure of light energy plants need to grow.

Photobiologists developed PAR watts as a measure of light energy plants use to produce food and sustain life. PAR watts are a truly impartial measure of light energy plants consume. To illustrate, a 400-watt incandescent bulb yields approximately 24 *actual* watts; a 3-K*, 400-watt halide produces about 160 *actual* watts. PAR watts are directly associated to the actual energy produced by a lamp which is defined in joules**. Almost 130 PAR watts are generated by a 400-watt HP sodium lamp. This simple example shows that a 400-watt (3-K) metal halide bulb produces 30 more PAR watts than a 400-watt HP sodium. That's about 20 percent more useable light produced by the halide, even though the HP sodium produces more lumens!

---

*Color temperature is expressed in degrees Kelvin. A 3-K lamp is 3000 degrees Kelvin. The Kelvin scale is an absolute measurement of temperature that indicates the color generated at different temperatures. Each lamp has an aggregate Kelvin temperature that denotes the bulb's color output.

**Energy, measured in "joules", is called a watt when one joule per second is produced. For instance, a 100-watt incandescent bulb uses 6 joules-per-second. This bulb is rated at 6 percent efficient – 6 percent of the electricity is converted into light-energy, the rest of the electricity dissipates as heat. High Intensity Discharge lamps convert 30 – 40 percent of the electricity they consume into light energy or watts. However, plants use just part of this light energy.

Photons are also a measure of light energy. Photons are single particles or packets that have no mass, zero electrical charge and an eternal life. Light energy is radiated and assimilated in photons. Photosynthesis is activated by the assimilation of photons. To find out how fast photosynthesis is happening, scientists measure the number of photons that fall on the surface of a leaf each second. The photons in the PAR section of the spectrum stimulate photosynthesis and are the only ones that are counted.

"**Radiant flux**" or "radiant flux of photons" is the term photobiology scientists use to describe the photons that fall on a leaf surface per second. Radiant flux of photons precisely describes the quantity of usable light that falls on a leaf's surface. Radiant flux of photons is even more complex. It is the base of measuring light energy known as Photosynthetic Photon Flux or PPF. This system counts the exact number of photons that fall on one square meter of surface each second.

Light measurement gets even more precise. Yield Photon Flux Photosynthetically Active Radiation (YPF PAR) measures how effectively a plant uses photons.

Both PPF and YPF PAR are measurement systems based on minute photons. Besides being super small, a HID generates a trillion photons every second. This is why scientists express PPF and YPF PAR in micromoles (micro = millionth and mole = atomic weight) of photons. A single mole (μmol) equals 6×10^{23} photons. Light energy, measured in watts per square meter or micromoles of photons per square meter per second, is shortened to micromoles of photons per meter^2 per second to μmol$^{-2 \cdot s1}$.

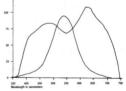

Micro-Einstein's" (Es) are occasionally used to indicate one mole per square meter per second. One micro-Es = 6×10^{23} photons that fall on one square meter of leaf surface. Using this system, the amount of radiant flux that initiate photosynthesis can be defined in micro-Einsteins, μmol$^{-2 \cdot s1}$ or PAR watts per square meter.

To further complicate light energy relative to photosynthe-

The single humped line in the center of the graph represents the visible light spectrum seen by the human eye. The dual humped line represents the spectrum plants need to grow; predominately blue light promotes vegetative growth and predominately red-orange spectrum encourages flowering and frutation.

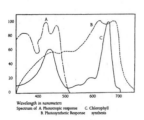

This chart shows the exact level that A. Phototropic response, B. Photosynthetic response and C. Chlorophyll synthesis take place.

sis, blue photons are worth more PAR watts than red photons, but scientists have difficulty measuring exactly how much.

To date, measuring a plant's use of light energy is in the beginning stages. Scientists continue to learn about how plants use specific portions of the light spectrum. The PAR system of measurement is here to stay and we will learn much more about it in the future. Gardeners who gauge a plant's light energy use in PAR will get the best use from their lights. To keep abreast of the newest developments in lighting technology, see earlier internet references in the Introduction and read magazines such as *Growing Edge, Practical Hydroponics and Greenhouses, Future Grow* and *Maximum Yield.*

PAR watts are the most accurate way to measure useable light for plant growth, even though virtually all light is measured in foot-candles, lux or lumens. Foot-candles and lux measure light visible to the human eye. The human eye sees much less of the light spectrum than plants "see". The eye is most sensitive to light between 525 – 625 nanometers. The importance of the blue and red portions in the spectrum is diminished greatly when light is measured in foot-candles, lux or lumens. A foot-candle is a unit of illumination equal to the intensity of one candle at a distance of one foot. The "lux" scale is similar to that of the foot-candle; one foot-candle is equal to 10.76 lux.

According to two scientifically controlled studies that compared plants grown under metal halide and HP sodium lamps; they were non-conclusive. When asked, a very big commercial indoor lettuce gardener who had tested most of the bulbs on the market for the last five years, which bulb he liked the best and why. He said, "I love the 1000-watt SunMaster Warm White. It outperformed all other bulbs hands down." To counter this empirical "fact," HP sodium bulbs grow outstanding flowers and vegetables, too. We continue our quest for more qualitative evidence on metal halides and HP sodiums.

Phototropism is the movement of a plant part (foliage) towards illumination. Positive tropism means the foliage moves towards the light. Negative tropism means the plant part moves away from the light. Positive tropism is greatest in the blue end of the spectrum at about 450 nm. At this optimum level, plants lean towards the light, spreading their leaves out horizontally to absorb the maximum amount of illumination possible.

Measuring Light

Humans "see" light differently than plants do. Compare the graphs above to see how light you "see" differs from the light a plant "uses" to grow. Plants use the photosynthetically active response or PAR portion of the spectrum. Humans use the central portion of the spectrum, while plants are able to use some portions of the spectrum that is not measured by popular light meters.

Light is also measured in spectrum with Kelvin temperature expressing an exact color the bulb emits. Bulbs with a Kelvin temperature from 3000 to 5500 are best for growing plants indoors. The PAR section explains that plants use specific portions of the spectrum, a complete range from blues to reds. Lamps that have a similar spectrum to PAR-rated bulbs can use Kelvin temperature of a bulb to ascertain the approximate PAR rating of the lamp. Kelvin temperature renders the color of the light. Color spectrum is a result of a specific mix of different colors. HID bulbs are similar in spectrum, with few surprises. That is, the same amount of halogen or sodium metal is in the arc tube and the color rendition in similar bulbs (e.g. phosphor coated, clear, conversion).

Light Meters

Most commercial light meters measure light in foot-candles or lux. Both scales of light are the ones the human eye "sees." These meters measure only the light the human eye reacts to. They do not measure photosynthetic response to light, they measure intensity in relation to the human eye. See PAR watts.

I have seen many different studies that measure light using foot-candles and lux. These studies are very valuable because they record the amount of reflected light spread over a specific surface. The spectrum of the lamp is another matter entirely. Regardless of the lamp used, providing the arc tubes and outer envelopes are consistent, the amount of light reflected is always constant. Once the best reflective hood for the specific application is found and used with a PAR bulb should produce good results.

Although this simple light meter measures light in foot-candles rather than PAR, it still gives an accurate idea of light distribution.

Photoperiod

The photoperiod is the relationship between the duration of the light period and dark period. The photoperiod affects the life cycle of all plants. Many plants will stay in the vegetative growth stage as long as an 18 – 24-hour light and a 6 – 0-hour dark photoperiod is maintained. Eighteen hours of light per day will give photoperiodic responsive plants all the light needed to sustain vegetative growth. Plants need their "rest" just like people. Many plant functions "reverse" at night, which keeps them healthy. Oxygen and CO_2 cycles actually reverse to cleanse plants.

Photoperiodic reactive plants, also called short-day plants, are signaled by short days and long nights that autumn is coming and to start flowering and producing seed. Many plants fall into this classification, including chrysanthemums, Christmas cactus, some snapdragons, Napa cabbage and cockle burrs. Short-day plants bloom when the days are short (12 hours) and the nights are long (12 hours). Blooming can be stopped by giving short-day plants a few minutes of light during the long night period.

Rule of Thumb: *The photoperiod is the relation between night (dark) and day (light) in 24 hours. A 12-hour photoperiod induces short-day plants to bloom.*

Technical Stuff: *Keep chrysanthemums and Christmas cactus from blooming by turning on the lights during the dark period for a minute or more two or three times a night to keep them from flowering.*

The photoperiod signals plants to start flowering; it can also signal them to stay in (or revert to) vegetative growth. Short-day plants must have 12 hours of uninterrupted, total darkness to flower properly. Tests have shown that even dim light during the dark period in the pre-flowering and flowering stages prevents short-day plants from blooming. When the 12-hour dark period is interrupted by light, short-day plants get confused. The light is signaling plants: "it's daytime, start vegetative growth." Given this light signal, plants start vegetative growth and flowering is retarded or stops.

Short-day plants will not stop flowering if the lights are turned on for a few minutes once or twice during the flowering cycle. If a light is turned on or daylight enters the garden room during the dark period, it should be as dim as possible to cause the minimum effect. Short-day plants will stop flowering, reverting to vegetative growth, if they are exposed to light every night for several consecutive days. Smart gardeners play it safe and keep the lights out at night!

The smart way to visit a garden room during the dark period is to illuminate it with a green light. Short-day plants do not respond to the green portion of the light spectrum.

 Rule of Thumb: Use a green light when visiting a garden room at night.

Rule of Thumb: Short day plants must have 12 hours of uninterrupted, total darkness to flower properly.

Some gardeners prefer to leave the light on 24 hours a day. Most mature plants can process only 16 – 18 hours of light per day efficiently. After that, a point of diminishing returns is reached and the electricity is used inefficiently. I advise to turn lights off after 18 hours and give all plants at least 6 hours of darkness.

Experiments with short-day plants show that if the light is turned off for 6 hours and on for 12 hours, plants can actually live a faster life. That is, a short-day plant can actually live a 24-hour day in 18 hours. But, this bit of trivia is more scientific jousting than practical application, and no electricity is saved.

Intensity

HIDs are bright, very, very bright. Gardeners who manage the light intensity properly harvest bigger flowers and super size vegetables. Intensity is the magnitude of light energy per unit of area. It is greatest near the bulb and diminishes the further away from the source. The "light and distance" chart demonstrates how rapidly light intensity diminishes. The "light and distance chart" demonstrates that light diminishes to the square of the distance. For example, plants that are four feet from a lamp receive one-sixteenth the amount of light than plants one foot away! A metal halide that emits 115, 000 lumens yields a paltry 7,180 lumens four feet away. A 400-watt HP sodium that emits 50,000 initial lumens yields 3,100 lumens four feet away. Couple this meager sum with a poorly designed reflective hood and much light efficiency is lost! The closer plants are to a light source the more lumens they receive and the better they grow, as long as they are not so close that heat from the lamp burns foliage.

Super Size Secret*: Keep plants at least 12 inches away from a lamp on a light mover. The closer a lamp is to plants without burning them, the more light plants get.*

Technical Stuff*: Hang a small plastic bottle full of water near the canopy of the garden below the bulb. Measure the temperature of the water with a digital thermometer regularly. Move the light up and down so the water stays between 75 and 95 degrees. Do not let the water/foliage temperature climb above 104 degrees F., at this point essential oils volatize, stomata close and plant processes shut down.*

Rule of Thumb: *Hang 1000- and 600-watt bulbs 24 – 36 inches above plants, 400-watt bulbs 18 – 24 inches and smaller HIDs 6 – 12 inches above garden canopy.*

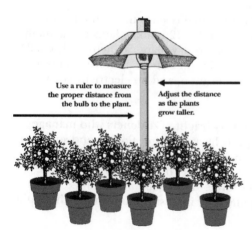

Use a ruler to measure the proper distance from the bulb to the plant.

Adjust the distance as the plants grow taller.

Tie a string 12 – 36 inches long to the HID reflector. Use the string to measure the distance between the bulb and plant canopy.

Intensity = light output/distance squared.

A 1,000-watt standard metal halide emits from 80,000 – 110,000 initial

Light strength diminishes exponentially as it moves away from the source.

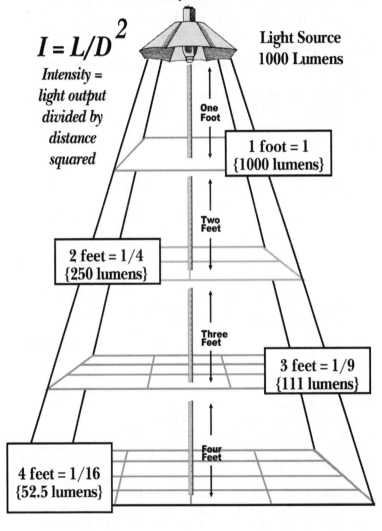

$$I = L/D^2$$

Intensity = light output divided by distance squared

**Light Source
1000 Lumens**

One Foot

1 foot = 1
{1000 lumens}

Two Feet

2 feet = 1/4
{250 lumens}

Three Feet

3 feet = 1/9
{111 lumens}

Four Feet

4 feet = 1/16
{52.5 lumens}

This is the most important graph in this book. Never forget that light intensity diminishes (exponentially) fast!

lumens and 65,000 – 88,000 average (mean) lumens. One lumen is equal to the amount of light emitted by one candle that falls on one square foot of surface one foot away. Super halides emit 115,000 initial lumens and 92,000 mean lumens. A 1000-watt HP sodium emits 140,000 initial lumens and a 600-watt HP sodium 90,000. Watt for watt, that's 7 percent more lumens than the 1000-watt HPS. Lumens *emitted* are only part of the equation. Lumens *received* by the plant are much more important.

Lumens received are measured in watts-per-square-foot or in foot-candles (f.c.). One foot-candle equals the amount of light that falls on one square foot of surface located one foot away from one candle.

A 175-watt HID yields enough light to supply all the light necessary to grow high light plants in a 2 x 2-foot. Notice how fast light intensity diminishes more than a foot from the bulb.

A 250-watt HID will illuminate up to a 3-foot square area. Keep the bulb from 12 – 18 inches above plants.

A 400-watt HID delivers plenty of light to illuminate a 4 x 4-foot area well. Hang the lamp from 12 – 24 inches above the canopy of the garden.

A 1000-watt HID illuminates a 6 x 6-foot area well. Some reflective hoods are designed to throw light over a rectangular area. Large 1000-watt HIDs can burn foliage if located closer than 24 inches from plants. Move HIDs closer to plants when using a light mover.

Watts-per-square-foot is easy to calculate, but an erroneous way to determine useable light for a garden. It measures how many watts are available from a light source in an area. For example, a 400-watt incandescent bulb emits the same watts-per-square-foot as a 400-watt metal halide. The effectiveness of the reflector is not considered in mounting height. Nor does it consider PAR watts or efficiency of the bulb.

Calculating foot-candles or lux is a more accurate way to estimate the amount of light plants receive, but still lacks the precision of measuring how much light is used by plants. If you start with a bulb that is rated in PAR watts, using a foot-candle or lux meter will suffice.

Super Size Secret: Try this simple test above. You will see how rapidly light intensity diminishes.

To demonstrate how dim light intensity retards plant development, check out an outdoor vegetable garden. Have you ever planted 65-day broccoli that took 100 days to mature? Most gardeners have suffered this fate. Did the plants get full sun all day long? The seed vendor assumes seeds were planted under perfect conditions – full sun and perfect temperature range. Plants that received less PAR light matured slowly and produced less than ones getting full sun all day long. It is the same in an indoor garden; plants that receive less light grow poorly.

Rule of Thumb: If plants get less intense or filtered light, they will yield less and mature slowly.

Lamp Spacing

When light intensity is low, plants s-t-r-e-t-c-h for it. Low light intensity is often the result of a lamp that is located too far away from plants. Dim light causes sparse foliage and spindly branches that are further apart on the stem.

Increase yield by giving growing area uniform light distribution. Uneven light distribution causes strong branch tips to grow towards the intense light. Foliage in dimly lit areas is shaded when light distribution is uneven.

Reflective hoods ultimately dictate the actual distance apart and how far above the plants lamps are spaced. Virtually all stationary lamps have bright (hot) spots that plants grow toward. Growing tips thrive in the bright spot around lamps.

HID light is most efficient when emitted from many points. Light is bound to the "Inverse Square Rule," it diminishes to the square of the distance; light fades very, very fast. Gardeners have several options to solve this problem:

Use high-wattage lights
Place lights closer to plants
Use more lights
Use efficient reflective hoods
Use white paint or reflective Mylar.

High-wattage lamps – 400, 600, 1000, 1100 watts – yield a higher lumen-per-watt conversion than smaller bulbs. Even if

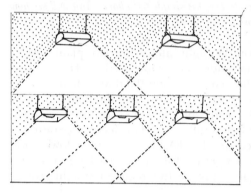

Three 600-watt HIDs actually deliver more light to plants than two 1000-watt HIDs. Smaller HIDs provide three points of light and can be located closer to plants.

large wattage lamps are spaced farther away from plants than 400- and 600-watt lamps, they still deliver more actual growing light.

Even though 400-watt lamps produce fewer lumens-per-watt, when properly setup, they actually deliver more useable light to plants. The 600-watt bulb has the highest lumen-per-watt conversion (150 LPW) and can be placed closer to the canopy of the garden than 1000- or 1100-watt bulbs.

Get the lamp as close as possible to the garden. But when using a 1000-watt HID lamp that emits lots of light, it also radiates lots of heat and the bulb must be farther away from the plants, so the heat it produces does not burn them. It is often more effective to use smaller wattage bulbs. For example, two 400-watt bulbs can be placed closer to plants than one 1000-watt bulb. The disadvantage is that two 400-watt systems cost more than one 1000-watt system.

 Super Size Secret: *Light intensity virtually doubles every 6 inches closer a HID is to the canopy of a garden.*

The benefits of using lower wattage bulbs include:

More point sources of light
More even distribution of light
Able to place bulbs closer to garden

Check out the diagrams that show the difference in useable light in different sized growing areas. Gardeners that use these drawings fine-tune the area with a hand-held light meter.

When we look at a few very simple mathematical examples, you will see how much more efficient it is to use lower wattage 400- and 600-watt lamps and space them properly.

For example, a 1000-watt lamp that produces 100,000 lumens at the source produces the following:

The goal is to give plants 10,000 lumens.

1000 watt (LPW = 140)
1 foot away	140,000 lumens
2 feet away	35,000 lumens
3 feet away	15,555 lumens
4 feet away	9,999 lumens

1000-watt HP sodium @ 4 feet = 10,000 lumens –
4 x 4 = ` square feet, 1000 watts / 16 square feet = **62.5 watts per square foot.**

1000 watt (LPW = 115)
1 foot away	115,000 lumens
2 feet away	28,750 lumens
3 feet away	12,777 lumens
4 feet away	8,214 lumens

1000-watt metal halide @ 3.25 feet = 10,000 lumens –
3.25 x 3.25 = 12.25 square feet, 1000 watts / 12.25 = **81.6 watts per square foot.**

600 watt (LPW = 150)
1 foot away	90,000 lumens
2 feet away	22,500 lumens
3 feet away	9,999 lumens
4 feet away	6,428 lumens

600-watt HP sodium @ 3 feet = 10,000 lumens –
3 x 3 = 9 square feet, 600 watts / 9 = **66 watts per square foot**

400 watt (LPW = 125)
1 foot away	50,000 lumens
2 feet away	12,500 lumens
3 feet away	5,555 lumens
4 feet away	3,571 lumens

400-watt HP sodium @ 2.25 feet = 10,000 lumens –
2.25 x 2.25 = 5 square feet, 400 watts / 5 square feet = **80 watts per square foot.**

400 watt (LPW = 100)

1 foot away	40,000 lumens
2 feet away	10,000 lumens
3 feet away	4,444 lumens
4 feet away	2,857 lumens

400-watt metal halide @ 2 feet = 10,000 lumens –
2 x 2 = 4 square feet, 400 watts / 4 = **100 watts per square foot**

If you use three 600-watt HP sodium lamps, you get a total of 270,000 lumens at a cost of $0.18 per hour (cost per KWH = $0.10)

If you use two 1000-watt HP sodium lamps, you get a total of 280,000 lumens at a cost of $0.20 per hour.

If using the examples above, you will see the 1000-watt HP sodium offers more watts per square foot to achieve the desired lumen output of 10,000. However, the bulb also produces a hot spot near the center of the illuminated area. Plants tend to grow into the hot spot and shade other plants.

Although lower wattage 400-watt lamps yield a lower lumen-per-watt conversion, they may be more efficient than higher wattage bulbs when used properly. One 1000-watt halide produces 115,000 initial lumens and a 400-watt halide only 40,000. This means each 400-watt lamp must be located closer to the canopy of the garden to get a similar amount of light. It also means that several different point sources keep light distribution intense and even.

Side lighting also helps light distribution. Side lighting is not as efficient as lighting plants from above. Light must penetrate the foliage of the side

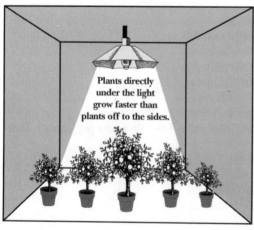

Light intensity is brightest directly under the bulb. Arrange plants under lamps so they receive the same

Plants directly under the light grow faster than plants off to the sides.

area is usually dense with foliage
that has a lower hormonal concentration. This area will grow more
slowly.

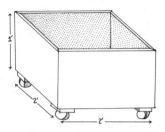

Rotating plants will help ensure
they get more even distribution of
light. Gardeners rotate plants every
day or two by moving them one
quarter to one-half turn. Rotating
keeps the plants growing evenly so
that foliage develops fully.

*Rotate and move plants in the gar-
den with wheels on a planter box.*

Move plants around under the lamp so that they receive the
most possible light. Move smaller plants toward the center and
taller plants toward the outside of the garden. Set small plants
up on a stand to even out the garden profile. Arranging plants
in a concave shape (stadium method) under the lamp so that
all plants receive the same amount of light. Placing the garden
on wheels makes moving heavy containers very easy.

Side lighting is another way to balance light. Of course this
uses more electricity, but increases the amount of light available to the plants. The lamps are mounted where light intensity is marginal, along the walls, to provide sidelight. If you are
really into getting the most light into the garden possible, you
may want to employ all of these methods: side lighting, a light
mover, white paint, Mylar, or other reflective materials.

You can also take advantage of the different levels of light
below the HID and place seedlings and cuttings that require
low light levels on the perimeter and high light flowering
plants under bright bulbs.

Some reflective hoods reflect light more evenly than others.
A reflector that distributes light evenly, with no hot spots, can
be placed closer to plants without burning them in a "hot
spot." These hoods are most efficient because the lamp is closer and the light more intense. Remember, light fades fast, and
the closer the light is to the plant, the better. The farther the
lamp is from the garden, the less light plants receive. For
example, a 1000-watt reflector with a "hot spot" must be placed
3 feet above the garden. A 600-watt lamp with a reflector that
distributes light evenly can be placed only 1.5 feet above the
garden. When placed closer a 600-watt system shines as much
light on the garden as the 1000-watt system!!

Rule of Thumb: *Keep HID 6 – 12 inches above garden.*
Tender clones, seedlings and transplants require 24 – 36 inches
and may require shading.

When light shines on a garden, the leaves near the top of
plants get more intense light than the leaves at the bottom.
The top leaves shade the bottom leaves, absorbing light energy,
making less light energy available to lower leaves. If the lower
leaves do not receive enough light, they yellow and die. Do
not pick off perfectly good leaves so lower foliage gets more
light! For example, tall 6 – 8-foot tomato plants take longer to
grow and yield more overall than shorter 4-foot plants. Taller
6-foot plants have large flowers and fruits on the top 3 – 4-feet,
and spindly growth nearer the bottom, due to lack of light.
Indoors with a lack of wind and rain to strengthen stems, tall
plants tend to develop flowers and fruit so heavy that the stem
cannot support the weight and staking is often necessary.
Short plants support the weight better.

Rule of Thumb: *High light plants more than 3 – 4 feet tall*
may need to be staked.

Young seedlings and cuttings can be huddled directly under
a single HID. The young plants will need more space as they
grow. If packed too closely together, plants sense the shortage
of space and do not grow to their maximum potential. Leaves
from one plant that shade another plant's foliage slow overall
plant growth. It is very important to space young plants just far
enough apart, so their leaves do not touch. This will keep
shading to a minimum and growth to a maximum. Check and
alter the spacing every few days.

Reflective Hoods

Reflective hoods increase available light by more than 30 percent. The proper reflective hood over the lamp and reflective
walls can double or triple the growing area. Gardeners who
use the most efficient reflective hoods can harvest up to twice
as much produce as those who don't.

Reflective hoods come in all shapes and sizes; some are more
efficient than others for specific applications. The trick is to
buy the proper reflective hood for the proper application.

Seedlings, cuttings and plants in the vegetative growth stage need less light than flowering plants, because their growth requirements are different. For the first few weeks of life, seedlings and clones can easily survive beneath fluorescent lights. Vegetative growth requires a little more light. Enough light for vegetative growth is easily supplied by a metal halide at the rate of:

Light requirements for plants

	Foot-candles	Lux	Hrs. of Light
Seedling	375	4000	16 – 24
Cutting	375	4000	18 – 24
Vegetative	2,500	27,000	18
Flowering	10,000	107,500	12

Reflective hoods are made from steel sheet metal, aluminum, even stainless steel. The steel is either cold rolled or pre-galvanized before a reflective coating is applied. Pre-galvanized steel is more rust resistant than cold rolled steel. This metal can be painted, polished or textured. White is the common color they are painted. Premium hood manufacturers apply white paint in a powder-coating process. Note: there are different shades of white and some whites are whiter than others. Flat titanium white is the most reflective color that diffuses light the best. Glossy white paint is easy to clean, but tends to create hot spots of light. Sheet metal hoods are less expensive than the same size of aluminum hood because materials cost less.

Textured aluminum reflective hoods are very reflective. Textured surfaces include:
Specular (mirror)
Semi-specular (dull mirror)
Pebble tone (fine dimples)
Hammer tone (large dimples)

The pebble and hammer tone surfaces offer good light diffusion and more surface area to reflect light. Hot spots are commonplace among highly polished, mirror-like surfaces. Mirror-polished hoods also scratch easily and create uneven lighting. Frosted bulbs tend to work best with mirror-polished reflectors.

Horizontal Reflective Hoods

Horizontal reflectors are the most efficient and the best value for frugal gardeners. A horizontal lamp yields up to 40

percent more light than a lamp burning in a vertical position. Light is emitted from the arc tube. When horizontal, half of this light is directed downward to the plants. Only half of the light needs to be reflected. Horizontal reflectors are inherently more efficient than vertical lamps/reflectors, because half of the light is direct and only half of the light must be reflected.

 Super Size Secret*: The most efficient horizontal reflective hoods produce up to 40 percent more light than most vertical reflectors.*

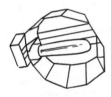

Horizontal reflective hoods can have various reflective shapes that direct the light downward. The closer the reflective hood is to the arc tube, the less distance light must travel before being reflected. Less distance traveled, means more light reflected.

Horizontal reflective hoods tend to have a hot spot directly under the bulb. To dissipate this hot spot of light and lower the heat it creates, some manufacturers install a light deflector below the bulb. The deflector diffuses the light and heat directly under the bulb. Reflective hoods with deflectors can be placed closer to plants because there is no hot spot.

 Super Size Secret*: PL reflective hoods (see drawings above) are computer designed for even light distribution.*

HP sodium lamps mounted horizontally use a small reflective hood for greenhouse culture. The hood is mounted just a few inches over the long horizontal HP sodium so that all the light is reflected down toward the plant beds but the small hood creates a minimum shadow. Several manufacturers hoods have a protective glass covering to protect the lamp from water spray when irrigating.

Vertical Reflective Hoods

Reflectors with vertical lamps are less efficient than horizontal ones. Like horizontal bulbs, vertically mounted bulbs emit light from the sides of the arc tube. This light must strike the side of the hood before it is reflected downward to plants. Reflected light is always less intense than original light. Light travels farther before being reflected in parabolic or cone reflective hoods. Direct light is more intense and more efficient.

 Rule of Thumb: Horizontal reflectors are the most effective and the best all round value.

Parabolic dome reflectors offer the best value for vertical reflectors. They reflect light relatively evenly, even though they throw less overall light than horizontal reflectors. Cone-shaped and other reflectors using a vertical bulb waste much light and are very inefficient. Gardeners that try to save money buying cone-shaped reflectors pay even more in lost efficiency.

Large parabolic dome hoods distribute light evenly and reflect enough light to sustain vegetative growth. The light spreads out under the hood and is reflected downward to plants. Popular parabolic hoods are inexpensive to manufacture and provide a good light value for the money.

Polished parabolic reflectors are dome shaped. They tend to concentrate the light directly under the source. They work best with light movers that concentrate intense light directly over plants.

 Technical Stuff: Parabolic dome reflective hoods distribute light quite evenly. They are inefficient in their use of light, but when growing clones and vegetative plants that require lower light levels, parabolic domes are a safe choice.

Four-foot parabolic hoods are usually manufactured in 9 parts. The smaller size facilitates shipping and handling. The customer assembles the hood with small screws and nuts.

For example, say you bought a cone reflective hood for $20 instead of the top of the line horizontal reflector for $40. First lets look at efficiency. The cone hood produces at 60 percent efficiency and the horizontal reflector at 100 percent, or 40 percent more. Each lamp costs $36 per month to operate 12 hours daily at $0.10 per kilowatt-hour. If 100 percent = $0.10 per kilowatt-hour, then 60 percent efficiency = $0.06, or a loss of $0.04 for each kilowatt-hour. With this information we can deduce that $36/$0.04 = 900 hours. In 900 hours (75 twelve-hour days) the horizontal reflector has recouped the extra $20 cost. Not only does the vertical cone yield 40 percent less light, it costs 40 percent more to operate! When this 75-day break-even point is reached, you will be stuck with an inefficient reflective hood that costs more overall for less lumens every second the lamp is using electricity! (See "Light Reflector Studies")

Lightweight reflective hoods with open ends or plenty of vents dissipate heat the best. Aluminum dissipates heat quicker than steel. Train a fan on reflective hoods that heat up and dissipate heat slowly. Extra air flows directly through the hood and around the bulb in open-end fixtures to cool the bulb and the fixture.

Because artificial light fades as it travels from its source (the bulb), the closer you put the reflector to the bulb, the more intensely light will be reflected.

Enclosed hoods with a glass shield that covers the bulb operate at higher temperatures but keeps water from causing damage to the lamp. The glass shield also serves as a barrier between plants and the hot bulb. Enclosed hoods must have enough vents; otherwise, heat builds up in the fixture causing premature bulb burnout. Many of these enclosed fixtures engage a special vent fan to evacuate hot air.

No Reflective Hood

One option is to remove the reflective hood if the garden is too tall. With no hood, the lamp burns cooler. You can paint the ceiling white to provide reflection, but somewhat less than a reflective hood. If the lamp is too close (less than 24 inches) to the ceiling, install a non-flammable heat shield to protect the ceiling. See Step Two in "Setting Up the Lamp,"

The Cage uses high-tech principles combined with simple pragmatic forces of nature to benefit growers. Direct un-reflected light from the bulb travels a short distance to illuminate plants and must penetrate a shallow mass of foliage only 6-8 inches deep. The

This vertical garden known as the "Cage" makes the best use of space and light.

bright intense light reaches more buds in this vertical garden than with conventional horizontal gardens.

Reflective Hood Study

Try the following experiment. Construct a black room, everything black inside, to measure the amount of light reflective hoods yield. Make the room 10 x 10-foot square and black. Cover the floor with black tar paper. Less than three percent light can be reflected from the black surfaces. There is no extra light in this room. Make measurements every 12 inches on a matrix marked on the floor. Mark the walls with one-foot increments.

I tried this experiment and used five different lamps in tests, a 1000-watt clear super metal halide, a 1000-watt HP sodium, a 600-watt HP sodium, a 400-watt super metal halide and a 400-watt HP sodium. The measurement to the floor was made from the bottom of the bulb and exactly three feet from the floor. Every lamp was warmed up for 15 minutes before taking measurements.

The foot-candle readings on the floor were taken every 12 inches and the results posted to a spreadsheet program. I used a simple spreadsheet graph program to present the graphic results. Some reflectors focus all the light in the center of the room and leave little for the perimeter. Other reflectors are very inefficient.

The studies show a huge difference between reflective hoods. Some of the companies developing the hoods do not test them before putting them on the market. To protect yourself and your garden, set up tests like the ones I did here to find out which reflector is the best for your needs. When making your tests, take your readings at the same locations.

When light distribution is even, the lamp can be placed closer to plants. The "Light and Distance Chart" shows that light diminishes very quickly. It shows that 3 feet from the bulb there is only one ninth as much light as 1 foot away! This evidence means that sun-loving high light flowers and vegetables grow best when a reflector that spreads the bright light in a large pattern over the garden and get the lamp as close as possible to the garden.

In general, the larger the wattage of the bulb, the more efficient it is. However, since light intensity diminishes so quickly, bulbs must be close to plants. This means that more lamps or point sources of light are necessary for even distribution of bright light.

Operating costs for three 600-watt HP sodiums are lower than the cost of operating two 1000-watt HP sodiums. The 600-watt sodiums produce more lumens for the same amount of money plus they can be closer to plants. There are also three point sources of light, which evens out distribution.

A heat vent outlet around the bulb helps dissipate heat into the atmosphere. Excessive heat around the bulb causes premature burnout. An oscillating fan pointed towards the bulb also helps and distributes heat around the room more evenly.

 Super Size Secret: *For maximum reflection, paint the inside of the reflector with titanium white paint. Titanium white reflectors produce 5 – 10 percent more light than average white paint.*

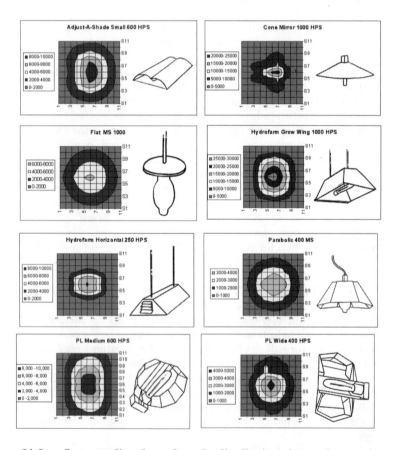

Light reflector studies above show the distribution of several types of light reflectors. The graphs clearly show horizontal reflectors deliver many more lumens than vertical setups.

Technical Stuff: *Check out the "Light Measurement Handbook" available free on the Internet. The 64-page technical book answers endless light questions. Download the book in a few minutes, photos and all: www.Intl-Light.com/handbook/.*

Water-Cooled Lamp Fixtures

Water-cooled and air cooled lamp fixtures are continuing to grow in popularity especially in hot climates. Lamps run cooler and can be moved closer to plants. Water-cooled bulbs are difficult for thermal imaging equipment to detect. Air-cooled fixtures are inexpensive to operate and easy to set up. The plastic shield around the bulb also lowers light output by as much as 10 percent. Keep outer jacket clean and avoid scratching.

Gardeners decrease bulb heat by 80 percent with a properly set up water-cooled bulb. The water and outer jacket account for a 10 percent lumen loss. Gardeners make up for the loss by moving bulbs closer to plants. On an average day, a 1000-watt bulb uses about 100 gallons to keep cool, if the water runs to waste. To recirculate the water requires a big, big reservoir. The water in the reservoir must also be cooled. Reservoir coolers can easily cost $1000. Cooling the reservoir can also solve many of your heat related problems when living in a hot climate.

Super Size Secret: *Check out the intensity "Light and Distance" chart to see what will happen if the lamps are one foot closer to plants.*

Air-Cooled Lamp Fixtures

Several air-cooled lights are on the market today. Some use a reflective hood with a protective glass face and squirrel cage blowers to move air through the sealed reflective hood cavity. The air is forced to travel around corners, which causes a higher velocity of air than necessary. The other air-cooled reflectors have no turns for the airflow so the air is evacuated quickly and efficiently.

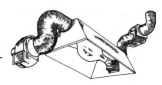

Air-cooled fixtures are economical to set up and operate. Heat from the bulb is easily channeled and vented discretely.

Reflective Light

Reflective light increases light in the growing area. Even though reflected light is less intense than original light, it is still makes gardens grow. For example, take a look at any one of the charts in the "Light Reflector Studies". Less intense light that is on the perimeters of the matrixes is wasted unless it is reflected back onto foliage. If 90 percent of 1000 foot-candles is reflected back to the garden, that's 900 foot-candles that would have been wasted. If you add 900 foot-candles per square foot of a 6 x 6-foot garden (36 square feet) you get 32,400 total foot-candles (36 x 900 = 32,400). That's light that has been paid for and light that's yours for the taking!

Reflective walls should be 12 inches or less from the plants for optimum reflection. The "Light and Distance Chart" rules also apply to reflected light. Ideally, take walls to the plants. Close walls always provide the optimum amount of reflection. The easiest way to install mobile walls is to hang the lamp near the corner of a room. Use the two corner walls to reflect light. Move the two outside walls as needed. Make the mobile walls from lightweight plywood, Styrofoam, white Visqueen plastic or Mylar.

 Super Size Secret: Flat white walls will increase light to the perimeter of the garden by 10 percent or more.

Using **white Visqueen plastic** to "white out" a room is quick and causes no damage to the room. Visqueen plastic is inexpensive, expandable, removable and reusable. It can also be used to fabricate walls, which is very handy when making partitions between rooms. Visqueen walls can expand as the garden grows, creating more reflection. Waterproof Visqueen protects the walls and floor from water damage. Lightweight Visqueen is easy to cut with scissors or a knife and can be stapled, nailed or taped.

To make the white walls opaque, hang black Visqueen on the outside. The dead air space between the two layers of Visqueen also increases insulation.

 Super Size Secret: White Visqueen walls are easy to move close to plants so they reflect the maximum amount of light.

The only disadvantages of white Visqueen plastic are that it is not as reflective as flat white paint, it may get brittle after a few years of use under a HID lamp and it can be difficult to find at retail outlets.

Using **flat white paint** is one of the simplest, least expensive, most efficient ways to create optimum reflection. Artists or titanium white paint is more expensive, but more reflective yet. While easy to clean, semi-gloss white is not quite as reflective as the flat white. Regardless of the type of white used, a fungus-inhibiting agent should be added when the paint is mixed. Choose a fungus-inhibiting agent that is not toxic to plants. Ask the paint man to add the fungus inhibitor! A gallon of good flat white paint costs less than $25. One gallon should be enough to "white out" the average garden room. But do not paint the floor white, the reflection can be detrimental to tender leaf undersides. Use a primer coat to prevent bleed through of dark colors, stains or if walls are rough and unpainted. Install the vent fans before painting. Fumes are unpleasant and can cause headaches. Painting is labor-intensive and messy, but it's worth the trouble. It helps control fungus and moisture problems and increases the usable growing area.

According to an engineer that measures light for a living, adding reflective Mylar around a garden is comparable to having other HID lights shine in from the sides. In other words, reflective light will increase the illumination at the edges of the garden substantially. For example, if 500 foot-candles is escaping from the edge of the garden and it is reflected at the rate of 50 percent, then 250 foot-candles will be available on the edge of the garden. Note the tests above used black walls so that no reflective values were recorded. This is why corner and perimeter readings diminish rapidly.

Technical Stuff: When light shines on a green object, green pigment in the object absorbs all colors but green from the spectrum and the green light is reflected. This is why we see the color green. Flat white contains little or no light absorbing pigment. Flat white absorbs virtually no light, it is almost all reflected, except for a little bit that somehow gets lost. Flat white is whiter and reflects better than glossy white. Glossy white is manufactured with more light absorbing varnish. The glossy surface lends itself to bright spots and glare. Flat white contains less varnish and inhibits the path of reflective light much less. It also has a mat texture, actually providing more reflective surface.

Foylon™ is a reflective material that reflects light and heat in an evenly dispersed pattern. I like Foylon™ because it is durable and it reflects about 95 percent of the light that hits it. The material is plied with rip-stop fiber and is thick enough to act as an insulator. It's also quite heat and flame resistant. This is good stuff and I highly recommend it. For more information on Foylon™, see www.greenair.com.

Reflective Mylar provides one of the most reflective surfaces possible. Mylar looks like a very thin mirror. Unlike light absorbing paint, reflective Mylar reflects almost all light. To install reflective Mylar, simply tape or tack to the wall. To prevent rips or tears, place a piece of tape over the spot where the staple, nail or tack will be inserted. Although expensive, it is preferred by lots of gardeners. The trick to setting it up is to get it flat against the wall. When affixed to surfaces loosely, light is reflected poorly. Keep it clean to increase effectiveness. Use frosted bulbs to prevent hot spots. Mylar is flammable and becomes explosive at high temperatures (above 1000 degrees F) so keep flames or hot bulbs a safe distance away.

Aluminum foil is one of the worst reflective surfaces possible. The foil always crinkles up, reflecting light in the wrong directions, actually wasting light. When light hits these crinkles, it is reflected in the wrong direction and never reaches foliage. It also reflects more ultraviolet rays than other surfaces, which are harmful to chloroplasts in leaves. Take a look at the reflective chart below.

Mirrors also reflect light, but much less than Mylar. Light must first pass through the glass in the mirror, before it is reflected back through the same glass. Light is lost when passing through the glass.

Reflective Chart

Material	Percent Reflected
Foylon	94 – 95
Reflective Mylar	90 – 95
Flat white paint	85 – 93
Semi-gloss white	75 – 80
Flat yellow	70 – 80
Aluminum foil	70 – 75
Black	less than 10

More Free Growing Light

Any unused light is wasted. There are several ways to get light without adding more watts including:

Use several 400- or 600-watt lamps instead of 1000s
Manually rotate plants regularly
Add a shelf
Install rolling beds
Grow a perpetual crop
Use a light mover.
Use white paint, Foylon or Mylar on walls and ceilings

Even though the lumen-per-watt conversion is lower with 400-watt bulbs than 1000-watt bulbs, hanging ten 400-watt lamps over the same area that four, 1000-watt lamps cover, provides more even distribution of light and minimizes shading. Three 600-watt lamps that produce 270,000 lumens from three point sources, instead of two 1000-watt HP sodiums yielding 280,000 lumens from two points, lowers total light output by 10,000 lumens, but increases the number of sources of light. Lamps can be placed closer to plants, increasing efficiency even more.

Manually rotating plants helps them fill out better so that the plant is evenly developed. The longer plants are in the flower-

ing growth stage, the more light they need. The first three to four weeks of flowering, plants process a little less light than the last three to four weeks. Plants flowering the last 3 – 4 weeks are placed directly under the bulb where light is the brightest and

Shelving and spacing account for much additional garden room space. Remember, plants grow wherever the light shines.

plants that have just entered the flowering stage can stay on the perimeter until the more mature plants are moved out. This simple trick can easily increase harvests by 5 – 10 percent.

When plants get big or are tied up, it can become laborious to rotate them. Difficult jobs often go undone. Save the strain and use a light mover or put the containers on wheels.

Add a **shallow shelf** around the perimeter of the garden to use light that is eaten by the walls. This sidelight is often very bright and very wasted. Use brackets to put up a 4 – 6-inch-wide shelf around the perimeter of the garden. The shelf can be lined with plastic to form a runoff canal and the shelf built on a slight angle. Pack small plants in 4 – 6-inch pots along the shelf. Rotate them so they develop evenly. These plants can either flower on the short shelf or moved under the light.

Installing **rolling beds** will remove all but one walkway from the garden. Greenhouse gardeners learned long ago to save space. We can use the same information to increase usable grow space in a garden room. Gardens that have one or more elevated growing beds often light walkways with HID light. This light is wasted. To make more growing area, place two 2-inch pipes or wooden dowels below the growing bed. The pipe allows the beds to be rolled back and forth so that only one walkway is open at a time. This simple trick usually increases growing space by about 25 percent.

Growing a **perpetual crop** and flowering only a portion of the garden allows for more plants in a smaller area and a higher overall yield. More plants receive intense light and no light is wasted in such a garden.

Light Movers

The most efficient way to replicate the movement of the sun through the sky is with a light mover. A light mover is a device that moves lamps back and forth or in circles across the ceiling of a garden room. Motorized or manual, light movers replicate the sun's path through the sky even though it does not consistently move east to west. The linear or circular path distributes light evenly. Slower moving light movers are generally more reliable than fast moving types. The fast movers often cause lightweight reflectors to wobble or list.

Light movers make bright light distribution more even. Uniform light distribution makes plants grow evenly. Branches tend to grow toward and around stationary HIDs. Some of them grow extra foliage and shade other foliage. A lamp, moving overhead increases the intense light more plants receive. This is not a substitute for more lumens from an additional lamp. It is a more efficient way to use each HID, especially 1000-watt lamps. Since the lamp will be directly overhead more plants, they all will receive more direct intense light.

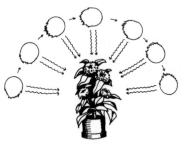

Light movers transport the HID over the canopy of the garden simulating the path of the sun. Moving bulbs can be closer to plants, which increases intensity.

 Super Size Secret: Use a light mover to get lights closer to plants. A closer light is a brighter light!

Light from a stationary bulb always shines the same intensity in the same spot. If upper foliage shades lower leaves, growth slows and is uneven. Light, received by plants from several directions, shines more intensely on more foliage. The light energy is being processed by more foliage and promotes even growth. In nature, as the sun arcs overhead, the entire plant gets full benefit of the light. This is the most efficient configuration for the plant to grow. Light gets all the way to the center of plants as well as to all outside parts.

Commercial light movers supply more intense light to more plants for less money. Gardeners report that light movers make it possible to use fewer lamps and get the same yield. Light movers increase intense light coverage by 25 – 35 percent. According to some gardeners, three lamps mounted on motorized light mover(s) will do the job of four lamps.

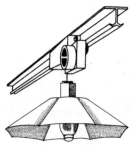

Reliable linear light movers offer an exceptional value to indoor gardeners. Light intensity increases exponentially when bulbs are moved closer to the garden using a light mover.

Gardeners prefer motorized light movers because they keep an even garden profile. Since the HID is already drawing about 9.2 amperes and is hooked up to a 15 or 20 ampere circuit, it would take another circuit to hang up another HID. The commercial mover is easily plugged into the same timer and socket as the lamp. Since the motor for the mover uses about one ampere (75 – 100 watts) of current it may be attached to the same circuit as the lamp with little risk of overload.

Benefits of a light mover:

Bulbs can be placed closer to the canopy of the garden.
Increases bright light to more plants.
Delivers light from different angles providing even lighting.
Increases intense light coverage about 25 percent.
Economical use of light.

Linear systems move in a straight line simulating the sun's path through the heavens. A linear system increases intense light to plants in a linear oval. The area covered by a light mover depends on the length of the track and the number of lamps. The systems use a track that affixes to the ceiling. The lamp moves back and forth across the ceiling, guided by the track. The lamp is fastened to the mover with an adjustable chain or cord. These units vary as to the length and speed the lamp travels. Some are designed for one lamp, while others are able to move 6 lamps efficiently. A 6-foot-linear light mover increases optimum coverage of light from 36 to 72 square feet.

 Rule of Thumb: *Young clones and seedlings might stretch, to get more light, becoming leggy, if the lamp travels too far away. Start using the light movers after the plants are 12 inches tall and have several sets of leaves. Light movers are most effective when plants are not receiving enough light from a stationary lamp.*

Homemade light movers work best for gardeners that are able to move the lamp when they look after their garden two or three times a day. These movers should be strong and move the light hood easily. Overhead rigging must be able to support the weight of the lamp and hood. If the system were to come crashing down on the garden, it would be unpleasant at best, maybe even start a fire. Make sure it is secured to the ceiling! The electric cord should not slow down or affect the movement of the light mover in any way.

Watch out for the following:
Stretched or leggy plants.
Weak or yellowing plants.
Foliage burned directly under the bulb.
Uneven lighting.
Light mover binding or getting hung up.

Construct a homemade light mover similar to a clothesline. Attach eyebolts at opposite ends of the ceiling or ceiling corners. Connect pulleys to the eyebolts. Between the pulleys, string a small diameter, heavy-duty nylon cord into a loop. Attach the HID to the bottom of the cord loop. This light mover is just like clothesline on pulleys. After the lamp is mounted on the looped cord, you can move it back and forth as often as desirable. You can also make another variation of this light mover by stretching a cord or rope between eyebolts anchored in the ceiling. Attach a single pulley to the cord. Attach the lamp to the pulley. Move the lamp back and forth on the pulley overhead. One industrious gardener made a light mover out of an old garage door opener. The possibilities are endless! When using these types of units, make sure to watch the plant profile and give the garden the most even distribution of light possible.

Homemade movers do not have a particular cycle to complete. The bulb can be placed wherever desired.

Seedlings and cuttings are huddled below the HID when small and moved into larger containers when they are crowding one another. When they are far enough apart that the light does not afford complete coverage, it is time to employ a light mover. Before this time, a light mover might not give them enough intense light and high light plants may become leggy.

Setting up a Light Mover Step-by-Step

A Sun Twist™ moves bulbs in circles above plants increasing bright light plants receive from many different angles.

Choose the right place. Affix board to the ceiling. Mount light mover track on board. Attach Sun Twist™ units to a board that is screwed into ceiling joists.

Run electrical cord via timer to light mover.

Attach supporting electrical wires with cable ties alongside track. May need to use eyelets alongside light track.

Reduce vibrations by backing the mounting board with a vibration-absorbing material.

Planter boxes or containers on wheels offer a good alternative to the light movers. The containers are rotated daily. The wheels make this job a snap. The light reaches every corner of the garden without having to move the lamp. This method has essentially the same effect as moving the lamp overhead, but is more work because all plants have to be moved, rather than only one or two lamps.

The 400-watt bulbs offer more even light distribution and the lamp can be closer to the plants since they have less heat build up than 1000-watt HIDs. The 400-watt bulbs offer certain advantages, especially if space is a problem. One gardener uses two of them in a narrow 4 x 8-foot room with amazing success. Another gardener has the brightest closet in town! The 400-watt halides do have a longer life than the 1000-watt lamps, but share the same lumen maintenance curve. For the amount of lumens produced, their initial cost is much higher. However, their life is twice as long, about 20,000 hours. Do not use a 400-watt lamp in a 1000-watt system! It will work for the first day or even a month, then it could stop working, rupture, or even explode. Use a ballast that is built for the type of bulb you have. A 400-watt bulb works with a ballast built specifically for 400-watt lamps. A 430-watt lamp works best in a specific ballast made for 430-watt bulbs, etc. Check out "Side Lighting" above for another way to add more light.

High Intensity Discharge (HID) Lights

Gardeners use HID lamps to replace natural sunlight indoors and grow strong healthy flowers and vegetables. HID lamps out-perform all other lamps in their lumen-per-watt efficiency, spectral balance and brilliance. The spectrum and brilliance of HIDs helps gardeners replicate growth responses induced in plants by natural sunlight. Compare charts on HID spectral emission with the chart on photosynthetic response, chlorophyll synthesis and positive tropism.

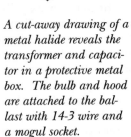

A cut-away drawing of a metal halide reveals the transformer and capacitor in a protective metal box. The bulb and hood are attached to the ballast with 14-3 wire and a mogul socket.

The HID lamp family contains mercury vapor, metal halide, High Pressure (HP) sodium, and conversion bulbs. Metal halide, HP sodium and conversion lamps have a spectrum similar to actual sunshine and can be used to grow plants efficiently. Mercury vapor lamps were the first widespread streetlights and the first HIDs on the market. Obsolete mercury vapor lamps are inefficient electrically and produce a poor spectrum for plant growth. Now most all mercury vapor lamps have been retrofitted with more efficient HIDs.

Popular HID's wattages include 150, 175, 250, 400, 430, 600, 1000 and 1100. A 1500-watt metal halide is also available but not practical for growing. The 1500-watt lamp is designed for stadium lighting and generates too much heat

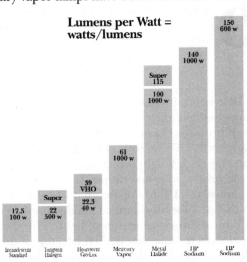

Lumens per Watt = watts/lumens

Incandescent bulbs are the least efficient and 600-watt HP sodium lamps are the most efficient.

and light to be used efficiently indoors. Smaller 150 – 250-watt bulbs are popular for small gardens measuring up to 3 feet square. Brighter 400 – 1100 lamps are favorites for larger gardens. The 400- and 600-watt bulbs are most popular among Europeans and North Americans favor 600- and 1000-watt bulbs. Super efficient 1100-watt metal halides were introduced in 2000.

The above bar graph shows the lumen-per-watt conversion of different lamps. Notice that except for the 600-watt HPS, the lumen-per-watt conversion factor increases with higher wattage bulbs. The lumen-per-watt formula is used to measure the lamps efficiency: the amount of lumens produced for the quantity of watts (electricity) consumed. The power (watts) not converted to light produces heat.

Originally developed in the 1970s, metal halides and HP sodiums were characterized by one main technical limitation, the larger the bulb, the higher the lumen-per-watt conversion. For example, watt for watt, a 1000-watt HP sodium produces about 12 percent more light than a 400-watt HPS and about 25 percent more light than a 150-watt HPS. Savvy scientists overcame this barrier when they developed the 600-watt HP sodium. Watt for watt a 600-watt HPS produces 7 percent more light than the 1000-watt HPS.

Warning! *The outer arc tube contains virtually all of the ultraviolet light produced by HIDs. Never look at the arc tube if the outer bulb breaks. The sudden, extreme exposure to UV light could be blinding. Turn off immediately!*

HID lamps produce light by passing electricity through vaporized gas enclosed in a clear ceramic arc tube under very high pressure. Ceramic and quartz arc tubes in HID lamps let dangerous UV rays pass. The glass in the outer bulb or envelope blocks UV light, which makes them safe. The color spectrum produced is determined by the dose or combination of chemicals sealed in the arc tube. The diverse mix of chemicals in the arc tube allows metal halide lamps to yield the broadest and most diverse spectrum of light. The spectrum of HP sodium lamps is somewhat limited because of the narrower band of chemicals used inside the arc tube. The arc tube is contained within a larger glass bulb. Most of the ultraviolet (UV) rays produced in the arc tube are filtered by the outer bulb. Some bulbs have a phosphor coating inside the bulb. This coating makes them produce a little different spectrum.

HID bulbs are manufactured by: General Electric, Iwasaki, Lumenarc, Osram/Sylvania, Philips and Venture. These companies construct many bulbs with the exact same technical statistics. According to some gardeners, certain brands of bulbs are better than others because of where they are manufactured. They usually come to this conclusion because they purchased two different brands of (1000-watt) bulbs and had better luck using one of the bulbs. What these gardeners don't know is that many of the manufacturers buy and use the same components, often manufactured by competitors!

Pulse-start metal halides, unavailable in North America, but common where they use 220-277 volts, harbor the starter in the ballast box and not in the arc tube. These systems employ physically smaller reactor ballasts that keep original line voltage within 10 percent of the voltage in the arc tube. Venture is currently working on such a system for North America, but at the time of publication they were still having trouble with uneven heating of horizontal arc tubes.

Rule of Thumb: Buy the entire HID system, ballast, lamp, socket, bulb, connecting wiring and timer all at the same time from a reputable supplier to ensure the ballast and lamp go together. Make sure to get a written guarantee from the dealer. Timers should be rated for at least 1850 watts, 15 amps at 120 volts.

The electricity or line voltage (1) flows through the ballast (2). The ballast is the box that contains a capacitor (3) that provides a high, fast, charge of electricity to start the lamps. Getting the electricity to flow between the electrodes (7) and (9) in the arc tube (10) requires a high voltage, charge or current. This current is sent through the starting mechanism of the lamp (5). In the HP sodium lamps, the starting electrode and the operating electrode are one in the same.

The electricity is then arced or literally shot across the arc tube (10) from

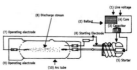

This HID system diagram shows how it functions starting with the input of electricity or line voltage.

the starting electrode (6) to the operating electrode (9) at the other end of the arc tube. As soon as the arc is established and the gasses vaporize, the arc jumps from the starting electrode to the operating electrodes (7) and (9). Once the electricity is flowing across the tube, the elements slowly vaporize into the discharge stream (8).

When the discharge stream (8) is working and the lamp warms up, the line voltage could run out of control, since there is an unrestricted flow of electricity between the two electrodes. The ballast (2) regulates this line voltage via a wire coil wrapped around an iron core (4). By employing this core (4) the lamp is assured of having a constant and even supply of electricity.

 Super Size Secret: *New metal halide pulse start lamps by SunMaster remove the starter from the bulb and place it with the transformer. This gives lamps much more efficiency and makes them burn brighter.*

About Ballasts

HID lamps all work on the same principle. However, each lamp has specific starting requirements, line voltage, operating characteristics and physical shape. Do not try to mix and match ballasts and lamps. Just because a lamp fits a socket attached to a ballast, does not mean that it will work properly in it. If you use the wrong ballast, capacitor or starter with a lamp, the lamp will not produce the rated amount of light and it will burn out sooner. The wrong lamp plugged into the wrong ballast adds up to a burn out!

All HIDs require a ballast. Wattages from 150 – 1100 use old-fashioned coil transformer-type ballasts. Smaller wattages – below 100 – use energy efficient electronic ballasts. Electronic ballasts run cool and quiet. Scientists continue to develop electronic ballasts for larger wattage HIDs and have finally succeeded. It is very important to buy the proper ballast for your HID. Whenever possible buy the assembled unit from a retailer or manufacturer. Buy a component parts kit if low on money and you want to assemble it yourself. Ballast kits may be ordered from GE, Sylvania and Universal. Assembly instructions are in the form of a wiring diagram glued to the top of the transformer.

If the white tip of a kitchen match ignites when touched to a hot ballast box, it's running too hot!

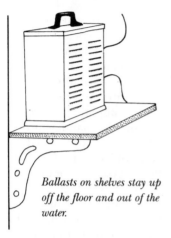

Ballasts on shelves stay up off the floor and out of the water.

The "core" or transformer consists of metal plates stuck together by resin and wound with copper wire. The capacitor can is on the right under the connecting wires. It has two terminals and is rated in microfarads (mfd) and voltage.

Electronic Ballasts

Electronic ballasts such as the one pictured here, manufactured by Sunburst/Western Water Farms, will soon become commonplace. Now at competitive prices, the ballast regulates electrical line voltage and power electronically which takes virtually no energy. The "core-based" ballasts create electrical resistance and heat, electronic ballasts make no resistance and create virtually no heat. Electricity is managed electronically. Electronic ballasts run cool and quiet. They have several other unique qualities. For example, this single ballast can be used with metal halide or HP sodium for wattages ranging from 400 to 1100! The ballast will work under 50 (Europe) or 60 (America) cycle current. That's right, one ballast for different wattages! Incredible! The ballast also has a telephone jack so it can easily be controlled by a remote signal generated by a computer. Ask your local hydroponic retailer for information or dial the manufacturer direct: 1-604-533-9301.

This electronic ballast will run 400 to 1100-watt metal halide or HP sodium bulbs all over the world.

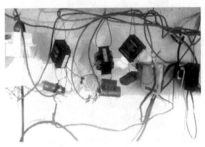

This is one of my favorite "disaster" scenes. This gardener saved money by hanging transformers and capacitors from a wire line. Do not try this at home!

Ballast kits contain a transformer core, cooling capacitor, (HPS and some metal halides) starter, enclosure box and sometimes wire. You can purchase components separately, from the manufacturers – Jefferson, Advance, GE, Sola, and Venture Lighting Power Systems – but it is a bigger hassle than it's worth. Capacitor manufacturers include Cornell, GE, Duviler and Dayton. If unfamiliar with electrical component assembly and reading wiring diagrams, purchase the assembled ballast in a package containing the lamp and hood from one of the many HID distributors.

Do not buy used parts from a junk yard or try to use a ballast if unsure of its capacity. Just because a bulb fits a socket attached to a ballast, does not mean that it is the proper system. The best way to grow a miserable garden is to try to save money on the ballast. One of the most wretched gardens I have ever seen was grown with mercury vapor streetlights and makeshift reflective hoods.

Even though HIDs have specific ballasting requirements, the ballasts have a good deal in common. The most common characteristics ballasts share are noise and heat. This noise could drive some people to great fits of paranoia! Ballasts operate at 90 to 150 degrees F. Touch a "strike anywhere" kitchen match to the side to check if it is too hot. If the match lights, the ballast is too hot and should be taken into the shop for assessment. A ballast that runs too hot is noisy and could cause problems or burn out. Heat is the number one ballast destroyer! Ballasts are manufactured with a protective metal box. This outer shell safely contains the core, capacitor, (starter) and wiring. If you build another box around a ballast to dampen noise, make sure there is plenty of air circulation. If the ballast runs too hot it will be less efficient, burn out prematurely and maybe even start a fire!

More expensive ballasts are equipped with ventilation fans to maintain cool operating temperatures. Air vents allow a ballast

to run cooler. The vents should protect the internal parts and
not let water splash in.

Some industrial ballasts are sealed in fiberglass or similar
material to make them weather proof. These ballasts are not
recommended. They were designed for outdoor use where
heat buildup is not a problem. Indoors the protection of the
sealed unit from weather is not necessary and creates excessive
heat and inefficient operation.

Make sure the ballast has a handle. A small 400-watt halide
ballast weighs about 30 pounds and a large 1000-watt HP sodium ballast tips the scales at about 55 pounds. This small, heavy
box is very awkward to move with no handle.

Most ballasts sold by HID stores are "single tap" and set up
for a 115-volt household current in North America or 220 volts
in Europe, Australia and New Zealand. North American ballasts run at 60 cycles per second while European, Australian
and New Zealand models run at 50 cycles per second. A ballast
from Europe, Australia or New Zealand will not work properly
at 60 cycles per second. Some "multi-tap" or "quad-tap" ballasts are ready for 115- or 220-volt service. Single-tap ballasts
accommodate only one voltage, usually 115. Multi-tap ballasts
accommodate either 115- or 220-volt service.

It is usually easiest to use the regular 115-volt system because
their outlets are more common. The 220-volt systems are normally used when several lamps are already taking up space on
other 115-volt circuits. Changing a "multi-tap" ballast from 115
volts to 220 volts is matter of moving the wire from the 115-volt
tap to the 240-volt tap and changing the plug to mate with a
220-volt receptacle. "Single-tap" ballasts cannot change operating voltages. Consult the wiring diagram found on each transformer for specific instructions. There is no difference in the
electricity consumed by using either 115- or 220-volt systems.
The 115-volt system draws about 9.6 amperes and a HID on a
220-volt current draws about 4.3 amperes. You save a little
when using 220-volt power. A 220-volt line looses only one
quarter as much power as does a 120-volt line. Work out the
details yourself using:

Ohms Power Law: Volts x Amperes = Watts.

The ballast has a lot of electricity flowing through it. Do not
touch the ballast when operating. Do not place the ballast
directly on a damp floor or any floor that might get wet and

conduct electricity. Always place it up off the floor and protect it from possible moisture. The ballast should be suspended in the air or on a shelf attached to the wall. It does not have to be very high off the ground, just far enough to keep it dry.

Place the ballast on a soft pad to absorb vibrations and lower decibel sound output. Vibrations caused by loose components inside the ballast can be tightened to further deaden noise. Most noise produced by a ballast is caused by vibrating laminated steel sheets in the transformer. Tightening old transformers with clamps often quiets them down.

 Super Size Secret: Set ballasts on a thick foam pad to lessen vibrations. Train a fan on ballasts to cool them. Cooler ballasts are more efficient and bulbs burn brighter.

Ballasts can be attached to the light fixture or be remote. The remote ballast offers the most versatility and is the best choice for most indoor gardens. A remote ballast is easy to move. Help control heat by placing it on or near the floor to radiate heat in a cool portion of the garden room or move the ballast outside the room if it is too hot. Attached ballasts are fixed to the hood, require more overhead space, are very heavy and tend to create more heat around the lamp. Industrial high bay ballasts are common in warehouses and large commercial buildings. These systems are designed to light a large area from 15 to 20 feet above.

Ballasts may be manufactured with an attached timer. These units are very convenient, but the timer should be constructed of heavy-duty heat-resistant materials. If it is lightweight plastic, it could easily melt under the heat of the ballast.

A good ballast manufacturer will place a 10-ampere fuse inside the ballast. This is a double safeguard against anything happening and destroying the lamp or causing a fire.

There are also ballasts that are sold to run both metal halide and HP sodium systems. These dual-purpose ballasts have evolved to the point that most are fail-safe. If you have a limited budget and can only afford one transformer, a switchable ballast is a good idea. Check out www.sunlightsupply.com for more information on switchable ballasts. Or you could use a conversion bulb (See "Conversion Bulbs") to change the spectrum from growing to flowering.

About HID Bulbs

Many new HID bulbs have been developed since this book was last updated. The most notable have been the 430-watt HP sodium, pulse start metal halides, SunMaster PAR bulbs and the 1100-watt metal halide. HID bulbs

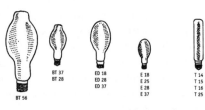

HID bulbs come in different sizes and shapes. Below each bulb are the numbers industry uses to define their shape and size.

are also available with many different outer envelopes so that bulbs can fit into more confining reflective hoods.

HID bulbs are rated by wattage and by the size of the outer envelope or bulb.

HID bulbs are designed to be tough and durable. They survive being shipped thousands of miles by uncaring carriers. New bulbs are tougher than used bulbs. Once the bulb has been used a few hours, the arc tube blackens and the internal parts become somewhat brittle. After a bulb has been used several hundred hours, a good bump will substantially shorten its life and lessen its luminescence.

Never remove a warm lamp. Heat expands the metal mogul base within the socket. A hot bulb is more difficult to remove and it must be forced. Special electrical grease is available to lubricate sockets (Vaseline works too). Lightly smear a tad of the lubricant around the mogul socket base to facilitate screwing it in and out.

 Rule of Thumb: Smear a little Vaseline on the bulb threads to facilitate insertion into the mogul socket.

If a HID should happen to break when inserting or removing, unplug the ballast immediately and avoid contact with metal parts to avoid electrical shock.

Always keep the bulb clean. Wait for it to cool and wipe it off every 2 – 4 weeks with a clean cloth. Dirt will lower lumen output substantially. Bulbs get covered with insect spray and salty water vapor residues. This dirt dulls lamp brilliance just as clouds dull natural sunlight.

Hands off bulbs! Touching bulbs leave them with your hand's oily residue. The residue weakens the bulb when it is baked into it. Most gardeners clean bulbs with Windex® or rubbing alcohol and use a clean cloth to remove filth and grime. But PL Lighting advises to clean bulbs with nothing more than a clean cloth.

Lumen output diminishes over time. This is not an excuse to use old bulbs; it is always better to use newer bulbs. However, it is a way to get a few more months out of an otherwise worthless bulb.

Write down the day, month and year you started using the bulb so you can better calculate when to replace it for best results. You can go blind staring at a dim bulb trying to decide when to replace it. Remember, your pupils open and close to compensate for different light levels!

 Super Size Secret: *Write down the date each bulb started service. Replace metal halides after 12 months of operation and HP sodium bulbs after 18 months.*

One way to determine when to replace a bulb is to examine the arc tube. When the arc tube is very cloudy or very blackened, it is most likely time to replace it.

Store HIDs that are not being used in the same box that they were purchased.

Please read the rules of disposal before laying a faithful HID to rest.

Place the bulb in a dry container and place it in the trash.

Lamps contain materials that are harmful to the skin. Avoid contact and use protective clothing.

Do not place the bulb in a fire.

Metal Halide Systems

The metal halide HID lamp is the most efficient source of artificial white light available to the horticulturist today. It comes in 175, 250, 400, 1000, 1100 and 1500-watt sizes. They may be either clear or phosphor coated and all require a special ballast. The smaller 175- or 250-watt halides are very popular for small growing situations. The 400-, 1000- and 1100-watt bulbs are very popular with most indoor gardeners. The 1500-watt halide is also avoided due to its relatively short 2000 to 3000 hour life and incredible heat output. American gardeners generally prefer the larger 1000-watt lamps and Europeans almost exclusively 400- and 600-watt lamps.

Six major metal halide manufacturers are General Electric (Multivapor), Osram/Sylvania (Metalarc) and Westinghouse (Metal Halide), Iwasaki (Eye), Venture (SunMaster) and Philips (Son Agro). Each manufacturer has a super halide, each of which fit and operate in standard halide ballasts and fixtures. They produce about 15 percent more lumens than standard halides. Super halides cost a few dollars more than standards, but are well worth the money.

SunMaster, a division of Venture Lighting, has developed new horticultural metal halide bulbs. The new bulbs are brighter and provide a spectrum better suited to plant growth. Gardeners prefer the Warm Deluxe bulbs. Check out their web site: www.sunmastergrowlamps.com.

Clear halides are the most commonly used by indoor gardeners. Clear super metal halides supply the bright lumens for plant growth. Clear halides work well for seedling, vegetative and flower growth.

Phosphor coated 1000-watt halides give off a more diffused light and are easy on the eyes, emitting less ultraviolet light than the clear halides. They produce the same initial lumens and about 4,000 fewer lumens than the standard halide and have a slightly different color spectrum. Phosphor-coated halides have more yellow, less blue and ultraviolet light. Phosphor-coated bulbs used to be popular among gardeners, but this trend has waned over the last 10 years, because they are not as bright as clear bulbs.

The 1000-watt super clear halides are the most common halides used in indoor gardens. Compare energy distribution charts and lumen output of all lamps to decide which lamp offers the most light for your garden. Typically, a home gardener starts with the one super metal halide.

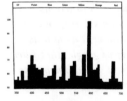

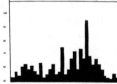

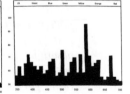

The light spectrum emitted by this clear metal halide is perfect for plant growth.

Phosphor-coated metal halides produce a little more yellow/orange light than clears.

The 5K metal halide yields fewer overall lumens, but is high in the blue end of the spectrum.

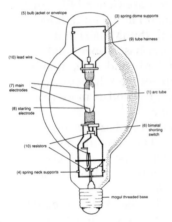

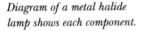

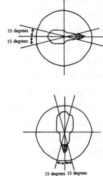

Base Up (BU) and Base Down (BD) metal halide lamps must be vertical to operate properly. Horizontal (H) lamps must orient the arc tube horizontally to burn brightest. Universal (U) bulbs burn in all positions 360 degrees. Be careful when purchasing Universal bulbs because they seldom burn as bright as a Horizontal bulb.

Diagram of a metal halide lamp shows each component.

Construction and Operation

Technical Stuff*: The metal halide lamps produce light by passing or arcing electricity through vaporized argon gas, mercury, thorium iodide, sodium iodide and scandium iode inside the quartz arc tube (1). At the end of the arc tube is a heat reflecting coating to control temperature during operation. Spring supports in the neck (4) and dome (3) of the outer bulb or envelope (5) mount the arc tube frame (9) in place. The bimetal-shorting switch (6) closes during lamp operation, preventing voltage drop between the main electrode (7) and the starting electrode (not pictured). Most bulbs are equipped with a resistor (10) that keeps the bulb from shattering under temperature stress. The outer bulb functions as a protective jacket, contains the arc tube and starting mechanism, keeping them in a constant environment as well as absorbing ultraviolet radiation. Protective goggles that filter out ultraviolet rays are a good idea if you spend much time in the garden room or if you are prone to staring at the HID!*

Initial vaporization takes place in the gap between the main electrode (7) and the starting electrode (8), when a high starting voltage is applied. When there is enough ionization, electricity will arc between the main electrodes (7). As the lamp warms up, the metal iodide additives begin to enter the arc stream. After they are in their proper concentrations in the arc tube, the characteristic bright white light is emitted. This process takes about 3 – 5 minutes.

Warning! If outer bulb shatters, turn off (unplug) lamp immediately. Do not look at or get near the lamp until it cools. When the outer bulb breaks, it is no longer able to absorb ultraviolet radiation. This radiation is very harmful and will burn skin and eyes if exposed. Be careful!!

Technical Stuff: The metal halide arc system is very complex and requires a seasoning period of 100 hours operation for all of its components to stabilize.

Technical Stuff: If a power surge occurs and the lamp goes out or the lamp is turned off, it will take 5-15 minutes for the lamp to restart. The gasses inside the arc tube must cool before restarting.

When the lamp is started, incredible voltage is necessary for the initial ionization process to take place. Turning the lamp on and off more than once a day causes unnecessary stress on the HID system and will shorten its life.

The metal halides operate most efficiently in a vertical + / - 15-degree position (see previous page). When operated in positions other than + /- 15-degree of vertical, lamp wattage, lumen output and life decrease; the arc bends, creating non-uniform heating of the arc tube wall, resulting in less efficient operation and shorter life. There are special lamps made to operate in the horizontal or any other position other than + / - 15 degrees (see previous page). These bulbs have "HOR" stamped on the crown or base. "HOR" is not an abbreviation for horticulture. It refers to horizontal.

Lumen Maintenance and Life

Metal halides have very good lumen maintenance and a long life. The decline in lumen output over the lamp's life is very gradual. The average life of a halide is about 12,000 hours, almost 2 years of daily operation at 18 hours. Many will last even longer. The lamp reaches the end of its life when it fails to start or come up to full brilliance. This is usually caused by deterioration of lamp electrodes over time, loss of transmission of the arc tube from blackening, or shifts in the chemical balance of the metals in the arc tube. I do not advise to wait until the bulb is burned out before changing it. An old bulb is inefficient and costly. Replace bulbs every 8 – 9 months or 5,000 hours. Electrode deterioration is greatest during starting and is usually the reason for the end of lamp life.

Super Size Secret: *Bulbs are cheap! Throw another one in and you will be happy!*

Rule of Thumb: *Start the lamp only once a day and always use a timer.*

The halide may produce a stroboscopic (flashing) effect. The light will appear bright, then dim, bright, dim, etc. This flashing is the result of the arc

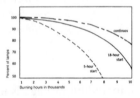

Average lumen maintenance curve for metal halide lamps shows they burn out quicker when started frequently.

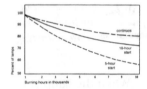

The average mortality curve of metal halide lamps shows the more frequent a lamp is turned on, the shorter the life.

being extinguished 120 times every second. Illumination usually remains constant, but it may pulsate a little. This is normal and nothing to worry about.

Metal Halide Ballasts

Read "About Ballasts". The ballast for a 1,000-watt halide will operate standard, clear and phosphor coated and super, clear and phosphor coated halides on a 115- or 220-volt current. Different ballasts are required for each wattage – 150, 250, 400, 1000, 1100 and 1500. The ballast for each wattage will operate all halides, super or standard, clear or phosphor coated of the same wattage. Each ballast must be specifically designed for the 150-, 250-, 400-, 1000-, 1100-, or 1500-watt halides, because their starting and operating requirements are unique.

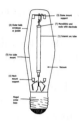

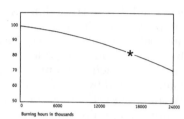

The arc tube of a HP sodium lamp is long emitting light along the entire length.

I placed a star where most gardeners finally decide to change bulbs. After 16,000 hours, a 1000-watt HP sodium runs at 80 percent brilliance.

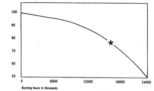

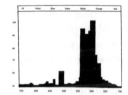

This mortality curve shows the lifespan of a 1000-watt HP sodium bulbs was 24,000 hours.

The color spectrum of HP sodium lamps are concentrated in the yellow/orange range.

Metal Halide Bulbs

Universal metal halide bulbs designed to operate in any position, vertical or horizontal, supply up to 10 percent less light and often have a shorter life. The brighter the halide the better.

SunMaster Warm Deluxe Grow Lamps emit balanced light similar to a 3000° Kelvin source. The enhanced orange-red component promotes flowering, stem elongation and germination while a rich blue content assures healthy vegetative growth.

Venture manufactures the AgroSun for Hydrofarm. It is an enhanced metal halide bulb with more yellow/orange in the spectrum. To find out more about this lamp, hit the Venture Lighting site: www.growlights.com.

High Pressure Sodium Systems

The most impressive fact about the 600-watt high-pressure sodium lamp is that it produces 90,000 initial lumens. That's a lot of light! The HP sodium is also the most efficient HID lamp available. It comes in 35, 50, 70, 100, 150, 200, 250, 310, 400, 600 and 1000 wattages. Virtually all of the HP sodium bulbs used in indoor gardens are clear. All HP sodium vapor lamps have their own unique ballast. HP sodium lamps are manufactured by: GE (Lucalox), Sylvania (Lumalux) and Westinghouse (Ceramalux), Philips (Son Agro), Iwasaki (Eye), Venture (High Pressure Sodium). American gardeners use 1000- and 600-watt HP sodiums most often while European gardeners love 400- and 600-watt HP sodiums.

HP sodium lamps emit an orange-like glow that could be compared to the harvest sun. The color spectrum is highest in the yellow, orange and red end. For many years, scientists believed this spectrum promoted flower production. However, with the new PAR technology, scientists are rethinking old theories. Most plant's light needs change when flowering; they no longer need to produce so many vegetative cells. Vegetative growth slows and eventually stops during blooming. All the plant's energy and attention is focused on flower, fruit and seed production so it can complete its annual life cycle. Light from the red end of the spectrum stimulates floral hormones within the plant, promoting flower production. According to some gardeners, flower volume and fruit weight can increase by as much as 20 percent when using HP sodium lights. Other compelling evidence shows the SunMaster metal halides to be superior. Gardeners using a 10 x 10-foot room often retain the 1000-watt halide and add a 1000-watt sodium during flowering. Flowering plants need more light to produce tight, full flower buds. Adding a HP sodium lamp not only doubles available light it increases the red end of the spectrum. This 1:1 ratio (1 halide and 1 HP sodium) is a popular combination many gardeners prefer during flower and fruiting.

Operation and Construction

Technical Stuff: The HP sodium lamp produces light by passing electricity through vaporized sodium and mercury within an arc tube. A little bit of xenon gas, used for starting, is also included in the arc tube. The HP sodium lamp is totally different from the metal halide in its physical, electrical and color spectrum `characteristics. An electronic starter works with the magnetic component of the ballast to supply a short, high voltage pulse. This electrical pulse vaporizes the xenon gas and initiates the starting

Lighting

Top: You can see this beautiful indoor hydroponic display garden at B & B Hydroponics in Ottawa, ON, Canada.

Middle: Rick Middlebrook from Underhill, Vermont, shovels a path to the church he converted into Green Thumb Hydroponics.

Bottom: This stylish indoor hydroponic garden by Hydroculture Guy Dionne can be seen in a growing number of Montreal homes and offices.

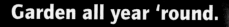

Left: This is an inside view of Sunlight Supply, one of the principal manufacturers of horticultural lighting in North America.

Lighting

Right: Bright new 95-watt compact fluorescent bulbs make indoor gardening in small spaces economical.

Above: High quality ventilation systems have diaphragm flow regulators, like this one found at Urban Flora, Portland, Oregon.

Lighting

The capacitor on the left works perfectly. The one on the right suffered heat damage. Note the swelling around the seal.

New Gavita lamp has the reflective hood inside of the gull-wing shaped bulb and is inherently more efficient.

Light strength diminishes exponentially as it moves away from the source.

$I = L/D^2$

Intensity = light output divided by distance squared

Light Source 1000 Lumens

One Foot
1 foot = 1
{1000 lumens}

Two Feet
2 feet = 1/4
{250 lumens}

Three Feet
3 feet = 1/9
{111 lumens}

4 feet = 1/16
{52.5 lumens}

Four Feet

Left: The Light Strength Chart shows how light strength dimishes the further away the source is from the plants.

Below: Here is a greenhouse full of Gavita lights in action.

Lighting

Top: This popular grow chamber lit by compact fluorescents supplies plenty of light to grow a thriving indoor garden.

Left: Al Disterhoff shows his prototype fiber optic horticultural lighting system. Fiber optic systems could change indoor gardening forever.

Below: The transformer on the left is in mint condition. The transformer on the right shows heat damage and no longer works.

Electronic ballasts are the wave of the future. Until recently, ballasts for larger HID lamps were unavailable. This single ballast will operate both HPS and metal halide lamps of different wattages that range from 400 to 1100.

Lighting

Middle: Grow incredible flowers year round with HID lights, courtesy Worm's Way, Bloomington, IN.

Lower Left: Find Optimum hydroponic systems like this at Brite-Lite in Montreal, PQ, Canada.

Lighting

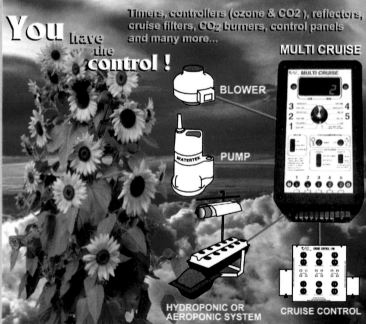

process that takes 3 – 4 minutes. Electricity passes or arcs between the two main electrodes (6) and (7). If the lamp is turned off, or power surge occurs and the lamp goes out, the gasses in the tube will usually need to cool 3 – 15 minutes before restarting is possible.

Similar to the metal halide, the HP sodium (see diagram page 61) has a two-bulb construction, with an outer protective bulb (2) and inner arc tube (1). The arc tube's frame is mounted (5) by spring supports in the dome (3) and neck (4). The outer bulb or jacket protects the arc tube from damage and contains a vacuum, reducing heat loss from the arc tube. The sodium, mercury and xenon gas are contained within the arc tube and have a constant operating temperature and the lamp may be operated in any position (360°). However, most prefer to hang the lamp overhead in a vertical operating position.

Life and Lumen Maintenance

HP sodium lamps have the longest life and best lumen maintenance of all HIDs. Eventually the sodium coats the arc tube. Over a long period of daily use, the sodium to mercury ratio changes, causing the voltage in the arc to rise. Finally the arc tube's operating voltage will rise higher than the ballast is able to sustain. At this point, the lamp will start, warm-up to full intensity, and go out. This sequence is then repeated over and over, signaling the end of the lamps life. The life of a 1000-watt HP sodium lamp will be about 24,000 hours, or 5 years, operating at 12 hours per day. As with other HIDs, HP sodiums should be replaced before the end of their rated life.

Sodium Ballasts

Read "About Ballasts." A special ballast is required specifically for each wattage of HP sodium lamp. Each wattage of lamp has unique operating voltages and currents during start-up and operation. These voltages and currents do not correspond to similar wattages of other HID lamps. Sodium ballasts contain a transformer that is larger than that of a metal halide, a capacitor and an igniter or starter. Purchase HID systems complete at a store rather than in a component kit.

HP Sodium Bulbs

HP sodium bulbs are everywhere you look. The most common bulbs are used for industrial, residential and horticultural lighting. The bulbs are inexpensive and readily available.

Discount building stores often carry 250- and 400-watt lamps.
All HP sodium lamps will grow an indoor garden. Even
though they are brighter, the spectrum contains little blue and
more yellow/orange. Lack of color balance makes plants
stretch between internodes, but does not necessarily diminish
overall harvest.

Philips designed and manufactures the 430-watt Son Agro
specifically to augment natural sunlight and grow plants. The
bulb produces a little more blue light in the spectrum. Adding
a touch more blue light helps prevent most plants from becoming leggy. The other enhanced performance HP sodium bulb,
is the Hortilux by Eye (Iwasaki).

 Super Size Secret: *The 600-watt HP sodium bulb is the most
efficient bulb available today. It produces more lumens per
watt than any other bulb in the world!*

Two HP sodium bulbs changed the way gardeners look at
light. The 600-watt HP sodium increased the lumen-per-watt
(LPW) efficiency of high intensity bulbs by 7 percent. The
430-watt Son Agro HP sodium bulbs have more blue in the
spectrum and run a little hotter than their 400-watt counter-
part. The Son Agro bulbs are the choice of European gardeners.

One European gardener loves the 430-watt bulbs because the
extra blue in the bulb attracts insects. The bugs go for the
bulb and explode into space!

Successful gardeners get the most brilliance for the buck
with a SunMaster Warm Deluxe Grow or 600-watt HP sodium.

Gavita Bulb

The Gavita bulb is like no other bulb on the market.
Headquartered in Norway, Gavita lighting has commandeered
the rights to a bulb that sprang from the Russian space program. The bulb needs no external hood because the reflector
is contained within the outer glass (envelope) of the lamp.
The reflector is actually built into the glass on the top half of
the bulb. The glass on the top of the bulb is shaped like a gull
wing and the silvery reflective material extends across the top
half of the bulb. The Gavita bulb is available in HP sodium
only – 400 and 600 wattages.

There are some inherent
benefits to such a bulb.
For example, light from the
arc tube is reflected directly
from the inside of the
outer envelope. Light does
not have to pass through
the glass envelope, hit the
external reflector and be
reflected back through the
glass envelope downward
toward plants. Reflection is

The Gavita bulb has the reflector built in to the top half of the bulb.

much more efficient and resourceful use of light makes more
of it available to plants.

The reflective surface is always parallel to the arc tube and
much closer than an exterior reflective hood. The bulb is said
to distribute more light better than any other. The factory was
recently moved to Hungary. The North American distributor,
Rambridge, Calgary, Alberta, Canada, Tel: 1-800-265-4769.

One of the independent parties testing the bulb said their
test bulb developed small pinholes after several weeks of use.
According to the manufacturer, the holes do not leak enough
light to measure and not all bulbs develop pinholes.

For more information about the Gavita bulb, contact local
hydroponic retailers or www.rambridge.com or www.gavita.no.

Conversion Bulbs

Conversion or retrofit bulbs increase flexibility. One type of
conversion bulb allows you to utilize a metal halide (or mercury vapor) system with a bulb that emits light similar to an HP
sodium bulb. The bulb looks like a blend between a metal
halide and a HP sodium. While the outer bulb looks like a
metal halide, the inner arc tube is similar to that of a HP sodium. A small igniter is located at the base of the bulb. Other
conversion bulbs retrofit HP sodium systems to convert them
into a virtual metal halide system.

Conversion bulbs are manufactured in 150-, 215-, 360-, 400-,
880-, 940- and 1000-watt sizes. You do not need an adapter or
any additional equipment. Simply screw the bulb into a compatible ballast of comparable wattage. Conversion bulbs operate at a lower wattage and are not as bright as HP sodium

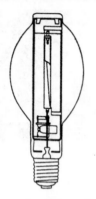

Conversion bulbs make it possible to have both metal halide and HP sodium spectrums at the expense of electrical efficiency.

bulbs. Although conversion bulbs have less blue, they are up to 25 percent brighter than metal halide systems and their lumen-per-watt conversion is better than that of super metal halides. The 940-watt conversion bulb has a lumen-per-watt rating of 138. Similar to the HP sodium lamp, the conversion bulb has a life expectancy of up to 24,000 hours. Unlike most high-pressure sodium lamps which flicker on and off near the end of their lives, conversion bulbs go off and remain off at the end of their lives.

Although conversion bulbs are not inexpensive, they are certainly less expensive than an entire HP sodium system. For gardeners who own a metal halide system, or who deem metal halide the most appropriate investment for their lighting needs, conversion bulbs offer a welcome alternative for bright light. C.E.W. Lighting distributes Iwasaki lights in the United States. Look for their Sunlux Super Ace and Sunlux Ultra Ace lamp.

Rule of Thumb: *Conversion bulbs are a relatively inexpensive way to change light spectrum. The bulbs are less efficient than dedicated HP sodium or metal halide bulbs.*

Venture, Iwasaki and Sunlight Supply manufacture bulbs for conversion in the opposite direction, from high-pressure sodium to metal halide. Venture's White-Lux and Iwasaki's White Ace are metal halide lamps which will operate in a HP sodium system. The 250-, 400-, 1000-watt conversion bulbs can be used in compatible HPS systems with no alterations or additional equipment. If you own a high-pressure sodium system, but need the added blue light which metal halide bulbs produce, these conversion bulbs will suit your needs.

Many gardeners have great success using conversion bulbs. If you have a metal halide system, but want the extra red and yellow light of an HP sodium to promote flowering, simply buy a conversion bulb. Instead of investing in both a metal halide and an HP sodium system, you can rely on a metal halide system and use conversion bulbs when necessary, or vice versa.

The disadvantage of conversion bulbs is that they lose some efficiency through the conversion process.

HP Sodium to Metal Halide

The Sunlux Super Ace and Ultra Ace (Iwasaki) and Retrolux (Philips) produce a HP sodium spectrum with a metal halide system. These bulbs make it possible to use a metal halide ballast and get the same spectrum as a HP sodium lamp. Lumen-per-watt efficiency is traded for the convenience of using these bulbs. A 1000-watt HP sodium bulb produces 140,000 initial lumens. A MH to HPS conversion bulb produces 130,000 initial lumens. If you want only one lamp, a conversion bulb is a fair choice.

Metal Halide to HP Sodium

The White Ace (Iwasaki) and White Lux (Venture) are conversion bulbs. They have a metal halide spectrum and are used in a HPS system. Converting from HPS to MH nets 110,000 initial metal halide lumens.

Mercury Vapor Lamps

The mercury vapor lamp is the oldest and best-known member of the HID family. The HID principle was first used with the mercury vapor lamp around the turn of the century, but it was not until the mid 1930s that the mercury vapor lamp was really employed commercially.

As the lumen-per-watt chart shows, the mercury vapor lamps produce only 60 lumens-per-watt. A comparison of the spectral energy distribution of the mercury vapor and the photosynthetic response chart will show you this is a poor lamp for horticulture. Not only is it expensive to operate, it produces most of its color in areas that are not helpful to plant growth.

Rule of Thumb: Mercury Vapor bulbs are the original HID bulbs. Mercury lamps are outdated, inefficient and grow spindly plants.

The old mercury vapor lamps produce light by arcing electricity through mercury and a little argon gas, which is used for starting. Lamps are available in sizes from 40 to 1000 watts. Bulbs have fair lumen maintenance and a relatively long life. Most wattages last up to three years at 18 hours of daily operation.

Mercury vapor bulbs usually require separate ballasts, however, there are a few low wattage bulbs that have a self-contained ballast. Uninformed gardeners on a budget occasionally try to scrounge a mercury vapor ballast from junk yards or who-knows-where and use it in place of the proper halide or HP sodium ballast. Unwise gardeners who used or tried to modify these ballasts for use with another HID, had all kinds of problems and still had to buy the proper ballast in the end. Attempting to save money on a ballast is usually realized at the expense of the garden.

In summary, the mercury vapor lamp produces a color spectrum that is not as efficient as metal halides or HP sodiums for indoor cultivation. It is not the lamp to use if you want any kind of garden at all! Gardeners that have used them paid more for electricity and their garden yielded much less.

Fluorescent Lamps

Fluorescent and low-pressure (LP) sodium lamps create light by passing electricity through gaseous vapor under low pressure.

Before the mid 1970s, fluorescent tubes were the most efficient and widely used artificial light available to the indoor gardener. Some fluorescents boast a spectrum almost identical to the sun, but they are just not bright enough to grow high light plants efficiently. Today, these lamps are most efficiently used as a light source to root cuttings. Fluorescent lamps are long glass tubes and found in many commercial and residential buildings. They come in a wide variety of lengths, from 1 to 12

Fluorescent lamps are great for rooting cuttings. Some people even use them to grow high light flowers.

feet. Most gardeners have found the 4- and 8-foot tubes the easiest to handle and most readily available. Eight-foot fluorescent tubes must be shipped by truck.

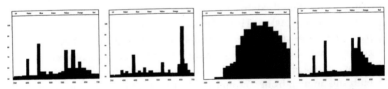

The four spectral emission charts show the color spectrum output of four different fluorescent bulbs.

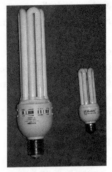

Fluorescent tubes come in several different wattages or outputs and require specific ballasts. Several companies make both tubes and ballasts. The standard or regular tubes use about 10 watts per linear foot. A four-foot tube uses about 40 watts; 8 foot, 80 watts, etc. Standard fluorescents have specific ballasting requirements and require specific ballasts. High Output (HO) tubes use about 50 percent more watts per linear foot and emit about 40 percent more light than the standard. HO fluorescents require their own specific ballast. Very High Output (VHO) use almost three times the electricity and produce more than twice as much light as the standard fluorescent. VHO fluorescents are more expensive and more difficult to find. VHO tubes also require a special ballast. They may be ordered from manufacturers or purchased from wholesalers.

Compact fluorescent lamps now offer a viable alternative for gardeners on a budget.

 Super Size Secret: *Fluorescent lights start robust cuttings with strong roots. Keep lamps 2–4 inches from foliage.*

Fluorescent lamps work very well for rooting cuttings. They supply cool, diffused light in the proper color spectrum to promote root growth. Gardeners use just about any "daylight spectrum" fluorescent lamp for rooting. Fluorescents, like HIDs, diminish in intensity the further away from the light source. Since standard fluorescents produce much less light than

Compact Fluorescent Lamps

Compact fluorescent lamps have been around for some time, but they were always too small to affect plant growth much. Now, they manufacture "flood" compact fluorescent lamps in larger wattages. I first saw them in 2001 at Home Depot. Now, you can find new compact fluorescent lamps in 65, 70 and 95 and 125 wattages. They do generate heat, but much less than their HID counterparts of similar wattage. Foliage should be able to be within two inches of the 95w bulb and an inch from 65w bulbs. The supply is somewhat sporadic and some bulbs are available in a reddish spectrum (2700 degrees Kelvin) or natural sunlight (6400 degrees Kelvin).

The new 95w EnviroLite is easy to suspended vertically in the center of a 2 x 2 x 4-foot box. I took light measurements around the perimeter of the box (about one foot from the bulb) with a high quality foot-candle meter. Foot-candle readings were between 1000 and 5000 everywhere in the box. The majority of the readings were at or above 2000 foot-candles. A 430w HP sodium lamp under a good horizontal hood suspended 3 feet above a 4 x 4-foot matrix lays down from 6,000 to 12,000 foot-candles. This amount of light will grow good flowers and vegetables. One foot away, the 95w compact fluorescent generates about a quarter as much light as a 430w HP sodium lamp at a distance of 3 to 4 feet. But, the 95w compact fluorescent generates enough light to grow relatively well-formed flowers and fruits. Although this much light will not grow plants as well as natural sunshine or even a larger HID, it will grow plants to maturity.

You could easily grow four tomato plants in shallow containers. Each plant would easily fit into one square foot of the 2 x 2-foot floor space and grow around the vertically mounted bulb. The bulb generates some heat and could burn foliage if plants touch it too long. An alternative light setup would be two 65w (65 x 2 = 130w) lamps, which would actually cost less than one 95w EnviroLite. Some of the 65w lamps come in a rigid fixture in which the ballast is mounted. A small fan is usually necessary to extract the extra heat and humidity in the small area. Holes near the bottom of the 2 x 2 x 4-foot box could pull in air and holes in the top could vent out hot air. The natural flow of cooler air from the bottom and hot air out the top will help keep humidity and temperature in check. The fan should be turned on during the nighttime to expel humid air.

The new compact fluorescent lamps are distributed by Sure Growth, Delta, BC, Canada, Tel: 1-604-515-3926 or check their web site: www.fearlessgardener.com or call 1-604-515-3926.

HIDs, they must be very close (2 – 4 inches) to the plants for best results.

A few gardeners hang extra fluorescent lamps with HIDs to increase light intensity. This works OK, but I have found fluorescents to be more trouble than they are worth for anything but rooting cuttings. When using them in conjunction with HIDs, fluorescents must be very close to plants to provide enough intense light to do any good. Fluorescents may also shade plants from HID light and generally get in the way.

 Technical Stuff*: You can grow an entire high light garden under fluorescent lights. The flowers will be small but, with enough fluorescent light, plant will mature. The garden will have to literally be lined with fluorescents to supply enough light.*

Power twist or grove type lamps offer additional lumens in the same amount of linear space. The deep wide groves gives more glass surface area and more light output! Several companies market these power-twist type fluorescents.

Fluorescent bulbs and fixtures are relatively inexpensive. Two 4-foot bulbs and a fixture will usually cost from $20 to $30. Cuttings root best with 18 – 24 hours of light.

Fluorescents have a wide variety of spectrums. Sylvania has the GroLux and the Wide Spectrum GroLux. The Standard GroLux is the lamp to use for starting clones or seedlings. It is designed for use as the only source of light, having the full spectrum necessary for photosynthesis and chlorophyll production. The Wide Spectrum GroLux is designed to supplement natural light and covers the blue to far-red regions. Westinghouse has the AgroLight that produces a very similar spectrum to the sun. Warm White and Cool White bulbs used together, make excellent lamps to root clones under, especially if they are VHO.

Construction and Operation

Like the HID family, the fluorescents require an appropriate fixture, containing a ballast (much smaller than the HID ballast) and the ordinary 115-volt house current. The fixture is usually integrated into the reflective hood. There are several types of fixtures. Some have one pin on each end while others are two pin types. If purchasing new tubes, make sure the bulb fits the fixture. The fixture may contain 1, 2 or 4 tubes.

The ballast, which is contained in the fixture, radiates almost all of the heat produced by the system. The ballast is located far enough away from standard tubes that plants can actually touch them without being burned. VHO tubes might burn tender plants if they get too close.

The ballast or transformer regulates electricity. Most ballasts and fixtures are for use with standard 40 or 80-watt tubes. Special ballasts are required for HO and VHO fluorescent tubes. The operating requirements of HO and VHO lamps are greater, due to the increase in current, than the standard fluorescents. Order the VHO ballast, fixture and tubes at the same time and from a reputable supplier.

The ballast reduces the current in the tube to the operating voltage required by a particular lamp. The ballast will normally last 10 – 12 years. Used fluorescent fixtures (unlike used mercury vapor ballasts) are generally acceptable to use. The end of life is usually accompanied by smoke and a foul chemical odor. When the ballast burns out, simply remove it (or take the entire fixture to the nearest electrical supply store) and buy a new one to replace it. Be very careful if the ballast has brown slime or sludge on or around it. This sludge could possibly contain PcBs. If the ballast contains the sludge, throw it away! Most modern fluorescents are self-starting, but older fluorescents require a special starter. This starter may be integrated into the body of the fixture and hidden from view, or be a small metal tube (about 1 inch in diameter and fi-inch long), located at the end of the fixture on the underside. The latter starters are replaceable, while the former require a trip to the electrical store.

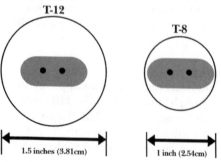

Most electrical supply stores are able to test starters. If your fluorescent fixture does not work and you are not well versed on fluorescent troubleshooting, simply take it to the nearest electric store and ask for advice. Make sure

The end view of a standard T-12 flourescent bulb compared to the modern T-8 design. Drawing to scale.

they test each component and tell you why it should be replaced. It might be less expensive to buy another fixture.

The tubular glass bulb is coated on the inside with phosphor. The mix of phosphorescent chemicals in the coating and the gasses contained within determine the spectrum of colors emitted by the lamp. The bulb contains a blend of inert gasses: argon, neon or krypton and mercury vapor, sealed under low pressure. Electricity arcs between the two electrodes, located at each end of the tube, stimulating the phosphor to emit light energy. The light emission is strongest near the center of the tube and somewhat less at the ends. If rooting just a few cuttings, place them under the center of the fixture for best results. Inside a fluorescent bulb most of the energy is given off at ultraviolet frequencies (235 nanometers) being predominant. The phosphors on the inside of the glass envelope convert the UV energy into visible light. Efficiency is about 22 percent, the rest is heat.

Once the fluorescent is turned on, it will take a few seconds for the bulb to warmup before an arc can be struck through the tube. Fluorescents blacken with age, loosing intensity. I recommend replacing bulbs when they reach 70 percent of their stated service life listed on the package or label. A flickering light is about to burn out and should be replaced. Life expectancy ranges from 9,000 hours (1.25 years at 18 hours daily operation) with VHO tubes to 18,000 hours (2.5 years at 18 hours daily operation) with the standard.

Other Lamps

Several other lamps deserve a mention, however, they grow plants poorly. Incandescent lamps are inefficient, tungsten halogen lamps are bright but inefficient and low-pressure sodium lamps are efficient but have a limited spectrum.

Incandescent Lamps

The incandescent lamp is the electric lamp invented by Thomas Edison. Light is produced by sending electricity through the filament, a super fine wire inside the bulb. The filament resists the flow of electricity, heating it to incandescence, causing it to glow. The incandescent bulbs work on ordinary home current and require no ballast. Filaments may be of many shapes and sizes, but are nearly always made of the tough heat resistant tungsten. They come in a wide range of wattages and constructions for special applications. Most lamps used in homes for Christmas trees, interior lighting and refrigerators are incandescent lamps. Their efficiency is between 8 and 12 percent, the rest is heat.

Technical Stuff: Incandescent bulbs are as old as Thomas Edison and the least efficient of all lamps. It's got the wrong spectrum too!

There are many types of incandescent lamps. They usually use a tungsten filament with a glass bulb construction and threaded base that fits household sockets. The bulb is usually under a vacuum or contains some type of gas to minimize wear on the filament.

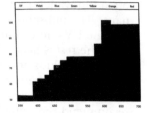

Most incandescents have a spectrum in the far-red end, but there are some incandescent grow lamps that have a more even spectrum. Incandescent lamps are so expensive to operate and produce so few lumens-per-watt, that they are not really worth using. They are most efficiently used as a source of bottom or soil heat for rooting cuttings or growing seedlings under cool fluorescents. A few gardeners use incandescents during flowering to help promote more and heavier tops.

The light spectrum of an incandescent lamp will grow plants, but is best suited to generating heat.

Tungsten Halogen Lamps

The tungsten halogen lamp was originally called Iodine Quartz lamp. This is because the outer tube is made of heat resistant quartz and the main gas inside the quartz tube was iodine, one of the five halogens. (The five halogens are any of the five elements: fluorine, chlorine, bromine, iodine and astatine.) There are many variations to this quartz halogen or quartz tungsten lamp (See drawing). Today, bromine, one of the halogens, is used most often in the lamps, so the name

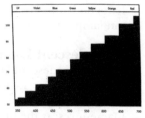

Tungsten halogen bulbs really crank in the red end of the spectrum. Too bad they are so inefficient.

halogen covers all of the gasses in the arc tube. The tungsten
lamps are very similar to the incandescents. They use a tungsten wire filament, use a sealed bulb and are very expensive to
operate; their lumen-per-watt output is very low. Tungsten
halogens, like incandescents, run on a 115-volt current and
require no ballast. They are as inefficient to operate as the
incandescents. Their color spectrum is in the far-red end with
10 – 15 percent in the visible spectrum. They are used for spot
lights and fog lights on cars.

LP Sodium Lamps

Low Pressure (LP) sodium lamps come in 55, 90, 135 and
180 wattages. Their lumen-per-watt conversion is the highest
of all lamps on the market today. More careful inspection of
the color spectrum chart, on the previous page, shows that it is
monochromatic or only produces light in one very narrow portion of the spectrum, at 589 nm. The LP sodium lamp emits a
yellow glow. Colors are not distinguished and appear as tones.

Westinghouse supplies LP sodium lamps. Their main use in
industry has been for security or ware-
house light.

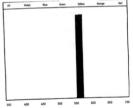

Each lamp wattage requires its own
unique ballast and fixture. The ballast
or transformer regulates electric current and is located inside the fixture.
The fixture for a 180-watt lamp is just a
little larger than a fixture for two 40-
watt, 4-foot fluorescent tubes.

Westinghouse (Phillips Corp.) is the
sole supplier of LP sodium lamps. The
ballast and fixture for a LP sodium cost
about $200. As with other lamps, I
advise to purchase the lamp, ballast
and fixture from a reputable supplier
and in the same package.

*LP sodium lamps have the
highest lumen-per-watt conversion of any lamp, but
their monochromatic spec-
trum makes them virtually
useless for growing.*

Technical Stuff: *The LP sodium lamp is super efficient, but
monochromatic in the yellow portion of the spectrum.*

Fiber Optic Lamps

Fiber optic lamps could possibly revolutionize the indoor
lighting industry. Fiber optic cables are able to transport light
from one end of the cable to the other without loss of transmission intensity or spectrum. This inventor has assembled

this rough prototype of a fiber optic lighting system for a small garden. The ingenious system uses a 150w projection lamp focused on to fiber optic cables. The cables are then directed to an even plane where they are all arranged over a crop of tomatoes. Preliminary tests showed the distribution of light very even and nearly as intense as a 400-watt HID. Amazing but true!

Light guided by fiber\optic cables can be placed much closer to garden foliage, because there is no heat where the light shines. The closer it is to foliage the brighter the light. This little fiber optic system needs a little bit more research and development before taking a strong place in the market. For more information, see our web site www.gardeningindoors.com.

About Electricity

The basics of electricity really do not need to be understood to garden indoors, but understanding the basics will save you money, time and possibly the shock of your life. First, simple electrical concepts and terms are defined and briefly discussed. Once these terms are understood, you will be able to see the purpose of fuses, wire thickness (gauge), amperes on a circuit, the importance of a ground and the necessity to develop safe habits.

Before you touch anything electrical, please remember the rule below.

Rule of Thumb: *Work backwards when installing electrical components or doing wiring. Turn off the power first! Start at the bulb and work towards the plug-in. Always plug in the power cord in last!*

Water and electricity don't mix. Always work with a grounded system and keep all standing water off the floor!

Super Size Secret: *GFI outlets are easy to install and stop electrical problems before they get started. They must have a ground circuit (three wires) to operate properly.*

Warning! *Be careful when working around electricity. It can kill!*

Ampere (amp) – is the measure of electricity in motion, the actual "flow of electrons". Electricity can be looked at in absolute terms of measurement just as water can. A gallon is an absolute measure of a portion of water; a coulomb is an absolute measure of a portion of electricity. Water in motion is measured in gallons per second and electricity in motion is measured in coulombs per second. When an electrical current flows at one coulomb per second, we say it has one ampere. We could say coulomb per second, but it would sound a little weird, because everybody uses amperes!

A ground-fault interrupt (GFI) outlet will let you sleep easier at night.

Overload Chart

Ampere Rating	Amperes Available	Amperes for Overload
15	13	14
20	16	17
25	20	21
30	24	25
40	32	33

A circuit is overloaded when 80 percent of the available amps (amperes) are used. For example, a 20-amp circuit is maximized when 16 amperes are used.

Breaker Box – Electrical circuit box containing circuit breakers.

Breaker Switch – ON/OFF safety switch that will turn the electricity OFF when the circuit is overloaded.

Circuit – the circular path that electricity travels. If this path is interrupted, the power will go off. If this circuit is given a chance, it can through your body! Never give it a chance!

Conductor – something that is able to carry electricity easily. Copper, steel, water and your body are good electrical conductors.

Current – the flow of electricity in coulombs per second. The symbol for current = "I".

Fuse – Electrical safety device consisting of a fusible metal that melts and interrupts the circuit when overloaded. Never replace fuses with pennies or aluminum foil! They will not melt and interrupt the circuit when overloaded. This is an easy way to start a fire.

Fuse Box – Electrical circuit box containing fuses.

Ground – a means to connect electricity to the ground or earth. Safety is the reason for a ground. If a circuit is properly grounded and the electricity travels somewhere it is not supposed to, it will go via the ground wire into the ground (earth) and rendered harmless. Electricity will travel the path of least resistance. This path must be along the ground wire. A ground wire should be connected to a cold water pipe or a copper stake in the earth nearby.

Warning! The HID lamp operating on an overloaded circuit will blow fuses, switch off the breakers and burn wiring. It could wreck the HID system and start a fire. Pay attention!

Rule of Thumb: Use only one 1000-watt HID for each 15/20-ampere circuit.

The ground is formed by a wire, (usually green or bare copper), that runs parallel to the circuit and is attached to a metal ground stake. All circuits are then attached to the ground stake, via ground wires . Metal water and sewer pipes also serve as excellent conductors for the ground. They are all attached to one another. Water pipes conduct electricity well and are all in good contact with the ground. Plastic water pipes in newer houses do not make good grounds.

The entire system – pipes, copper wire and metal ground stake – conduct any misplaced electricity safely into the ground.

The ground wire is the third wire with the big round prong. The ground should run all the way through the ballast and all the way to the hood.

HID systems must have a ground that runs a continual path from the socket, through the ballast to the main fuse box, then to the house ground.

GFI – Ground Fault Interrupt outlets are required anywhere water is used in a home or business. Install GFI outlets in garden rooms to provide an instant safe electrical shut off when necessary. They will only operate on a 3-wire grounded system.

Hertz – Fluctuations or cycles of electricity within a conductor (wire). In the United States, electricity runs at 60 HERTZ or cycles per second.

Ohm's Power Law – A law that expresses the strength of an electric current: Volts x Amperes = Watts. (P = E x I).

Resistance – The impediment of wires or a load to current flow, like a valve is to water. The symbol the symbol is "R" and is measured in ohms.

Short Circuit – A side or unintentional circuit formed when conductors (wires) cross. A short circuit will normally blow fuses trip circuit breakers.

Volts – Air, water, and gas virtually anything can be put under pressure. Pressure is measured in pounds per square inch (PSI). Electricity is also under pressure or electrical potential; this pressure is measured in volts. The symbol for volts = "E" (for electromotive force). Most home wiring is under the pressure of approximately 115 or 220 volts.

Watts – Are a measure of work. Watts measure the amount of electricity flowing in a wire. When amperes, (units of electricity per second), are multiplied by volts (pressure) we get watts: 1000 watts = 1 kilowatt. The symbol for watts = "P".

A halide lamp that draws about 9.2 amperes x 120 volts = 1104 watts. Remember Ohms Power Law: Amps x Volts = Watts. This is strange, the answer was supposed to be 1000 watts. What is wrong? The electricity flows through the ballast, which uses energy to run. The energy drawn by the ballast must amount to 104 watts. There is also voltage loss in wires, called "IR drop".

Watt-hours measure the amount of watts that are used during an hour. One watt-hour is equal to one watt used for one hour. A kilowatt-hour is 1000 watt-hours. A 1000-watt HID will use roughly one kilowatt per hour and the ballast will use about 100 watts. Electrical bills are based on how many KWH are used (See chart "Cost of Electricity").

Electrical wire comes in many sizes (gauges), indicated by number. The higher the number, the smaller the wire; the lower the number, the larger the wire. Most household circuits are connected together with 14-gauge wire. Wire thickness is important for two reasons (1) ampacity (2) voltage drop. Ampacity is the amount of amperes a wire is able to carry safely. Electricity flowing through wire creates heat. The more

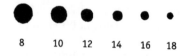

8   10   12   14   16   18

The diameter of electrical wire grows thicker as the gauge number decreases. Notice how much thicker a 14 gauge wire is than a 16.

amps flowing, the more heat created. Heat is wasted power. Avoid wasting power by using the proper thickness of well-insulated wire (14 gauge) and use a ground wire (3-wire circuit).

Using too small of a wire not only forces too much power (amperes) through a wire, it also causes voltage drop; voltage (pressure) is lost in the wire. For example: by forcing an 18-gauge wire to carry 9.2 amperes at 120 volts, it would not only heat up, maybe even blowing fuses, but the voltage at the outlet would be 120 volts while the voltage 10 feet away could be as low as 108. This is a loss of 12 volts. Would you like to pay for this? The ballast and lamp run less efficiently with fewer volts. The further the electricity travels, the more heat that is generated and the more voltage drops. This is measured as IR drop. The power that is wasted goes up rapidly with smaller wire because $P = I^2 R$. Twice the current = 4 x the loss of power because of I^2 (current squared).

Voltage drop is wasteful and causes lamps to function very

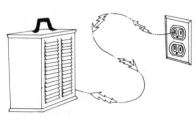

The voltage drops if electricity travels more than 10 feet from the outlet to the ballast. The longer the distance, the greater the voltage- drop. Ballasts are underpowered when voltage is low, causing the bulb to dim.

inefficiently. A lamp that was designed to work at 120 volts, that receives only 108 volts (90 percent of the power it was intended to operate at) would produce only 70 percent of the normal light. Use at least 14-gauge wire for any extension cords and if the cord is to carry power more than 60 feet, use 12-gauge wire.

Warning! A voltage drop of 10 percent causes light output to drop up to 30 percent!

Wires are usually:

Black = Hot
White or Red = Common
Bare, Blue or Green = Ground

When wiring a plug-in or socket:

The hot wire attaches to the brass or gold screw.
The common wire attaches to the aluminum or silver screw.
The ground wire always attaches to the ground prong (usually green).
Take special care to keep the wires from crossing and creating a short circuit.

Plug-ins and sockets must have a solid connection. If they are jostled around and the electricity is allowed to jump, electricity is lost in the form of heat, the prongs will burn and a fire could result. Check plug-ins periodically to ensure they have a solid connection. If they feel warm or hot, a problem is starting.

If installing a new circuit or breaker box, hire an electrician, or purchase *Wiring Simplified* by H.P. Richter and W.C. Schwan. It costs about $10 and is available at most hardware stores. Installing a new circuit in a breaker box is very easy, but installing another fuse in a fuse box is more complex. Best leave this bit of handiwork to a professional electrician. You could save yourself the shock of your life!

About Electricity Consumption

Super Size Secret: Electricity and lumens-per-watt are usually the limiting factor indoors. Grow as many blossoms or as much weight per watt of light as possible to get the most from your garden.

Cost of electricity chart

Cost per KWH	12-hour days day	month	18-hour days day	month
$0.05	0.60	18.00	0.90	27.00
$0.06	0.72	21.60	1.08	32.40
$0.07	0.84	25.20	1.26	37.80
$0.08	0.96	28.80	1.44	43.20
$0.09	1.08	32.40	1.62	48.60

$0.10	1.20	36.00	1.80	54.00
$0.15	1.80	54.00	2.70	81.00
$0.20	2.40	72.00	3.60	108.00
$0.25	3.00	90.00	4.50	135.00

There are many ways to help conserve electricity when using a HID light to garden indoors. One gardener moved into a home that had all electric heat and a fireplace. He installed three HID lamps in the basement that generated quite a bit of heat. The excess heat was dispersed via a vent fan attached to a thermostat/humidistat. He turned off the electric heat, bought a fireplace insert and started heating with wood. Even running three lamps, consuming three kilowatts per hour, the electric bill was less than it had been with electric heat! Electric bills are controlled and generated with a computer. The monthly energy consumption is often displayed on a bar graph for the previous 12 months. This graph makes it easy to see fluctuations in electricity consumption.

A 1 – 3 bedroom home can run 2 – 3 1000-watt lamps and a 4 – 5 bedroom home can operate 3 – 5 lamps with little or no problem. Any more lamps usually require new incoming circuits or the use of present circuits are severely limited.

 Rule of Thumb: *One 1000-watt lamp per bedroom does not draw as much power as a portable heater.*

The amount of normal electricity consumption and the size of the home are proportional. Often an increase in electric consumption is normal. For example, electric bills always go up if there is a baby in the home or there are more residents living there. Changing to gas or wood heat and a gas stove and water heater will also lower the electricity bill. Some friends bought a new, efficient water heater and saved $17 per month! Just by changing water heaters, they were able to add another 600-watt lamp. Another horticulturist set her water heater for 130 degrees instead of 170 degrees. This simple procedure saved about 25 KWH per month!

 Warning! *Do not turn the water heater any lower than 130 degrees F. Harmful bacteria can grow below this safe point!*

The electric company might call to ask if you were aware of your increased electricity bill. This is nothing to worry about. Simply reply that you are aware of the electricity being used. If you like to make excuses, some appliances that draw a lot of electricity are: electric pottery kiln, arc welder and hot tub. If the situation warrants, take showers at a friend's house or at a gym, use a laundromat and never use any appliances that use a lot of electricity. The less electricity you use the better!

The meter reader may think it is strange to see a meter spinning like a top during the middle of the day when nobody is home. As often as every 10 years, some electric companies will change the electric meter to update technology, replace old worn out mechanical parts or to improve efficiency. If there is an increase in electric consumption the power company often chalks it up to a defective meter, and they change the meter.

Super Size Secret: use a surge protector manufactured by Western Water Farms, Langley, BC to cut your electrical bill up to 40 percent!

The Equalizer saves BIG BUCK$ on electricity.

This gadget is a godsend from BC that is guaranteed to reduce garden room electricity bills from 5 to 40 percent. It is most effective when used in conjunction with a 10-light (10,000 watt) or bigger garden. I've been watching this little box for more than a year. At first, I thought it was such a good deal that it had to be illegal. Now it is CSA and UL approved! But, how does this thing work? How does it save 40 percent on electricity bills? Will this miracle box really solve the garden room energy crisis?

I'm not going to go into everything here and now, look for more specific information in upcoming issues of magazine articles. For now, I'll lay out the basics: how it works and where to get one.

Electricity travels in waves. It is most efficient when delivered at a constant rate without disruption; ballasts, bulbs and capacitors function at maximum efficiency. Trouble is, electricity is transported in wires that adulterate electrical waves, as do the bulbs, ballasts and capacitors on the receiving end. Much of the electricity is "consumed" in transmission; lost when sent from point A to point B. Electricity is also adulterated by localized oscillations, as well as fluctuations in relation to its location within the electrical grid. This is usually due to inductive leads, like turning on large motors or solenoids.

The Equalizer, a little black box, modulates and cleans up the electricity before it hits your electrical panel. It increases the Power Factor (PF): a measure of how efficiently electrical power is being used. The static, surges, spikes and fluctuations (some of which actually send electricity back to the electric company!) are removed to supply a constant stream of efficient electricity. Bottom line? Clean electricity is efficient electricity and your bill drops like a rock. The more electricity you use, the more saved. With this box, gardeners that fire up 10 lights are only billed for six! Cost is less than $1000 US ($1400 CDN) with a no-questions-asked money-back guarantee. Payback is quick; at $0.10 per KWH, a 10-light setup pays for the box in 70 days. To get hooked up, give Western Water Farms in BC, Canada a call: 1-800-533-9301, Ext. 1.

Generators

Generators are popular among people that live "off the power grid". Some of the things to consider when purchasing a generator are reliability, ampere output and the noise. A loud generator can destroy domestic harmony!

Buy the generator new. It should be water cooled and fully automated. Any major brand is OK, but check its noise output and listen to it run before purchasing. Always buy a generator that is big enough to do the job. A little extra cushion will be necessary to allow for power surges. Allow about 1300 watts per lamp to be run by the generator. The ballast consumes a few watts as does the wire, etc. A 5500-watt Honda generator will run four lamps with ease.

Generators provide complete "off the grid" autonomy. Check into their consumption and maintenance before purchasing one. Some models make are loud and must be muffled.

Honda generators are the most often used because they are the least expensive, dependable and quiet. Diesel motors are more economical to run, but noisy and the fumes are toxic. Always make sure a gasoline-powered generator is vented properly. The exhaust produces carbon monoxide, which is toxic to plants and humans. The exhaust from the muffler must go outside into the atmosphere.

The gasoline generator motor may be converted to propane, which burns much cleaner and the exhaust may be used as a source of CO_2. A carbon monoxide monitor should measure these gasses before use.

Diesel generators for truck and train car refrigerators are fairly easy to acquire and last for years. Once set up, a big generator can run an entire home or farm, including an indoor garden. Check with wholesale railway and truck wrecking yard outlets for such generators. With a good exhaust system and baffling around the motor, the sound is soon dissipated. Muffling the exhaust and expelling the fumes is a little complex, but very effective. The exhaust must be able to escape freely into the atmosphere.

Generators require a lot of maintenance and must run for many hours. The generator needs fuel monitoring and maintenance to keep it in top shape.

Timers

A timer is an inexpensive investment that turns lights and other appliances on and off at regular intervals. Using a timer ensures that your plants will receive a controlled light period for the same duration every day.

Purchase a heavy duty grounded timer with an adequate amperage and power rating to

The large box is full of solenoid switches that turn lamps on and off. The timer (left) sends on/off instructions to the solenoid switches on normal household wire (12-14 gauge). Wire connects the breaker box to all the outlets.

This set of timers control everything you need to run a garden room.

meet your needs. Some timers have different amperage rating for a
given load; it is often lower than that of the timer. Timers that control more than one lamp are more expensive because they require
the entire force of electricity to pass through it. Many pre-wired
timers are available at stores that sell HID lights. In the simplest
setup, only control lamps on a lamp timer. Adding a pump, heater,
fan, etc., adds extra amperage (load) and could cause an overloaded
circuit. Add up the power requirements to stay below the power rating of the timer.

Always remember to ask how many lights (total watts) the timer
will handle. If you are running more than 2000 or 3000 watts, you
may want to attach the lamps to a relay or solenoid switch and control the relay with a timer. The advantage of a relay is it offers a path
for more electricity without having to change the timer. There are

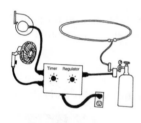

numerous sophisticated timers on the
market that will solve every need you may
have.

Setting up the HID System – Step-by-Step

Step One: Before setting up the HID system, read "Setting Up the Garden Room" in
Chapter One and complete the step-by-step
instructions.

*This controller is just one
of many different timers
available at indoor garden
stores.*

Step Two: Both the lamp and ballast radiate quite a bit of heat. Take care when posi-
tioning them so they are not so close (6 – 12
inches) to plants or flammable walls and ceil-

ing that they become hazardous. If the room has limited space, with a
low ceiling, place a protective, non-flammable material, like metal
between the lamp and ceiling to protect from heat. An exhaust fan will

*Garden room controllers offer com-
plete control of every aspect of the
room.*

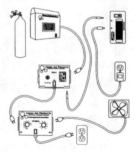

*Precise garden room control is
easy with the controllers available today.*

be necessary to keep things cool in virtually all garden rooms. It is most effective to place the remote ballast near the floor to keep things cool. It may also be placed outside the garden room if the temperature is too high, which is unlikely when a good vent fan is used. When hanging the lamp on the overhead chain or pulley system, make sure electrical cords are unencumbered and not too close to any heat source.

Step Three: Buy a good timer and use it. Mother Nature allows for each day to start and end roughly at the same time. Changes in day length are always slow and subtle. If the photoperiod bounces around it will confuse plants. A decent timer will cost from $20 to $30.

Step Four: To plug-in the HID lamp, it will be necessary to find the proper outlet. A 1000-watt HID lamp will use about 9.5 amperes (amps) of electricity on a regular 115-volt current.

A typical home has a fuse box or a breaker box. Each fuse or breaker switch controls an electrical circuit in the home. The fuse or breaker switch will be rated for 15-, 20-, 25-, 30-, or 40-amp service. Circuits are considered overloaded when more than 80 percent of the amps are being used (See "Overload Chart"). The fuse will have its amp rating printed on its face and the breaker switch will have its amp rating printed on the switch or on the breaker box. To find out which outlets are controlled by a fuse or breaker switch, remove the fuse or turn the breaker switch off. Test each and every 115-volt outlet in the home to see which ones do not work. All the outlets that do not work are on the same circuit. All outlets that work are on another circuit. When you have found a circuit that has few or no lights, radios, TV's, stereos, etc., plugged into it, look a the circuits amp rating. If it is

The mechanical timer on the left will operate several lamps at the same time. The digital timer on the right operates a single 1000-watt HID.

rated for 15 amps, just plug one HID into it. A leeway of 5.5 amps is there to cover any power surges or irregularities in electricity. If the circuit is rated for 20 or more amps, it may be used for the HID lamp as well as a few other low amp appliances and lights. To find out how many amps are drawn by each appliance, add up the number of watts used by each appliance, then divide by 120.

Example:
A circuit with a 20-amp fuse, containing the following items
1400-watt toaster oven
100-watt incandescent light bulb + 20-watt radio

1520 total watts divided by 120 = 12.6 amps in use

The above example shows 12.6 amps are being drawn when everything is on. By adding 9.2 amps, drawn by the HID to the circuit, we get 21.8 amps drawn – an overloaded circuit! There are three solutions to this problem:

Remove one or all of the high-amp drawing appliances and plug them into another circuit.

Find another circuit that has few or no amps drawn by other appliances.

Install a new circuit. A 220-volt circuit will make more amps available per circuit if using several lamps.

Never put a larger fuse in the fuse box than it is rated for. The fuse is the weakest link in the circuit. If a 20-amp fuse is placed into a 15-amp circuit, the fuse is able to conduct more electricity than the wiring. When this happens, the wires burn, rather than the fuse. An overloaded circuit may result in a house fire.

Use an extension cord that is at least 14-gauge wire or heavier if the plug will not reach the outlet desired. The thicker 14-gauge extension cord is more difficult to find and may have to be constructed. A smaller 16- or 18-gauge cord will not conduct adequate electricity and will heat up, straining the entire system. Cut the 14-gauge extension cord to the exact length; the further electricity travels, the weaker it gets and the more heat it produces, which also strains the system.

Step Five: Always use a 3-prong grounded plug. If your home is not equipped with working 3-prong grounded outlets, buy a 3-prong grounded plug and outlet adapter. Attach the ground wire to a grounded ferrous metal object like a grounded metal pipe, a heavy copper stake, driven into the earth to a form a ground or screw the ground into the plug-in face. Or install a GFI outlet (See "About Electricity"). You will be working with water under and around the HID system. Water conducts electricity about as well as the human body; guaranteed to give you a charge!

Step Six: Once the proper circuit is selected, the socket and hood mounted overhead, the ballast in place on the floor (but not plugged in) screw the HID bulb finger tight into the socket. Make sure the bulb is secured in the socket tightly, but not too tight and make certain there is a good connection. When secure, wipe off all smudges on the bulb to increase brightness and prevent etching of the glass by body oil.

Step Seven: Plug the 3-prong plug into the timer that is in the OFF position. Plug the timer into the grounded outlet. Set the timer at the desired photoperiod and turn the timer on. Shazam! The ballast will hum; the lamp will flicker and slowly warm up, reaching full brilliance in about 5 minutes.

Soil and Containers

Soil

Soil is made up of many mineral particles mixed together with living and dead organic matter that incorporate air and water. Four basic factors contribute to the plant's ability to grow in a soil: texture, pH, water and nutrient content.

Soil texture is governed by the size and physical make-up of the mineral particles. The proper soil texture is required for adequate root penetration, water and oxygen retention and drainage, as well as many other complex chemical processes. Clay or adobe soil is made up of very small flat mineral particles. When it gets wet, these minute particles pack tightly together, slowing or stopping root penetration and water drainage. Roots are unable to breathe because very little or no space is left for oxygen. Water has a very difficult time penetrating these tightly packed soils, and once it does penetrate, drainage is slow. Sandy soils have much larger particles. They permit good aeration (supply of air or oxygen) and drainage. Frequent watering is necessary because water retention is very low. The soil's water and air-holding ability, as well as root penetration, are a function of texture.

To check soil texture, pick up a handful of moist (not soggy) soil and gently squeeze it. The soil should barely stay together and have a kind of sponge effect when you slowly open your hand to release pressure. Indoor soils that do not fulfill these requirements should be

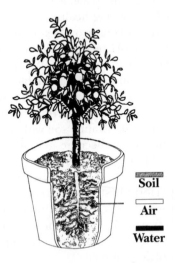

Soil

Air

Water

This cut away drawing shows how roots penetrate soil. There must be enough air trapped in the soil to allow biological activity and absorption of nutrients.

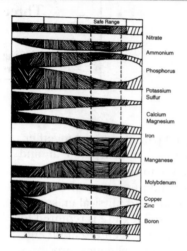

This pH chart shows the "Safe Zone" for soil is between 5.8 and 6.8.

thrown out or amended. See "Soil Amendments."

pH

pH is a scale from 1 to 14 that measures acid-to-alkaline balance. One is the most acidic, 7 is neutral and 14 is most alkaline. Every full point change in pH signifies a ten-fold increase or decrease in acidity or alkalinity. For example: soil or water with a pH of 5 is 10 times more acid than water or soil with a pH of 6. Water with a pH of 5 is 100 times more acidic than water with a pH of 7. With a ten-fold difference between each point on the scale, accurate measurement and control is essential to a strong healthy garden.

Most plants grow best in soil with a pH from 5.8 – 6.8. For specific pH recommendations for different plants see listings in the back of this book. Within this range, plants can properly absorb and process available nutrients most efficiently. If the pH is too low (acidic), acid salts bind nutrients chemically, and the roots are unable to absorb them. An alkaline soil with a high pH causes nutrients to become unavailable. Toxic salt build up that limits water intake by roots also becomes a problem. Hydroponic solutions perform best in a pH range a little lower than for soil. The ideal pH range for hydroponics is from 5.8 – 6.8. Some gardeners run the pH at lower levels and report no problems with nutrient uptake.

Measure pH with a soil test kit, litmus paper or electronic pH tester, all of which are available at most nurseries and hydroponic stores. When testing pH, take two or three samples

An inexpensive electronic pH tester is easy to use.

and follow instructions supplied by the manufacturer to the letter. Soil test kits measure soil pH and primary nutrient content by mixing soil with a chemical solution and comparing the color of the solution to a chart. Every one of these kits I have seen or used are difficult for novice gardeners to achieve accurate measurements. Comparing the color of the soil/chemical mix to the color of the chart is often confusing. If you use one of these kits, make sure to buy one with a good set of directions that are easy to understand and ask the sales clerk for exact recommendations on using it. A simple way to measure pH with a meter or litmus paper is to soak some soil in distilled water, put it in a paper towel and squeeze the water out into a cup and measure the water.

 Rule of Thumb: *The pH level is much more important in organic soil gardens than in chemical hydroponic gardens. The pH dictates the environment of bacteria necessary to the uptake of organic nutrients.*

If using litmus paper, collect soil samples that demonstrate an average of the soil. Place the samples in a clean jar and moisten the soil samples with distilled water. Place two pieces of the litmus paper in the muddy water. After 10 seconds, remove one of the strips of litmus paper. Wait a minute before removing the other one. Both pieces of litmus paper should register the same color. The litmus paper container should have a pH color chart on the side. To learn the pH, match the color of the litmus paper with the colors on the chart to get a pH reading. Litmus paper will accurately measure the acidity of the substance to within a point. The pH readings will not be accurate if altered by water with a high or low pH, and litmus paper could give a false reading if the fertilizer contains a color tracing agent.

Electronic pH testers are economical and convenient. Less expensive pH meters are accurate enough for casual use. More expensive models are quite accurate. Pay special attention to the soil moisture when taking a pH test with an electronic meter. The meters measure the electrical current between two probes and are designed to work in moist soil. Good pH meters use a permeable glass ball on the sensing end. Use a pH buffer to check the calibration and keep the

glass ball in storage solution or pH 4 buffer solution. If the
soil is dry, the probes do not give an accurate reading. Most
gardeners prefer electronic pH meters over the reagent test
kits and litmus paper because they are convenient, economical
and accurate. Once purchased, you can measure pH thousands of times with an electronic meter, while the chemical test
kits are good for about a dozen tests. Some meters measure
the pH perpetually.

 Rule of Thumb: *Always test the pH of raw water and*
drainage water with a pH meter.

For an accurate pH test with an electronic pH meter:
1. Clean the probes of the meter after each test and wipe
   away any corrosion.
2. Water soil with distilled or neutral pH water before testing.
3. Pack the soil tightly around the probes.

Check the pH of irrigation water. In dry climates, such as
the desert Southwest in the US and Australia, irrigation water is
often alkaline with a pH above 7.0. The water in rainy climates, such as the Pacific Northwest of North America, the UK
and maritime Northern Europe, is often acidic with a pH
below 6. After repeated irrigation, water with a pH that is too
high or low will change the pH of the growing medium, especially in organically amended soils. Climatic conditions can
also affect irrigation water pH. For example, the pH can
become more acidic in late autumn, when leaves fall and
decompose. Large municipalities carefully monitor and correct pH, and there are few water quality problems. Nonetheless,
be on the lookout for any major environmental changes that
could affect water pH. Check pH at least once a week.

 Rule of Thumb: *Raw water pH above 6.0 helps keep fertilizer*
mixes from becoming too acidic.

Most plants flourish when the pH is between 6.0 and 7.0.
Commercial potting soil almost never has a pH above 7.5. A
lower pH is more common, even as low as 5.5. Some potting
soils purchased at a nursery are pH balanced and near a neu-

tral 7. However, most potting soils have a tendency to be acidic. The easiest way to stabilize soil pH is to mix in one cup of fine dolomite lime per cubic foot of potting soil. Mix dolomite lime thoroughly into dry soil. Remix the soil in the container after it has been watered.

A few gardeners place charcoal in the bottom of containers to absorb excess salts and maintain sweet soil if plants are grown more than a few months.

Fine Dolomite Lime has been a favorite pH stabilizer of gardeners for years. It is difficult to apply too much as long as it is thoroughly mixed into soil. Dolomite has a neutral pH of 7 and can never raise the pH beyond 7. It stabilizes the pH safely. Compensate for acidic soil by mixing dolomite with soil before planting. It will help keep the pH stable, but correct the pH of acidic fertilizers before applying to growing medium. Dolomite, a compound of magnesium (Mg) and calcium (Ca), is popular among indoor gardeners. Dolomite does *not* prevent toxic salt accumulation in the growing medium caused by impure water and fertilizer buildup. A proper fertilizer regimen and regular leaching flush away toxic salts. When purchasing, look for dolomite flour, the finest, fastest-acting dust-like grade available. Coarse dolomite could take a year before it becomes available for uptake by roots. Mix fine dolomite thoroughly with the growing medium before planting. Improperly mixed, dolomite will stratify, forming a cake or layer that burns roots and repels them.

Rule of Thumb: When planting, add one cup of fine dolomite lime to each cubic foot (one ounce per gallon) of planting medium to stabilize the pH and provide calcium and magnesium.

Hydrated Lime contains only calcium and no magnesium. As the name hydrated implies, it is water-soluble. Fast-acting hydrated lime alters the pH quickly. Mix it thoroughly with warm water and apply with each watering for fastest results. Many gardeners use a mix of a quarter cup hydrated lime and three quarters cup dolomite lime. Hydrated lime is immediately available. Slower acting dolomite buffers the pH over the long term. Do not use more than one half cup of hydrated

lime per cubic foot of soil. The larger quantity is released so
fast that it can toxify soil, stunt or even kill plants. The beauty
of hydrated lime is that it washes out of the soil in about two
weeks. Leach it quicker by flushing pots with copious quantities of water. Hydrated lime is also used as a garden room fungicide. Sprinkle it on the floor and around the room. It kills
fungus on contact.

Do not use **quicklime**; it is toxic to plants. Calic lime (quicklime) contains only calcium and is not a good choice. It does
not have the buffering qualities of dolomite, nor does it contain any magnesium. Some growers use quicklime that is highly diluted in water.

Raise the pH of a growing medium or irrigation water by
adding some form of alkali, such as calcium carbonate, potassium hydroxide or sodium hydroxide. Both hydroxides are caustic and require special care when handling. These compounds
are normally used to raise the pH of hydroponic nutrient solutions but can be used to treat acidic nutrient solutions applied
to soil. The easiest and most convenient way to raise and stabilize soil pH is to add fine dolomite lime and hydrated lime
before planting. Do not use baking soda, it contains sodium.

 Rule of Thumb: *To raise the pH one point, add 3 cups of fine
dolomite lime to one cubic foot of soil. An alternate faster acting mix would be to add 2.5 cups of dolomite and one half
cup of hydrated lime to one cubic foot of soil.*

Pulverized eggshells, clam or oyster shells and wood ashes
have a high pH and raise soil pH. Eggshells and oyster shells
take a long time to decompose enough to effect pH; wood
ashes have a pH from 9 – 11 and are easy to over apply. Ashes
are often collected from fireplaces or wood stoves that have
been burning all kinds of trash and are, therefore, unsafe. Do
not use wood ashes on indoor gardens unless you know their
origin, pH and nutrient content.

Commercial potting soils and soilless mixes are generally
acidic and seldom need to be lowered. Fertilizers are naturally
acidic and lower the pH of the growing medium. Sulfur will
lower the pH if necessary, but it is tricky to use. I advise to use

an acid to alter the pH, but do not advise to use vinegar. Those that choose to, add distilled white vinegar at the rate of one teaspoon per gallon of irrigation water. Allow the water to sit for a few minutes and recheck. The pH should drop by a full point. If it does not, add more vinegar in small increments. Often when using vinegar, the pH drifts up overnight. Check the pH the next day. Hydroponic gardeners use phosphoric and nitric acid to lower pH. Keep a close eye on the pH and control it accordingly. After altering the pH, check it, and then check it again the next day and once or twice the following week to make sure it remains stable. Calcium nitrate can also be used, but is less common.

Aspirin also lowers the pH.

Rule of Thumb: *If new soil pH is under 5 or above 8, it is easiest and less expensive in the long run, to change soil rather than experimenting with changing the pH.*

Potting Soil

Potting soil fresh out of the bag often fulfills all of the requirements for a growing medium: good texture that allows good root penetration, water retention and good drainage, a stable pH (around 6.0) and a minimum supply of nutrients. Premium fast-draining soils with good texture that will not break down quickly are the best choice. Potting soils found at nurseries are formulated to retain water (contain a wetting agent) and air evenly, drain well and allow easy root penetration. Organic potting soil is becoming very popular. These soils are often fortified with organic nutrients including readily available high-nitrogen worm castings. Potting soils are very heavy and transportation costs tend to keep them somewhat localized. There are many good brands of high quality potting soil. Ask your nursery person for help in selecting one for fast-growing flowers and vegetables.

Many potting soils supply seedling transplants and clones with enough food (fertilizer) for the first two to four weeks of growth. After that, supplemental fertilization is necessary to retain rapid, robust growth. Add fine grade dolomite lime to buffer and stabilize the pH. Trace elements in "fortified" soil and soilless mixes can leach out and should be replenished with chelated nutrients. Organic gardeners often add their own blends of trace elements in mixes that contain seaweed, guanos and manures.

Do not reuse potting soil for another crop of flowers or vegetables. If used for more than one crop, undesirable microorganisms, insects and fungus start growing; nutrients are depleted, water and air retention are poor, causing compaction and poor drainage. Some gardeners mix their old potting soil with new potting soil to stretch their mix and save a few dollars. Cutting corners this way most often costs them more in problems.

 Warning! Potting soils containing more than 30 percent lightweight pumice or perlite may float and stratify when saturated with water before planting. Mix water-saturated soil thoroughly with your hands until it is evenly mixed before planting or transplanting if necessary.

Mushroom Compost

Mushroom compost is an inexpensive potting soil and soil amendment that is packed with organic goodies. Mushroom compost is sterilized chemically to provide a clean medium for mushroom growth. After serving its purpose as a mushroom growing medium it is discarded. Laws usually require that it sit fallow for two years or more to allow all the harmful sterilants to leach out. After lying fallow for several years, mushroom compost is very fertile and packed with beneficial microorganisms. The high-power compost could also foster anti-fungicidal and anti-bacterial properties in foliage and below the soil line, which helps guard against disease. Mushroom compost is packed with beneficial bacteria that hasten nutrient uptake. The texture, water holding and drainage in some mushroom compost should be amended with perlite to promote better drainage. Check your local nursery or extension service for a good source of mushroom compost. Some of the most abundant harvests I have seen were grown in mushroom compost.

Soilless Mix

Soilless mixes are very popular, inexpensive, lightweight sterile growing mediums. They have been used in commercial nurseries for decades. The mixes are generally made from a combination of the following: pumice, vermiculite, perlite, sand, peat moss and coconut coir. Pre-mixed commercial soilless mix is a favorite growing medium for many indoor gardeners. It allows for strong root penetration and even growth. Fertilizer concentration, moisture level and pH are very easy to control with precision in a soilless mix.

Soilless mix is inexpensive in 4-cubic-foot bails.

Soilless mixes are the preferred substrate for many bedding plant and vegetable seedling commercial gardeners. The commercial mixes are regaining ground against soil and other hydroponic mediums. Successful gardeners know that soilless mixes have good texture, hold water and drain well. Unless fortified with nutrients, soilless mixes contain no nutrients and are pH balanced near 6.0 – 7.0. Coarse soilless mixes drain well and are easy to force plants into growing faster with heavy fertilization. The fast-draining mixes can be leached efficiently so nutrients have little chance of building up to toxic levels. Look for ready-mixed bags of fortified soilless mixes, such as Jiffy Mix®, Ortho Mix®, Sunshine Mix®, Terra-Lite®, etc. To improve drainage, mix in 10 – 30 percent coarse perlite before planting. Fortified elements supply nutrients up to a month. I still recommend using a complete fertilizer designed for hydroponics that contains chelated trace elements.

Soilless components can be purchased separately and mixed to the desired consistency. Ingredients always blend together best when mixed dry and wetted afterwards using a "wetting agent," a detergent that improves water penetration and retention. Mix small amounts right in the bag. Larger batches should be mixed in a wheelbarrow or on a concrete slab. Blending your own soil or soilless mix is a dusty, messy job that takes a little space. To cut down on dust, lightly mist the pile with water several times when mixing. Always wear a respirator to avoid inhaling dust.

Rule of Thumb: *Mix dry soilless amendments outdoors and wear a respirator.*

Texture of soilless mix should be coarse, light and spongy. Such texture allows drainage with sufficient moisture and air retention, as well as providing good root penetration qualities. Fine soilless mix holds more moisture and works well with smaller containers. Soilless mixes using more perlite and sand drain faster, making them easier to fertilize heavier without excessive salt buildup. Vermiculite and peat hold water longer and make good ingredients in small pots to root clones or situations that require good water retention.

pH is generally near neutral, 7.0. If using more than 15 percent acidic peat, add appropriate dolomite or hydrated lime to correct and stabilize pH. Check the pH every week. Soilless mixes are composed mainly of mineral particles that are not affected by organic decomposition, which could change pH. The pH is affected by acidic fertilizers or by water with a high or low pH. Check the pH of the runoff water to ensure the pH in the medium is not too acidic.

Cutting and Seedling Cubes and Mixes

Rockwool root cubes, peat pellets and Oasis® blocks are pre-formed containers that make rooting cuttings, starting seedlings and transplanting them easy. Root cubes and peat pots also encourage strong root systems. Peat pellets like Jiffy-7, are small compressed peat moss containers with an outside expandable plastic netting wall. The flat pellets pop up into a seedling pot when watered.

Place a seed or cutting in a moist peat pot or root cube. If the little container does not have a planting hole make one with a pencil or a chopstick or a large nail. Set the seed or clone stem into the hole. Crimp the top over the seed or around the stem so constant contact is made with the medium. In one to three weeks, roots grow and show through the side of the cube. Cut the nylon mesh from peat pots before they get entangled with roots. To transplant, set the peat pot or root cube into a hole in larger pot. The beauty of using root cubes and peat pots is virtually no transplant shock. For rockwool cubes, break a small corner off with tweezers and put it in the hole over the seed.

Check moisture levels in peat pots and root cubes daily. Keep them evenly moist, but not drenched. Root cubes and peat pots do not contain any nutrients. Seedlings do not require nutrients for the first week or two. Feed seedlings after the first week and clones as soon as they are rooted with half strength nutrient solution.

Coarse, sharp sand, fine vermiculite and perlite work well to root cuttings. Sand and perlite are fast-draining, which helps prevent damping-off. Vermiculite holds water longer and makes sticking cuttings easier. A good mix is one third of each – sand, fine perlite and fine vermiculite. Premixed seed starter mixes sold under such brand names as Sunshine Mix® and Terra-Lite® are the easiest and most economical mediums to root clones and start seedlings. Soilless mix also allows for complete control of critical nutrient and root stimulating hormone additives for cuttings, essential to asexual propagation.

Soil Temperature

Raising the soil temperature speeds chemical process and hastens nutrient uptake. Ideally, the soil temperature should range from 65 – 75 degrees F for the most chemical activity. Warm the soil with soil heating cables or a heating pad. Most all soil heating cables have a built-in waterproof thermostat set for 72 degrees F. They should be placed on the bottom of starter trays and immersed under wet soil or nutrient solution in hydroponics. Fasten soil heating cables to a board or table and set a heat-conducting pad on top of the cables to distribute heat evenly. Set cuttings and seedlings in shallow flats or growing trays on top of the heat-conducting pad. The added heat speeds root growth by several days.

Soil heating cables cost much less than soil heating pads but must be installed, whereas the pads are ready to use. Most commercial nurseries handle cables and hydroponic stores carry heating pads. When rooting cuttings, a heating pad or cables virtually ensures success and expedites root growth.

Cold soil slows water and nutrient uptake and stifles growth. Gardeners often over-water when the soil is too cold or the garden room cools unexpectedly, further slowing growth. Pots on cold concrete floors stay as cold as the concrete, which is always colder than the ambient temperature. Increase soil tempera-ture by moving pots up off the floor a few inches. Set them on an insulating board or piece of Styrofoam™.

Soil temperatures that climb above 75 degrees F dehydrate roots and at higher temperatures, the roots actually cook! I advise to use a thermometer to check soil or nutrient solution temperature. Not all thermostats or heating controllers are accurate. It is relatively easy to heat the soil in a pot if you first heat the solution. Use heater to warm water/nutrient solution to 75 degrees F. Set pots in warm water/nutrient solution. If the light or any heat source is too close to small pots, it can easily heat up the outside layer of soil where the majority of the feeder roots are located. Once destroyed, feeder roots take one or two weeks to grow back.

Soil Amendments

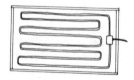

An inexpensive soil warming cable can be tacked to the bottom of a drawer lined with plastic to make a seed or cutting bed.

Soil amendments increase the soil's air and water retaining ability. Soil amendments fall into two cate-gories: mineral and organic.

Mineral amendments are all near neutral on the pH scale and contain few, if any, available nutrients. Mineral amendments decompose through weathering and erosion. They have the advantage of creating no bacterial activity to alter nutrient content and pH of the growing medium. Dry mineral amendments are also very lightweight and much easier to move in and out of awk-ward spaces.

Super Size Secret: *Add perlite, pumice or expanded clay to soil and soilless mixes to augment air and increase drainage.*

Perlite is sand or volcanic glass expanded by heat, like pop-corn. It holds water and nutrients on its many irregular sur-faces and works especially well for aerating the soil. This is a good medium to increase drainage during vegetative and flow-ering growth and does not promote fertilizer salt buildup. Versatile perlite is available in three main grades: fine, medium and coarse. Most gardeners prefer the coarse grade as a soil amendment. Perlite should make up one third or less of any mix to keep it from floating and stratifying the mix.

Pumice, volcanic rock, is very light and holds water, nutrients and air, in its many catacomb-like holes. It is a good amend-ment for aerating the soil and retaining moisture evenly. But like perlite, pumice floats and should constitute less than a third of any mix to avoid problems.

Vermiculite is mica processed and expanded by heat. It holds water, nutrients and air within its fiber and gives body to fast draining soils. Fine vermiculite holds too much water for cuttings, but does well when mixed with a fast draining medi-um. This amendment holds more water than perlite or pumice. Used in hydroponic wick systems, vermiculite holds and wicks much moisture. Vermiculite comes in three grades: fine, medium and coarse. Use fine vermiculite as an ingredi-ent in cloning mixes. If fine is not available, crush coarse or medium between your hands, rubbing palms back and forth. Coarse is the best choice as a soil amendment.

Organic soil amendments contain carbon and break down through bacterial activity, slowly yielding humus as an end product. Humus is a soft, spongy material that binds minute soil particles together, improving the soil texture. New actively composting organic soil amendments require nitrogen to carry on bacterial decomposition. If they do not contain at least 1.5 percent nitrogen, the organic amendment will get it from the soil, robbing roots of valuable nitrogen. When using organic amendments, make sure they are thoroughly composted (at least one year) and releasing nitrogen rather than using it from the soil. A dark rich color is a good sign of fertility.

Rich thoroughly composted organic matter amends texture and supplies nutrients. Leaf mold, garden compost (at least one year old) and many types of thoroughly composted manure, usually contain enough nitrogen for their decomposition needs and are releasing nitrogen, rather than using it. Purchase quality organic amendments at a reputable nursery. Look carefully at the descriptive text on the bag to see if it is sterilized and is guaranteed to contain no harmful insects, larvae, eggs, and fungi or bad microorganisms. Contaminated soil causes many problems that are easily averted with a clean mix.

Rule of Thumb: Properly grown organic vegetables have a very sweet aroma and taste.

Garden compost and leaf mold are usually rich in organic nutrients and beneficial organisms that speed nutrient uptake, but they can be full of harmful pests and diseases, too. For example, compost piles are a favorite breeding ground for cutworms and beetle larvae. Just one cutworm in a container means certain death for the defenseless plant.

Manure: Barnyard manure, a great fertilizer for outdoor gardens, often contains toxic levels of salt and copious quantities of weed seeds and fungus spores that disrupt an indoor garden. If using manure, purchase it in bags that guarantee its contents. There are many kinds of manure, cow, horse, rabbit and chicken, etc. All of which help retain water and improve soil texture when used as soil amendments. When mixing manures as amendments, do not add more than 10 – 15 percent to avoid salt buildup and over-fertilization. The nutrient content of manures varies, depending upon animal diet and decomposition factors.

Peat is the term used to describe partially decomposed vegetation; the decay has been slowed by the wet and cold conditions of the northern U.S. and Canada, where it is found in vast bogs. The most common types of peat are formed from sphagnum and hypnum mosses. These peats are harvested and used to amend soil and used as a growing medium. Peat moss is very dry and difficult to wet the first time, unless you bought it wet. Wet peat is heavy and awkward to transport. When adding peat moss as a soil amendment, cut your workload by dry-mixing all of the components before wetting. Use a wetting agent. Another trick to mixing peat moss is to kick the sack a few times to break the bale up before opening.

Sphagnum peat moss is light brown and the most common

peat found at commercial nurseries. This bulky peat gives soil
body and retains water well, absorbing 15 to 30 times its own
weight. It contains essentially no nutrients of its own and the
pH ranges from 3 – 5. After decomposing several months, the
pH could continue to drop and become very acidic. Counter
this propensity for acidity and stabilize the pH by adding fine
dolomite lime to the mix.

Hypnum peat moss is more decomposed and darker in color
with pH from 5.0 – 7.0. This peat moss is less common and
contains some nutrients. Hypnum peat is a good soil amendment, even though it cannot hold as much water as sphagnum
moss.

Coconut fiber is also called coir, palm peat, coco peat, cocos
and kokos. Coir is coconut pith, the fibery part just under the
heavy husk. Pith is soaked in water up to nine months to
remove salts, natural resins and gums in a process called "ret-
ting". Next, they beat the straw-brown coir to extract the husk.

Coir is biodegradable and a good medium for propagation
through flowering and fruit growth. Coir holds lots of water
while maintaining structure. It is durable, rot resistant and a
good insulator too.

*Super Size Secret: Coconut coir is becoming very popular
indoors. It is inexpensive, easy-to-control and holds lots of
air.*

Washed, pressed blocks or bricks of coir are virtually inert.
Bricks weigh about 600 grams (1.3 pounds) to one kilogram
(2.2 pounds). The pH is between 5.5 and 6.8. Some of the
best coconut coir is from the interior of the Philippine Islands,
where the environment is not packed with coastal salts. Quality
coconut coir is guaranteed to have sodium content of less than
50 PPM.

Gardeners use coir by itself or mixed 50/50 with perlite or
expanded clay to add extra drainage to the mix. Some gardeners sprinkle coconut coir on top of rockwool blocks to keep the
top from drying out.

Flake and break dry bricks of coconut coir apart by hand or
soak the bricks in a bucket of water for 15 minutes to expand
and wet. One brick will expand to about 9 times its original

size. Growing in coconut coir is similar to growing in any
other soilless medium. Coconut coir may stay a little too wet
and require more ventilation and air circulation.

Soil Mixes

Some gardeners mix their own soil. Too often misguided
novices go out to the back yard and dig up some good-looking
dirt that drains poorly and retains water and air unevenly. The
problems are compounded when they mix the dirt with garden
compost packed with harmful microorganisms and pests. This
lame soil mix grows sickly plants. By saving a few bucks on soil,
such gardeners create unforeseen problems and pay for their
savings many times over with low harvest yields. Avert problems with soil mixes by purchasing all of the components. Use
garden soil or compost only if they are top quality and void of
harmful pests and diseases. Use only the richest, darkest garden soil with a good texture. Amend the soil by up to 80 percent to improve water retention and drainage. Even a soil that
drains well in the outdoor garden needs amending to drain
properly indoors. Check the pH of the garden soil before dig-
ging to ensure it is between 6.0 and 7.0. Add fine dolomite to
stabilize and buffer pH. Check pH several times after mixing
to ensure it is stable.

Sterilize small amounts (a gallon or less) of outdoor garden
soil by spreading it out on a cookie sheet and bake in the oven
at 160 degrees F for 10 minutes. Heat bakes out all the bad
insects, bacteria and fungi, but leaves most of the good ones.
The stench can be horrible and playing with dirt in the kitchen
is messy. One friend swears by his backyard fire pit. He set a
barbeque grill on top of brick sides to form a soil cooker.

Compost

Some gardeners have no trouble with organic composts, but
others have bad luck and even lose their entire crop when
growing in backyard compost. Good compost recipes are available from monthly publications such as *Sunset, Organic
Gardening, Mother Earth News* or from the companies specializ-
ing in organic composts. Few gardeners use homemade compost.

A good compost pile includes manure, the older the better. Manure from horse stalls or cattle feed lots are mixed with straw or sawdust bedding. Sawdust uses available nitrogen and is also acidic and not recommended. Look for the oldest, rottenest manure. Well-rotted manure is less prone to have viable weed seeds and pests. Fresh nitrogen-packed grass clippings are one of my favorites to use in a compost pile. Put your hand down deep into a pile of grass clippings. Temperatures one or two feet down in such a pile range from 120 to 180 degrees F. Heat generated by chemical activity kills pests, breaks down the foliage and liberates the nutrients.

 Rule of Thumb: *Make sure all composts are well rotted and have cooled before mixing with indoor soil.*

Build compost piles high and keep turning them. Good compost pile recipes include the addition of organic trace elements, enzymes and the primary nutrients. The organic matter used should be ground up and in the form of shredded leaves and grass. Do not use large woody branches that could take years to decompose.

Before using compost, pour it through quarter-inch mesh hardware cloth (screen) to break up the humus before mixing with soil. Place a heavy-duty framed screen over a large garbage can or a wheelbarrow to catch the sifted compost. Return earthworms found on the screen to the medium and kill cutworms. For more information about composting, see *Let It Rot*, by Stu Campbell, Storey Press, Prowal, VT.

Some gardeners mix up to 30 percent perlite into organic potting soil that contains lots of worm castings. Heavy worm castings compact soil and leave little space for air to surround roots. Adding perlite or similar amendments aerates soil and improves drainage. Mix thoroughly by hand or with a trowel.

Containers

Container preference is often a matter of convenience, cost and availability. But the size and shape of a container can affect the size and health of a plant as well as the versatility of the garden. Containers come in all shapes and sizes and can be constructed of almost anything; clay, metal, plastic, wood

Mixes of compost and soil

1/2 compost	1/2 compost
1/2 soilless mix	1/2 coco coir
1/3 compost	1/3 compost
1/3 soilless mix	1/3 soilless mix
1/3 coconut coir	1/6 worm castings
	1/6 perlite

and wood fiber are the most common. Plants will grow in any clean container that has not been used for petroleum products or deadly chemicals. Clay fiber and wood containers breathe better than plastic or metal pots. Heavy clay pots are brittle and absorb moisture from soil inside, causing soil to dry out quickly. Metal pots are also impractical for garden rooms because they oxidize (rust) and bleed off harmful elements and compounds. Wood, although somewhat expensive, makes some of the best containers, especially large raised beds and planters on wheels. Plastic containers are inexpensive, durable and offer the best value to indoor gardeners.

Rigid plastic pots are the most commonly used containers in garden rooms. Growing in inexpensive, readily available containers is brilliant because they allow each plant to be cared for individually, controlling its specific water and nutrient regimen. Individual plants can also be moved. Turn the pots of plants receiving light on just one side every few days so foliage fills out evenly. Huddle small, containerized plants tightly together on the floor or on a bench under the brightest area below the HID lamp and move them further apart as they grow. Set small plants up on blocks to move them closer to the HID. Individual plants are easily quarantined or dipped in a medicinal solution. Weak, sick and problem plants are easily culled from the room.

Grow bags are my favorite containers. Inexpensive long lasting grow bags take up little space and are lightweight. A box of 100 3-gallon bags weighs less than 5 pounds and measures less than a foot square. One hundred 3-gallon grow bags can be stored in two 3-gallon bags. Imagine storing 100 rigid pots in the same space!

Grow bags are very easy to wash and reuse. Empty out the soilless mix and submerge bags in a big container of soapy water overnight. Wash each one by hand the next day and fill with soil. I like them much better than rigid pots because they are so practical.

The potting soil sack can be used as a container. They grow OK plants, but the roots do not make the best use of space and the growing medium. The moist soil inside the bag holds its shape well and bags expand and contract with the soil, lessening the chance of burned root tips that grow down the side of pots.

Fiber and paper-pulp pots are popular with gardeners who move their plants outdoors. The bottoms of the pots habitually rot out. Painting the inside of the fiber container with latex paint will keep the bottom from rotting for several crops.

Large planters set up on blocks or casters to allow air circulation underneath and make good garden beds. The soil stays warmer and maintenance is easier. Planters should be as big as possible, but still allow easy access to plants. The roots have more room to grow and less side surface for roots to run into and grow down. Roots are able to intertwine and grow like crazy.

Raised beds can be installed right on the earthen floor of a garage or basement. If drainage is poor, a layer of gravel or a dry well can be made under the bed. Some gardeners use a jackhammer to remove the concrete floor in a basement to get better drainage. An easier option is to cut a hole in the basement floor and install a dry well. But knocking holes in basement floors could cause water seepage where water tables are high. When it rains, the water may collect underneath. The garden seldom needs watering, but plants are kept too wet.

A raised bed with a large soil mass can be built up organically after several crops. To hasten organic activity within the soil, add organic seaweed and manure. When mixing soil or adding amendments, use the best possible organic components and follow organic principles. There should be good drainage and the soil should be as deep (12 – 24 inches) as possible.

You can treat the beds similar to outdoor soil beds, but when you irrigate heavily, water runs out on the floor and must be mopped up. Even with a good bank of soil, individual beds should be flushed at least once every four weeks to avoid nutrient buildup.

Much heat can be generated by decomposition of organic matter. Heat not only speeds nutrient uptake, but also helps warm the room. Ventilation lowers heat, humidity and helps keep the room free of pests and diseases. An organic soil garden sounds great, but it is a lot of work to replicate the great outdoors. Most "organic" gardeners opt for organic liquid fertilizers and a bagged commercial organic soil mix.

Containers must be:
   Clean
   Have adequate drainage holes
   Big enough to accommodate plant

Drainage

All containers need some form of drainage. Drainage holes allow excess water and nutrient solution to flow freely out the bottom of a container. They should let water drain easily, but not be so big that growing medium washes out onto the floor. Containers should have at least two half-inch holes per square foot of bottom. Most pots have twice this amount. To slow drainage and keep soil from washing out large holes, add a one-inch layer of gravel in the bottom of the pot. Surface tension created by the different size of soil and rock particles cause water to be retained at the bottom of the container. Or line pots with newspaper, nylon mesh window screen or broken pieces of clay pots if drainage is too fast or if soil washes out drain holes. This will slow drainage, so be wary!

 Rule of Thumb: Containers should have at least two fi-inch holes per square foot of bottom. When using a tray under a pot, do not let excess water sit in the tray for more than a day. Stagnant water causes root rot and fungi growth.

Put trays under containers to catch excess water. Leaving water-filled saucers under pots often retains too much moisture, which causes root rot. Set containers up an inch or two on blocks when using trays to avoid water logging soil and roots.

Nursery trays used for rooting cuttings and growing seedlings must have good drainage throughout the entire bottom. Once clones and seedlings are in place in the tray, the tray should always drain freely with no standing water in the bottom.

Container Shape, Size and Maintenance

Popular pot shapes include rectangular and cylindrical. Gardeners prefer taller pots, rather than wide squat containers, because the root system penetrates deeply. Of all the gardens I have visited, squat pots were few and far between. Gardeners I queried about them said they may hold more soil for their stature, but did not produce as extensive of a root system.

The volume of a container can easily dictate the size of a plant. For example, annual flowers and vegetables grow very fast and require a lot of root space for sustained vigorous development. Containers should be big enough to allow for a strong root system, but be just big enough to contain the root system before harvest. If the container is too small, roots are confined, water and nutrient uptake is limited and growth slows to a crawl. But if the container is too big, it requires too much expensive growing medium and becomes heavy and awkward to move.

Fast growing annual flowers and vegetable roots develop and elongate quickly, growing down and out, away from the main taproot. For example, about midsummer nurseries have unsold tomato plants that are still in small four inch and one-gallon containers. The stunted plants have blooming flowers and ripe fruit. But few branches extend much beyond the sides of the container; the plants are tall and leggy with curled down leaves and an overall stunted sickly appearance. These plants are pot or root-bound. Once a plant deteriorates to this level, it is often easier and more efficient to toss it out and replace it with a healthy one.

Roots soon hit the sides of containers where they grow down and matt up around the bottom. The unnatural environment inside the container often causes a thick layer of roots to grow alongside the container walls and bottom. This portion of the root zone is the most vulnerable to moisture and heat stress and is the most exposed!

When soil dries in a pot, it becomes smaller, contracting and separating from the inside of the container wall. This condition is worst in smooth plastic pots. When this crack develops, frail root hairs located in the gap quickly die when they are exposed to air whistling down this crevice. Water also runs straight down this crack and onto the floor. You many think the pot was watered, but the root ball remains dry. Avoid such killer cracks by cultivating the soil surface and running your finger around the inside lip of pots. Cultivate the soil in pots every few days and maintain soil evenly moist to help keep root hairs on soil perimeter from drying out.

Do not place containers in direct heat. If soil temperature climbs beyond 75 degrees F, it can damage roots. Pots that are in direct heat should be shaded with a piece of plastic or cardboard.

 Super Size Secret: Run your finger around the inside lip of each container to break up the soil and fill the crack along the inside of the pot. Water pot heavily so that soil fills gap and feeding root hairs stay moist.

Transplant before roots become pot bound and rapid growth is stunted. A stunted plant takes several weeks to grow enough new feeder roots to resume normal growth. Transplant at the proper time relative to a cutting's or seedling's growth stage and rate to keep them growing fast during all stages of life to ensure a strong healthy high-yielding crop.

Seedlings and cuttings can also be transplanted directly into a 3 – 5-gallon pot. It requires fewer containers, less work and less possible plant stress. The larger volume of soil holds water and nutrients longer and requires less frequent watering. Often when small cuttings and seedlings are transplanted directly into a 5-gallon container, the roots grow down and out toward the container walls and bottom. Roots do not grow into much of the soil in the container.

To get roots to develop a dense compact system, transplant just before roots have outgrown their container. Transplanting a well-rooted cutting in a root cube into a 4-inch pot and transplanting the 4-inch pot into a 3-gallon pot or grow bag causes roots to develop a more extensive system than in a small ball of growing medium. Successful transplanting generates mini-

Water & Nutrients

Nitrogen

Deficiency: Nitrogen is the most common nutrient deficiency. Symptoms include slower growth. Lower leaves cannot produce chlorophyll and become yellow between veins while veins remain green. Yellowing progresses through entire leaf, eventually causing it to die and drop off. Stems and leaf undersides may turn reddish-purple, but this could also be a sign of a phosphorus deficiency. Nitrogen is very mobile, dissipates into the environment quickly, and must be added regularly to sustain fast growing gardens.

Toxicity: An overdose of nitrogen will cause excessively lush foliage that is soft and susceptible to stress, including insect and fungal attacks. Stems become weak and may fold over easily. The vascular transport tissue breaks down and water uptake is restricted. In severe cases, leaves turn a brownish-copper color, dry and fall off. Roots develop super slowly and tend to darken and rot. Flowers are smaller and sparse. Ammonium toxicity is most common in acid soils, while nitrate toxicity is more prevalent in alkaline soil.
For more information see page 130 in the text.

Phosphorus

Deficiency: A lack of phosphorous causes stunted growth. Leaves are smaller, bluish-green and often with blotches. Stems, leaf stems (petioles) and main veins on some plants may turn reddish-purple starting on leaf underside. NOTE: The reddening of stems and veins is not always well pronounced. Leaf tips of older leaves turn dark and curl downward. Leaves severely affected develop large purplish-black necrotic (dead) blotches. These leaves later become bronzish-purple, dry, shrivel up, contort and drop off. Flowering and fruit set are often delayed, buds are uniformly smaller, seed yield is poor and plants become very vulnerable to fungal and insect attack. Stunted and very slow growth.

Toxic signs of phosphorus may take several weeks to surface, especially if excesses are buffered by a stable pH. Most annual flowers and vegetables use a lot of phosphorus throughout life and many varieties tolerate high levels. Excessive phosphorus interferes with calcium, copper, iron, magnesium and zinc stability and uptake. Toxic symptoms of phosphorous manifest as a deficiency of zinc, iron, magnesium, calcium and copper; zinc is the most common.

For more information see page 131 in the text.

Potassium

Deficiency: Potassium-starved plants initially appear healthy. Symptoms include: older leaves, first browning on the tips and margins, followed by whole leaves turn dark yellow and die; sStems often become weak and sometimes brittle; plants become susceptible to disease. Potassium is usually present in soil, but can be locked up by high salinity. First, leach the toxic salt out of the soil, and then apply a complete N-P-K fertilizer. A potassium deficiency causes the internal temperature of foliage to climb and protein in the cells burn or degrade. Evaporation is normally highest on leaf edges and that's where burning takes place.

Toxicity: Occurs occasionally and is difficult to diagnose because it is mixed with the deficiency symptoms of other nutrients. Too much potassium impairs and slows the absorption of magnesium, manganese and sometimes zinc and iron. Look for signs of toxic potassium buildup when symptoms of magnesium, manganese, zinc and iron deficiencies appear, water uptake affected similar to high saline conditions; leaf burn and wilting.

See page 132 in the text for more information.

Magnesium

Deficiency: Magnesium deficiency is common indoors. Lower and later middle leaves develop yellow patches between darker green veins and rust-brown spots appear on leaf margins, tips and between veins as deficiency progresses. The brownish leaf tips usually curl upward before dying. The entire plant could discolor in a few weeks, and if severe, turn a yellow-whitish tinge before browning and dying. A minor deficiency causes little or no problems with growth. However, minor deficiencies escalate and cause a diminished harvest as flowering progresses.

Toxicity: Magnesium toxicity is rare and difficult to discern with the naked eye. If extremely toxic, magnesium develops a conflict with other fertilizer ions, usually calcium, especially in hydroponic nutrient solutions. Toxic buildup of magnesium in soils that are able to grow most fast growing annuals is uncommon.

See page 135 in the text for more information.

Get the whole family working for you.

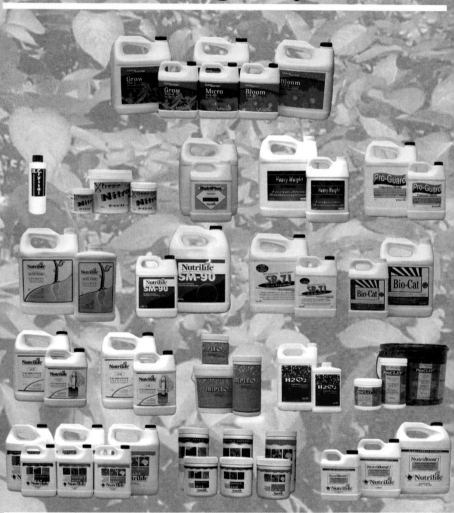

Iron

Deficiency: Iron deficiencies are common when the pH is above 6.5 and uncommon when the pH is below 6.5. Symptoms may appear during rapid growth or stressful times and disappear by themselves. Young leaves are unable to draw immobile iron from older leaves, even though it is present in soil. First symptoms appear on smaller leaves as interveinal chlorosis where veins remain green and areas between veins turns yellow or white. Note that interveinal chlorosis starts at the opposite end of the leaf tip, the apex of the leaves attached by the petiole. As the deficiency progresses, the chlorosis becomes more acute. Leaves and buds fall off in severe cases. Iron deficiency is sometimes traced to an excess of copper. See "Copper."

Toxicity: Excess iron is rare. High levels of iron do not damage most plants, but it can interfere with phosphorus uptake and other elements. An excess of iron causes leaves to turn bronze accompanied by small, dark-brown leaf spots. If iron chelate is over-applied, it will kill the plant in a few days.
Treat excess iron by leaching plants heavily.

See page 143 for more information.

Sulfur

Deficiency: Young leaves turn lime-green to yellowish. As shortage progresses leaves yellow interveinally and lack succulence. Veins remain green. Leaf stems, petioles, turn purple. Leaf tips can burn, darken and hook downward. In some plants the youngest leaves yellow first, but in other plants, the symptoms are most obvious in the older leaves. Sulfur deficiency resembles a nitrogen deficiency. Acute sulfur deficiency causes elongated stems that become woody at the base. Sulfur deficiency occurs indoors when the pH is too high or when there excessive calcium present and available.

Toxicity: An excess of sulfur in the soil causes no problems if the EC tively low. At a high EC plants tend to take up more "available" sulfur, which blocks uptake of other nutrients. Excess sulfur symptoms include overall smaller plant development and uniformly smaller dark green foliage. Leaf tips and margins could discolor and burn when severe. Saline toxicity, wilting (some plants) non-salt tolerant.

See page 138 for more information and treatments.

GROTEK

SCIENCE
FOR PLANTS

Grotek.net

Zinc

Deficiency: Zinc is the most common micronutrient found deficient. First younger leaves exhibit interveinal chlorosis. New leaves and growing tips develop small thin blades, contort and wrinkle. This condition is called "resetting" or "little leaf". Leaf tips, and later margins, discolor and burn. These symptoms are often confused with a lack of manganese or iron, but when zinc deficiency is severe, new leaf blades contort and dry out. Flowers can also contort into odd shapes, turn crisp, dry and are often hard. A lack of zinc stunts all new growth.

Treat zinc deficient plants by flushing growing medium with a dilute mix of a complete fertilizer containing chelated trace elements, including zinc, iron and manganese. Or add a quality brand of a hydroponic micronutrient mix containing chelated trace elements.

Toxicity: Zinc is extremely toxic in excess. Severely toxic plants die quickly. Excess zinc interferes with iron's ability to function property and causes an iron deficiency. Leaves are small, dark and wilt.

See page 141 for more information.

Manganese

Deficiency: Young leaves show symptoms first. They become yellow between veins – interveinal chlorosis – veins remain green. Symptoms spread from young to older leaves as deficiency progresses. Necrotic (dead) spots develop on severely affected leaves before they fall off. Overall plant growth is stunted and maturation may be prolonged. Severe deficiency looks like a severe lack of magnesium. Treat with small amount of magnesium sulfate of chelate.

Toxicity: Young and newer growth develops chlorotic dark orange to dark rusty brown mottling on leaves. Tissue shows on young leaves before progressing to older leaves. Growth is slower, overall vigor is lost. Toxicity is compounded by low humidity. The additional transpiration causes more manganese to be drawn into foliage. An excess of manganese causes a deficiency of iron and zinc.

See page 142 for more information.

Water & Nutrients

In the Netherlands, where hydroponics is big business, they use big water systems as well. These large tanks hold lots of nutrient solution at a rather stable temperature, because of the mass involved. Inside the control box is a PC linked to keypads at the end of the garden rows throughout this greenhouse. Nutrient flow and temperature can be adjusted section by section remotely, or from a central control station.

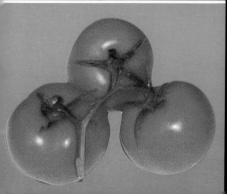

Strong root systems like these are common in hydroponically grown tomatoes.

Water & Nutrients

Catching a glimpse of the future in a pool of nutrient solution, these students could be the future farmers of the world.

mum stress. Annual indoor
flower and vegetable gardens are
in the ground for such a short
time that transplant shock slows
growth and costs valuable recu-
peration time.

Transplant cuttings and
seedlings into raised beds and
large planter boxes directly from
4-inch pots. As many as 20

*Cultivating soil surface with your
fingers or a fork increases water
penetration.*

plants can be transplanted into a 24 by 24 by 12-inch planter,
but 6 – 12 plants will yield about the same. Once plants start
crowding and shading one another, bend stems outwards and
tie them to a trellis attached to the planter. Large planters
require less maintenance. The larger mass of soil retains water
and nutrients much longer and more evenly. One downside is
that all plants must receive the same water and diet. Choose
plants that will grow together well and receive the same water
and nutrient regimen.

 Super Size Secret: *Transplant well-rooted cutting into a 4-
inch pot; transplant the 4-inch pot into a 3-gallon container.
Proper transplanting causes roots to develop in the small pot
first.*

Three-gallon containers are the ideal size for 2 – 3-foot
plants. Larger pots are best for plants that grow more than
three feet tall. Smaller 2 – 3-gallon pots are easy to move and
work with. However, smaller containers require daily watering
and a more vigilant eye.

Larger plants that grow longer than a few months require
containers up to 30 gallons in size, especially if growing for a
year or longer.

 Rule of Thumb: *Allow 1 – 1.5 gallons of soil or soilless mix
for each month the plant will spend in the container. A 2 –
3-gallon pot supports a plant for up to three months. 3 – 6–
gallon containers are good for 3 – 4 months of rapid plant
growth.*

Plant age	Container size
0 – 3 weeks	root cube
2 – 6 weeks	4-inch pot
6 – 8 weeks	2-gallon pot
6 – 8 weeks	3-gallon pot
2 – 3 months	4-gallon pot
3 – 8 months	5-gallon pot
6 – 18 months	10-gallon pot

How to Pot a Seed, Step-by-Step

Step One: Acquire the desired number of clean pots.

Step Two: Fill the pot with well-mixed growing medium to about one inch from the top.

Step Three: Water with warm water until soil is completely saturated and excess water runs freely out the drain holes. Wait 15 minutes and repeat watering to ensure saturation.

Step Four: With your finger or pencil, make a small hole fi-inch deep in the surface. Place a (sprouted) seed in each hole and cover with moist soil. Point the rootlet down. Pack it gently, but firmly in place. Place a paper towel over the planted area to keep the soil surface moist and to keep soil from washing away.

Step Five: Sprinkle water on the surface. Make sure seeds remain at proper depth and do not wash out.

Step Six: Maintain soil surface evenly moist. Check twice daily.

Step Seven: Remove paper towel as soon as growing shoots break ground.

Step Eight: Grow a strong, healthy plant. Keep moist and use half-strength fertilizer for the first 2 – 3 weeks of growth.

Water and Nutrients

Water, the "universal solvent," provides a medium to transport nutrients necessary for plant life and make them available for absorption by the roots. Water quality is essential to this process working at maximum potential. The laws of physics govern plant water uptake. Applying these laws, a gardener can provide precise, properly balanced components to grow outstanding indoor gardens.

Microscopic root hairs absorb water and nutrients in the presence of oxygen in the growing medium and carry them up the stem to the leaves. This flow of water from the soil through the plant is called the transpiration stream. A fraction of the water is processed and used in photosynthesis. Excess water evaporates into the air, carrying waste products along with it, via the stomata in the leaves. This process is called transpiration. Some of the water also returns manufactured sugars and starches to the roots.

Roots support plants, absorb nutrients and provide the initial pathway into the vascular system. A close up look at a root reveals the xylem and phloem core vascular tissue that is enveloped by a cortex tissue, the layer between the internal vascular and the external epidermal tissue. The microscopic root hairs are located on the epidermal tissue cells. These tiny root hair follicles are extremely delicate and must remain moist. Root hairs must be protected from abrasions, drying out, extreme temperature fluctuations and harsh chemical concentrations. Plant health and vigor is contingent upon strong healthy roots.

Nutrient absorption begins at the root hairs and the flow continues throughout the plant via the vascular system. Absorption is sustained by diffusion and osmotic pressure. In the process of diffusion, water and nutrient ions are uniformly distributed throughout the plant. The intercellular spaces, aproplasts and connecting protoplasm, symplast, are the pathways that allow the water and nutrient ions and molecules to pass through the epidermis and cortex to the xylem and phloem's vascular bundles. The xylem channels the solution via capillary action and active transport through the plant while phloem tissues distribute foods manufactured by the plant. Once nutrients are transferred to plant cells, each cell accumulates the nutrients they require to perform their specific function.

The solution transported through the vascular bundles or veins of a plant has many functions. This solution delivers nutrients and carries away waste products. It also provides pressure to help keep the plant structurally sound. The solution also cools the plant by evaporating water via leaf stomata.

Osmosis

Roots draw nutrient solution up by the process of osmosis, the amount of dissolved salts present. Osmosis is the tendency of fluids to pass through a semi-permeable membrane and mix with each other until the fluids are equally concentrated on both sides of the membrane. Semi-permeable membranes located in root hairs allow specific nutrients dissolved in water to enter the plant while other nutrients and impurities are excluded. Since salts and sugars are concentrated in roots, the EC inside roots should always be higher than that outside the roots. If the opposite is true, such as too high a concentration of fertilizer salts, water is sucked out of the roots causing plants to wilt and die. Nutrient transport by osmosis works because it depends on relative concentrations of each individual nutrient on each side of the membrane. For nutrients to be drawn in by roots via osmosis, the strength of individual elements must be greater than that inside the roots.

But, the transport of water (instead of nutrients) across the semi-permeable membrane depends on EC. For example, if EC is greater outside the roots than inside, the plant dehydrates as water is drawn out of the roots. In other words, salty water with a high EC can dehydrate plants.

Reverse osmosis (RO) machines are used to separate dissolved solids from water. These machines move the solvent (water) through the semi-permeable membrane, but the process is reversed; it moves from lower concentrations to higher. The process is accomplished by applying pressure to the "tainted" water to force only "pure" water through the membrane. The water is not totally "pure" with an EC of "0", but most of the dissolved solids are removed. The efficiency of the reverse osmosis depends on the type of membrane, the pressure differential on both sides of the membrane and the chemical composition of the dissolved solids in the tainted water.

Unfortunately, common tap water often contains high levels of sodium, calcium, alkaline salts, sulfur and chlorine. The pH could also be out of the acceptable 5.8 – 6.8 range. Water containing sulfur is easily smelled and tasted. Saline water is a little more difficult to detect. Water in coastal areas is generally full of salt that seeps inland from the ocean. Dry regions that have less than 20 inches annual rainfall also suffer from alkaline soil and water that is often packed with alkaline salts. When water evaporates, the salt is left behind and gets concentrated such as in the Great Salt Lake in Utah or the Dead Sea in Israel.

Table salt, sodium chloride (NaCl), is added to many household water systems. A small amount of chlorine, below 140 PPM, does not affect the health of most plants, but higher levels cause foliage chlorosis and stunt growth. Remember, sodium (Na) is toxic to plants. Do not use salt-softened water. Salty, brackish and salt-softened water is detrimental to most plants. Chlorine also tends to acidify soil after repeated applications and is toxic to plants in all but very small doses. The best way to get chlorine out of water is to let it sit one or two days in an open container. The chlorine will evaporate (volatize) as a gas when it comes in contact with air. If chlorine noticeably alters soil pH, adjust it with a commercial "pH UP" product or hydrated lime.

The metric system facilitates the measurement of "dry residue per liter". Measure dry residue per liter by pouring a liter of water on a tray and allow it to evaporate. The residue of dissolved solids that remains after all the water evaporates is the "dry residue per liter". The residue is measured in grams. Try this at home to find out the extent of impurities. Fertilizers have a difficult time penetrating root tissue when they must compete with resident dissolved solids.

Water that is packed with high of levels of dissolved solids (salts in solution) is possible to mange but requires different

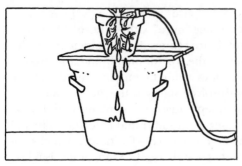

Flushing plants with plain water will wash out most built up toxic salts. Flush again with a dilute nutrient solution.

tactics. Highly saline water that contains sodium will block the uptake of potassium, calcium and magnesium. Salt-laden water will always cause problems. If water contains 300 PPM or less dissolved solids, allow at least 25 percent of the irrigation water to drain out the bottom of containers with each watering. If raw water contains more than 300 PPM of dissolved solids, use a reverse osmosis device to purify the water.

Dissolved salts caused by saline water and fertilizer build up to toxic levels quickly in container gardens. Excessive salts inhibit seed germination, burn root hairs, tips and edges of leaves and stunt the plant. Flush excess salt built up from growing mediums by applying 2 gallons of water per gallon of medium. Repeat leaching using a mild pH-corrected fertilizer solution. Leach growing medium every 2 – 4 weeks if using soft water or saline water. Hard water and well water in dry climates is often alkaline and usually contains notable amounts of calcium and magnesium. Many fast growing flowers and vegetables use large quantities of both nutrients, but too much calcium or magnesium can buildup in soil. In general, water that tastes good to people, also "tastes" good to plants.

Hard Water

The concentration of calcium and magnesium indicate how "hard" the water is. Water containing 100 to 150 milligrams of calcium ($CaCO_3$) per liter is acceptable to grow most plants. "Soft" water contains less than 50 milligrams of calcium per liter and should be supplemented with calcium and magnesium.

Sodium Chloride and Water Quality

Water with high levels of chloride frequently contains high levels of sodium, but the opposite is not true. Water with high levels of sodium does not necessarily contain excessive levels of chloride.

At low levels, sodium appears to bolster yields, possibly acting as a partial substitute for potassium deficiencies. But when excessive, sodium is toxic and induces deficiencies of other nutrients, primarily potassium, calcium and magnesium.

Chloride (chlorine) is essential to the use of oxygen during photosynthesis and is necessary for root and leaf cell division. Chloride is vital to increase cellular osmotic pressure, modify stomata regulation and augment plant tissue moisture content. A solution concentration of less than 140 PPM is usually safe for most fast growing annuals, but some may show sensitivity when foliage turns pale green and wilts. Excessive chlorine causes leaf tips and margins to burn and leaves to turn a bronze color.

Super Size Secret: *Run water with more than 300 PPM dissolved solids through a reverse osmosis machine.*

Super Size Secret: *Add nutrients to pure water and avoid many nutrient problems.*

Simple water filters do not clean dissolved solids from the water. Such filters remove debris emulsified (suspended) in water. Releasing dissolved solids from their chemical bond is more complex. A reverse osmosis machine uses small polymer semi-permeable membranes that let pure water pass through and filters out dissolved solids from water. Reverse osmosis machines are the easiest most efficient means to clean contaminated water.

Irrigation

Large plants use more water than small plants, but there are many more variables than size that dictate a plant's water consumption. The age of the plant, container size, soil texture, temperature, humidity and ventilation all contribute to water needs. Change any one of these variables and water consumption will change. Good ventilation is essential to promote a free flow of fluids, transpiration and rapid growth. The healthier a plant, the faster it grows and the more water it needs.

 Rule of Thumb: *Plants process tepid (70 – 80 degrees F) water rapidly and it penetrates the growing medium more easily. Tepid water does not shock tender root hairs or leaves.*

 Rule of Thumb: *Water early in the day so excess water will evaporate from soil surface and leaves during the daytime. This increases humidity around the plants during hot days and cools them by evaporation of the water. Leaving foliage and soil wet overnight invites a fungal attack.*

Small plants with a small root system in small containers must be watered often. Frequent fertilization and irrigation is necessary as soon as the soil surface dries out.

Irrigate soil and soilless mixes when it is dry one-half inch below the surface. As long as drainage is good, it's difficult to over-water fast growing annuals. Four-week-old cuttings flowering in 2 – 3-gallon containers need daily irrigation. In fact, many gardeners prefer smaller containers because they are easier to control.

 Super Size Secret: *Use plenty of water, mix fertilizer solution properly and allow 25 percent runoff during each watering.*

 Rule of Thumb: *Irrigate small seedlings and cuttings when the soil surface is dry. If using a humidity dome, watering is necessary every 4 – 6 days. Cuttings and seedlings grown in the open air need watering more often.*

 Rule of Thumb: *Irrigate larger plants in the vegetative and flowering stages when soil is dry one inch below the surface. Flowering and fruiting plants use high levels of water to carry on rapid floral and fruit formation. Withholding water actually stunts flower and fruit formation.*

A moisture meter takes most of the guesswork out of irrigating. They can be purchased for less than $30 and are well worth the money. The meter can tell exactly how much water the soil contains at any level or point. Often soil will not hold water evenly and develops dry pockets. Checking moisture with a finger is an educated guess and disturbs the root system. A moisture meter will give an exact moisture reading without disturbing roots too much.

 Rule of Thumb: *Line pots up when irrigating so you can keep track of watered pots.*

Cultivating the soil surface allows water to penetrate evenly and guards against dry soil pockets. It also keeps water from running down the crack between the inside of the pot and the soil and out the drain holes. Gently break up and cultivate the top half-inch of soil with your fingers or a salad fork. Be careful not to disturb tiny surface roots.

The trick is to apply enough water so all of the soil gets wet and not let too much run out the drain holes, which will cause a leaching effect, carrying away nutrients. Nonetheless, a little drip (at least 10 percent) out the drain holes is beneficial.

Over-watering is a common problem, especially with small plants. Too much water drowns roots by cutting off their supply of oxygen. If you have symptoms of over-watering, buy a moisture meter! It will let both you and your garden breathe easier. Sometimes, parts of the soil are over-watered and other soil pockets remain bone dry. Cultivating the soil surface, allowing even water penetration and using a moisture meter will overcome this problem. One of the main causes of over-watering is poor air ventilation! The plant needs to transpire water into the air. If there is nowhere for this wet, humid air to go, gallons of water are locked in the garden room atmosphere. Well-ventilated air carries this

A moisture meter takes the guesswork out of watering.

moist air away, replacing it with fresh dry air. If using trays to
catch runoff water, use a turkey baster, large syringe or sponge
to draw the excess water from the tray. Signs of over-watering
are: leaves curl down and yellow, waterlogged soggy soil, fungal
growth and slow plant growth. Over-watering symptoms are
often subtle and inexperienced gardeners may not see any bla-
tant symptoms for a long time.

Fast growing annuals do not like soggy soil. Soil kept too wet
drowns roots, squeezing out oxygen. This causes slow growth
and possible fungal attack. Poor drainage is most often the
cause of soggy soil. It is compounded by poor ventilation and
high humidity.

 ***Rules of Thumb** – About watering: (1) large plants transpire
more than small ones, (2) maintain good ventilation and (3)
check the soil of each plant for moisture. This will be a base
to work from in developing your watering skill.*

Under-watering is less of a problem. However, it is fairly
common if small (1 – 2-gallon) pots are used, or if small pots
are used by gardeners that do not realize the water needs of
rapidly growing plants. Small containers dry out quickly and
may need daily watering. If forgotten, poor water-starved
plants become stunted. Once tender root hairs dry out, they
die. Most gardeners panic when they see their plants wilted in
bone-dry soil. Dry soil, even in pockets, makes root hairs dry
up and die. It seems to take forever for the roots to grow new
root hairs and resume rapid growth.

 ***Rule of Thumb:** Add a few drops of biodegradable liquid dish soap
concentrate to irrigation water. Detergent makes water penetrate soil
more thoroughly.*

If the soil is nearly or completely dry, take the following
steps: Add a few drops (one drop per pint) of a biodegradable,
concentrated liquid soap like Castille® or Ivory® to the water.
It will act as a wetting agent, helping the water penetrate soil
more efficiently and guard against dry soil pockets. Most soluble fertilizers contain a wetting agent. Apply about a quarter to
half as much water/fertilizer as the plant is expected to need,

wait 10 to 15 minutes for it to totally soak in, then apply more water/fertilizer until the soil is evenly moist. If trays are underneath the pots, let excess water remain in the trays a few hours or even overnight before removing it with a large turkey baster.

Another way to thoroughly wet pots is to soak them in water. This is easy to do with small pots. Simply fill a 5-gallon bucket with 3 gallons of water. Submerge the smaller pot inside the bigger pot for a minute or longer until the growing medium is completely saturated. Wetting plants thoroughly ensures against dry soil pockets.

Having a readily accessible water source is very convenient and saves time and labor. A 10 x 10-foot garden, containing 24 healthy plants in 6-gallon pots, could need 10 to 30 gallons of water per week. A garden the same size with 80 plants in 3-gallon containers could use in excess of 50 gallons a week. Water weighs eight pounds a gallon (30 gallons x 8 pounds = 240 pounds!). That's a lot of containers to fill, lift and spill. Carrying water in containers from the bathroom sink to the garden is OK when plants are small, but when they get large, it is a big, sloppy, regular job. Running a hose into the garden saves much labor and mess. A lightweight half-inch hose is easy to handle and is less prone to damage plants. If the water source has hot and cold water running out the same tap and is equipped with threads, attach a hose and irrigate with tepid water. Use a dishwasher coupling if the faucet has no threads. The hose should have an on/off valve at the outlet so water flow can be controlled while watering. A rigid watering wand will save many broken branches while leaning over to

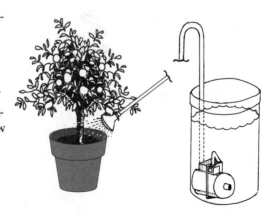

Place a pump attached to a garden hose and watering wand with an on/off valve to water individual plants efficiently by hand.

A water wand with a "breaker" head mixes air with irrigation water just before applying.

water in tight quarters. Buy a water wand at the nursery or construct one from plastic PVC pipe. Do not leave water under pressure in the hose for more than a few minutes. Garden hoses are designed to transport water, not hold it under pressure, which may cause it to rupture.

To make a siphon or gravity fed watering system, place a barrel at least 4 feet high in the garden room. If humidity is a problem, put a lid on the can or move it into another room. The attic is a good place because it warms the water and promotes good pressure. Place a siphon hose in the top of the tank or install a PVC on/off valve near the bottom of the barrel. It is easy to walk off and let the barrel overflow. An inexpensive device that measures the gallons of water added to the barrel is available at most hardware stores. You can also install a float valve in the barrel to meter out water and retain a constant supply.

Drip systems deliver nutrient solution one drop at a time or in low volume via low-pressure plastic pipe with friction fittings. Water flows down the pipe and out the emitters, one drop at a time or at a very slow rate. The emitters are attached to the main hose are either spaghetti tubes or a nozzle/dripper actually emitting from the main hose. Many drip irrigation kits are available or you can construct your own system from component parts. Drip irrigation kits are available at garden stores and building centers.

Rule of Thumb: *Use a filter with drip systems!*

Drip systems offer several advantages. Once set up, drip systems lower watering maintenance. Fertilizer may also be injected into the system. This facilitates fertilization, but gives the same amount of water and nutrient to each plant.

When setting up a drip system, make sure the growing medium drains freely to prevent soggy soil or salt buildup. If growing cuttings that are all the same age and size, a drip system would work very well. However, if you are growing a lot of different types of plants, they may need different fertilizer regimens. Hand-watering selected plants can remedy this problem.

 Rule of Thumb: *Drip systems make watering more consistent, but each pot still has to be checked for moisture.*

The convenience and constant feeding ability of a drip system is wonderful, and you can fertilize with mild nutrient solution simply by mixing nutrient solution in a reservoir and pumping it through feeder hoses. Using a drip system, cuttings and seedlings can be grown in smaller containers. Root growth is strong and consistent because nutrients and water are in constant supply.

A drip system attached to a timer disperses nutrient solution at regular intervals. If using such a system check the soil for water application daily. Check several pots daily to ensure they are watered evenly and that all soil gets wet. Drip systems are very convenient and indispensable when you have to be away for a few days. However, do not leave a drip system on it's own for more than four consecutive days or you could return to a surprise! Test the system first to make sure it will "behave" and not flood you out!

Drip systems cost a few dollars to set up, but the consistency they add to a garden is often paid off in a bountiful yield. Be careful! Such an automated system could promote negligence! Remember gardens need daily care! If everything is automated, it still needs monitoring. All the vital signs – moisture, pH, ventilation, humidity, etc., still need to be checked and adjusted daily. Automation adds consistency, uniformity and usually a higher yield when applied properly.

Misdiagnosed Disorders

Many indoor garden problems are misdiagnosed as a lack of fertilizer. Disease and insects can cause other problems. Problems can also be caused by an imbalanced pH of the growing medium and water. A pH between 6.5 and 7 in soil (5.8 – 6.5 in hydroponics) will allow nutrients to be chemically avail-

Drip irrigation makes watering and fertilizing a snap.

able. Above or below this range, several nutrients become less available. For example, a full point movement in pH represents a tenfold increase in either alkalinity or acidity. This means that a pH of 5.5 would be ten times more acidic than a pH of 6.5. In soil, a pH below 6.5 may cause a deficiency in calcium, which causes root tips to burn and leaves could get fungal infections (leaf spot). A pH over 7 could slow down the plant's iron intake and result in chlorotic leaves with yellowing between the veins on younger leaves.

Incorrect pH contributes to most nutrient disorders in organic soil gardens. Many complex biological processes occur between organic fertilizers and soil during nutrient uptake. The pH is critical to these activities. When the pH fluctuates in a hydroponic garden, the nutrients are still available in solution for uptake and the pH is not as critical. EC (Electrical Conductivity) is the most critical indicator of plant health and nutrient uptake in hydroponics. An EC or PPM meter can measure this, the dissolved salt content.

Once a plant shows symptoms, it has already undergone severe nutritional stress. It will take time for the plant to resume vigorous growth. At first sign of trouble, you should thoroughly flush the system or soil with dilute nutrient solution. Adjust the pH and use half-strength nutrients. Correct identification of each symptom as soon as it occurs is essential so plants retain vigor. Some indoor crops are harvested so fast that plants do not have time to recover from nutrient imbalances. One small imbalance could cost a week of growth.

Do not confuse nutrient deficiencies or toxicities with insect and disease damage, or poor cultural practices.

Damage from Cultural Practices:
Lack of ventilation
Lack of light
Humidity – too high or too low
Temperature – too high or too low
Spray application damage
Ozone or carbon monoxide damage
Over-watering – soggy soil
Under-watering – dry soil
Light burn (light too close)
Indoor air pollution – leaching of chemicals from
pressboard
Pets or pests

The temperature within the leaf can climb to excess of 114 degrees F. It happens easily because the leaf stores the heat radiated by the lamp. At 114 degrees F the internal chemistry of a plant leaf is disrupted; manufactured proteins and essential oils are broken down and become unavailable to the plant. As the internal temperature of leaves climb, they are forced to use and evaporate more water. Higher temperatures (110 degrees F.) close the leaf stomata and the plants wilt. About 70 percent of the plants energy is used in evaporation.

The basic elements of the environment must be checked and maintained at specific levels to avoid problems. Check each of the vital signs – air, light, soil, water, temperature, humidity, etc., and fine-tune the environment, especially ventilation, before deciding that plants are nutrient deficient.

Nutrient deficiencies are less common when using fresh potting soil fortified with micronutrients. If the soil or water supply is acidic, add dolomite lime to buffer the pH and keep soil sweet. Fresh planting mix, coupled with a regular fertilization schedule, averts many problems.

Most common ailments are averted when you use clean water, the proper complete nutrient solution, maintain EC and pH and flush the system with fresh water, then replenish nutrients every two weeks.

Nutrients

Nutrients are elements that plants need to live. Carbon, hydrogen and oxygen are absorbed from air and water. The rest of the elements, called nutrients, are absorbed from the growing medium and nutrient solution. Supplemental nutrients supplied in the form of fertilizer allow plants cultivated under HID lights to reach maximum potential. Nutrients are grouped into two categories: macronutrients or primary nutrients, secondary nutrients and micronutrients or trace elements. Each nutrient in the above categories can be further classified as either "mobile" or "immobile."

Mobile nutrients – nitrogen, (N), phosphorus (P), potassium (K), magnesium (Mg) and zinc (Zn) – are able to re-translocate, move from one portion of the plant to another, as needed. For example, nitrogen accumulated in an older leaf re-translocates to a younger leaf to solve a deficiency. The result, deficiency symptoms appear on older, lower leaves first.

Immobile nutrients – calcium (Ca), boron (B), chlorine (Cl), cobalt (Co), copper (Cu), iron (Fe), manganese (Mn), molybdenum (Mo), selenium (Se), silicon (Si) and sulfur (S) – do not re-translocate to new growing areas as needed. They remain deposited in their original place in older leaves. This is why deficiency symptoms usually appear first in the upper new leaves on top of the plant.

Chart of Mobile and Immobile Nutrients

Nitrogen (N)	mobile
Phosphorus (P)	mobile
Potassium (K)	mobile
Magnesium (Mg)	mobile
Zinc (Zn)	mobile
Calcium (Ca)	immobile
Boron (B)	immobile
Chlorine (Cl)	immobile
Cobalt (Co)	immobile
Copper (Cu)	immobile
Iron (Fe)	immobile

Manganese (Mn)	immobile
Molybdenum (Mo)	immobile
Selenium (Se)	immobile
Silicon (Si)	immobile
Sulfur (S)	immobile

Mobile nutrients re-translocate within a plant. They move to the specific part of the plant where they are needed causing older leaves to show deficiencies first.

Immobile nutrients stay deposited in their original destination causing new young leaves to show deficiencies first.

Macronutrients

Macronutrients are the elements plants use the most. Fertilizers show the nitrogen (N), potassium (P), phosphorous (K) as (N-P-K) percentages in big numbers on the front of the package. They are always listed in the same N-P-K order. These nutrients must always be in an available form to supply plants with the building blocks for rapid growth.

 ## Nitrogen (N) – mobile

Practical Stuff: Flowers and vegetables love nitrogen and require high levels during vegetative growth and lower levels during the balance of life. Nitrogen is easily washed away and must be replaced regularly, especially during vegetative growth. Excess levels of nitrogen in harvested vegetables do not enhance flavor.

Technical Stuff: Nitrogen regulates a plant's ability to make proteins essential for new protoplasm in the cells. It is essential for the production of amino acids, enzymes, nucleic acids, chlorophyll and alkaloids. This important nutrient is mainly responsible for leaf and stem growth, as well as overall size and vigor. Nitrogen is most active in young buds, shoots and leaves. **Ammonium** (NH_4+) This form of nitrogen is the most readily available. Be careful when using too much of this form, it can burn plants. **Nitrate** (NO_3-) The nitrate form of nitrogen is much slower to assimilate than ammonium. Hydroponic fertilizers use this nitrogen compound as slower acting and mix it with ammonium.

Deficiency: Nitrogen is the most common nutrient deficiency. Symptoms include slower growth. Lower leaves cannot produce chlorophyll and become yellow between veins while veins remain green. Yellowing progresses through entire leaf, eventually causing it to die and drop off. Stems and leaf undersides may turn reddish-purple, but this could also be a sign of a phosphorus deficiency. Nitrogen is very mobile, dissipates into the environment quickly, and must be added regularly to sustain fast growing gardens.

Progression of deficiency symptoms at a glance:
> Older leaves yellow between veins (interveinal chlorosis).
> Older bottom leaves turn entirely yellow.
> More and more leaves yellow. Severely affected leaves drop.
> Leaves might develop reddish-purple stems and veins on leaf undersides.
> Progressively younger leaves develop interveinal chlorosis.
> All foliage yellows and leaf drop is severe.

Treat deficiency by fertilizing with N or complete N-P-K fertilizer. You should see results in 4 – 5 days. Fast-acting organic sources of nitrogen include seabird guano, fish emulsion and blood meal. Gardeners also report excellent results by adding bio-fertilizers (see "Additives") to stimulate the uptake of nitrogen.

Toxicity: An overdose of nitrogen will cause excessively lush foliage that is soft and susceptible to stress, including insect and fungal attacks. Stems become weak and may fold over easily. The vascular transport tissue breaks down and water uptake is restricted. In severe cases, leaves turn a brownish-copper color, dry and fall off. Roots develop super slowly and tend to darken and rot. Flowers are smaller and sparse. Ammonium toxicity is most common in acid soils, while nitrate toxicity is more prevalent in alkaline soil.

Progression of toxicity symptoms at a glance:
    Excessively dark green foliage
    Weak stems that fold over (also could be lack of light)
    Slow root development
    Flowers grow slowly and are smaller
    Leaves brown, dry and fall off

    Treat toxicity by flushing the growing medium of affected plants with a very mild complete fertilizer. Severe problems require more water be flushed through the growing medium to carry away toxic elements. Flush a minimum of three times the volume of water for the volume of growing medium. Do not add more fertilizer containing nitrogen for one week, so the excess nitrogen in foliage can be used. If plant remains excessively green, cut back on nitrogen dose.

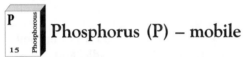

Phosphorus (P) – mobile

    Practical Stuff: Fast growing annuals use highest levels of phosphorus during the germination, seedling, cloning and flowering. "Super Bloom" fertilizers designed for flowering have high levels of phosphorus.

    Technical Stuff: Phosphorus is necessary for photosynthesis and provides a mechanism for energy transfer within the plant. Phosphorus, a component of DNA, many enzymes and proteins, and is associated with overall vigor and seed production. Highest concentrations of phosphorus are found in root growing tips, growing shoots and vascular tissue.

    Deficiency: A lack of phosphorous causes stunted growth. Leaves are smaller, bluish-green and often with blotches. Stems, leaf stems (petioles) and main veins on some plants may turn reddish-purple starting on leaf underside. NOTE: The reddening of stems and veins is not always well pronounced. Leaf tips of older leaves turn dark and curl downward. Leaves severely affected develop large purplish-black necrotic (dead) blotches. These leaves later become bronzish-purple, dry, shrivel up, contort and drop off. Flowering and fruit set are often delayed, buds are uniformly smaller, seed yield is poor and plants become very vulnerable to fungal and insect attack.

Phosphorus deficiencies are aggravated by clayey acidic and soggy soil.

Deficiencies are somewhat common and often misdiagnosed. Deficiencies are most common: (1) growing medium pH is above 7 and phosphorus is unable to be absorbed properly (2) the soil is acidic (below 5.8) and/or there is an excess of iron and zinc (3) the soil has become fixated (chemically bound) with phosphates.

Progression of deficiency symptoms at a glance:
Stunted and very slow growth.
Dark bluish-green leaves often with dark blotches.
Plants are smaller overall.
When blotches overcome leaf stem, leaf turns bronzish-purple, contorts and drops.

Treat phosphorous deficiency by lowering the pH to 5.5 – 6.2 (hydroponics), 6 – 7 for clay soils and 5.5 – 6.5 for potting soils so that it will become available. If soil is too acidic, and an excess of iron and zinc exist, phosphorous becomes unavailable. If growing in soil, mix complete fertilizer containing phosphorous thoroughly into growing medium before planting. Fertilize with an inorganic complete hydroponic mix that contains phosphorous. Mix in organic nutrients – bat guano, steamed bone meal, natural phosphates or barnyard manure – to add phosphorus to soil. Always use finely ground organic components that are available quickly.

Toxic signs of phosphorus may take several weeks to surface, especially if excesses are buffered by a stable pH. Most annual flowers and vegetables use a lot of phosphorus throughout life and many varieties tolerate high levels. Excessive phosphorus interferes with calcium, copper, iron, magnesium and zinc stability and uptake. Toxic symptoms of phosphorous manifest as a deficiency of zinc, iron, magnesium, calcium and copper; zinc is the most common.

Treat toxicity by flushing the growing medium of affected plants with very mild complete fertilizer. Severe problems require more water be flushed through the growing medium. Flush a minimum of three times the volume of water for the volume of growing medium.

K
19 Potassium

Potassium (K) – mobile

Practical Stuff: Potassium is used at all stages of growth. Soils with a high level of potassium increase a plant's resistance to bacteria and mold.

Technical Stuff: Potassium is essential to the manufacture and movement of sugars and starches, as well as growth by cell division. It increases chlorophyll in foliage and helps regulate stomata openings so plants make better use of light and air. Potassium is essential in the accumulation and translocation of carbohydrates. It also encourages strong root growth and is associated with disease resistance and water intake. The potash form of potassium oxide is (K_2O). Potassium nitrate is normally used and is highly water soluble.

Deficiency: Potassium-starved plants initially appear healthy. Symptoms include: older leaves, first browning on the tips and margins; followed by whole leaves turn dark yellow and die; stems often become weak and sometimes brittle; plants become susceptible to disease. Potassium is usually present in soil, but can be locked up by high salinity. First, leach the toxic salt out of the soil, and then apply a complete N-P-K fertilizer. A potassium deficiency causes the internal temperature of foliage to climb and protein in the cells burn or degrade. Evaporation is normally highest on leaf edges and that's where burning takes place.

Progression of deficiency symptoms at a glance:
> Plants appear healthy with dark green foliage.
> Leaves loose luster.
> Branching may increase, but branches are weak and scrawny.
> Leaf margins turn gray and progress to a rusty brown, curl up and dry.
> Yellowing of older leaves accompanied by rust-colored blotches.
> Leaves curl up, rot sets in and older leaves drop.
> Flowering, fruit set and growth retarded or greatly diminished.

Treat deficiency of potassium by fertilizing with a complete N-P-K fertilizer. Occasionally a gardener will add potassium directly to the nutrient solution. Organic gardeners add potassium in the form of soluble potash (wood ashes) mixed with water. Be careful when using wood ash, the pH is normally above 10. Use a pH lowering mix to bring the pH to around 6.5 before application. Foliar feeding to cure a potassium deficiency is not recommended.

Toxicity: Occurs occasionally and is difficult to diagnose because it is mixed with the deficiency symptoms of other nutrients. Too much potassium impairs and slows the absorption of magnesium, manganese and sometimes zinc and iron. Look for signs of toxic potassium buildup. Symptoms of magnesium, manganese, zinc and iron deficiencies appear; water uptake affected similar to high saline conditions; leaf burn and wilting.

Treat toxicity by flushing the growing medium of affected plants with very mild complete fertilizer. Severe problems require more water be flushed through the growing medium. Flush a minimum with three times the volume of water for the volume of growing medium.

Secondary Nutrients

Secondary nutrients - magnesium, calcium, and sulfur - are also used by plants in large amounts. Rapid growing indoor flower and vegetable crops are able to process more secondary nutrients than most "general purpose" fertilizers are able to supply. Many gardeners opt to use high quality two and three part hydroponic fertilizers that supply all the secondary and trace elements necessary. But be careful, these three nutrients may be present in high levels in ground water. It is important to consider these values when adding nutrient supplements. If growing in soil or soilless mix with a pH below 7, such as "Peat-Lite", incorporating one cup of fine (flour) dolomite lime per gallon of medium ensures adequate supplies of calcium and magnesium.

Mg	
12	Magnesium

Magnesium (Mg) – mobile

Practical Stuff: Fast growing annuals use a lot of magnesium and deficiencies are common, especially in acidic (pH below 7) soils. Adding dolomite lime to acidic potting soils before planting will stabilize pH, plus add magnesium and calcium to the soil. Add Epsom salts with each watering to correct magnesium deficiencies if no dolomite was added when planting.

Technical Stuff: Magnesium is found as a central atom in every chlorophyll molecule and is essential to the absorption of light energy. Magnesium aids in the utilization of nutrients. It also neutralizes soil acids and toxic compounds produced by the plant.

Deficiency: Magnesium deficiency is common indoors. Lower and later middle leaves develop yellow patches between darker green veins and rust-brown spots appear on leaf margins, tips and between veins as deficiency progresses. The brownish leaf tips usually curl upward before dying. The entire plant could discolor in a few weeks, and if severe, turn a yellow-whitish tinge before browning and dying. A minor deficiency causes little or no problems with growth. However, minor deficiencies escalate and cause a diminished harvest as flowering progresses.

Most often magnesium is in the soil but unavailable to the plant because the root environment is too wet, cold or acidic and cold. Magnesium is also bound in the soil if there is an excess of potassium, ammonia (nitrogen) and calcium (carbonate). Small root systems are also unable to take in enough magnesium, so make sure there is an adequate supply. A high EC, denoting high salt content, slows water evaporation and will also diminish magnesium availability.

Progression of deficiency symptoms at a glance:
No deficiency symptoms are visible during the first 3 – 4 weeks
The fourth to sixth week of growth show the first signs of deficiency. Interveinal yellowing and irregular rust-brown spots appear on older and middle-age leaves. Younger leaves remain healthy.

Leaf tips turn brown and curl upwards as deficiency progresses.

Rust-brown spots multiply and interveinal yellowing increases.

Rust-brown spots and yellowing progress from the bottom to the top of the entire plant.

Youngest leaves develop rust-colored spots and interveinal yellowing.

Leaves dry and die in extreme cases.

Treat Deficiency by watering with two teaspoons of Epsom salts (magnesium sulfate) per gallon of water. For fastest results, spray foliage with a 2 percent solution of Epsom salts. If the deficiency progresses to the top of the plant, it will turn green there first. In 4 – 6 days, it will start moving down the plant, turning lower leaves progressively greener. Continue regular watering schedule with Epsom salts added until symptoms totally disappear. Adding Epsom salts regularly is not necessary when fertilizer contains available magnesium. Another option is to apply magnesium sulfate monohydrate in place of Epsom salts. Add fine dolomite lime to soil and soilless mix to add a consistent supply of both calcium and magnesium over the long term. Always use the finest dolomite available.

Control the room and root zone temperatures, humidity, pH and EC of the nutrient solution. Keep root zone and nutrient solution 70 – 75 degrees F. Keep ambient air temperature at 75 degrees day and 65 degrees night. Use a complete fertilizer with an adequate amount of magnesium. Keep soil pH above 6.5, keep hydroponic pH above 5.5, and lower high EC for a week.

Extra magnesium in soil is generally not harmful but can inhibit calcium uptake. Signs of excess magnesium are described below.

Toxicity: Magnesium toxicity is rare and difficult to discern with the naked eye. If extremely toxic, magnesium develops a conflict with other fertilizer ions, usually calcium, especially in hydroponic nutrient solutions. Toxic buildup of magnesium in soils that are able to grow most fast growing annuals is uncommon.

Ca 20 Calcium | Calcium (Ca) – immobile

Practical Stuff: Fast growing flowers and vegetables require nearly as much calcium as other macronutrients. Avert deficiencies in soil and most soilless mixes by adding fine dolomite lime or using soluble hydroponic fertilizers containing adequate calcium.

Technical Stuff: Calcium is fundamental to cell manufacture and growth. Calcium is necessary to preserve membrane permeability and cell integrity. Plants must have some calcium at the growing tip of each root.

Deficiency of calcium is somewhat uncommon indoors. Frequently, plants can process more calcium than is available. Deficient signs start with very dark green foliage and exceptionally slow growth. Young leaves are affected and show signs first. Severe calcium deficiency causes new growing shoots to develop yellowish to purple hues and disfigure before shriveling up and dying. Bud development is inhibited, plants stunted and harvest diminished. Growing tips could show signs of calcium deficiency if humidity is maxed out. At 100 percent humidity the stomata close, which stops transpiration, to protect the plant. Calcium, transported by transpiration, becomes immobile.

Treat deficiencies by dissolving one-half teaspoon of hydrated lime per gallon of water. Water deficient plants with calcium-dosed water as long as symptoms persist. Or use complete hydroponic nutrient that contains adequate calcium. Keep the pH of the growing medium stable.

Progression of deficiency symptoms at a glance:
Slow growth and young leaves turn very dark green.
New growing shoots discolor.
New shoots contort, shrivel and die.
New bud development slows rapidly.
Flowers fall off, little or no fruit set.

Toxicity is difficult to see in foliage. It causes wilting. Toxic levels also exacerbate deficiencies of potassium, magnesium, manganese and iron. The nutrients become unavailable, even though they are present. If excessive amounts of soluble calcium are applied early in life, it could also stunt growth. If growing hydroponically, an excess of calcium will precipitate with sulfur in solution, which causes the nutrient solution to become cloudy. Once calcium and sulfur combine (flocculate), they form a residue (gypsum) that settles to the bottom of the reservoir. This reaction is irreversible for all practical purposes. When using 2 or 3 part hydroponic formulas, dissolve each part separately with adequate water before combining. Do not mix concentrates!

Sulfur (S) – immobile

Practical stuff: Many fertilizers contain some form of sulfur, and it is seldom deficient. Gardeners avoid elemental (pure) sulfur in favor of sulfur compounds such as magnesium sulfate. Nutrients combined with sulfur mix better in water.

Technical stuff: Sulfur is an essential building block of many hormones, proteins and vitamins including vitamin B[1]. Sulfur is also an indispensable element in many plant cells and seeds. The sulfate form of sulfur buffers water pH. Virtually all ground, river and lake water contains sulfate. Sulfate is involved in protein synthesis and is part of the amino acids, cystine and thiamine, which are the building blocks of proteins. It is active in the structure and metabolism in the plant. It is essential for respiration and the synthesis and breakdown of fatty acids. Hydroponic fertilizers separate sulfur from calcium in an "A" container and "B" container. If combined in a concentrated form sulfur and calcium will form crude insoluble gypsum (calcium sulfate) and settle as residue to the bottom of the tank.

Deficiency: Young leaves turn lime-green to yellowish. As shortage progresses leaves yellow interveinally and lack succulence. Veins remain green. Leaf stems, petioles, turn purple. Leaf tips can burn, darken and hook downward. In some plants the youngest leaves yellow first, but in other plants, the symptoms are most obvious in the older leaves. Sulfur deficiency resembles a nitrogen deficiency. Acute sulfur deficiency causes elongated stems that become woody at the base.

Sulfur deficiency occurs indoors when the pH is too high or when there is excessive calcium present and available.

Progression of deficiency symptoms at a glance:
> Similar to nitrogen deficiency; older leaves turn pale green.
> Leaf stems turn purple. More leaves turn pale green.
> Entire leaves turn pale yellow.
> Interveinal yellowing.
> Acute deficiency causes more and more leaves to develop purple leaf stems and yellow leaves.

Treat sulfur deficiency by fertilizing with a hydroponic fertilizer that contains sulfur. Lower the pH to 5.5 – 6. Add inorganic sulfur in a fertilizer that contains magnesium sulfate (Epsom salts). Organic sources of sulfur include mushroom composts and most animal manures. Make sure to apply only well-rotted manures to avoid burning roots.

Toxicity: An excess of sulfur in the soil causes no problems if the EC is relatively low. At a high EC, plants tend to take up more "available" sulfur, which blocks uptake of other nutrients. Excess sulfur symptoms include overall smaller plant development and uniformly smaller dark green foliage. Leaf tips and margins could discolor and burn when severe. Saline toxicity, wilting (some plants) non-salt tolerant.

Treat toxicity by flushing the growing medium of affected plants with very mild, complete fertilizer. Check the pH of the drainage solution. Correct input nutrient solution pH to 6.0. Severe problems require more water be flushed through the growing medium. Flush a minimum of three times the volume of water for the volume of growing medium.

Micronutrients

Micronutrients, also called trace elements or trace nutrients, are essential to chlorophyll formation and must be present in minute amounts. They function mainly as catalysts to plant processes and utilization of other elements. For best results, use fertilizers designed for hydroponics to ensure a complete range of trace elements are available. High quality hydroponic fertilizers use food-grade ingredients that are completely soluble and leave no residues. If using an inexpensive fertilizer that does not list a specific analysis for each trace element on the label, it's a good idea to add soluble trace elements in a chelated form. Chelated micronutrients are available in both powdered and liquid form. Add and thoroughly mix micronutrients into the growing medium before planting.

Micronutrients are often added to commercial potting soils and soilless mixes. Check the ingredients on the bag to ensure trace elements were added to the mix. Trace elements are necessary in minute amounts and reach toxic levels easily. Always follow the manufactures instructions to the letter when applying micronutrients because they are easy to over apply.

 Rule of Thumb: *Micronutrients are easy to over apply. Be careful!*

 **Zinc, iron and manganese are the three most common micronutrients found deficient.**
Deficiencies of these three micronutrients plague many gardens. Often deficiencies of all three occur simultaneously, especially when soil or water pH is above 6.5. Deficiencies are most common in arid climates, such as the Southwest in the USA and Australia, with alkaline soil and water. All three have the same initial symptoms of deficiency: interveinal chlorosis of young leaves. It is often difficult to distinguish which element – zinc, iron, or manganese – is deficient, and all three could be deficient. This is why treating the problem should include adding a chelated dose of all three nutrients.

A chelate, Greek for claw, is an organic molecule that forms a claw-like bond with free electrically charged "metal particles." This property keeps metal ions, such as zinc, iron, manganese, etc., soluble in water and the chelated metal's reactions with other materials is suppressed. Roots take in chelated metals in a stable soluble form that are used immediately.

Natural chelates such as humic acid and citric acid can be added to organic soil mixes. Roots and bacteria also exude natural chelates to promote the uptake of metallic elements. Man-made chelates are designed for use in different situations. DTPA is most effective in a pH below 6.5, EDDHA is effective up to pH 8, EDTA chelate is slow to cause leaf burn.

Chelates decompose rapidly in low levels of ultraviolet (UV) light, including that produced by HID bulbs and sunlight. Keep chelates out of the light to protect them from rapid decomposition.

 ## Zinc (Zn) – mobile

Practical Stuff: Zinc is the most common micronutrient found deficient in arid climates and alkaline soils.

Technical Stuff: Zinc works with manganese and magnesium to promote the same enzyme functions. Zinc cooperates with other elements to help form and retain chlorophyll. It is fairly common to find zinc deficient plants. Deficiencies are most common in alkaline soils.

Deficiency: Zinc is the most common micronutrient found deficient. First younger leaves exhibit interveinal chlorosis. New leaves and growing tips develop small thin blades, contort and wrinkle. This condition is called "resetting" or "little leaf." Leaf tips, and later margins, discolor and burn. These symptoms are often confused with a lack of manganese or iron, but when zinc deficiency is severe, new leaf blades contort and dry out. Flowers can also contort into odd shapes, turn crispy, dry and are often hard. A lack of zinc stunts all new growth.

Progression of deficiency symptoms at a glance:
Interveinal chlorosis of young leaves
New leaves develop thin wispy leaves
Leaf tips discolor, turn dark and die back
New growth contorts horizontally
New bud and leaf growth stops

Treat zinc deficient plants by flushing growing medium with a dilute mix of a complete fertilizer containing chelated trace elements, including zinc, iron and manganese. Or add a quality brand of a hydroponic micronutrient mix containing chelated trace elements.

Toxicity: Zinc is extremely toxic in excess. Severely toxic plants die quickly. Excess zinc interferes with iron's ability to function property and causes an iron deficiency. Leaves are small, dark and wilt.

Mn | Manganese (Mn) – immobile
87 | Manganese

Practical Stuff: Manganese deficiency is relatively common indoors.

Technical Stuff: Manganese is engaged in the oxidation-reduction associated with photosynthetic electron transport. This element activates many enzymes and plays a fundamental part in the chloroplast membrane system.

Deficiency: Young leaves show symptoms first. They become yellow between veins – interveinal chlorosis – veins remain green. Symptoms spread from young to older leaves as deficiency progresses. Necrotic (dead) spots develop on severely affected leaves before they fall off. Overall plant growth is stunted and maturation may be prolonged. Severe deficiency looks like a severe lack of magnesium. Treat with small amount of magnesium sulfate of chelate.

Progression of deficiency symptoms at a glance:
Interveinal chlorosis of young leaves.
Interveinal chlorosis of progressively older leaves.
Dead spots develop on acutely affected leaves.
Overall growth is stunted.

Toxicity: Young and newer growth develops chlorotic dark orange to dark rusty brown mottling on leaves. Tissue shows on young leaves before progressing to older leaves. Growth is slower, overall vigor is lost. Toxicity is compounded by low humidity. The additional transpiration causes more manganese to be drawn into foliage. An excess of manganese causes a deficiency of iron and zinc.

Fe
26
Iron (Fe) – immobile

Practical Stuff: Iron is available in a soluble, chelated form that is immediately available for absorption by roots. Deficiency indoors is common in alkaline soils.

Technical Stuff: Iron is fundamental to the enzyme systems and to transport electrons during photosynthesis and respiration. A catalyst for chlorophyll production, iron is necessary for nitrate and sulfate reduction and assimilation. Iron colors the earth from brown to red (rust colored) according to concentration. Rust is not an available source of iron to plants. It is iron oxide and insoluble. Plants often have a difficult time absorbing iron. Acidic soils normally contain adequate iron for most plants to grow well.

Deficiency: Iron deficiencies are common when the pH is above 6.5 and uncommon when the pH is below 6.5. Symptoms may appear during rapid growth or stressful times and disappear by themselves. Young leaves are unable to draw immobile iron from older leaves, even though it is present in soil. First symptoms appear on smaller leaves as interveinal chlorosis where veins remain green and areas between veins turns yellow or white. Note that interveinal chlorosis starts at the opposite end of the leaf tip, the apex of the leaves attached by the petiole. As the deficiency progresses, the chlorosis becomes more acute. Leaves and buds fall off in severe cases. Iron deficiency is sometimes traced to an excess of copper. See "Copper."

Progression of deficiency symptoms at a glance:
Younger leaves and growing shoots turn pale green and progress to yellow in between veins starting at petiole. Veins remain green.

More and more leaves yellow and develop interveinal chlorosis.

Larger leaves finally yellow and develop interveinal chlorosis.

In acute cases, leaves and flower buds develop necrosis and drop.

Treat iron deficiencies by lowering the soil pH to 6.5 or less. Avoid fertilizers that contain excessive amounts manganese and zinc, which inhibit iron uptake. Improve drainage, excessively wet soil holds little oxygen to spur uptake. Increase root zone temperature. Apply chelated iron or ferrous sulfate in liquid form to root zone at the rate of 0.5 tablespoon per gallon of water. Note: chelates are decomposed by light (deep in the dark container) and must be thoroughly mixed with the growing medium to be most effective. Leaves should "green up" in four or five days. Complete balanced hydroponic nutrients contain iron and deficiencies are seldom a problem. Organic sources of iron as well as chelates include cow, horse and chicken manure. Use only well-rotted manures to avoid burning plants.

Toxicity: Excess iron is rare. High levels of iron do not damage most plants, but it can interfere with phosphorus uptake and other elements. An excess of iron causes leaves to turn bronze accompanied by small, dark-brown leaf spots. If iron chelate is over-applied, it will kill the plant in a few days.

Treat excess iron by leaching plants heavily.

The following group of micronutrients is seldom found deficient. Avoid deficiencies by using a high-quality hydroponic fertilizer that contains chelated micronutrients.

Boron (B) – immobile

Practical Stuff: Usually causes no problems.

Technical Stuff: Boron deficiencies seldom occur indoors. Boron is still somewhat of a biochemical mystery. Scientists have collected evidence to suggest boron helps with synthesis, a base for the formation of nucleic acid (RNA uracil) formation. Strong evidence also supports boron's role in cell division, differentiation, maturation and respiration, as well as a link to pollen production.

Deficiency: Stem tip and root tip grow abnormally. Root tips often swell, discolor and stop elongating. Growing shoots look burned and may be confused with a burn from being too close to the HID. First the top shoot contorts and/or turns pale yellow/white, later followed by progressively lower growing shoots. When severe, growing tips die. Leaf margins discolor and die back in spots. Necrotic spots develop between leaf veins. Root tips are stubby and brown. Root steles (insides) often become mushy and become a perfect host for rots and disease. Deficient leaves become thick, distorted and wilt with chlorotic and necrotic spotting. Deficiency causes "heart rot" in beets and "stem crack" in celery.

Treat boron deficient plants with one tenth (0.05 grams) teaspoon of boric acid per gallon of water. You can apply this solution as a soil drench to be taken up by roots. You can also apply hydroponic micronutrients containing boron. Hydroponic gardeners should keep boron dosage below 20 parts per million (PPM), because boron quickly becomes toxic if concentrated in solution.

Toxicity: Leaf tips first yellow and as toxic conditions progress, leaf margins become necrotic. After leaves yellow they fall off, leading to wilting and death of the plant.

Chlorine (Chloride) (Cl) – immobile

Practical Stuff: Chloride is found in many municipal water systems. Most plants tolerate low levels of chlorine. It is usually not a component of most fertilizers and almost never deficient in gardens.

Technical Stuff: Chlorine in the form of chloride is fundamental to photosynthesis and cell division in roots and foliage. It also increases osmotic pressure in cells, which opens and closes stomata to regulate moisture flow within plant tissue.

Deficiency: Deficiency is uncommon. Young leaves pale and wilt. As deficiency progresses leaves become chlorotic and develop a characteristic bronze color. Roots develop thick tips and become stunted. NOTE: Both severe deficiency and excess of chloride have the same symptoms: bronze-colored leaves.

Treat chlorine deficiencies by adding chlorinated water or one quarter tablespoon of potassium chloride per gallon.

Toxicity: Young leaves are small and dark and develop burnt leaf tips and margins. Very young seedlings and cuttings are the most susceptible to damage. As plants mature, symptoms progress throughout the plant. Characteristic yellowish-bronze leaves are smaller and slower to develop. Severe toxicity causes saline poisoning and wilt.

Treat toxic signs of chlorine by letting heavily chlorinated water set out overnight and stirring occasionally. Chlorine will vaporize and disappear into the atmosphere. Use this water to mix nutrient solution or irrigate garden.

Co 27 Cobalt | Cobalt (Co) - immobile

Practical Stuff: This nutrient is seldom mentioned as necessary for plant growth and most fertilizer labels do not include cobalt. Cobalt is virtually never deficient in indoor gardens.

Technical Stuff: Cobalt is necessary for countless beneficial bacteria to grow and flourish. Scientific evidence suggests this element is linked to enzymes needed to form aromatic compounds. It is required in very small amounts for nitrogen fixation and DNA synthesis. It is also involved in the formation of vitamin B-12 (lack of B-12 causes pernicious anemia). B-12 cobalazion and only two micrograms are needed per day by people. Vitamin B-12 is found only in meat and dairy products.

Deficiency: affects nitrogen utilization and causes nitrogen deficiency. Add a small pinch of cobalt nitrate (0.01 grams) per gallon.

Toxicity: Quick wilting and death of plant.

Cu 29 Copper | Copper (Cu) – immobile

Practical Stuff: Copper is also used as a fungicide.

Technical Stuff: Copper is a component of numerous enzymes and proteins. Necessary in very minute amounts, copper helps with carbohydrate metabolism, nitrogen fixation, iron utilization and in the process of oxygen reduction. Copper helps to keep plants healthy and ward off plant diseases.

Deficiency: Copper deficiencies are rare. Young leaves and growing shoots wilt. Leaf tips and margins develop necrosis and turn a dark coppery-gray. Occasionally an entire copper-deficient plant wilts, drooping even when adequately watered. Growth is slow and yield decreases.

Treat copper deficiency by applying a copper-based fungicide such as copper sulfate. Do not apply if the temperature is above 75 degrees F to avoid burning foliage. Apply a complete hydroponic nutrient containing copper. Indoor plants seldom develop a copper deficiency. Throw a penny in the holding tank or watering can. Copper sulfate or chelate can be used, too, at the rate of 0.01 grams per gallon of water.

Toxicity: Copper, although essential, is extremely toxic to plants in excess. Toxic levels slow overall plant growth. As toxic level climbs, symptoms include interveinal iron chlorosis (deficiency), stunted growth, fewer branches grow and roots become dark, thick and slow growing. Toxic conditions accelerate fastest in acidic soils. Hydroponic gardeners must monitor their solution carefully to avoid copper excesses.

Treat Toxicity: Flush soil or growing medium to expel excess copper.

Mo 42 Molybdenum | Molybdenum (Mo) – immobile

Practical Stuff: Molybdenum is seldom deficient.

Technical Stuff: Molybdenum is a part of two major enzyme systems that converts nitrate to ammonium. This essential element is used by plants in very small quantities and operates to oxidize sulfur.

Deficiency: This micronutrient is almost never found deficient indoors. First, older and middle-aged leaves yellow; some develop interveinal chlorosis. Leaves continue to yellow and develop rolled up margins as the deficiency progresses. Acute symptoms cause leaves to become long and narrow, severely twisted, die and drop. Overall growth is stunted. Deficiencies are worst in acidic soils. A deficiency of molybdenum will cause a sulfur deficiency. Correct by adding a small pinch (0.01 grams) of molybdic acid or ammonium molybdate per gallon of water.

Toxicity: Excess is very uncommon in indoor gardens. An excess of molybdenum causes a deficiency of copper and iron. Toxic above 200 PPB (parts per billion). Horsetail reeds contain high levels of silicic acid (H_2SiO_3).

Si
ilicon
Silicon – (Si)

Practical Stuff: Silicon is readily available in most soils and water. It does not cause most indoor plants any complications due to deficiencies or excesses.

Technical Stuff: Silicon is absorbed by plants as silicic acid. It is found mainly in epidermal cell walls where it collects in the form of hydrated amorphous silica. It also accumulates in walls of other cells. A lack of silicon has been proven to decrease yields of some fruits and cause new leaves to deform. Scientists are still studying the effects of silicon on plants.

Other Elements

Other elements are needed by some plants in very small quantities. These include selenium, vanadium, iodine, fluorine, tellurium and rubidium. They usually need sub-microgram quantities and are found as impurities in ordinary plant fertilizers in sufficient quantities. Excesses are deadly.

Fertilizers

The goal of fertilizing is to supply plants with proper amounts of nutrients for vigorous growth without creating toxic conditions by over-fertilizing. A 5 – 6 gallon container full of rich fertile potting soil will supply all the necessary nutrients for the first month of growth, but the development might be slow. After the roots have absorbed most of the available nutrients, they must be added to sustain vigorous growth. Unless fortified, soilless mixes require fertilization from the start. Start fertilizing fortified soilless mixes after the first week or two of growth. Some commercial soilless mixes are fortified with trace elements.

A plants metabolism changes as it grows older and so do its fertilizer needs. All the minerals a plant needs are in the seed until the first true leaves appear. During germination and seedling growth, intake of phosphorus is fairly high. The vegetative growth stage requires larger amounts of nitrogen for green leaf growth; phosphorus and potassium are also necessary in substantial levels. During this leafy vegetative growth, use a "general purpose" or a "grow" fertilizer with high nitrogen content. In the flowering stage, nitrogen takes a backseat to potassium, phosphorus and calcium intake. Using a "super bloom" fertilizer, with less nitrogen and more potassium, phosphorus and calcium, promotes strong flowers and fat fruit. Plants need some nitrogen during flowering, but very little. With no nitrogen, buds do not develop to the fullest potential for the first few weeks of growth. You should fertilize at half strength.

 Rule of Thumb: *Read the entire fertilizer label and follow directions.*

Now we come to the confusing part about the "guaranteed analysis" of commercial fertilizer mixes. Federal and state laws require nutrient concentrations to appear prominently on the face of fertilizer packages, even though the values are dubious in accuracy; they can be over but not under the percentages listed on the package.

Do you think the N-P-K numbers on the label give the percentages of nitrogen, phosphorous, and potassium? Well, yes and no. The government measures nutrients with different scales. Nitrogen is listed as "total combined elemental". Most hydroponic fertilizers break nitrogen into slower acting nitrate (NO_3) and ammonium (NH_4). Phosphoric anhydride (P_2O_5) is listed as the form of phosphorus, but this figure overstates phosphorus content by 44 percent. It gets worse! The balance, or 56 percent, of the phosphorus molecule is comprised of oxygen. Twenty percent P_2O_5 is 8.8 percent actual phosphorous. Potassium (K) is listed in the potash form (potassium oxide) (K_2O), of which 83 percent of the stated value is actually elemental potassium.

Magnesium is sometimes expressed as MgO (magnesium oxide), which is car-

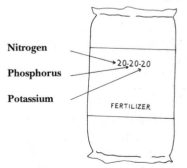

Fertilizers show the N-P-K (20-20-20) in big letters on the front of the package or container label.

cinogenic! Don't worry. It is not used in fertilizers; magnesium sulfate is used instead. When expressed as MgO, the magnesium content is only 60 percent of the amount quoted as MgO.

The rest of the mineral nutrients are listed in their elemental form that represents the actual content. Most often mineral elements used in fertilizer formulas are listed in chemical compounds on the label. Look at fertilizer labels to ensure that elements, especially trace elements, are "chelated" and readily available for root absorption. Also be careful about having too much sodium in your water/nutrient solution. The sodium will block potassium and several other nutrients, causing deficiencies and slow growth.

Nutrients in the United States are measured in parts-per-million (PPM), even though they are expressed as a percentage concentration on the label. The PPM scale is simple and finite, almost. The basics are simple: one part per million is one part of 1,000,000. Divide by one million to find parts per million. To convert percentages into PPM, multiply by 10,000. For example: 2 percent = 20,000 PPM. For more information on PPM and Electrical Conductivity see Chapter Five, Hydroponic Gardening. To convert PPM to percent, divide by 1,000,000. Remember, 2 percent is the decimal form for 0.02.

Fertilizers are either water soluble or partially soluble (gradual release). Both soluble and gradual release fertilizers can be organic or chemical.

 Super Size Secret: *Use high quality balanced soluble fertilizers that are immediately available for uptake.*

Element	Atomic Wt.	Limits	Average
Nitrogen (N)	14	150 – 1000	250
Calcium (Ca)	40	100 – 150	200
Magnesium (Mg)	24.3	50 – 100	75
Phosphorus (P)	31	50 – 100	80
Potassium (K)	39.1	100 – 400	300
Sulfur (S)	32	200 – 1000	400
Copper (Cu)	63.5	0.05 – 0.5	0.5
Boron (B)	10.8	0.5 – 5.0	1.0
Iron (Fe)	55.8	2.0 – 10	5.0

Manganese (Mn)	55	0.1 – 5.0	2.0
Molybdenum (Mo)	96	0.01 – 0.05	0.02
Zinc (Zn)	65.4	0.5 – 1.0	0.5

The chart above lists suggested soluble salts fertilizer recommendations for fast growing annuals. Values expressed in parts per million in solution. The atomic weights are not exact numbers because of naturally occurring isotopes (extra neutrons) involved. Atomic weights are used to determine elemental percents in mineral salts and chemical formulas.

For most hydroponic fertilizers, this generally means 2 teaspoons (10 grams) per gallon of water (powdered) or 4 teaspoons (20 grams) per gallon of water (concentrated liquid). The nutrient is only 0.5 percent of the nutrient solution (0.25 percent for powders) and the rest is 99.5 percent water (99.75 percent for powder fertilizer).

Chemical Fertilizers

The diversity of local hydroponic fertilizers is amazing and provides gardeners with fine-tuned fertilizers. Local storeowners know a lot about the local water and gardener needs. They are in a perfect position to develop their own nutrient solution or adapt one that works well with their water. A few manufacturers do not do their homework and make bad nutrients. Most manufacturers are conscious and manufacture excellent fertilizers.

Soluble chemical fertilizers are an excellent choice for indoor container cultivation. Soluble fertilizers dissolve in water and are easy to control; they can be added or washed (leached) out of the growing medium easily. You can control the exact amounts of nutrients available to plants in an available form with water-soluble fertilizers. Soluble fertilizer may be applied in a water solution to the soil. In general, high quality hydroponic fertilizers that use completely soluble food-grade nutrients are the best value. Avoid low-quality fertilizers that do not list all necessary micronutrients on the label. Some elements may not be listed on a hydroponic nutrient because of "minimum" government requirements, and elements like copper are below that minimum but are present.

Chemical granular fertilizers can be over applied easily, creating toxic soil. They are almost impossible to leach out fast enough to save the plant.

Osmocote™ chemical fertilizers are time-release and used by many nurseries because they are easy to apply and only require one application every few months. Using this type of fertilizer may be convenient, but exact control is lost. They are best suited for ornamental containerized plants where labor costs and uniform growth are the main concerns.

Organic Fertilizers

Enthusiasts say organically-grown vegetables have a sweeter taste, but implementing an organic indoor garden requires horticultural know how. The limited soil, space and the necessity for sanitation must be considered when growing organically. Outdoors, organic gardening is easy because all the forces of nature are there for you to seek out and harness. Indoors, few of the natural phenomena are free and easy. Remember, you are Mother Nature and must create everything! The nature of growing indoors does not lend itself to long-term organic gardens, but some organic techniques have been practiced with amazing success.

Most indoor organic gardens use potting soil high in worm castings, peat, sand, manure, leaf mold, compost and fine dolomite lime. In a container, there is little space to build the soil by mixing all kinds of neat composts and organic nutrients to cook down. Even if it were possible to build soil in a container, it would take months of valuable growing time and could foster bad insects, fungi, etc. It is easiest and safest to throw old depleted soil outdoors, and start new plants with fresh organic soil.

Organic nutrients, manure, worm castings, blood and bone meal, etc., work very well to increase soil nutrient content, but nutrients are released and available at different rates. The nutrient availability may be tricky to calculate, but it is somewhat difficult to over-apply organic fertilizers. Organic nutrients seem to be more consistently available when used in combination with one another. Usually gardeners use a mix of about 20 percent worm castings with other organic agents to get a strong, readily available nitrogen base. They fertilize with bat guano, the organic super bloom, during flowering and fruiting.

An indoor garden using raised beds allows true organic methods. The raised beds have enough soil to hold nutrients, promote organic activity and when managed properly, ensure a constant supply of nutrients. The raised bed must have enough soil mass to promote heat and fundamental organic activity.

Alfalfa meal has 2.5 percent nitrogen, 5 percent phosphorus and about 2 percent potash. Outdoor gardeners use pelletized animal feed as a slow-release fertilizer.

Blood and bone meal, while wonderful organic fertilizers, could transport Mad Cow Disease and other maladies. Use them at your own risk!

Blood (dried or meal) is collected at slaughterhouses, dried and ground into a powder or meal. It's packed with fast-acting soluble nitrogen (12 to 15 percent by weight), about 1.2 percent phosphorus and under one-percent potash. Apply carefully because it's easy to burn foliage.

Bone meal is rich in phosphorus and nitrogen. The age and type of bone determine the nutrient content of this pulverized slaughterhouse product. Older bones have higher phosphorus content than young bones. Use bone meal in conjunction with other organic fertilizers for best results. Its lime content helps reduce soil acidity and acts fastest in well-aerated soil.

Raw, unsteamed bone meal contains 2 to 4 percent nitrogen and 15 to 25 percent phosphorus. Fatty acids in raw bone meal retard decomposition.

Steamed or cooked bone meal is made from fresh animal bones that have been boiled or steamed under pressure to render out fats. The pressure treatment causes a little nitrogen loss and an increase in phosphorus. Steamed bones are easier to grind into a fine powder and the process helps nutrients become available sooner. It contains up to 30 percent phosphorus and about 1.5 percent nitrogen. The finer bone meal is ground, the faster it becomes available.

Cottonseed meal is the leftover byproduct of oil extraction. According to the manufacturer, virtually all chemical residues from commercial cotton production are dissolved in the oil and not found in the meal. This acidic fertilizer contains about 7 percent nitrogen, 2.5 percent phosphorus and 1.5 percent potash. It should be combined with steamed bone meal and seaweed to form a balanced fertilizer blend.

Chicken manure is rich in available nitrogen, phosphorus, potassium and trace elements. Indoor gardeners most often prefer to purchase dry, composted chicken manure in a bag. Use it as a top dressing or mix with soil before planting. Often chicken manure collected from farms is packed with feathers that contain as much as 17 percent nitrogen, which is an added bonus. The average nutrient content of wet chicken manure is: N – 1.5%, P – 1.5%, K – 0.5% and dry: N – 4%, P – 4%, K – 1.5% and both have a full range of trace elements.

Coffee grounds are acid-loving and encourage acetic bacteria in the soil. Drip coffee grounds are the richest, containing about 2 percent nitrogen and traces of other nutrients. Add to the compost pile or scatter and cultivate in as a top dressing in moderation because they are very acidic.

Compost tea is used by many organic gardeners as the only source of fertilizer. Comfrey is packed with nutrients and many gardeners grow it just to make compost tea. Do not plant comfrey in a garden or flowerbeds; it will take over! Roots go so deep, even the smallest piece will sprout a new plant. Almost impossible to remove!

Cow manure is sold as "steer" manure but it is often collected from dairy herds. Gardeners have used cow manure for centuries, and this has led to the belief that it is a good fertilizer as well as a soil amendment. Steer manure is most valuable as mulch and a soil amendment. It holds water well and maintains fertility for a long time. The nutrient value is low and should not be relied upon for the main source of nitrogen. The average nutrient content of cow manure is N – 0.6%, P – 0.3%, K – 0.3% and a full range of trace elements. Apply at the rate of 25 – 30 pounds per square yard of soil.

Diatomaceous earth, the fossilized skeletal remains of fresh and saltwater diatoms, contains a full range of trace elements and is a good insecticide. Apply to the soil when cultivating or as a top dressing high in silica.

Dolomite lime adjusts and balances the pH and makes phosphates more available. Generally applied to "sweeten" or de-acidify soil. It consists of calcium and magnesium, sometimes listed as primary nutrients but generally referred to as the secondary nutrients. Quicklime is not the same and raises the pH very fast.

Feathers and feather meal contain from 12 to 15 percent nitrogen that is released slowly. Feathers included in barnyard chicken manure or obtained from slaughterhouses, are an excellent addition to the compost pile or as a fertilizer. Feathers are steamed under pressure, dried, then ground into a powdery feather meal. Feather meal contains slow-release nitrogen of about 12.5 percent.

Fish meal is made from dried fish ground into a meal. It is rich in nitrogen (about 8 percent) and contains around 7 percent phosphorus and many trace elements. It has an unpleasant odor, causing it to be avoided by indoor gardeners. It is a great compost activator. Apply to the soil as a relatively fast-acting top dressing. To help control odor, cultivate into the soil or cover with mulch after applying. Always store in an airtight container so it will not attract cats, dogs and flies. Fish meal and fish emulsion can contain up to 10 percent nitrogen. The liquid generally contains less nitrogen than the meal. Even when deodorized, the liquid form has an unpleasant odor.

Fish emulsion, an inexpensive soluble liquid, is high in organic nitrogen, trace elements and some phosphorus and potassium. This natural fertilizer is difficult to over-apply and is immediately available to plants. Even deodorized fish emulsion smells like dead fish. Inorganic potash is added to fish emulsion by some manufacturers and is "semi-organic".

Goat manure is much like horse manure but more potent. Compost this manure and treat as you would horse manure.

Granite dust or granite stone meal contains up to 5 percent potash and several trace elements. Releasing nutrients slowly over several years, granite dust is an inexpensive source of potash and does not affect soil pH. Not recommended indoors because it is too slow acting. There are many different kinds of granite, most contain feldspar which can contain sodium or calcium. All contain aluminum and silicon.

Greensand (glaucomite) is an iron potassium silicate that gives the minerals, in which it occurs, a green tint. It is mined from ancient seabed deposits of shells and organic material rich in iron, phosphorus, potash (5 to 7 percent) and numerous micronutrients. Much of it comes from New Jersey. Some organic gardeners do not use Greensand because it is such a

Bat guano has transformed into the organic super bloom fertilizer.

limited resource. Greensand slowly releases its treasures in about four years. Slow acting for indoor gardens.

Guano (bat) consists of the droppings and remains of bats. It is rich in soluble nitrogen, phosphorus and trace elements. The limited supply of this fertilizer, sometimes called soluble organic super bloom, makes it somewhat expensive. Mined in sheltered caves, guano dries with minimal decomposition. Bat guano can be thousands of years old. Newer deposits contain high levels of nitrogen and burn foliage, if applied too heavily. Older deposits are high in phosphorus and make an excellent flowering fertilizer. Bat guano is usually powdery and used as an organic "super bloom" or diluted in a tea. Do not breathe the dust when handling. It can cause nausea and irritation. As with any powdered ingredient, wear a mask!

Guano (sea bird) is high in nitrogen and other nutrients. The Humboldt Current along the coast of Peru and northern Chile keeps the rain from falling and decomposition of the guano is minimal. South American guano is the world's best. The guano is scraped off the rocks of arid sea islands. Guano is also collected from many coastlines around the world. Nutrient content varies.

Gypsum (hydrated calcium sulfate) is used to lower soil pH and improve drainage and aeration. It speeds the absorption of phosphorus. It is also used to hold or slow the rapid decomposition of nitrogen. Seldom used indoors. Plaster and plaster of Paris are made from gypsum.

Hoof and horn meal is an excellent source of slow-release nitrogen. Finely ground horn meal makes nitrogen available quicker and has few problems and does not attract fly maggots. Soil bacteria must break it down before it is available to roots. Apply two to three weeks before planting. It remains in the soil for six months or longer. Hoof and horn meal contains from 6 to 15 percent nitrogen and about 2 percent phosphorus.

Horse manure is readily available from horse stables and racetracks. Use horse manure that has straw or peat for bedding. Wood shavings could be a source of plant disease. Compost horse manure for two months or longer before adding to the garden. The composting process kills most weed seeds and helps make better use of the nutrients. Straw bedding often uses up much of the available nitrogen. Nutrient content of horse manure is N – 0.6%, P – 0.6%, K – 0.4% and a full range of trace elements. See "Blood and Bone Meal."

Kelp is the "Cadillac" of trace minerals. Kelp should be deep green, fresh and smell like the ocean. Seaweed contains 60 to 70 trace minerals that are already chelated (existing in a form that's water-soluble and mobile in the soil). Check the label to ensure all elements are not cooked out. See "Seaweed."

Oyster shells are ground and normally used as a calcium source for poultry. They contain up to 55 percent calcium and traces of many other nutrients that release slowly. Not practical to use indoors, because they break down too slowly.

Paper ash contains about 5 percent phosphorus and over 2 percent potash. It is an excellent water-soluble fertilizer, but do not apply in large doses because the pH is quite high. Paper ash is also full of toxic (oil-based) inks. Use ash from a barbeque or fireplace sparingly.

Pigeon manure has a very high concentration of nitrogen but is difficult to find. It can be used in the same fashion as chicken manure.

Rabbit manure is also excellent fertilizer but can be difficult to find in large quantities. Use rabbit manure as you would chicken or pigeon manure. According to one friend, rabbit poop is the best. Bunnies Rule!

Potash rock supplies up to 8 percent potassium and may contain many trace elements. It releases too slowly to be practical indoors.

Rock phosphate (hard) is calcium or lime based phosphate rock that is finely ground to the consistency of talcum powder. The rock powder contains over 30 percent phosphate and a menagerie of trace elements, but it is available very, very slowly. Super phosphate is made by adding gypsum to finely ground rock phosphate.

Colloidal phosphate (powdered or soft phosphate) is a natural clay phosphate deposit that contains just over 20 percent phosphorus (P_2O_5), calcium and many trace elements. But it yields only 2 percent phosphate by weight the first few months.

Rock potash should be avoided as a source of potassium, because it is too slow acting for short-lived indoor crops.

Seaweed meal and kelp meal is harvested from the ocean or picked up along beaches, cleansed of salty water, dried and ground into a powdery meal. It is packed with potassium (potash), numerous trace elements, vitamins, amino acids and plant hormones. The nutrient content varies according to the type of kelp and growing conditions. Seaweed meal is easily assimilated by plants and contributes to soil life, structure and nitrogen fixation. It may also help plants resist many diseases and withstand light frosts. Kelp meal also eases transplant shock.

Seaweed (liquid) contains nitrogen, phosphorus, potash; all necessary trace elements in a chelated form as well as plant hormones. Apply dilute solution to the soil for a quick cure of nutrient deficiencies. Liquid seaweed is also great for soaking seeds and dipping cuttings and bare roots before planting.

Sheep manure is high in nutrients and makes a wonderful tea. The average nutrient content is: N – 0.8%, P – 0.5%, K – 0.4% and a full range of trace elements. Sheep manures contain little water and lots of air. They heat up readily in a compost pile. Cow and pig manures are cold because they hold a lot of water and can be compacted easily, squeezing out the air.

Shrimp & crab wastes contain relatively high levels of phosphorus.

Sulfate of potash is normally produced chemically by treating rock powders with sulfuric acid, but one company, Great Salt Lake Minerals and Chemicals Company produces a concentrated natural form. The sulfate of potash is extracted from the Great Salt Lake. Potassium sulfate is also extracted from the Dead Sea in Israel.

Swine manure has a high nutrient content, but is slower acting and wetter (more anaerobic) than cow and horse manure. The average nutrient content of pig manure is: N – 0.6%, P – 0.6%, K – 0.4% and a full range of trace elements.

Wood ashes (hardwood) supply up to 10 percent potash and softwood ashes contain about 5 percent. Potash leaches rapidly. Collect ash soon after burning and store in a dry place. Apply in a mix with other fertilizers at the rate of one-quarter cup per 3-gallon pot. The potash washes out of wood ash quickly and can cause compacted, sticky soil. Avoid using alkaline wood ashes in soil with a pH above 6.5.

Worm castings are excreted digested humus and other (decomposing) organic matter that contain varying amounts of nitrogen as well as many other elements. They are an excellent source of non-burning soluble nitrogen and an excellent soil amendment that promotes fertility and structure. Mix with potting soil to form a rich fertile blend. Pure worm castings look like coarse graphite powder and are heavy and dense. Do not add more than 20 percent worm castings to any mix. They are so heavy, root growth can be impaired. Worm castings are very popular and easy to obtain at commercial nurseries and garden supply centers.

Note: The nutrients in organic fertilizers may vary greatly depending upon source, age, erosion, climate, etc. For exact nutrient content, consult the vendor's specifications.

Organic Teas

Organic tea concoctions contain soluble organic nutrients diluted in water. Fish emulsion is the most readily available commercial "organic tea". Old goldfish water is another example of organic tea. Soluble seaweed, molasses, worm castings, high in nitrogen, and bat guano, high in phosphorus, are the most common ingredients in U-mix organic teas because nutrients are immediately available. If bringing bat guano, cow manure or any kind of feces into the home, then mixing it with water and pouring it on plants is repulsive to you, the only solution is to not garden organically in your home. A greenhouse, shed or barn is better. Fish Farms – another form of organic tea is the recent use of fish excrement collected from raceways, troughs and ponds at fish farms. Many fish farms now have gardens, even hydroponic greenhouses next to them and use these ingredients in conjunction with normal hydroponic fertilizers.

Fill a nylon stocking with organic nutrients and soak in a bucket for a few days to make an organic nutrient solution that will not clog emitters or filters.

To make an organic mix, combine the organic nutrient(s) with water, let it sit for a few days and stir occasionally. Strain out the heavy stuff; pour the solution through an old nylon stocking before applying. Apply the diluted tea often at each watering. Make an organic tea bag by filling the foot of an old nylon with organic nutrients and soak in water.

Mixing Fertilizers

To mix, dissolve powder, crystals or liquid into a little warm (90 – 100 degree F) water; make sure it is totally dissolved, before adding the balance of the tepid water. This will ensure that the fertilizer and water mix evenly.

Containers have very little growing medium in which to hold nutrients, and toxic salt build-up may become a problem. Follow dosage instructions to the letter. Adding too much fertilizer will not make plants grow faster. It could change the chemical balance of the soil and supply too much of a specific nutrient or lock up other nutrients, making them unavailable to the plant.

Fertilizer Application

Determine if plants need fertilizing by visual inspection, taking an N-P-K soil test, or experimenting on a test plant(s). No matter which method is used, remember, plants in small containers use available nutrients quickly and need frequent fertilizing, while plants in large planters have more soil, supply more nutrients and require less frequent fertilizing.

A brix meter will give you an exact indication of how well plants are using fertilizers.

Computer Nutrient Mixing

The Nutron 2000 is a program that calculates nutrient formulations. The inexpensive CD-ROM program developed by a New Zealand company, Suntec, calculates every element (fertilizer salt) in your mix and factors in water quality, pH and application rates. The exact two-part formulation is calculated in nanoseconds. Gardeners can blend their own specific nutrient mix best suited to individual growing environments. Blending nutrients saves money in big grow operations, as well as helping gardeners dial in an exact nutrient mix suited to their conditions. Use the CD with Windows 95 or higher.

The Nutron 2000 calculates nutrient quantities down to grams per liter, ounces per gallon, PPM and mmol concentrations. It further calculates in relation to any EC, dilution rate, stock solution volume, salt element content and water supply. The program renders complete EC and pH assessment.

The Nutron 2000 will teach you everything you need to know to mix your own nutrients from scratch.

Check out the Casper Publishing site:
www.hydroponics.com.au.
Distributed in America, by DB Distributing,
Tel. 1-888-321-7249

Brix Meter

A Brix meter or refractometer is one of the most useful tools any gardener can own. The simple refractometer measures natural brix (sugar) content in foliage. The quick and easy test is a measure of fertilizer uptake and plant health. Winemakers use a brix meter to determine the sugar content in grapes. Indoor gardeners are starting to use brix meters to get a quick read on individual plant's health.

Super Size Secret: *A brix meter measures foliage sugar content, which estimates the effectiveness of fertilizers. Brix level is the key to plant health and a big harvest*

Unlike EC measurements that can measure only the strength of a nutrient solution before it enters the plant, a brix reading measures the actual sugar content within the plant after nutrients are applied.

Determining plant health with the refractometer is simple and straight forward. The higher the level of sugar within plant tissue, the stronger the plant and better it will yield. Using the meter, gardeners can learn about nutrient problems in days, or weeks before they are visible in foliage. A brix reading below 10 indicates a lack of nutrients. Low brix readings are common even though nutrients are in abundant supply in the soil. A reading above 12 indicates a strong healthy plant. Gardeners can fine tune nutrient uptake with the help of a brix meter. Ensuring that nutrients are supplied and actually being used by a plant is a key to growing great plants.

To test brix content, pick a leaf and roll it into a ball. Compress the balled-up leaf with a pair of clean pliers to extract a few drops of juice. Drip the fresh leaf juice on the inclined glass plane of the refractometer. Take the reading by looking through the viewfinder to see which number the sugar content registers. At the time of this writing Brix meters were available from Western Water Farms, Langley, BC, Canada, Tel. 1-604-533-9301 and from Peaceful Valley Farm Supply, www.groworganic.com.

Visual Inspection: If plants are growing well and have deep green healthy leaves, they are probably getting all necessary nutrients. The moment growth slows or leaves begin to turn pale green, it is time to fertilize. Do not confuse yellow leaves caused by a lack of light with yellow leaves caused by a nutrient deficiency. Light green (almost yellow) leaves at the top center of a fast-growing plant (meristematic) zone is actually a good sign. It means plants are growing so fast, they have yet to produce chlorophyll.

Taking an N-P-K soil test will reveal exactly how much of each major nutrient is available to the plant. The test kits mix a soil sample with a chemical. After the soil settles, a color reading is taken from the liquid, and matched to a color chart. The appropriate amount of fertilizer is then added. This method is very exact, but can be more trouble than it is worth. Simply flush and re-fertilize with a complete fresh mix.

Experiment on two or three test plants. This method yields experience and develops horticultural skills. Cuttings are perfect for this type of experiment. Give the test plants some fertilizer and see if they green up and grow faster. If it is good for one, it should be good for all.

Now, it has been determined the plants need fertilizer, but how much? The answer is simple. Mix fertilizer, as per instructions, and water as normal or dilute fertilizer and apply more often. Remember, small plants use much less fertilizer than large ones. Fertilize early in the day, so plants have all day to absorb and process the fertilizer.

It is almost impossible to explain how often to apply fertilizer. We know that large plants use more nutrients than small plants. The more often fertilizer is applied, the less concentrated it should be. Frequency of fertilization is one of the most widely disagreed upon subjects among gardeners. Many indoor containerized plants can be pushed to incredible lengths; they can absorb amazing amounts of fertilizer and grow well. Lots of gardeners add as much as one tablespoon per gallon (Peters™ (20-20-20) or (10-30-20)) with each watering! This works best with growing mediums that drain readily and are easy to leach. Other gardeners use only rich organic potting soil with fine dolomite lime added. No supplemental fertilizer is applied until a super-bloom formula is needed for flowering.

 Rule of Thumb: *The faster a plant grows, feed it more and more often. The slower a plant grows, feed it less and less often.*

You can use a siphon applicator, found at most nurseries, to mix soluble fertilizers with water. The applicator is simply attached to the faucet with the siphon submerged in the concentrated fertilizer solution and the hose attached to the other end. Often, applicators are set at 1:15 ratio for every 1 unit of liquid concentrate fertilizer, 15 units of water will be mixed with it. Sufficient water flow is necessary for the suction to work properly. Misting nozzles restrict this flow. When the water is turned on, the fertilizer is siphoned into the system and flows out the hose. Fertilizer is generally applied with each watering, since a small percentage of fertilizer is metered in.

A garbage can with a garden hose fitting at the bottom, set 3 – 4 feet off the floor will act as a gravity flow source for fertilizer solution. The container is filled with water and fertilizer. This works OK for drip systems.

When it comes to fertilization, experience with specific plants and growing systems tell gardeners more than anything else. There are hundreds of N-P-K mixes and they all work! When choosing a fertilizer, make sure to read the entire label and know what the fertilizer claims it can do. Do not be afraid to ask retail clerks questions or contact the manufacturer with questions.

Once you have an idea of how often to fertilize, put the garden on a regular feeding schedule. A schedule usually works very well, but it must be combined with a vigilant, caring eye that looks for over-fertilization and nutrient deficiency signs.

Rule of Thumb: Leach soil with 1 – 3 gallons of mild nutrient solution per gallon of soil every 1 – 2 months. This is the best form of preventive maintenance against toxic salt build-up in the soil.

Foliar Feeding

Virtually all liquid foliar fertilizers including fish emulsion, contain nitrates. Plant leaves convert nitrates to carcinogenic N-nitrosamines! This is why foliar feeding is not recommended.

Over-fertilizing can become one of the biggest problems for indoor gardeners. Too much fertilizer causes a build up of nutrients (salts) to toxic levels and changes soil chemistry. When over-fertilized, growth is rapid and lush green until the toxic levels are reached. When toxic fertilizer levels are reached, leaves spot, margins and tips often burn, and if severe, the leaves will curl under like a bighorn sheep's horns. Plants wilt and die if severe.

Chance of over-fertilization is greater in a small amount of soil that can hold only a small amount of nutrients. A large pot or planter can hold much more soil and nutrients safely, but it will take longer to flush if overdone. It is very easy to add too much fertilizer to a small container. Large containers have good nutrient holding ability.

To treat severely over-fertilized plants, leach soil with 2 gallons of diluted nutrient solution per gallon of soil, so as to wash all the excess nutrients out. The plant should start new growth and look better in one week. If the problem is severe and leaves are curled, the soil may need to be leached several times. After the plant appears to have leveled off to normal growth, use normal diluted fertilizer solution.

Hydroponic Gardening

Hydroponics is the science of growing plants without soil, most often in a soilless mix. In fact, many gardeners are already cultivating hydroponically and don't even know it. Growing cuttings in rockwool, peat moss, coconut fiber, or growing mature plants in soilless Sunshine Mix™ or Terra-Lite™, even when watered by hand, is hydroponic gardening. With hydroponics, nutrient uptake and grow medium oxygen content can be totally controlled. Manage these two factors along with a few other requirements to grow a bumper crop every harvest.

The inert soilless hydroponic medium contains essentially no nutrients. All the nutrients are supplied via the nutrient solution. This solution passes over or floods around roots at regular intervals, later draining off. The extra oxygen trapped in the soilless medium and around the roots speeds nutrient uptake by tiny root hairs. Plants grow fast hydroponically, because the roots are able to take in food as fast as it can be used. In soil, as in hydroponics, the roots absorb nutrients and water. Even the best soil rarely has as much oxygen in it as a soilless hydroponic medium. Damp roots with a thin layer of nutrient solution surrounded by atmospheric oxygen (O_2) grows plants the fastest.

Contrary to popular belief, hydroponic gardens often require more care than soil gardens. If growing hydroponically, expect to spend more time in the garden. Extra maintenance is necessary, because plants grow faster, and there are more things to check and more can go wrong. In fact, some people do not like hydroponic gardening because it requires too much additional care. Good automatic systems, however, can be easy to maintain and a joy to behold

Super Size Secret: *Hydroponic gardens require more care because plants grow faster. Nutrient levels, temperature, light and pH must be checked and kept optimized to a "hydroponic balance".*

Novice gardeners frequently get so excited about their first garden that they try to do too much, too soon. They buy too many new little gadgets to solve problems they didn't know they had, and they start more projects than they can manage. One of the biggest problems gardeners have when purchasing hydroponic units is following the directions to assemble the system. Before a gardener decides to invent their own hydroponic system, they should be able to follow the assembly directions of another hydroponic system. It takes a month or two to work out most of the bugs in a commercial system and even longer for a homemade unit. Remember, just because a hydroponic garden cost hundreds of dollars, does not guarantee success.

Hydroponic gardening is very exacting and not forgiving like soil gardening. Soil works as a buffer for nutrients and holds them longer than the inert hydroponic growing medium. In fact, advanced aeroponic systems do not use a soilless mix; they use nothing at all! Roots are suspended in the air and misted with nutrient solution. The misting chamber is kept dark to keep algae from competing with roots.

Plants grow less foliage and more flowers and vegetables when the fertilizer regimen is tightly controlled. Hydroponically grown plants flower and fruit faster and can be harvested a few days or weeks earlier than if soil-grown.

Small flowering plants grow well in small containers and horizontal tubes. For example, determinate tomatoes, bananas, peppers, etc., that take longer to grow are best suited to a large bucket system, which allows room for root development. The root system on many plants is easily contained in the bucket, and they are able to produce numerous flowers and fruits during their lifetime. Plants with large root systems take in lots of nutrients to keep up with heavy flower and fruit production. The root system, to above ground plant size, changes with hydroponics. In soil, it is normally 50/50 but in hydroponics, it can be 90/10 (90 percent above ground, 10 percent below). This is because the nutrients are brought to the roots instead of the roots having to go out and "find" nutrients and water.

Most garden rooms have two limiting factors: (1) the number of plants in the garden and (2) the electrical consumption expressed in watts. For example, if growing 12 large tomato plants in a five-gallon bucket hydroponic system, the main garden room should be illuminated with two 600-watt HP sodium lamps. A 40-watt fluorescent fixture could be used to root cuttings or start seedlings.

A wick system is simple and low maintenance. The wick carries nutrient solution up to the roots.

Different Systems

Hydroponic systems are distinguished by the way the nutrient solution is applied. The first distinction is whether the nutrient solution is applied in an "active" or "passive" manor.

Passive systems rely on capillary action to transfer the nutrient solution from the reservoir to the growing medium. Nutrient solution is passively absorbed by a wick and transported to the growing medium and roots. Absorbent growing mediums such as vermiculite, sawdust, peat moss, etc., are ideal for passive systems. The growing medium stays very wet in passive systems. Soggy substrates hold less air and deprive roots of rapid nutrient uptake. Although most passive gardens are not "high performance," they do fill a need. Wick systems have no moving parts. Seldom does anything break or malfunction. A low initial cost and low maintenance enhance wick system's popularity. Wick systems are efficiently used to root cuttings and sustain mother plants starting seedlings. Large plants are usually transferred to larger containers or growing trays, using flood and drain or gravity-flow hydroponic systems.

The soilless medium used, the number of wicks, their gauge and texture are the main variables involved in a wick system. Increase the number of wicks and roots are supplied with more nutrient solution.

Active hydroponic systems actively move the nutrient solution. Examples of active systems are: flood and drain and top feed. Fast growing plants are best suited to active hydroponic systems.

Active hydroponic gardens are considered a "recovery" system if the nutrient solution is recovered and reused after irrigation. A "non-recovery" system applies the nutrient solution once and it runs to waste. The solution is not reused. Non-recovery systems have few complications, but are not practical for many indoor gardens. Also out of favor with commercial gardeners, "run-to-waste" systems are avoided because they pollute ground water with high levels of nitrates, phosphates and other elements. Indoor gardeners seldom use non-recovery systems because they require disposing of so much nutrient solution. Many are now banned in Europe.

Active recovery hydroponic systems, such as the flood and drain (ebb and flow), top feed and nutrient film technique (NFT) are the most popular and productive available today. All three systems cycle reused nutrient solution into contact with roots. Recovering and reusing the nutrient solution makes management more complex, but with the proper nutrient solution and schedule, it is easy to manage. Active recovery systems use growing mediums that drain rapidly and hold plenty of air, including pea gravel, pumice rock, crushed brick, rockwool and coconut coir. Most use a pump and timer.

Flood and drain hydroponic systems are popular because of their proven track record of a low maintenance easy-to-use garden. Ebb and flow systems are versatile, simple by design and very efficient. Individual plants in pots or rockwool cubes are set on a special table. The table is actually a growing bed that can hold an inch or more of water. A maze of drainage gullies directs runoff solution back to the catchment tank. Nutrient solution is pumped into the table or growing bed. The rockwool blocks or containers are flooded from the bottom, which pushes the oxygen-poor, air out. As the growing medium drains, new oxygen-rich air is drawn into contact with the roots. A timer turns the pump on and off at appropriate times.

Top feed hydroponic systems are very efficient and productive. The nutrient solution is delivered via spaghetti tubing or emitters to the base of individual plants. Aerated nutrient solution flows over the nutrient solution and roots. The nutrient solution is directed back to the reservoir as soon as it drains from the growing medium. Rockwool, gravel, coconut coir, expanded clay and expanded

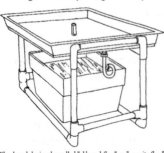

Flood and drain also called "ebb and flow" or "gravity flow" gardens pump water into a tray full of plants before draining back into the reservoir.

mica are the most common growing mediums found in top feed systems. Versatile top feed systems can be used with individual containers, long beds or tables. Aeration of the nutrient solution can be increased with an aquarium air pump and air stones or bubble wands in the holding tank.

Top feed systems apply nutrient solution via an emmiter near the stem.

NFT hydroponic systems are high performance gardens. Nutrient Film Technique (NFT) is a relatively new form of hydroponics. Seedlings or cuttings are placed on capillary matting in a covered channel. Nutrient solution flows down the channel over and around the roots and back to the reservoir. Irrigation is most often constant, 24 hours a day. Roots receive virtually all the oxygen they need to absorb the nutrient solution. Growth is super fast when everything is fine-tuned. Although high performance, NFT systems offer practically no buffering ability, unfortunately no room for error. In the absence of a growing medium, roots must be kept perfectly moist by the nutrient solution all the time. If a pump fails, roots die. If the system dries out for a day or longer, grave consequences result. The system is very easy to clean up and lay out after each crop. Only gardeners with several years experience should try a NFT system if working alone. With help, they are easier to master.

Adding a growing medium such as Leca clay, rockwool or pea gravel can add some buffering and make things less critical. A timer is then usually added. These "hybrid" systems are easier to operate and function great.

NFT (nutrient film technique) systems grow roots on capillary matting in troughs. Nutrient solution flows over the roots.

Aeroponic systems use no growing medium and offer the highest performance possible. The root zone is

Aeroponic systems mist roots suspended in air.

suspended in a dark growth chamber. No growing medium is used. The roots are misted at regular intervals. The humidity in the chamber remains at or near 100 percent. The roots have the maximum potential to absorb nutrient in the presence of air. Only air and nutrient solution fill the growth chamber. Phenomenal growth can be achieved with this system, but it can be very touchy to use. There is no growing medium to act as a water/nutrient bank. If the pump fails, the roots soon dry out and plants die. If the pH and the nutrient solution concentration become imbalanced, there is nothing to help stabilize them. Check on them often. Saddle sprayers or misting nozzles provide a fine spray or mist. PVC pipe and fittings are normally used to transport the nutrients, and high pressure, low volume pumps are normally used.

Rooted cuttings and seedlings grown in aeroponic systems develop exceptionally fast. To grow cuttings, simply insert cutting stems into the growth chamber and turn it on. The roots will grow in a perfect environment to develop roots. Rockwool cubes can be used as support. Large plants need to be supported or tied up.

Growing Mediums

Soilless growing mediums provide support for the root system, as well as, hold and make available oxygen, water and nutrients. Three factors contribute to plant root's ability to grow in a substrate: texture, pH and nutrient content, measured in EC or PPM.

The texture of any substrate is governed by the size and physical structure of the particles that constitute it. Proper texture promotes strong root penetration, oxygen retention, nutrient uptake and drainage. Growing mediums that consist of large particles permit good aeration and drainage. Increased irrigation frequency can be used to compensate for low water retention. Water and air holding ability and root penetration are a function of texture. The smaller the particles, the closer they pack together and the slower they drain. Larger particles drain faster and retain more air.

If you are going to use other substances like pumice or coral, put some in a glass of water and boil it for 20 or so minutes. Measure the pH and EC (PPM) of the water. If it is fairly neutral (pH 6.5-7.5) and has a PPM of under 100, it should be OK to use. Do not use mine tailings that may contain toxic metals.

Irregular shaped substrates, such as perlite and some expanded clays, have more surface area and hold more water than round soilless mediums. Avoid crushed gravel with sharp edges that cut into roots if the plant falls or is jostled around. Round pea gravel, smooth, washed gravel, crushed brick and lava rocks are excellent mediums to grow plants in an active recovery system. Use igneous (volcanic) based rock because it is inert, tends to have a neutral pH, and does not break up or shed system-clogging dust.

Wash clay and rock growing mediums thoroughly to get out all the dust that turns to sediment.

Fibrous materials like vermiculite, peat moss, rockwool and coconut coir retain large amounts of moisture within their cells. Such substrates are ideal for passive hydroponic systems that operate via capillary action.

 Rule of Thumb: *A fast-draining growing medium is essential to the success of an active recovery hydroponic system.*

Mineral growing mediums are inert and do not react with living organisms or chemicals to change the integrity of the nutrient solution. Coconut coir and peat mosses are also inert, although some peat moss contains 15 percent N and can be acidic.

Non-inert growing mediums cause unforeseen problems. For example, gravel from a limestone quarry is full of calcium carbonate and old concrete is full of lime. When mixed with water, calcium carbonate will raise the pH and it will be very difficult to make it go down. Growing mediums made from reconstituted concrete bleed out so much lime they soon kill the garden.

Avoid substrates found within a few miles of the ocean or large bodies of salt water. Most likely such mediums are packed with toxic salts. Rather than washing and leaching salts from the medium, it is easier and more economical to find another source of substrate.

Coconut fiber: (also called coir, the fibrous outer husk) is an excellent hydroponic medium. See "coconut fiber" under Soil Amendments in Chapter Three.

Expanded clay: This medium is made by many different manufacturers. It is an excellent medium to mix with Peat-Lite™ and to grow plants in large containers. I like the way it drains so well and still retains nutrient solution while holding lots of oxygen. Examples of expanded clay include commercially available Hydroton®, Leca®, Grorox™, and Geolite™.

Expanded mica: Similar to expanded clay. For lots of exacting information on how and why this stuff works so well, check out www.hydroponics.com. Vermiculite is expanded mica. Stay away from "thermalite", which contains both mica and asbestos, a carcinogen. It is used for attic insulation.

Foam rubber: The jury is still out on this medium. I have seen it used with fair results. It holds a lot of water and does not wick as well as many other mediums. Roots do not penetrate very well.

Gravel: This is one of the original hydroponic mediums, although heavy. Gravel is inert, holds plenty of air, drains well and is inexpensive. Still popular today, gravel is difficult to over-water. It holds moisture, nutrient and oxygen on its outer surfaces. Use pea gravel or washed river gravel with round edges, that do not cut roots when they jostle about. Gravel should be one-eighth to three eights-inches in diameter, with more than half of the medium about a quarter-inch across.

Lava Rock: Naturally occurring, this porous lightweight rock holds moisture and air in the catacomb-like surfaces. Light and easy to work with, lava rock, called pumice, occasionally floats and sharp edges can grind on roots. Still it is a good medium and acts similar to expanded clay. See "Pumice" under "Soil Amendments."

Peat moss: This is partially decomposed vegetation. Decomposition has been slow in the northern regions where it is found. Sphagnum and hypnum mosses form the most common types of peat. For more information on peat moss, see "Sphagnum" and "Hypnum" peat moss under "Soil Amendments."

Perlite: This is puffed glass or quartz sand, it drains fast but it's very light and tends to float when flooded with water. See "Perlite" under "Soil Amendments."

Rockwool: This is an exceptional growing medium. It is an inert, sterile, porous, nod-degradable growing medium that provides good root support. Rockwool is probably the most popular hydroponic growing medium in the world. Check out *Gardening Indoors with Rockwool*, G. F. Van Patten and A. Bust, $14.95 for all you need to know about rockwool. Brand names include Grodan®, General Hydro™, HydroGro™ and Vacrok™. It is made out of igneous basalt or rhyolite melted at high temperature. It is dripped onto spinning disks that spin out fine strands like making cotton candy.

Sand: I love sand! Sand is the only medium I would use to grow cuttings for years. Make sure to use sharp river sand. Do not use ocean or salty beach sand. Sand drains quickly but still retains moisture. It's a bit heavy but I still love it.

Sawdust: This medium holds too much water for many fast growing plants to flourish, and is too acidic. It can be mixed with three quarters vermiculite, perlite, straw and sand to make a good soilless mix.

Vermiculite: Holds a lot of water and is best suited for rooting cuttings when it is mixed with sand or perlite. Vermiculite, along with perlite, are used in wick systems. See "Vermiculite" under "Soil Amendments."

pH

The pH of the nutrient solution controls the availability of ions the plant needs to assimilate nutrients. Most plants grow well hydroponically within a pH range of 5.5 – 6.5, with 5.8: 6.0 being ideal. The pH in hydroponic gardens requires a somewhat vigilant eye. All of the nutrients are in solution and more available than when in soil. The pH of the solution can fluctuate a half point and not cause any problems. A buffered nutrient solution, like Ecogrow, will not drift so much in pH. The choice of ingredients is critical. If the ingredients that alter pH are used up the same rate, the pH will not drift. For example, nitrate nitrogen (75 percent) and amonical nitrogen (25 percent) is a buffered ratio that prevents pH drift.

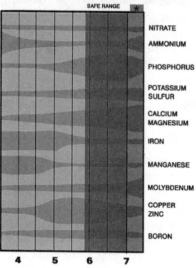

HOW PH AFFECTS YOUR NUTRIENT

The pH in hydroponic systems should run a little lower than in soil gardens.

Roots take in nutrients at different rates, which cause the ratios of nutrients in solution to change the pH. When the pH is above 7 or below 5.5 some nutrients are not absorbed as fast as possible.

Rule of Thumb: *Check the pH every day or two to make sure it is at or near the perfect level.*

Deviations in pH levels often affect element solubility. Values change slightly with different plants, grow mediums and hydroponic systems. Overall, hydroponic gardens require lower pH levels than that of soil. The best pH range for hydroponic gardens is from 5.5 to 6.5. Different mediums perform best at different pH levels. Follow manufactures guidelines for pH level and correct the pH using the manufacturers suggested chemicals, because they will react best with their fertilizer. The pH can easily fluctuate up and down one full point in hydroponic systems and cause little or no problem with nutrient uptake.

Adjust Nutrient Solution pH Levels With

pH Up
Potassium hydroxide
*Do not use
dangerous and caustic
sodium hydroxide
to raise pH.*

pH Down
Nitric acid
Phosphoric acid
Citric acid
Vinegar

Buy pH Up
and pH Down
rather than
making
your own from
concentrated
acids.
Commercial
mixes are
buffered
and safe
to use.

Follow the directions on the container and remember to mix adjusters into the reservoir slowly and completely. Fertilizers are normally acidic and lower the pH of the nutrient solution. But nutrient solution is still taken in by plants and water transpires and evaporates into the air, which also causes the pH to climb. You should stabilize the pH of the water BEFORE adding the fertilizer. Make corrections to pH only of readings vary by +/- a half point.

EC, TDS, DS, CF, PPM

Pure distilled water has no resistance and conducts no electrical current. However, when impurities are added to pure distilled water, it conducts electricity. Your water analysis will indicate the impurities or dissolved solids found in household tap water. These impurities conduct electricity. For instance, when you add fertilizer to pure water, the EC climbs. All these units of measure can be converted to any other. They all measure the electrical conductivity of the nutrient solution in ohms (or its reciprocal, the MHO). Some nutrient ingredients like urea (46 percent nitrogen) and the chelates do not conduct electricity and, even though present, will not register on these instruments.

TDS stands for Total Dissolved Solids. This is just one of the ways to arrive at EC, Electrical Conductivity. EC is the most consistent measure of gross nutrient solution strength.

Nutrient (salt) concentrations are measured by their ability to conduct electricity through a solution. Dissolved ionic salts create electrical current in solution, the main constituent of hydroponic solutions is ionic salts. Several scales are currently used to measure how much electricity is conducted by nutrients including: EC = Electrical Conductivity, CF = Conductivity Factor, PPM = Parts Per Million, TDS = Total Dissolved Solids and DS = Dissolved Solids. Most American gardeners use PPM, to measure overall fertilizer concentration.

The difference between EC, CF, PPM, TDS and DS is more complex than originally meets the eye. Different measurement systems all use the same base, but interpret the information differently. First, let's start with EC, the most accurate and consistent scale.

> **EC = Electrical Conductivity**
> **CF = Conductivity Factor,**
> **PPM = Parts Per Million,**
> **TDS = Total Dissolved Solids,**
> **DS = Dissolved Solids,**

EC is measured in: (a) Milli-siemens per Centimeter (MS/CM) or (b) Micro-siemens per Centimeter (US/CM). One Micro-siemen/CM = 1000 Milli-siemens/CM.

PPM testers actually measure in EC and convert to PPM. Unfortunately the two scales (EC and PPM) are not directly related. Each nutrient or salt gives a different electronic discharge reading. To overcome this obstacle, an arbitrary standard was implemented which assumes "a specific EC equates to a specific amount of nutrient solution." Consequently, the PPM reading is not precise, it is only an approximation, a ball park figure!

It gets worse! Nutrient tester manufacturers use different standards to convert from EC to the PPM reading.

1. Hanna	1 MS/CM = 500 PPM
2. Eutech	1 MS/CM = 640 PPM
3. New Zealand Hydro.	1 MS/CM = 700 PPM

PPM recommendations are inaccurate and confusing! To help you through this confusion, Graemme Plummer from Australia has compiled the following easy reference conversion chart. Note that high quality meters are calibrated to eliminate this non-linear discrepancy, like Electro Scientific (ESI), soil test.

1 MS/CM = 10 CF e.g. 0.7 EC = 7 CF.

Conversion scale from PPM to CF and EC.

EC MS/CM	Hanna 0.5	Eutech 0.64	Truncheon 0.70	CF 0
0.1	50 PPM	64 PPM	70 PPM	1
0.2	100 PPM	128 PPM	140 PPM	2
0.3	150 PPM	192 PPM	210 PPM	3
0.4	200 PPM	256 PPM	280 PPM	4
0.5	250 PPM	320 PPM	350 PPM	5
0.6	300 PPM	384 PPM	420 PPM	6
0.7	350 PPM	448 PPM	490 PPM	7
0.8	400 PPM	512 PPM	560 PPM	8
0.9	450 PPM	576 PPM	630 PPM	9
1.0	500 PPM	640 PPM	700 PPM	10
1.1	550 PPM	704 PPM	770 PPM	11
1.2	600 PPM	768 PPM	840 PPM	12
1.3	650 PPM	832 PPM	910 PPM	13
1.4	700 PPM	896 PPM	980 PPM	14
1.5	750 PPM	960 PPM	1050 PPM	15
1.6	800 PPM	1024 PPM	1120 PPM	16
1.7	850 PPM	1088 PPM	1190 PPM	17
1.8	900 PPM	1152 PPM	1260 PPM	18
1.9	950 PPM	1260 PPM	1330 PPM	19

2.0	1000 PPM	1280 PPM	1400 PPM	20
2.1	1050 PPM	1344 PPM	1470 PPM	21
2.2	1100 PPM	1408 PPM	1540 PPM	22
2.3	1150 PPM	1472 PPM	1610 PPM	23
2.4	1200 PPM	1536 PPM	1680 PPM	24
2.5	1250 PPM	1600 PPM	1750 PPM	25
2.6	1300 PPM	1664 PPM	1820 PPM	26
2.7	1350 PPM	1728 PPM	1890 PPM	27
2.8	1400 PPM	1792 PPM	1960 PPM	28
2.9	1450 PPM	1856 PPM	2030 PPM	29
3.0	1500 PPM	1920 PPM	2100 PPM	30
3.1	1550 PPM	1984 PPM	2170 PPM	31
3.2	1600 PPM	2048 PPM	2240 PPM	32

Every element in a multi-element solution has a different conductivity factor in these approximate measurements. Pure water will not conduct electrical current. But as elemental salts/metals are added, electrical conductivity increases proportionately. Simple electronic meters measure this value and interpret it as total dissolved solids (TDS). Nutrient solutions used to nurture fast growing annuals generally range between 500 and 2000 parts per million (PPM). If the solution concentration is to high, the internal osmotic systems can reverse and actually dehydrate the plant. For general purpose, try to maintain a moderate value of approximately 800 to 1200 PPM. Nutrient solution concentration levels are affected by nutrient absorption by roots and by water evaporation. The solution weakens as plants use nutrients, but water also evaporates from the solution, which increases the nutrient concentration. Adjust the concentration of the solution by adding fertilizer or diluting with more water.

 Super Size Secret: *Use an EC meter to check the overall strength of your nutrient solution. EC is the most consistent measure of overall solution strength.*

Then you can run your nutrient at the same level, regardless of the meter purchased. You will see by the scale of the PPM reading you obtain from your meter can gave quite drastic differences, depending on which brand of meter you use.

Many factors can alter the EC balance of a garden. For example, if under-watered or allowed to dry completely, the EC reading will rise. In fact, the EC may increase to two or three times as high as the input solution when too little water is applied to rockwool. This increase in slab EC causes some nutrients to build up faster than others. For example, when the EC doubles, the amount of sodium can increase as much as four to six-fold under the right conditions!

NOTE: There should not be any sodium present in your garden, unless it is in the water supply, and it should not be in excess of 50 PPM. If you use city water, they probably have an analysis of what's in it for the asking.

Let 10 – 20 percent of the nutrient solution drain from the rockwool after each irrigation cycle. This will help retain stability of the Conductivity Factor. The runoff carries away any excess fertilizer salt build-up in the growing medium.

If the EC level of a rockwool solution is too high, increase the amount of run-off you create with each flush. For example, instead of a 10–20 percent run-off, flush so 20–30 percent of the solution runs off. To raise the EC, add more fertilizer to the solution or change the nutrient solution.

A dissolved solids (DS) measurement indicates how many parts per million (PPM) of dissolved solids exist in a solution. A reading of 1800 PPM means there are 1800 parts of nutrient in one million parts solution, or 1,800/1,000,000, or 0.18 percent, a very small amount. This means the solution is 99.82 percent water.

An EC meter works well to measure the overall volume or strength of elements in your water or solution. A digital LCD (Liquid Crystal Display) screen displays the reading or the EC of the electrical current flowing between the two electrodes in the meter. Pure rainwater has an EC close to 0. Check the pH and EC of rainwater to find out if it is acidic (acid rain) before using it.

Distilled bottled water from the grocery store often registers a small amount of electrical resistance because it is not perfectly pure. Pure water with no resistance is very difficult to obtain and not necessary for a hydroponic nutrient solution.

EC measurement is temperature sensitive and high quality meters have automatic and manual temperature adjustments.

Temperature must be factored into the EC reading to retain accuracy. Calibrating an EC meter is similar to calibrating a pH meter. Simply follow manufacturer's instructions. For an accurate reading, make sure your nutrient solution and stock solution are the same temperature. Inexpensive meters have a short life span (about one year) and expensive meters can last for many years. The life of an EC meter, regardless of cost, is contingent upon regular maintenance. The probes must be kept moist and clean at all times. This is the most important part of keeping the meter in good repair. Read all the instructions thoroughly on care and maintenance. Watch for corrosion build-up on the probes of your meter. When the probes are corroded, you will not get an accurate reading. Clean with fine abrasive and toothbrush.

An EC measurement is only an overall reading of all the nutrients mixed together. EC readings do not delineate specific nutrients. For example, an EC reading of 1.0 could mean there are sodium and sulfur in a solution. On the other hand, the same 1.0 EC could also measure a complete and balanced solution, which contains all necessary nutrients in the proper proportions. EC is only a valid measurement when you start with the proper ratio of nutrients in your solution and you know the dissolved solids in your water.

 Rule of Thumb: *Check the EC of your water, slab, and runoff regularly.*

To check the EC, collect nutrient solution samples from both the reservoir and the rockwool. Save time and effort and collect EC and pH samples simultaneously. Collect samples with a syringe or baster at least two inches deep in the rockwool. Collect a separate sample from the reservoir. Place each sample in a clean jar. Use an EC meter to measure the samples. Under normal conditions, the EC in the slab should be a bit higher than the nutrient solution in the reservoir. If the EC of the solution drawn from the rockwool is substantially higher than the one from the reservoir, there is a salt buildup in the rockwool. Correct the imbalance by flushing rockwool thoroughly with fresh water or a dilute nutrient solution and replace with a fresh nutrient solution.

Sterilizing

To reuse a growing medium, it must be sterilized to remove destructive pests and diseases. Sterilizing is less expensive and often easier than replacing the growing medium. Sterilizing works best on rigid growing mediums that do not loose their shape, such as gravel, expanded clay and mica. Avoid sterilizing and reusing substrates that compact and loose structure, such as rockwool, coconut coir, peat moss, perlite and vermiculite. Avoid problems caused by compaction and dead roots by replacing such mediums. Once sterilized, the medium is free of harmful microorganisms, including bacteria, fungi, pests and their eggs.

Remove roots from the growing medium before sterilizing. A 3 – 4-month-old tomato plant has a root mass about the size of an old desk telephone. Try to separate most of the roots from the medium. Fewer decaying roots cause fewer pest and disease problems, and decreases incidences of clogged feeder tubes.

To remove roots and sterilize the growing medium:

Manually remove the mat of roots that are entwined near the bottom of the bed and shake loose any attached growing medium. It may be easier to add more medium than trying to pick it from between the matted roots

Pour growing mediums, such as expanded clay and gravel, through a screen placed over a large bucket. Most of the roots will stay on the screen.

The roots in this 5-gallon bucket hydroponic system have been growing just over three months.

Lay growing medium out on the floor and train an oscillating fan on it to dry out remaining roots.

Substrate can also be washed in a large container such as a barrel or bathtub. Washing works best with lighter substrates, such as expanded clay or mica. Stir well, roots will float to the top and are readily skimmed off and removed.

Once roots are removed, soak the substrate in a sterilant

such as a 5 percent bleach solution for at least an hour. Pour,
drain or pump off the sterilant and flush the medium with
plenty of fresh water until you can no longer smell the chlorine. A bathtub and a shower nozzle on a hose are perfect for
washing substrate. Place the substrate in the bathtub, set a
screen over the drain and use the showerhead on a hose to
spray and wash down the medium. It may be necessary to fill
the tub with fresh water and drain it a couple of times to rinse
any residual sterilants from the substrate.

Note: Some gardeners elect to use rockwool and coconut
coir for a second crop. Some have had good results. Others
have had problems with diseases and pests. In general, I recommend reusing a medium only if it does not deteriorate or
compact. Examples include: pea gravel, expanded clay, lava
rock, sand, etc.

To sterilize a hydroponic garden, remove the nutrient solution from the reservoir. Pump the solution into the outdoor
garden. Avoid pumping it down household drains, and defi-
nitely, do not pump it into a septic tank. The nutrients will disrupt the chemistry! It is still 90 percent good, so re-use it on
flowers, gardens or shrubs. There are certain outdoor plants
you should not use spent nutrients on. Bamboo can take over
your flowerbed, lawn and house foundation. Ivy can get under
wood siding and rip shingles off roof. Wisteria can grow 3 feet
a day and strangle large trees up to 150 feet high. Blackberries
can take over everything.
Mix a sterilizing solution of laundry bleach (calcium or sodium hypochlorite) at the rate of one part bleach to 9 parts
water. Or substitute hydrochloric acid, the kind used in hot
tubs and swimming pools.
Flood the growing medium with the sterilizing solution for at
least one half-hour, let drain and flush again. Pump the bleach
solution out of the system and down the drain. Do not dump
sterilant outdoors; it will defoliate wherever it is dumped. Use
lots of fresh water to leach and flush the entire system, including beds, connecting hoses, drains and reservoir. Make sure all
toxic chemicals are gone by flushin the entire system for at
least one hour – two intervals of one-half hour each. Remove

TIME MANAGEMENT 101

Simplicity, Quality & Expandability

LET'S FACE IT...

Sometimes we all need a little control. The all new Light Rail 3.5 Intelli Drive, with Solid State Advanced Controls fully integrated PCB Circuitry, will give you the control you are looking for. With an adjustable 0-60 second time delay, you can "fine tune" the length of delay at each end of your lamp's travel to meet your garden's ever changing needs.

ALL NEW

LIGHT RAIL™ 3.5
SELF-PROPELLED, TRACK MOUNTED LIGHT MOVER

PAT.

"INTELLI DRIVE"

LIGHT RAIL 3.5 Products Available:

6' Intelli Drive System – Cycle time down and back on a 6 foot rail; between 6 and 7 minutes, as you adjust time delay.

9' Intelli Drive System – Cycle time down and back on a 9 foot rail; between 5.5 and 6.5 minutes, as you adjust time delay.

12' Add-a-Lamp System – The LightRail 3.5 "Add-a-Lamp" package will accommodate 2 lamps running in line over a 12 foot span.

"Robo Stik"
The all new adjustable Lamp Attaching device that positions, balances and stabilizes your lamp as you mount it to your Light Rail 3.5 Intelli Drive.

Design Features:

✓ Instrument grade drive motor totally sealed from the environment runs on only 5 watts

✓ Self clutch drive design with automatic traction control

✓ Light weight, easy to install, extendable 6' aluminum track

✓ No sprockets or chains

✓ Sliding switch stops for adjustable travel distance

✓ Heavy duty carrier wheels

✓ Travels 2 feet per minute for closer plant to lamp tolerances

✓ Solid State Advanced Controls fully integrated PCB circuitry with a 0-60 second adjustable time delay

✓ 2 Year Limited Warranty on Drive Unit!

Fragrant showy flowers are easy to grow hydroponically.

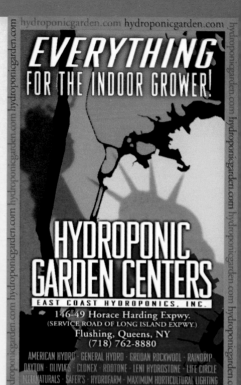
Hydroponics

Cucumbers as long as your arm are easy to grow in northern climates hydroponically.

Keypads at the end of each row control the flow of nutrients in this high-tech Dutch greenhouse.

Above: Grow great currants hydroponically and manage production with complete environmental control.

Right: Towering pepper plants sport huge prolific fruit when grown hydroponically.

Below: Tomatoes cascade over the table in this easy to manage hydroponic garden.

Hydroponics

This NFT system mounted on a wall is a great way to have fresh lettuce year round at home! Photo courtesy American Hydroponics.

Tomato 30 days after planting into the Aeromax 1200 note massive flowering!

Foothill Hydroponics
call 800-83 HYDRO
for a free catalog / info 116 pages
www.foothillhydroponics.com

Hydroponics

Left: Rick Middlebrook (left) and a friend peer from behind a hedge of cucumbers that are producing fruit in February.

Above: You can grow and enjoy hydroponic lettuce like this every day of the year at home.

Hydroponics

Right: This AAS winner 'Fanfare' was started indoors and moved outdoors to a sunny patio, and produced an early crop of cukes in May.

Below: Dutch growers pioneered hydroponic basil production. You can put their knowledge to work at home.

Hydroponics

Above: Hydroponic berries are bursting with flavor when vine ripened.

Background: Gerberas are one of the most responsive flower crops you can grow hydroponically.

Below: This hydroponic greenhouse filled with fuchsias, roses and begonias can be grown indoors with HID lights.

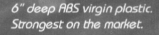

Hydroponics

Above: Thousands of support lines hold up this bountiful yield of peppers and tomatoes grown hydroponically indoors in the Netherlands.

Right: Super strong root systems in this NFT system absorb more nutrients faster.

OPTIMUM PRODUCTS FOR OPTIMUM RESULTS

OPTIMUM™
HYDROPONIX

SUPERMAX B1

ALTITUDE 7" DOME

**2-PART HYDROPONIC NUTRIENT
GROW AND BLOOM
1L, 4L, 12L and 20L**

**CLIMAX SERIES
CLIMATE CONTROLLER**

CLIMAX SERIES

**HUMEX AND FULVEX
(HUMIC AND FULVIC ACID)
1L and 4L**

X-TRA AIR

GROW TRAYS

**CLIMAX SERIES
CO2 MANAGER**

**AIR-COOLED REFLECTOR
WITH 8" OPEININGS**

CAMEL RESERVOIR

SUPERNOVA+

**EBB AND FLOW KITS
WITH CAMEL RESERVOIR AND
GROW TRAYS**

**ROOTING GEL
60g and 120g**

**ASSEMBLED LIGHT KITS
HPS and MH 120v & 240v**
(* bulb and reflector not included)

HYDROPONIX™ • ORGANIX™ • SCIENTIFIX™ • ELECTRONIX™

THESE FINE PRODUCTS AVAILBLE AT:
Brite-Lite and Qué-Pousse Indoor Garden Centres and many other gardening stores.

WWW.HYDROPONIX.COM

OPTIMUM HYDROPONIX™ INC. Laval QC Canada H7S 2G2, (450) 669-3803 or 1-800-489-2215, contact@hydroponiX.com

Gardening Indoors

Dorothy Turner in one of her greenhouses shows off the masses of beautiful orchids she grew hydroponically under HID lights and natural sunlight.

Orchid's roots are flourishing in this hydroponic system at Urban Flora in Portland, OR.

Hydroponics

Right: Large yet compact nutrient tanks make indoor gardening convenient, even for small indoor gardeners.

Below: A mountain of seedlings gets a head start on the growing season under a single HID lamp.

Hydroponics

Ed Sweet, owner of Sweet Hydroponics in Renfrew, ON, Canada, is a pioneer in accessible indoor gardening for all.

This brand new garden at Everybody's Garden Center in Portland, OR, will soon explode into a lush patch of green.

Cuttings
Step-by-step

1. Trim extra leaves from stem.

2. Cut stem at 45-degree angle.

3. Dip cutting in rooting gel.

4. Make a hole in the growing medium with a pencil. Note the line on the pencil to mark depth of the hole.

5. Insert cutting into the rooting medium.

IONIC Nutrients for Hydroponics

IONIC GROW and IONIC BLOOM are SINGLE PACKS for ease of use.

They contain every element needed for successful hydroponic growing.

The pH is stabilised and rarely needs correction.

Special HW formulations are available for hard water.

IONIC Nutrients for Soil & Coco

IONIC nutrients especially formulated for SOIL and COCO growers.

Contains complex ORGANIC plant acids for improved soil fertility and explosive growth.

IONIC BOOST

Formulated with the crucial elements needed for production of heavy buds and flowers. BOOST should be added to nutrients for soil, coco and hydroponics. Use throughout the flowering period.

Super concentrated.

Clonex Rooting Gel

Clonex is a powerful blend of hormones, vitamins and crucial plant nutrients.

It is the ultimate cloning agent in a rich, translucent gel.

Used for intensive root production on clones.

GreenMyst Humic

GreenMyst Humic contains pure Humic and Fulvic acids. These are the crucial organic growth promoters that are missing from hydroponic systems as well as from most soils. GreenMyst Humic will enhance nutrient uptake, supercharging growth and greatly improving quality and yield.

Formulex

Formulex is especially formulated for seedlings, young plants and clones. It contains the pure mineral elements needed for strong, bushy, vegetative growth.

Formulex is a gentle nutrient and will not burn young plants.

Formulex gives young plants the best possible start.

Nitrozyme

Nitrozyme is rich in natural growth enhancers. It is used by commercial growers worldwide. It can be added to nutrient solutions, and watered into soil or coco. It is also highly effective when used as a foliar spay.

Our products are designed by professionals ... and fine-tuned by experience.

Available from retailers everywhere – contact us for more information:
info@growthtechnology.com

Growth Technology

This massive greenhouse in Holland sports a computerized plant moving system. Trays revolve around the room several times per hour in a slow majestic dance. Insets show how plants move forward and sideways on mechanized tracks.

Greenhouses

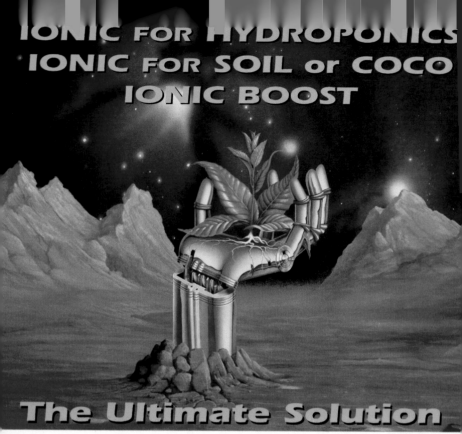

IONIC FOR HYDROPONICS
IONIC FOR SOIL or COCO
IONIC BOOST

The Ultimate Solution

Ionic for Hydroponics contains pure mineral elements bonded together in a highly stable single pack Solution. Ionic, the most precise hydroponic formulation ever achieved, guarantees quality, consistency and ease of use.

Ionic for Soil or Coco is a single part formulation designed for all stages of growth. It contains soluble mineral salts and crucial organic components including humates and highly active plant acids. This combination of minerals and organic materials follows the pattern of natural systems and will produce strong and healthy plants.

Ionic Boost is a supplement designed to promote heavy flowering and should be used in conjunction with Ionic Bloom or with any full spectrum nutrient solution.

HYDRODYNAMICS
INTERNATIONAL

www.hydrodynamicsintl.com

Greenhouses

This high tech Dutch greenhouse has computer-controlled skylights with screens to exclude pests and interior solar blankets that roll across the ceiling to retain heat at night.

This inset shows the interior of the greenhouse that produces high yield-ing of hydroponic vegetables.

all of the solution from the tank and scrub away any visible signs of salt buildup with a big sponge. Have a bucket of clean water handy to rinse the sponge.

An alternate sterilization method is to "solarize" the rockwool. In a sunny location, set dry slabs of rockwool outside on a sheet of black plastic, and cover with black plastic. Let the sun bake the layer of slabs or flock for several days. The temperatures in the rockwool will climb to 140 degrees or more, enough to sterilize for most all harmful diseases and pests.

Hydroponic Nutrients

High quality hydroponic formulations are soluble, contain all the necessary nutrients and leave no impure residues. Always use the best hydroponic fertilizer you can find. There are many excellent commercial hydroponic fertilizers that contain all the nutrients in a balanced form to grow great plants. Hydroponic fertilizers packed in a two or three part formula should have all of the necessary macro- and micronutrients necessary for rapid assimilation and growth. Cheap fertilizer, with low quality impure components, contain residue and sediments that buildup readily and cause extra maintenance. High quality soluble hydroponic nutrients properly applied are immediately available for uptake. Exact control is much easier when using pure, high-grade nutrients.

 Super Size Secret: Always use high quality (food grade) hydroponic nutrient components. Low-grade components are packed with impurities.

Nutrients are necessary for plants to grow and flourish. These nutrients must be in ionic form and broken down chemically within the plant, regardless of origin. The nutrients could be derived from a natural organic base without being heated or processed to change form, or they could be simple chemical elements and compounds. When properly applied, each type of fertilizer should produce the same results.

For a complete background on nutrients and fertilizers, see Chapter Four, "Water and Nutrients." Many of the same principles that apply to soil, apply to the hydroponic medium.

Nutrient Solutions

As a general guideline, change the nutrient solution at least every two (at the most every three) weeks. Remember to change the solution more often when plants are big, because they use more nutrients. It can go longer, but imbalances soon result. Some gardeners change the solution every week to avoid toxic conditions and head off nutrient excesses and deficiencies. Plants absorb nutrients at different rates and some of them run out before others, which causes more complex problems. The best form of preventative maintenance is to change the solution often. Skimping on fertilizer can cause stunted growth. The nutrient imbalances also cause the pH to fluctuate, usually drop. Nutrients used at different rates create an imbalanced formulation. Avert problems by using pure nutrients and flushing the soilless medium thoroughly with fresh tepid water between nutrient solutions.

Rule of Thumb: *Change the nutrient solution every two weeks.*

Super Size Secret: *Change the nutrient solution every week.*

Hydroponics gives the means to supply the maximum amount of nutrients a plant needs, but it can also starve them to death or over-fertilize them rapidly. Remember, this is a hot or fast high performance system. If one thing malfunctions, say the electricity goes off, the pump breaks, the drain gets clogged with roots, or there is a rapid fluctuation in the pH, all of these things could cause severe problems with the garden. A mistake could kill or stunt plants so badly they never fully recover.

Solution Maintenance

Plants use so much water that nutrient solutions need to be replenished regularly. Water is used at a much faster rate than nutrients, so casually "topping off" the reservoir with pH-balanced water works will keep the solution relatively balanced for a week or two. Never let the nutrient solution go for more than four weeks before draining the system and adding new fresh solution. Smart gardeners change their solution every week or two. They leach the entire system with weak nutrient solution for a couple of hours between changing the reservoir. Wipe down the entire system with the solution.

Super Size Secret: Do not flush with plain water. Flushing with mild (quarter-strength) nutrient solution will actually remove more excess fertilizer than plain water.

Rule of Thumb: Check EC of reservoir, growing medium and runoff nutrient solution at the same time every day.

Use an electronic EC pen to monitor the level of dissolved solids in the solution. Occasionally, you will need to add some more fertilizer concentrate to maintain the EC level in the reservoir during the "topping off" times. Keep the reservoir full at all times. The smaller the reservoir, the more rapid the depletion and the more critical it is to keep full. Smaller reservoirs should be refilled daily.

Nutrient Solution Composition

The chart below is a guideline of satisfactory nutrient limits expressed in PPM. Do not deviate too far from these ranges to avert nutrient deficiencies and excesses.

ELEMENT	Range	Average	Plant Usage
Nitrogen	150-1000	250	high
Calcium	100-500	200	medium high
Magnesium	50-100	75	high
Phosphorus	50-100	80	medium
Potassium	100-400	300	medium low
Sulfur	50-200	90	low
Copper	0.1-0.5	0.05	low
Boron	0.5-5.0	1.0	low
Iron	2.0-10	5.0	medium high
Manganese	0.5-5.0	2.0	medium
Molybdenum	0.01-0.05	0.02	medium low
Zinc	0.01-2.0	1.5	medium
Chlorine	10-50	30	medium low

Soluble Salts Range Chart

Electrical conductivity (EC) as milli-siemen (mS) and total dissolved solids (TDS) as parts per million (PPM)

RANGE
DESIRABLE	PERMISSIBLE	PROBABLE SALT DAMAGE
	(but potential for concern)	
EC as mS		
0.75 to 2.0	2.0 to 3.0	3.0 and up TDS as PPM
500 to 1300	1300 to 2000	2000 and up

For nutrient solutions determinations: one (1) mS (milli-siemen) or one mMho/cm^2 is equivalent to approximately 650 PPM total dissolved solids.

For a blooming formula, nitrogen and phosphorus numbers are usually reversed. Growth slows, produce is maximized and the plants won't push your roof off!

Reservoirs

Reservoirs should be as big as possible, the more volume, the better. Forgetting to replenish the water supply and/or nutrient solution could result in crop failure! Plants use a lot of water, and water also evaporates from the system. Gardens use from 5 – 25 percent of the nutrient solution every day. More water is lost to arid rooms packed with plants. Flood and drain systems also evaporate a lot of water into the air when the table is flooded. Water will evaporate faster at higher temperatures and lower humidity.

Keep a top on the reservoir to quell evaporation. When the water is used, the concentration of elements in the solution increases; there is less water in the solution and nearly the same amount of nutrients.

Sophisticated systems have a float valve that controls the level of water in the reservoir. If not already on the reservoir, make a full line or float indicator on the inside of the reservoir tank to show when the solution is low. Add water as soon as the solution level drops. The reservoir should contain at least 25 percent more nutrient solution than it takes to fill the beds, to compensate for daily use and evaporation. The greater the volume of nutrient solution, the more forgiving the system, and the easier it is to control. On flood and drain systems, an overflow tube is advisable to prevent overfilling of the bed due to timer errors or multi table/buckets supplied by a common pump. Overflow should go back into the holding tank.

 Rule of Thumb: *Check the level of the reservoir daily and replenish if necessary.*

The pump should be set up to lift the solution out of the reservoir. Set reservoirs up high enough so spent nutrient solution can be siphoned or gravity-flowed into a separate container for use on soil plants. Reuse it or pump it to the outdoor garden.

Reservoir Temperature

The temperature of the nutrient solution should stay somewhere in the 60 – 75 degrees F range. Heating the nutrient solution instead of the air in a room will save energy and money. Heat the nutrient solution with a submersible aquarium heater or grounded propagation heating cables. The heaters might take a day or longer to heat a large volume of solution. Do not leave heaters in an empty reservoir. They will soon overheat and burn out. Aquarium heaters seldom have ground wires, a seemingly obvious oversight. But I have yet to learn of an electrocution by aquarium heater. Avoid submersible heaters that give off harmful residues. Put glass aquarium heaters in a separate jar filled with water or nutrient solution to keep it from burning out.

 Super Size Secret: *Nutrient solution with a 60 – 65-degree F temperature holds much more oxygen than 75-degree solution.*

When air is warmer than water, moisture evaporates into the air rapidly: the greater the temperature differential, the higher the relative humidity. Maintaining the nutrient solution temperature around 60 degrees F will help control transpiration and humidity. It will also help with the uptake of nutrients. Cooler nutrient solution holds more oxygen, which is necessary for nutrient uptake.

Warning! *Never let the nutrient solution temperature climb above 85 degrees. Hot roots attract fatal pests and diseases and diminish oxygen uptake severely.*

Remix nutrient solution with 60-degree water.   Warmer water dissolves nutrients more quickly, but holds less oxygen.

An air pump submerged in the reservoir will help level out the temperature differential between ambient air and reservoir.

Never let the water temperature get warmer than 85 degrees F. Roots are easily damaged by heat. Heat-damaged roots are very susceptible to rot, wilts and fungus gnat attacks. Ideally, the air temperature should be 10 degrees F. above the nutrient temperature.

Irrigation Cycles

Irrigation cycles depend on plant size, climate conditions and the type of medium used. Large, round, smooth particles of substrate drain rapidly and need to be irrigated more often; 4 – 12 times for 5 to 30 minute cycles every day. Slow draining fibrous mediums, such as vermiculite with irregular surfaces drain slowly and require less frequent watering, often just one irrigation per day. The water comes to within one-half inch of the top of the gravel and should completely drain out of the medium at each watering. Top feed systems cycle for about 5 minutes or longer and should be irrigated at least three times daily. Often gardeners "feed" 24 hours a day, especially when growing in fast draining expanded clay or similar mediums and in NFT systems. Nutrient solution should raise no faster than one inch per minute and drain out at the same or a slower rate to prevent root disturbance.

Rule of Thumb: Irrigation cycles are often more frequent and shorter lived. Overhead irrigation in fast-draining mediums is continual. Drip irrigation in coco coir is four or five times daily. Flood and drain irrigation cycles are 3 – 10 times daily, depending on the size of plants depth of the growing medium and temperature.

During and soon after irrigation, the nutrient content of the bed and the reservoir are the same concentration. As time passes between irrigations, EC and pH gradually change. If enough time passes between waterings, the nutrient concentration might change so much that the plant is not able to draw it in.

There are many variations on how often to water. Experimentation will tell you more than anything else. One gardener explained to me, "After a while you kind of get the feel for it." It took this hydroponic horticulturist several crops to get it together. Whatever you discover "works," stick with it.

 Super Size Secret: Speed biological activity by keeping the nutrient solution at 60 – 70 degrees.

Nutrient Disorders

When the hydroponic garden is on a regular maintenance schedule, and the gardener knows the crop well, nutrient problems are usually averted. If nutrient deficiency or excess affects more than a few plants, check the irrigation fittings to ensure nutrient-challenged plants are receiving a full dose of nutrient solution. Next check the substrate around affected plants to ensure nutrient solution is penetrating all medium and all roots are wet. Then check the root zone to ensure roots have not plugged drainage conduits and are not standing in stagnant solution. Check the roots and root hairs for disease. They should be white to light tan, not dark and not gelatinous (shiny, with no root hairs). Use hand lens or jewelers loupe.

Change the nutrient solution, if there is a good flow of nutrient solution through the root zone, but plants still appear sickly. Make sure the pH of the water is within the acceptable 5.5 – 6.5 range before adding new nutrients.

If changing solution does not solve the problem, changing to a new brand of fertilizer may do the trick. Check out color drawings of specific nutrient deficiencies and excesses, to determine the exact problem, and add 10 to 20 percent more of the deficient nutrient in a chelated form until the disorder has disappeared. Leach growing medium heavily to solve simple overdose nutrient problems.

Hydroponic gardens have no soil to buffer the uptake of nutrients causing disorders to manifest in discolored foliage, slow growth, spotting, etc., at a rapid rate. Novice gardeners must learn how to recognize nutrient problems in their early stages to avoid serious problems that cost valuable time for plants to recoup. Treatment for a nutrient deficiency or excess must be rapid and certain. But once treated, plants take several days to respond to the remedy.

Nutrient deficiency or excess diagnosis becomes difficult when two or more elements are deficient or in excess at the same time. Symptoms might not point directly at the cause. Solve unknown nutrient deficiency syndromes by changing the nutrient solution, and hope the change will do the plants good! Plants do not always need an accurate diagnosis when the nutrient solution is changed. Sometimes you have to be a detective.

 Rule of Thumb: *If the garden has a nutrient disorder, flush the growing medium and change the nutrient solution.*

Over-fertilization, once diagnosed, is easy to remedy. Drain the nutrient solution. Flush the system at least twice with fresh diluted (10 percent) nutrient solution to remove any lingering sediment and salt buildup. Replace with properly mixed solution.

Nutrient disorders often show in all of the same variety at the same time when they are receiving the same nutrient solution. Different varieties often react differently to the same solution. Do not confuse other problems – wind burn, lack of light, temperature stress, fungi and pest damage – with nutrient deficiencies. Plants with such problems usually appear on individual plants that are most affected. For example, foliage next to a heat vent might show signs of heat scorch, while the rest of the garden looks healthy. Or a plant on the edge of the garden would be small and leggy because it receives less light. For more information see "Nutrient Disorders."

Hydro-Organic

Hydro-Organic is becoming so popular that it qualifies as a buzzword. Hydro-organic means growing plants without soil (in a soilless medium, air or water) and feeding them with a soluble organic liquid nutrient solution. Organic fertilizers are most often defined as containing substances with a carbon molecule or a natural unaltered substance, such as ground up rocks.

Dedicated gardeners spend the time and trouble it takes to grow hydro-organically, because the natural nutrients brings out a sweet organic taste. Indoor gardens grown for a couple of months do not have time to wait for organic nutrients to be broken down. Organic nutrients must be soluble and readily available.

An exact balance of organic nutrients can be achieved with constant experimentation and attention to details. Even when you buy a ready-mixed commercial, like Earth Juice or Fox Farm, you will need to try different feeding amounts and schedules to get the exact combination to grow top quality flowers and vegetables.

Taking an accurate EC reading or mixing the exact amount of a specific nutrient is very difficult in organic hydroponics. Chemical fertilizers are easy to measure out and apply. It is easy to give plants the specific amount of fertilizer they need in their stage of growth.

Organic nutrients have a complex structure and measuring content is difficult. Organics are difficult to keep stable too. Some manufacturers, including Fox Farm and Earth Juice, have managed to stabilize their fertilizers. When buying organic nutrients, always buy from the same supplier and find out as much as possible about the source.

You can use premixed soluble organic fertilizers mixed with other organic fertilizers to make your own blend. Gardeners experiment to find the perfect mix for their system. Adding too much fertilizer can toxify soil and bind up nutrients, so they are not available. If the condition is severe, plants burn. The growth always slows and harvest diminishes.

You can flush soluble organic fertilizers out of the growing medium fairly effectively. Like chemical fertilizers, organic fertilizers easily build to toxic levels. Look for the same symptoms as in soil: burned leaf tips, discolored misshapen leaves, brittle leaves, etc. Organic nutrients require heavier flushing. Rinse medium with three gallons of water for every gallon of medium. Some gardeners flush the entire last two weeks of flowering to get all fertilizer taste out of vegetables and leaf crops.

A balanced seaweed mix with macronutrients, as well as primary and secondary nutrients is necessary. The amount of primary and secondary nutrients is not as important as the menagerie of trace elements that are found in an available form in the seaweed. Major nutrients can be applied via soluble fish emulsion for nitrogen, phosphorous and potassium supplied by bat guano, bone meal and manures. More and more organic gardeners are adding growth stimulators, such as humic acid, trichoderma and hormones. Many also mix organic "tea" with hydroponic nutrients. Experiment with a few plants first.

Getting Started

Start seeds and cuttings in small propagation blocks. Starting seeds in coarse growing mediums like gravel or expanded clay is almost impossible. Tiny seeds easily wash away, get too deep or dry out. Transplant the pot or cube into the hydroponic medium when roots show out the side of the cube. When cuttings are placed into the hydroponic medium, the root cube will be able to hold the extra moisture it needs for the dry times in between waterings.

Transplanting root cubes and peat pots is easy in hydroponics. Simply move root filled cube into the growing medium. Young plants suffer less transplant shock than older plants. Transplant before roots protrude more than one-half inch from the cube to avoid shock from bruising and breaking. After transplanting, scoop up some of the nutrient solution, or mix a B[1] solution and pour it over the new transplant two or three times. Manually cycle the nutrient solution through the system, so the young transplant roots get good and damp.

Air

Fresh air is at the heart of all successful indoor gardens. Think about the atmosphere in the great outdoors and how different the air is indoors. Outdoor air is abundant and packed with carbon dioxide (CO_2) necessary for plant life. For example, the level of CO_2 in the air over a field of rapidly growing corn could be only a third of normal on a very still day. The wind blows in fresh new CO_2-rich air and (acid) rain, washes air and plants of dust and pollutants. Outdoors, the atmosphere creates a fantastic environment for plant growth. Put a garden in a small room, and the air must be meticulously controlled to replicate the air of the great outdoors. Indoors, none of the natural elements to make CO_2-rich air are available, and the horticulturist must take on the task.

Carbon dioxide and oxygen provide basic building blocks for plant life. Oxygen is used for respiration, burning carbohydrates and other foods to provide energy. Carbon dioxide must be present during photosynthesis. Without CO_2 a plant will die. Plants get all their carbon from CO_2. They do not take it up at the roots. Carbon is a major nutrient. CO_2 combines light energy with water to produce sugars. These sugars are used to fuel the growth and metabolism of the plant. With reduced levels of CO_2, growth slows to a crawl. A plant releases more oxygen than is used. It uses much more carbon dioxide than it releases, except during darkness when more oxygen is used and their "day" cycle is actually somewhat reversed.

Roots use air too. Oxygen must be present, along with water and nutrients, for the roots to be able to absorb nutrients. Compacted water-saturated soil leaves roots little or no air and nutrient uptake stalls.

Smoke, polluted stale air, is sucked out of the room immediately with this in-line fan.

> ***Super Size Secret***: *Precise control of atmospheric humidity, temperature, ventilation, circulation, CO_2 level and airborne fungal spores yields the heaviest crops.*

Plants and animals (people are animals, too) complement one another in a symbiotic relationship. Plants give off oxygen, essential to animal life, as a by-product. Animals inhale air, using oxygen to carry on life processes, and exhale carbon dioxide as a by-product. Animals give off carbon dioxide as a by-product, making it available to plants. Without plants, animals could not live, and without animals, plants could not live. Almost all of the oxygen in our atmosphere was created by plants.

Air Movement

Air ventilation and circulation are essential to a healthy harvest. Without fresh air, stomata are stifled and plants stunted. Indoors, fresh air is one of the most overlooked factors contributing to a healthy garden and a bountiful harvest. Fresh air is the least expensive essential component that can create a bumper crop. Experienced gardeners understand the importance of fresh air and take the time to set up an adequate ventilation system. Three factors affect air movement: stomata, ventilation and circulation. You should see some movement of plant leaves to have good ventilation and circulation.

Leaf Cross-Section
showing stomata

Microscopic stomata located on leaf undersides must remain clean and unstifled by humidity to promote rapid growth.

Stomata

Stomata are microscopic pores on leaf undersides that are similar to an animal's nostrils. Animals regulate the amount of oxygen inhaled. Carbon dioxide along with other elements are exhaled through the nostrils via the lungs. In plants, oxygen and carbon dioxide flows are regulated by the stomata. The larger the plant, the more stomata it has to take in carbon dioxide and release oxygen. The greater the volume of plants, the more fresh CO_2-rich air they will need to grow fast. Dirty clogged stomata do not work properly and restrict airflow. Stomata are easily clogged by dirt from polluted air and sprays that leave filmy residues. Outdoors, stomata are cleaned by rain and wind. Indoors, the horticulturist must make rain with a sprayer and wind with a fan to ensure a healthy plant environment.

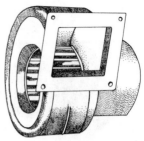

A blower moves a lot of air, but they can be noisy!

 Rule of Thumb: Wash or spray plants with clean, tepid water on both sides of the leaves at least once a month.

Circulation

Plants use all of the CO_2 around the leaf within a few minutes. New CO_2-rich air must replace the used air for rapid growth to resume. When no new CO_2-rich air replaces the "used" CO_2-depleted air, a dead air space forms around the leaf, stifling the stomata and virtually stopping growth. The air around leaves stratifies, if it is not actively moved. Warm air stays near the ceiling and cool air settles near the floor. Air circulation breaks up these air masses, mixing them together. Avoid all of these would-be problems by opening a door, window and/or installing an oscillating circulation fan. Air circulation also helps prevent harmful pest and fungus attacks. Omnipresent mold spores don't land and grow as often when air is stirred up by a fan. Insects and spider mites find

Venitilation is important

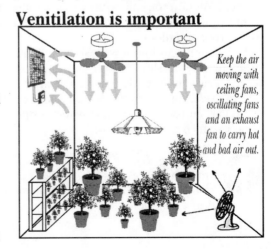

Keep the air moving with ceiling fans, oscillating fans and an exhaust fan to carry hot and bad air out.

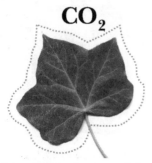

CO₂

CO2 is quickly used up around the leaves of a plant and must be replaced every few minutes for rapid growth.

it difficult to live in an environment that is constantly bombarded by air currents.

Super Size Secret: Make sure the air around each leaf on all plants changes regularly to prevent stratification and CO₂ depletion. You want to see some leaf movement.

Ventilation

Fresh air is easy to obtain and inexpensive to maintain. The appropriate exhaust fan positioned properly exhausts hot humid air. An intake vent is necessary to create a flow of fresh air in the room.

A 10 x 10-foot garden will use from 10 to 50 gallons or more of water every week. Most of this water is transpired (evaporated) into the air. Every day and night, rapidly growing plants transpire more and more moisture into the air. If this moisture is left in the garden room, humidity increases to 100 percent, which stifles stomata and causes growth to screech to a halt. It also opens the door for pest and disease attacks. Replace moist air with fresh, new dry air and transpiration increases, stomata function properly, and growth rebounds. A vent fan that pulls or extracts air from the garden room is the perfect solution to remove this humid stale air. New fresh air is drawn in through the intake vent. High humidity can also be a problem indoors.

Ventilation is as important as water, light, heat and fertilizer. In many cases fresh air is even more important. Most greenhouses have large ventilation fans. Garden rooms are very similar to greenhouses and their example should be followed. Most garden rooms have an easy-to-use opening, such as a window, in which to mount a fan.

Warning! Lack of air ventilation stifles growth and is the precursor to numerous other problems including: nutrient deficiencies, pest and disease attacks, over-watering, high humidity and temperature.

A baffle that turns air around a corner, or a vent fan with louvers that close when the fan is not in use, keep undesirable outdoor backdrafts from entering the garden room. A 4-inch flexible dryer hose will help prevent backdrafts in small garden rooms. Larger 8-, 10-, and 12-inch galvanized heat duct pipe is ideal to move a larger volume of air in larger gardens. Place one end of the hose outdoors. It should be placed high enough that it vents off hot air near the ceiling. One of the best vents is the chimney. The outlet can be a dryer hose, wall outlet. The other end of the hose is attached to the vent fan. The vent fan is then placed near the ceiling, so it vents off hot, humid air. Check for leaks. Set the fan up; go outdoors after dark to inspect for light leaks. See 'Setting Up the Vent Fan."

Super Size Secret: Ventilation is the key to temperature and humidity control. Change the air in the garden room at least twice an hour to ensure a heavy harvest.

Greenhouse fans are equipped with baffles (flaps) to prevent backdrafts. During the cold and hot weather, undesirable backdrafts could change the room temperature and usher in a menagerie of pests and diseases into the growing area. Eliminate backdrafts by installing a vent fan with flaps.

All garden rooms require some sort of ventilation system. This system could be an open door or window that supplies fresh air that circulates around the room. But, open doors and windows can be inconvenient and problematic. Most gardeners elect to install a ventilation system that employs at least one efficient vent fan. Others need to install an entire ventilation system, including ducting and several fans.

A vent fan is able to *pull* air out of a room at least four times more efficiently than a fan is able to *push* it out. Vent fans are rated by the amount of air, measured in cubic feet per minute (CFM), they can move. The fan should be able to replace the volume

This gardener built a wall below this vent fan to vent two rooms.

Roof fans and vents make venting a garden room easy.

In-line fans are the absolute best for indoor garden rooms. They are quiet and move a lot of air efficiently.

This big blower has to move air three stories up an 8-inch duct and needs extra power. Ingenious gardeners mounted the blower on flexible bungi cords and interfaced the exit hole with shock absorbing rubber to dampen vibrations and noise.

(length x width x height = total volume in cubic feet) of the garden room in less than 5 minutes. Once evacuated, new fresh air is immediately drawn in through an intake vent. Covering the intake vent with fine mesh silkscreen will help exclude pests from the garden room. An intake fan might be necessary to bring an adequate volume of fresh air into the room quickly. Some rooms are not tightly sealed and have so many little cracks for air to drift in and do not need an intake vent.

Do not set up a circulation fan in the room and expect it to vent the area by pushing air out a distant vent. The circulation fan must be very big to increase air pressure, enough to push enough air out of the vent and create an exchange of air. A vent fan, on the other hand, is able to change the pressure and air quickly and efficiently. Oscillating or circulation fans are only meant to exchange warm air near the ceiling with cooler air along the floor and keep a boundary-layer from forming around leaf stomata.

Squirrel cage blowers are very efficient at moving air, but very loud. Blowers with a balanced well-oiled wheel run quietest. Felt or rubber grommets below each foot of the fan will lower noise caused by vibrations. Run the motor at a low RPM to lessen noise.

In-line fans are designed to fit into a duct pipe and move air. The propellers are mounted to increase the flow of air quickly, effortlessly and quietly. In-line fans are available in high quality models that run smooth and quiet. Always buy a larger vent fan and ducting than you think necessary. Run the vent fan slower than its maximum rated speed, so it is quieter. A light-dimmer switch can regulate fan speed.

 Rule of Thumb: *Expel air with a large vent fan that moves slowly to decrease noise. Moving air fast is loud and resonates through the house.*

Warning! *Noise level increases in proportion to the velocity (RPM) of the fan. Move air slowly through large vents to decrease ventilation noise.*

Hot air rises. Adept gardeners locate air exit vents in the hottest peak of the room, so air is vented passively and silently. The bigger the diameter of the exhaust duct, the more air that can travel through it. By installing a large, slow-moving vent fan in this vent, hot, stale air is evacuated quietly and efficiently. A fan running at 50 RPM is quieter than one running at 200 RPM. Smart gardeners install 12-inch ducting and inline fans.

Propeller or muffin fans with large fan blades are most efficient and quietest when operated at a low RPM and expel through a large opening. A slow-moving propeller fan on the ceiling of a garden room will move much air out quietly and efficiently.

Temperature

An accurate thermometer, to measure the temperature, is a must for all garden rooms. The mercury or liquid type are typically more accurate than the spring or dial-type. An inexpensive thermometer is necessary to collect the most basic information. The ideal thermometer is a day-night or maximum/minimum type that measures how low the temperature drops at night and the maximum it reaches during the day. The maximum and minimum temperatures in a garden room are very important for many reasons that are explained below.

Under normal conditions, the ideal temperature range for indoor plant growth is 72 – 76 degrees F. At night, the temperature can drop 10 – 15 degrees with no noticeable effect on growth rate. The temperature should not drop more than 20 degrees F, or excessive humidity and mold might become problems. Daytime temperatures over 90 degrees F and below 60 degrees F slow growth. Maintaining the proper, constant temperature in the garden room promotes strong, even,

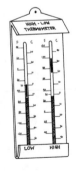

A simple maximum/minimum thermometer will tell you if it is getting too hot or cold in the garden room.

Knowing both Celsius and Fahrenheit makes garden room calculations more precise.

healthy growth. Make sure plants are not too close to a heat source, like a ballast or heat vent, or they may dry out, maybe even get heat scorch!

 Super Size Secret: Keep the temperature at 75 degrees F during the day and about 65 at night. Measure it perpetually to ensure consistency.

Temperatures above 85 degrees F are not recommended, except with CO_2 enrichment, when the temperature could go as high as 95 degrees (not recommended). Under the proper conditions, which are very demanding to maintain, higher temperatures step up metabolic activity and speed growth. The warmer it is, the more water the air is able to hold. This moist air often restrains plant functions and decelerates rather than speeding up growth. Other complications and problems often result from excess humidity and moisture condensation when the temperature drops at night.

Heat buildup during warm weather can catch gardeners off-guard and cause serious problems. Ideal garden rooms are located underground, in a basement, with the insulating qualities of the Mother Earth. With the added heat of the HID and hot humid weather outdoors, a room can heat up real fast. More than a few gardeners have lost plants to heat stroke during the Fourth of July weekend. This is the first big summer holiday and everybody in the city wants to get away to enjoy it. There are always some gardeners that forget to maintain good ventilation in the garden room while on vacation.

Temperatures can easily climb to 100 degrees or more in garden rooms that are poorly insulated and vented. The hotter it is, the more ventilation and water that's necessary.

Rule of Thumb: *Control the temperature in most garden rooms with a vent fan attached to a thermostat. Set the thermostat so the fan keeps the temperature at 75 degrees F.*

The cold of winter is the other extreme. Montreal, Quebec, Canada gardeners will remember the year of the big ice storm. Electricity went out all over the city and surrounding areas. Water pipes froze and the heat went off. Residents were driven from their homes until the electricity was restored some days later. Many gardeners returned to find their beautiful gardens wilted, with the deepest, most disgusting green only a freeze can bring. Broken water pipes and ice were everywhere! It's difficult to combat Acts of God that drive gardeners from their home. But if possible, always keep the garden room above freezing – 32 degrees F. If the temperature dips below this mark, the freeze will rupture plant cells and foliage will die back or at best, grow slowly. Growth slows when the temperature dips below 50 degrees F. Stressing plants with cold weather will make them produce poorly.

A thermostat controls a heating and/or cooling device(s) to regulate the temperature in a room. It measures the temperature, then turns a device that regulates a heating or cooling, on or off, so the temperature stays within a predetermined range. A thermostat can be attached to an electric or combustion heater. In fact, many homes are already setup with electric baseboard heat, with a thermostat in each room.

 Rule of Thumb: *Build a heat bank with jugs full of water. Place them under bench on uninsulated concrete floors to cool room. Place jugs full of water in a warmer location to absorb warm temperatures.*

A thermostat can be used to control cooling vent fans in all but the coldest garden rooms. When it gets too hot, the thermostat turns the vent fan on, evacuating the hot stale air out of the room. The vent fan remains on until the desired temperature is reached, then the thermostat turns the fan off. A thermostat-controlled vent fan offers adequate temperature and humidity control for many garden rooms. A refrigerated air conditioner can be installed if heat and humidity are a big problem. If excessive heat is a problem, but humidity is not a concern, use a swamp cooler. These evaporative coolers are inexpensive to operate and keep rooms cool in arid climates.

Common thermostats include single stage and two-stage. The single stage controls a device to keep the temperature the same, both day and night. A two-stage thermostat is more expensive, but can be set to maintain different day and night-time temperatures. This convenience can save money on heating since room temperature can drop 10 – 15 degrees at night with no effect on growth. HID lights can raise the room temperature 10 – 15 degrees F.

Many new garden room controllers have been developed in the last ten years. These controllers can operate and integrate every appliance in the garden room. More sophisticated controllers integrate the operation of CO_2 equipment, vent and intake fans. Relatively inexpensive computer controllers are also available for garden rooms. If temperature and humidity regulation are causing cultural (plant growth) problems in the garden room, consider purchasing a controller.

Uninsulated garden rooms or garden rooms that experience significant temperature fluctuations require special considerations and care. Before growing in such a location, make sure that it is the only choice. If forced to use a sun-baked attic that cools at night, make sure maximum insulation is in place to help balance temperature instability. Enclose the room to control heating and cooling.

This simple humidistat/thermostat controller is just one of many different time/controllers found at www.greenair.com. It is very easy to use and virtually fail proof.

When CO_2 is enriched to 0.12 – 0.15 percent (1200 – 1500 PPM), a temperature of 85 degrees F promotes a more rapid exchange of gases. Photosynthesis and chlorophyll synthesis are able to take place at a more rapid rate causing plants to grow faster. Remember, this extra 10 – 15 degrees increases water, nutrient and space consumption, so be prepared! Carbon dioxide-enriched plants still need ventilation to remove stale, humid air and promote plant health. Normal CO_2 levels are between 250 and 350 PPM.

Super Size Secret: *Increase the temperature 10 – 15 degrees when using CO_2. Also monitor and increase nutrient and water levels.*

Seeds germinate faster and cuttings root quicker when air temperature ranges from 80 to 85 degrees F. Increase the ambient air temperature by building a (plastic) tent to cover young germinating seeds or cuttings. The tent increases both temperature and humidity. Remove the tent cover as soon as the seeds sprout above the soil to allow for air circulation. Failure to remove the covering could result in seedlings damping-off. Cuttings, however, should remain covered throughout the entire rooting process. Always watch for signs of mold or rot when using a humidity tent with cuttings. Remove the tent several times a day to allow for new fresh air to circulate in the enclosure. Fresh air circulation and ventilation supply CO_2 and help prevent fungus.

Super Size Secret: *Cuttings root fastest when the air temperature is 72 – 75 degrees F and the growing medium is 78 – 80 degrees F.*

The temperature in the garden room tends to stay the same, top to bottom, when the air is circulated with an oscillating fan(s). In an enclosed garden room, HID lamps and ballasts keep the area warm. A remote ballast placed on a shelf or a stand near the floor also helps break up air stratification by radiating heat upwards. Garden rooms in cool climates stay warm during the day when the outdoor temperature peaks, but often cool off too much at night when cold temperatures set in. To compensate, gardeners turn the lamp on at night to help heat the room and off during the day. Aiming an oscillating fan at a HID bulb can easily distribute its heat evenly if extra heat is needed.

Sometimes it is too cold for the lamp and ballast to maintain satisfactory room temperatures. Garden rooms located in homes are frequently equipped with a central heating and/or air conditioning vent. The vent is usually controlled by a central thermostat that regulates the temperature of the home. By adjusting the thermostat to 72 degrees F and opening the door to the garden room, it can stay a cozy 72 degrees. Keeping the thermostat between 60 and 65 degrees F, coupled with the heat from the HID system, should be enough to sustain the 75-degree F temperature. Other supplemental heat, such as inefficient incandescent light bulbs and electric heaters are expensive and cause an extra electricity draw, but provide instant heat that is easy to regulate. Propane and natural gas heaters increase temperatures and burn oxygen from the air, creating CO_2 and water vapor as a by-product. This dual advantage makes using a CO_2 generator economical and practical.

Kerosene heaters also work to generate heat and CO_2. Look for a heater that burns its fuel efficiently and completely with tale-tale odor of the fuel in the room. Do not use old kerosene heaters or fuel oil heaters, if they burn fuel inefficiently. A blue flame is burning all the fuel cleanly. A red flame signifies that only part of the fuel is being burned. I'm not a big fan of kerosene heaters and do not recommend using them. The room must be vented regularly to avoid buildup of toxic carbon monoxide, also a byproduct of combustion. With a blue, white or clear flame, carbon monoxide is not a problem.

Diesel oil is a common source of indoor heat. Many furnaces use this dirty and polluting heat source. Wood heat is not the cleanest, but works well as a heat source. A vent fan is extremely important to bring new, fresh air into a room heated by a polluting furnace.

Insect populations and fungi are also affected by temperature. In general, the cooler it is, the slower the insects and fungus reproduce and develop. Temperature control is effectively integrated into many insect and fungus control programs.

Humidity

Humidity is relative, that is, air holds different quantities of water at different temperatures. Relative humidity is the ratio between the amount of moisture in the air and the greatest amount of moisture the air could hold at the same temperature. In other words, the hotter it is, the more moisture air can hold; the cooler it is, the less moisture air can hold. Relative humidity is measured with a wet-dry hygrometer. When the temperature in a garden room drops, the humidity climbs and moisture condenses. For example, an 800 cubic foot (10 x 10 x 8 feet) garden room will hold about 14 ounces of water when the temperature is 70 degrees F and relative humidity is at 100 percent. When the temperature is increased to 100 degrees F, the same room will hold 56 ounces of mois-

ture at 100 percent relative humidity. That's four-times as
much moisture! Where does this water go when the temperature drops? It condenses, just like dew condenses outdoors,
onto the surface of plants, garden room walls, and "weeping"
windows.

A 10 x 10 x 8 foot (800 cubic feet) garden room can hold:
4 oz. of water at 32 degrees F.
7 oz. of water at 50 degrees F.
14 oz. of water at 70 degrees F.
18 oz. of water at 80 degrees F.
28 oz. of water at 90 degrees F.
56 oz. of water at 100 degrees F.

Relative humidity increases when the temperature drops at
night. The more temperature variation, the greater the relative humidity variation. Supplemental heat or extra ventilation
is often necessary at night if temperatures fluctuate more than
15 degrees F.

Bright Idea – The moisture holding capacity of air doubles
with every 20° F increase in temperature.

Most plants grow best when the relative humidity range is
from 40 to 60 percent. As with temperature, consistent humidity promotes healthy, even growth. Relative humidity level
affects the transpiration rate of the stomata. When humidity is
high, water evaporates slowly. The stomata close, transpiration
slows and so does plant growth. Water evaporates quickly into
dryer air, causing stomata to open, increasing transpiration,
fluid flow and growth.

Warning! Air that holds 16 ounces of water at 75 degrees F,
but will hold only 10 ounces at 60 degrees, causing 6 ounces
of water to condense out of the air into the room.

Transpiration in arid conditions will be rapid only if there is
enough water available for roots to draw in. If water is inadequate, stomata will close to protect the plant from dehydration,
causing growth to slow. In severe cases, plants will wilt and die.

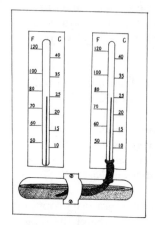

A hygrometer measures relative humidity. Measuring and controlling humidity in a garden room is essential to a bountiful harvest.

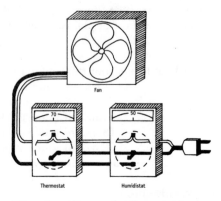

Wire a humidistat and a thermostat to a vent fan for garden room climate control.

Measuring Relative Humidity

Relative humidity control is an integral part of insect and fungus prevention and control. Humidity above 80 percent discourages spider mites but promotes fungus, root and stem rot. Humidity levels below 50 percent reduce the chances of fungus and rot.

Measure relative humidity with a hygrometer. This extremely important instrument will save you and your garden much frustration and fungus. By knowing the exact moisture content in the air, the humidity may be adjusted to a safe 50 percent level that encourages transpiration and discourages fungus growth.

There are two common types of hygrometers:

Spring type, which is accurate to within 5 – 10 percent. This hygrometer is inexpensive and adequate for most hobby garden rooms where the main concern is to keep the humidity near 50 percent.

A psychrometer (hygrometer) is more expensive but is very accurate. A psychrometer that measures relative humidity with a wet and dry bulb is an excellent way to keep an accurate vigil on relative humidity. But, today there are many high-tech gadgets that are exceptionally accurate, plus they have a memory!

A humidistat is similar to a thermostat, but regulates humidity instead of temperature. Humidistats are wonderful and make controlling the environment very easy. Humidistats cost less than $100 and are worth their weight in vine ripened tomatoes . A humidistat and thermostat wired "in line" to the vent fan (see drawing above). Each can operate the fan independently. As soon as the humidity (or temperature) gets out of the acceptable range, the fan turns on to vent the humid (or hot) air outdoors.

 Rule of Thumb: *A vent fan offers the best humidity control in most gardens.*

The HID lamp and ballast radiate heat, which lowers humidity. Heat from the HID system and a vent fan on a thermostat/humidistat are all the humidity control necessary for most garden rooms. Other dry heat sources, such heat vented from a furnace or wood stove, dry the air and lower humidity. Be careful. Do not let this warm dry air blow directly on foliage. It will dehydrate plants rapidly. One gardener with a small garden room uses the silicon packets that absorb moisture in camera cases to absorb excess moisture in the room. He sets the silicon packets out in the garden room to gather moisture every day and dries them out by placing them in a solarium for a few hours. An oven will also dry them out. These packets are called desiccants.

Increase humidity by misting the air with water or setting a bucket of water out to evaporate into the air. A humidifier is convenient and relatively inexpensive, but consumes precious electricity. Humidifiers evaporate water into the air to increase humidity. Just set the dial on a specific humidity and presto! The humidity changes to the desired level as soon as the humidifier is able to evaporate enough water into the air. A humidifier is not necessary unless there is an extreme problem with the garden room drying out. Problems seldom occur that can be remedied by a humidifier. All too often, there is too much humidity in the air as a result of irrigation and transpiration. If a ventilation system is unable to remove enough air to lower humidity, a dehumidifier could be just the ticket!

A dehumidifier removes moisture in a room by condensing it from the air. Once the water is separated from the air, it is captured in a removable container. This container should be emptied daily. It is easy to remove and catch 10 ounces of water in a 10 x 10 x 8-foot room when the temperature drops just 10 degrees F.

A dehumidifier can be used anytime to help guard against fungus. Just set the dial at the desired percent humidity and presto, perfect humidity. Dehumidifiers are more complex than humidifiers and cost more, but are worth the added expense to gardeners with extreme humidity problems that a vent fan has not yet cured. The best price on dehumidifiers has been found at Home Depot and other discount stores. Check the rental companies in the Yellow Pages for large dehumidifiers, if only needed for a short time.

Young seedlings and rooting cuttings thrive when the humidity is from 70 to 100 percent. Under arid conditions, the undeveloped root system is not able to supply water fast enough to keep cuttings alive. See "Cloning" for more specific information on humidity levels during different stages of clone propagation.

CO_2 Enrichment

Carbon dioxide (CO_2) is a colorless, odorless, non-flammable gas that is around us all the time. The air we breathe contains 0.03 – 0.04 percent (300 – 400 PPM) CO_2. Rapidly growing plants can use all of the available CO_2 in an enclosed garden room within a few hours. Photosynthesis and growth slow to a crawl when the CO_2 level falls below 0.02 percent (200 PPM).

CO_2 enrichment has been used in commercial greenhouses for more than 40 years. Adding more CO_2 to garden room air stimulates growth. Indoor growing is similar to conditions in a greenhouse and indoor gardeners apply the same principles. Most plants can use more CO_2 than the 0.03 – 0.04 percent (300 – 400 PPM) that naturally occurs in the air. By increasing the amount of CO_2 to 0.12 – 0.15 percent (1200 to 1500 PPM), the optimum amount widely agreed upon by professional gardeners, plants may grow two or three times as fast, providing that light, water and nutrients are not limiting. CO_2 enrichment has little or no affect on plants grown under fluorescent lights. Fluorescent tubes do not supply enough light for the plant to process the extra available CO_2. On the other hand, HID lamps supply ample light to process the CO_2-enriched air. A garden room using CO_2-enriched air, adequate light, water and nutrients, superlative results may be achieved. In fact, with this basic combination, most plants will grow much faster and more efficiently than they grow outdoors. The old wives tale, "talk to your plants, they will grow faster" is, in fact, true!

Warning! CO_2 can make people woozy when it rises above 5000 PPM, and can become toxic at super high levels. When CO_2 rises to such high levels, there is always a lack of oxygen! At these levels, plants are also adversely affected. Human and animal breath contains over 5000 PPM. Don't exhale directly on seedlings or cuttings under a humidity tent, it could kill them.

Super Size Secret: Enrich the air with CO_2 and monitor water, nutrient solution, temperature, humidity, etc., carefully to ensure they are always at optimum levels.

CO_2 enriched plants demand a higher level of maintenance than normal plants. Carbon dioxide enriched plants use nutrients, water and space up to twice as fast as un-enriched plants. A higher temperature, 85 degrees F, will help stimulate more rapid metabolism within the super enriched plants. Properly maintained, the garden will grow so fast and take up so much space, that flowering will have to be induced sooner than normal.

Like foliage, root growth is stimulated by CO_2 enrichment. CO_2 is taken in via the leaves and the overall growth, including root development, is stimulated.

CO_2 enriched plants use more water because of their accelerated growth rate. CO_2 is actually helpful in conserving water used by plants. Water rises from plant roots and is released into the air by the same stomata that plants use to absorb CO_2, during transpiration. To stay upright and turgid, a plant must balance the uptake of water with the amount released through transpiration. A plant that transpires water faster than it can be replaced, will wilt. Water rises in a plant beyond the point it would be supported by atmospheric pressure, because evaporation from its leaves produces a "suction" that actually pulls water up from the roots. Capillary action also helps.

CO_2 enrichment affects transpiration by causing the plants stomata to partially close. This slows down the loss of water vapor into the air. The leaves of plants that are enriched are measurably thicker and more turgid. They are also slower to wilt than leaves on un-enriched plants.

CO_2 affects plant morphology. Stems and branches grow faster and the cells of these plant parts are more densely packed in an enriched growing environment. Flower stems carry more weight without bending. Because of the increased rate of branching, flowers and vegetables have more flower initiation sites.

Some gardeners get frustrated using CO_2. It causes plants to grow so fast, unsuspecting gardeners are unable to keep up with them. With CO_2 enriched air, plants that do not have the support of the other critical elements for life, will not benefit at all and the CO_2 is wasted. The plant can be limited by just one of the critical factors. For example, the plants use water and nutrients a lot faster and if they are not supplied, they will not grow. They might even be stunted. Or, if plants need a larger pot but do not get it soon enough, they will not grow and be stunted.

 Rule of Thumb: CO_2 enrichment means more time in the garden and moving up the garden calendar 1 – 2 weeks.

Increasing light intensity by adding another HID lamp helps speed growth, but may not be necessary. The extra lamp just might make the garden grow so fast that it is impossible to keep up with. More CO_2 does not mean more hours of light per day. The photoperiod must remain the same as under normal conditions for healthy growth and flowering. Switch to a high-phosphorus bloom formula when plants are within 2.5 feet of a HID lamp or 3.5 feet of the ceiling. Change the photoperiod to slow vegetative growth. They will still grow a foot or two but should stay under control.

 Super Size Secret: CO_2 enrichment will increase yield from 20 – 30 percent when all other elements affecting growth are at optimum levels.

To be most effective, the CO_2 level must be kept near 1500 PPM everywhere in the room. To accomplish this, the garden room must be completely enclosed. Cracks in and around the walls over one-eighth inch should be sealed off to prevent CO_2 from escaping. Enclosing the room makes it easier to control the CO_2 content of the air within. The room must also have a vent fan with flaps or a baffle. The vent fan will remove the stale air that will be replaced with CO_2-enriched air. The flaps or baffle will help contain the CO_2 in the enclosed garden room. Venting requirements will change with each type of CO_2 enrichment system. Venting is discussed in detail in the "CO_2 Generator" and the "Compressed CO_2 Gas" sections. To distribute CO_2 evenly in the room, use an oscillating fan.

Measuring CO_2

Measuring and monitoring CO_2 levels in the air is a little expensive and often not necessary for small gardeners with few lights. Once the room grows to 10 plus lights, monitoring CO_2 levels really helps keep the levels consistent in the room. To learn all about the most recent products available to monitor CO_2, check out the web site: www.greenair.com.

Disposable comparative colorimetry CO_2 test kits are easy to use, accurate, and inexpensive. The test kits contain a syringe and test tubes. To use the kit, break off each end tip of the test tube and insert one end into the closed syringe. Pull 100 cubic centimeters into the syringe, and note the blue color change in the cylinder where the active ingredient reacts with the CO_2 in the air drawn through the cylinder. These kits are reliable to within 40 PPM, plenty accurate for indoor gardeners.

The kit includes a plastic syringe and a couple of test tubes and sell for a reasonable price about (US) \$30. Find the kits in your local hydroponic store.

Electrochemical sensing systems measure electrical conductivity of an air sample in either an alkali solution or distilled or de-ionized water. These systems are relatively inexpensive. They possess several drawbacks: limited accuracy, and sensitivity to temperature and air pollutants.

 Rule of Thumb: *It is less expensive to produce more CO_2 than needed than to purchase an expensive monitoring device.*

Infrared monitoring systems are more accurate and versatile. They measure CO_2 accurately and can be synchronized with controllers, which operate heat, ventilation, and CO_2 generators. Even though the initial cost for a monitor is high, they can solve many CO_2 problems before they occur and ensure optimum growing conditions. Specialty indoor garden stores sell the monitors for less than \$1,000.

Gardeners who do not want to spend the time and energy required to monitor CO_2, can use a set of scales and simple mathematics to determine the approximate amount CO_2 in the air. But this calculation does not account for ventilation, air leaks and other things that would skew the measurement. It is easier to measure the amount of CO_2 produced, rather than measuring the amount of CO_2 in the atmosphere of the garden room.

To measure the amount of fuel used, simply weigh the tank before it is turned on, use it for an hour, then weigh it again. The difference in weight is the amount of gas or fuel used. See the calculations below for more information on calculating the amount of CO_2 in the room.

 Rule of Thumb: *One third-pound of fuel produces 1 pound of* CO_2.

Producing CO_2

There are many ways to raise the CO_2 content of an enclosed garden room. CO_2 is one of the by-products of combustion. Gardeners can burn any fossil (carbon-based) fuel to produce CO_2, except for those containing sulfur dioxide and ethylene, which are harmful to plants. See "CO_2 Generators." A by-product of fermentation and organic decomposition is CO_2 gas. The CO_2 level near the ground of a rain forest covered with decaying organic matter could be 2 – 3 times as high as normal. But bringing a compost pile inside to cook down is not practical. Dry ice is made from frozen CO_2. The CO_2 is released when it comes in contact with the atmosphere. It can get expensive and be a lot of trouble keeping a large room replenished with dry ice.

 Rule of Thumb: *CO_2 generators are the most economical and practical for most garden rooms. CO_2 emitters are usually the best choice for one light rooms.*

There are lots of spin-offs to all of these principles and some work better than others. It is difficult to calculate how much CO_2 is released into the air by fermentation, decomposition or dry ice, without purchasing scientific measurement equipment that is more expensive than actually making the CO_2. Dry ice gets very expensive after prolonged use. Two pounds of dry ice will raise the CO_2 level in a 10 x 10-foot garden room to about

2000 PPM for about 24 hours. One chagrined gardener
remarked, "I can't believe that stuff melts so fast." A decaying
compost pile is simply out of the question indoors! Besides, a
new compost pile would need to be moved twice a day to
release enough CO_2.

Fermentation will create CO_2, but it is difficult to tell how
much is produced. It is also difficult to regulate the level of
CO_2 when it is a byproduct of fermentation. Here is a recipe
for brewing CO_2. A one-gallon plastic milk jug works best, but
any other container will do. Mix one cup of sugar and a packet of brewer's yeast with about 3.5 gallons of warm water. The
concoction smells horrid, but produces a fairly decent burst of
CO_2. This method is one of the least expensive ways of producing CO_2. It works best when used in a small growth chamber.
Seedlings that get started with CO_2 seem to get a head start
that is maintained throughout life. The CO_2 produced by the
fermentation is soon released in the enclosed chamber. The
concoction is changed one to four times daily. Half of the
solution is poured out, and 1.5 quarts of water and another
cup of sugar are added. The yeast will continue to grow during the fermentation process. The first packet of yeast is all
that needs to be added. This CO_2 mix is like a sourdough bat-
ter starter mix, do not let it die! As long as the yeast does not
die, this fermentation mix may be used continually to generate
CO_2. In fact, if a person were really into it, there could be several gallons, and one would be changed every couple of hours.
The smell would soon gag a maggot!

CO_2 Emitter Systems

Compressed CO_2 systems are virtually risk free, producing no
toxic gases, heat, or water. The system is also very precise,
metering an exact amount of CO_2 into the room. CO_2 is
metered out of a cylinder of compressed carbon dioxide with a
regulator-flow meter, a solenoid valve, and a short-range timer.
Two types of systems include: (a) continuous flow and (b)
short range. Metal carbon dioxide cylinders which hold the
gas under 1000 – 2200 pounds of pressure per square inch
(PSI) (depending upon temperature) can be purchased from
welding or beverage supply stores. The cylinders are often
available at hydroponic stores. Cylinders come in three sizes:
twenty, thirty-five and fifty pounds. They average between $100
and $200 (with refills costing about $30 US). Tanks must be

inspected annually and registered with a nationwide safety agency. Welding supply and beverage suppliers often require identification such as a driver's license. Most suppliers exchange tanks and refill them. Fire extinguisher companies and beverage supply companies normally fill CO_2 tanks on the spot. If you purchase a lighter and stronger aluminum tank, make sure to request an aluminum tank exchange. Remember the tank you buy is not necessarily the one that you keep. To experiment before purchasing equipment, rent a fifty-pound tank from a hydroponic store. A large fifty-pound cylinder is a little heavier, but will save you the time of returning to the store to have it refilled. When full, a fifty-pound steel tank weighs 170 pounds. A full twenty-pound steel tank weighs fifty pounds and might be too heavy for you to carry up and down stairs. A full 20-pound aluminum tank weighs about 50 pounds and a full 35-pound tank weights 75 pounds.

Rule of Thumb: Use CO_2 emitter systems in rooms with 1000 or fewer watts, or in rooms that stay too hot to use a CO_2 generator.

Buying a complete CO_2 emitter system at a hydroponic store is the best option for most closet gardeners. These systems offer a good value for small indoor gardeners. You can also make your own system as described below, but often these systems cost more than the pre-manufactured models.

Warning! Make sure CO_2 tanks have a protective collar on top to shield the valve. If the valve is knocked of by an accidental fall, there is enough pressure to send the top (regulator/flow meter, valve, etc.) straight through a parked car.

Welding suppliers also carry regulator-flow meters. Flow meters reduce and control the cubic feet per hour (CFH). The regulator controls the PSI. Models with smaller flow rates, 10-60 CFH, are preferable for gardening purposes. Buy a quality regulator-flow meter and buy all components at the same time and make sure they are compatible.

A regulator-flow valve is essential, but the solenoid valve and the timer are optional. However, gardeners that do not use a timer and solenoid valve waste CO_2. The solenoid valve and timer regulate the flow of CO_2, something you can do by hand, given the time and schedule flexibility. A solenoid valve is electrically operated and is used to start and stop the gas flow from the regulator-flow meter. The least expensive timer is plastic and is commonly used for automatic sprinkler systems. 115-, 24- and 12-volt systems are available. They cost about the same, but the lower voltages offer added safety from electrical shock.

To automate the system, you need a "short-range" timer to open the solenoid valve for brief periods several times a day. Ordinary timers have a minimum on/off period of one-half to one hour, way to long for a CO_2 system. Short-range timers have a cycle of ten minutes or less. Short-range timers and solenoid valves are available from hydroponic stores and most building supply stores.

Control the exact amount of CO_2 released into the garden room by altering the flow and duration of CO_2. To determine how long the valve should remain open, divide the number of cubic feet of gas required (See Example 1.) by the flow rate. If the flow meter is set at 10 cubic feet per hour, the valve will need to be open for 0.1 hours (1 divided by 10) or 6 minutes (0.1 hour x 60 minutes) to bring the room up to 1,500 PPM. Remember, CO_2 leaks out of the garden room. On average, the CO_2 level of the room returns to 300 PPM in

This CO_2 emitter system meters the heavier-than-air gas out evenly above the garden for even distribution.

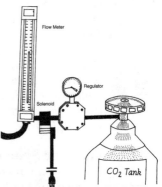

A setup consists of a tank of CO_2 gas, regulator, solenoid valve and a flow meter.

about three hours due to plant usage and room leakage. Split the amount of CO_2 released per hour into two or four smaller increments and dispersed more frequently to maintain a steady level of CO_2.

Distribute the CO_2 from the tank to the garden room by using (a) the tube method or (b) the fan method. Suspend lightweight perforated plastic from the ceiling to disperse the CO_2. The tubing carries CO_2 from the supply tank to the center of the garden room. The main supply-line is attached to several smaller branches that extend throughout the garden. CO_2 is heavier and cooler than air and cascades onto the plants below.

Rule of Thumb: *Construct your own CO_2 emitter system only if you cannot buy a ready-made unit from a hydroponic store.*

To make sure the CO_2 is dispersed from the tubing evenly, submerge the lightweight plastic tubing in water and punch the emission holes under water while the CO_2 is being piped into the line. This way you know the proper diameter holes to punch and where to punch them to create the ideal CO_2 flow over the garden.

Overhead fans help distribute CO_2 evenly throughout the room. The CO_2 is released directly below the fan into its air-flow. This evenly mixes the CO_2 throughout the air and keeps it recirculating across the plants.

Compressed CO_2 may be virtually risk-free, but it is expensive, especially for large gardeners. At roughly 50 cents per pound, compressed gas is much more expensive than fuels used in generators. Cost of equipment and fuel make compressed CO_2 enrichment systems less economical than generators.

Warning! *Be careful when using compressed CO_2. It is very cold when it is released from a bottle where it has been kept under pressure. Even a quick blast can do damage to skin or eyes. If the flow rate is above 20 cubic feet per hour, your regulator might freeze.*

CO_2 Generator Systems

CO_2 generators are used by commercial flower and vegetable growers. Green Air Products has introduced a complete line of reasonably priced CO_2 generators that burn natural gas or LP (propane) to produce CO_2. However, heat and water are by-products of the combustion process. Generators use a pilot light with a flow meter and burner. The inside of the generator is similar to a gas stove burner with a pilot light enclosed in a protective housing. The generator must have a cover over the open flame. You can operate the generators manually or synchronize them with a timer to operate with other garden room equipment, such as ventilation fans.

Rule of Thumb: *Use a CO_2 generator in rooms with one or more lights. If the temperature rises above 95 degrees, stop using the generator. It is creating too much heat.*

Warning! CO₂ generators produce hot exhaust gasses (CO₂ + H₂O). Even though CO₂ is heavier than air, it is hotter, and therefore, less dense and rises in a garden room. If you use CO₂ you must have good air circulation for even distribution of CO₂.

CO_2 generators can burn any fossil fuel – kerosene, propane, or natural gas. Low grades of kerosene can have sulfur content as high as one tenth of one percent, enough to cause sulfur dioxide pollution. Use only high quality kerosene even though it is expensive. Always use grade "1-K" kerosene. Maintenance costs for kerosene generators are high because they use electrodes, pumps, and fuel filters. For most garden rooms, propane and natural gas burners are the best choice.

In small rooms with ventilation, a kerosene lamp will burn enough oxygen from the air to create an excess of CO_2.

Spray soapy water around all propane gas connections to check for bubbles (leaks).

Green Air generators can burn either propane or natural gas, but must be set up for one or the other. They are inexpensive to maintain because they do not use filters or pumps. Hobby CO_2 generators range from $300-$500, depending on size. The initial cost of a generator is slightly higher than a CO_2 emitter system that uses small compressed gas cylinders. Nonetheless growers prefer propane and natural gas generators because they are about 4 times less expensive to operate than bottled CO_2 generators. One gallon of propane, which costs about $2, contains 36 cubic feet of gas and over 100 cubic feet of CO_2 (every cubic foot of propane gas produces 3 cubic feet of CO_2). For example, if a garden used one gallon of propane every day, the cost would be about $60 per month. In contrast bottled CO_2 for the same room would cost more than $200 per month!

A CO_2 generator increases harvests about 20 percent on average.

To determine how much fuel you will need when the room temperature is 68 degrees F:

1 pound of CO_2 displaces 8.7 cubic feet of CO_2.
0.33 pounds of fuel produces 1 pound of CO_2.

Divide the amount of CO_2 required by 8.7 and multiply by 0.33 to determine the amount of fuel needed. In our example we need 1 cubic foot* of CO_2 for an 800 cubic foot garden room.

L x W x H = room volume (cubic feet)
10 x 10 x 8 = 800 cubic feet

Desired CO_2 level is 1,200 PPM (0.0012 PPM)**
Multiply room volume by 0.0012 = desired CO_2 level
800 cubic feet x 0.0012 = 1 cubic foot CO_2

$$\frac{1 \text{ cubic foot of } CO_2}{8.7} = 0.115 \times 0.33 = 0.038$$

It will take three times this amount (3 x 0.038 = 0.114 pounds) of fuel dispersed over time to create enough CO_2 for the room for 12 - 18 hours.

To convert 0.114 pounds to ounces, multiply by 16, 0.114 x 16 = 1.82 ounces of fuel must be burned daily to keep the CO_2 level at 1500 PPM.

* Numbers are rounded up from 0.96 to 1.
** 1,500 PPM − 300 PPM ambient CO_2 = 1200 PPM

To find out how much CO_2 it will take to bring a grow room up to the optimum level, follow the example below and insert the appropriate figures in the blanks.

Example:

Total Volume = Length x Width x Height = total cubic feet

Total Volume = ____ x ___ x ____ = _____ total cubic fee

Total cubic feet x 1200 PPM = cubic feet CO_2 needed to bring level to 1200 PPM

_____ x 0.0012 = _____ cubic feet

_____ = _____ x 0.33 = _____ pounds of fuel needed
8.7

_____ x 16 = _____ ounces of fuel needed to bring the CO_2 level up to 1500 PPM.

CO_2 generators are less expensive to maintain and less cumbersome, they have some disadvantages too. One pound of fuel produces 1.5 pounds of water and 21,800 BTUs of heat. For garden rooms less than 400 cubic feet, this makes generators unusable. Even for larger garden rooms, the added heat and humidity must be carefully monitored and controlled so as not to affect plants. Gardeners in warm climates do not use generators because they produce too much heat and humidity.

Warning! Mix equal parts of water and detergent to check for leaks in burners. If bubbles appear, the system leaks. Do not use a leaky system! It is dangerous!

If fuel does not burn completely or cleanly, CO_2 generators can release toxic gases, including carbon monoxide into the garden room. Nitrous oxide, also a by-product of burning propane, can grow to toxic levels, too. Well-made CO_2 generators have a pilot and timer. They will turn off if leaks or problems are detected.

Warning! *Carbon monoxide is a deadly gas and can be detected with a carbon monoxide alarm; available at most hardware and building supply stores.*

 Warning! *A CO_2 monitor is necessary if you are sensitive to high levels of the gas. Digital alarm units or color change plates (used in aircraft) are an economical alternative.*

Check homemade generators, including kerosene or gas heaters frequently. Propane and natural gas produce a blue flame when burning efficiently. A yellow flame indicates unburned gas (which creates carbon monoxide) and needs more oxygen to burn cleanly. Leaks in a system can be detected by applying a solution of equal parts water and concentrated dish soap to all connections. If bubbles appear, gas is leaking. Never use a leaky system.

Oxygen is also burned and as this oxygen becomes deficient in the room the oxygen/fuel mixture changes. The flame burns too (oxygen) rich and turns yellow. This is why fresh air is essential.

 Rule of Thumb: *One pound of fuel releases 3 pounds of CO_2. Each pound of CO_2 displaces 8.7 cubic feet of air.*

 Warning! *When filling a new propane tank, first empty it of the inert gas, which is used to protect it from rust. Never completely fill a propane tank. Propane expands and contracts with temperature change and could release flammable gas from the pressure vent if too full.*

 Warning! *Do not drag tank around by the hose! This practice could break the hose and create a fire hazard. This may sound like a no-brainier, but it is more common than you think!*

Other Ways to Make CO_2

There are many ways to make CO_2. You can enrich small areas by burning ethyl or methyl alcohol in a kerosene lamp. Norwegians are studying using charcoal burners as a source of CO_2. When refined, the system will combine the advantages of generators and compressed gas. Charcoal is much less expensive than bottled CO_2 and is less risky than generators in terms of toxic by-products. Other companies are also studying using new technology to extract or filter CO_2 from the air and concentrating it.

Chemical Puck

This product is cool. It's a pressed puck that dissolves and releases CO_2 into the atmosphere. All you do is drop the puck in a paper cup and add water. Put the lid back on the cup and poke a few holes in the lid so the CO_2 does not disperse too quickly. The puck is available from www.fearlessgardener.com.

Compost and Organic Growing Mediums

Composing organic materials like wood chips, hay, leaves and manures release large amounts of CO_2. Although you can capture CO_2 from this decomposition because of the smell, it is most often impractical for indoor gardeners. For more information about collecting CO_2 via decomposition, see *Gardening Indoors with CO_2*, by George Van Patten and Alyssa Bust, 96 pages, $14.95.

This puck of compressed chemicals vaporizes into CO_2 gas when you add water.

Fermentation

Small-scale gardeners use fermentation to produce CO_2. Combine water, sugar and yeast to produce CO_2. The yeast eats the sugar and releases CO_2 and alcohol as by-products. Gardeners that brew beer at home can use a small-scale system to increase the CO_2 levels in a room. Non-brewers can mix one cup of sugar, a packet of brewer's yeast, and three quarts of warm water in a gallon jug to make CO_2. You will have to experiment a little with the water temperature to get it right. Yeast dies in hot water and does not activate in cold water. Once the yeast is activated, CO_2 is released into the air. Punch a small hole in the cap of the jug and place it in a warm spot (between 80 – 95 degrees F) in your garden room. Many gardeners buy a fermentation lock (available for under $10 at beer brewing stores). It keeps contaminants from entering the jug, and bubbles CO_2 through water so the rate of production can be observed. The hitch is that you must change the concoction every 2 – 3 days. Pour out half the solution and add 1.5 quarts of water and another cup of sugar. As long as the yeast continues to grow and bubble, the mixture can last indefinitely. When the yeast starts to die, add another packet. This basic formula can be adapted to make smaller or larger scale fermenters. Several jugs scattered around the garden room have a significant impact on CO_2 levels.

Fermentation is an inexpensive alternative to produce CO_2, releases no heat, toxic gases, or water, and uses no electricity. However, because it stinks, it is unlikely that a gardener could tolerate a large-scale fermentation process. In addition, because it is difficult to measure CO_2 production from this system, it is also difficult to maintain uniform levels throughout the day. The by-product of fermentation is ethyl alcohol.

Dry Ice

Large insulated tanks filled with dry ice can be used to add CO_2 to an indoor garden. Dry ice is carbon dioxide that has been compressed and frozen. As it melts, it changes from solid to gas. The gaseous CO_2 can be mixed into the air with fans so that it circulates among the plants. Dry ice works well on a smaller scale without a tank and converter. It is readily available (check out the Yellow Pages) and inexpensive. Because CO_2 is rare in the liquid stage, the transformation from solid to gas as the ice melts is clean and tidy. It's also easy to approximate the amount of CO_2 being released. A pound of dry ice is equal to a pound of liquid CO_2. Determining the thawing period for a particular size of dry ice will allow you to estimate how much CO_2 is released during a particular time period. To prolong the thawing process, put dry ice in insulating containers, such as a foam ice cooler and cut holes in the top and sides to release the CO_2. The size and number of holes allow you to control the rate at which the block melts and releases CO_2. Solid CO_2 has a cooling effect, so producing CO_2 by this method can lower the room temperature if heat is a problem.

Put dry ice in a plastic container with holes to slow evaporation of CO_2 gas.

Dry ice is economical and risk free; it releases no toxic gases, heat or water. Although dry ice is easier to handle than compressed CO_2 tanks, it is difficult to store. Melting can be slowed through insulation, but it cannot be stopped. Because it is extremely cold, dry ice can also cause tissue damage or burn the skin after prolonged contact.

Rule of Thumb: On the average, a 5-pound block of dry ice will last about 24 hours.

Baking Soda and Vinegar

Consider using vinegar and baking soda to produce CO_2 in a small garden room. This method eliminates excess heat and water vapor production and requires only household items. Create a system that drips vinegar (acetic acid) into a bed of baking soda. The main disadvantage of this system is the erratic levels of CO_2 produced. It takes a considerable amount of time for the CO_2 to build up to a level where it helps plants. However, once it reaches an optimum level, it can continue to rise until it reaches levels detrimental to plants. If you have time to experiment, it is possible to set up a drip system operated by a solenoid valve and a short-term timer. With such a system, CO_2 could be released in small increments periodically and coordinated with ventilation schedules.

Ozone Generators

Ozone generators add another molecule to the naturally occurring oxygen (O_2) in the air. Ozone molecules have three parts oxygen (O_3). This form of oxygen is very interesting and has many applications. Ozone is used at low levels to sterilize food and water as well as to remove odors from the air at the molecular level. Indoor gardeners have found that an ozone-treated atmosphere also kills fungi and pests, including spider mites. The generator produces ozone by saturating the air containing oxygen (O_2) with ultraviolet (UV) light.

UV light is can be dangerous in large doses. Exposure to intense UV light can burn your eyes and skin beyond repair. Do not look at the UV lamp in an ozone generator. High enough levels of ozone are capable of burning your lungs and nasal passages. At low levels there is no

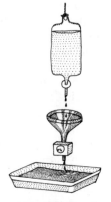

Although a bit of a trick to keep going all the time, pouring vinegar on baking soda is a fair source of CO_2.

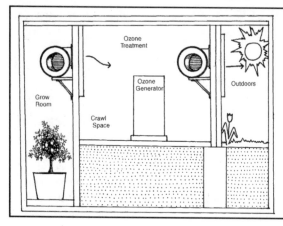

Mixing Ozone-treated air for a minute or more allows O_3 to shed a molecule and become O_2.

damage. Always consult manufacturers instructions and follow them to the letter.

 Warning! *Never look at high levels of UV light! Looking at bright ultraviolet (UV) light can burn retinas.*

Ozone has an unusual odor similar to the smell of the air after a good rain. Anybody who has smelled a recently ozoneated room knows the smell and will never forget it. Ozone is oxygen (O_2) with an extra oxygen molecule (O_3). The extra molecule is always a positively charged ion that is predisposed to attach to a negatively charged cation. Odors are usually negatively charged cations. When the extra oxygen ion attaches to the cation, they neutralize one another and the odor disappears! The chemistry takes a minute or longer to occur, so treated air must be held in a chamber to be treated effectively.

There are many ozone generators on the market today. Some of them are built better than others. When shopping for an ozone generator, look for one that is self-cleaning, easy to clean and easy and safe to replace the bulb. Make sure it has proper safety features built-in, such as a switch that turns off the lamp for maintenance and makes it impossible to look at the retina-searing UV rays. When UV light comes into contact with moisture in the air nitric acid is produced as a by-product. White-powdery nitric acid collects around the lamps at connection points. It is an unpleasant, very corrosive acid that will burn skin and eyes severely.

The Air Tiger™, manufactured by
Rambridge, www.rambridge.com, is an
excellent value for gardeners. It is one
of the safest available and easy to maintain. A deadman's switch makes direct
eye contact with the 10-inch-long UV
light tube impossible. Highly corrosive
ozone stays away from interior wiring
and little moisture can penetrate the
outer shell to combine with O_3 to form
powdery nitric acid.

*Ozone generators neu-
tralize odors in less
than a minute.*

Ozone generators are rated in the
number of cubic feet they are able to treat. Figure cubic feet
by multiplying the length x width x height of the room. Some
gardeners set the ozone generator up in the garden room and
let it treat all the air in the room. Once ozone is generated, it
takes a minute or two for the O_3 molecules to go to work.

 Warning! *Ozone can damage plants severely when overdone.
Excessive ozone causes chlorotic spots on leaves. The mottled
spots increase in size turning dark in the process. Leaves with-
er and drop and overall plant growth slows to a crawl.*

Setting Up the Vent Fan – Step-by-Step

Step One: Figure the total volume of the garden room. Length x
width x height = total volume. For example, a garden room that is 10 x
10 x 8 feet has a total volume of 800 cubic feet (10 x 10 x 8 feet = 800
cubic feet.)

Step Two: Use a vent fan that will remove the total volume of air in
the room in less than 3 minutes. Buy a fan that can easily be mounted to
the wall or "in line" in a duct pipe. "In line" fans move the most air and
make the least noise. It's worth spending a few extra dollars on an "in
line" fan. Small rooms can use a fan that can be attached to a flexible 4-
inch dryer hose. Many stores sell special duct fittings to connect high-
speed squirrel cage fans with the 4-inch ducting.

Step Three: Place the fan high on a wall or near the ceiling of the
garden room, so it vents off hot, humid air.

Step Four: If possible, cut a hole in the wall and secure the fan in
place over the hole. However, most locations require special installation.
See: 5 – 9 below.

Step Five: To place a fan in a window, cut a piece of one-half-inch plywood to fit the windowsill. Cover window with a lightproof dark-colored

paint or similar covering. Mount the fan near the top of the plywood, to blow air out. Secure the plywood and fan in the windowsill with sheet rock screws. Open the window from the bottom.

Step Six: Another option to make a lightproof vent is to use a 4-inch flexible dryer hose. Vent the hose outdoors and attach a small squirrel cage fan to the other end of the hose. Make sure there is an air-tight connection between the fan and hose by using a large hose clamp or duct tape. Stretch the hose so that it is as smooth as possible inside. Irregular interior surfaces cause air turbulence and diminish airflow.

Turning air around a corner keeps garden room from being affected by gusts of winds from outdoors and prevents outside light from entering during the dark period.

Step Seven: Another option is to vent the air up the chimney or into the attic. If using the chimney for a vent, first clean out the excess ash and creosote. Tie a chain to a rope. Lower the chain down the chimney, banging and knocking all debris inside to the bottom. There should be a door at the bottom to remove the debris. This door can also be used as the exhaust vent. See drawing.

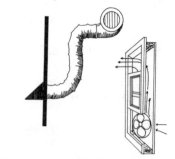

Step Eight: Attach the fan to a thermostat/humidistat or other temperature/humidity monitor/control

Remove hot stale air from the garden room and vent it out a hole already in the chimney.

device to vent hot, humid air outside. Set the temperature on 75 degrees F and the humidity on 50 percent. Most control devices have wiring instructions. More sophisticated controllers have electrical outlets and the peripherals are simply plugged in.

Step Nine: You can also attach the vent fan to a timer and run it for a specific length of time. This is the method that is used with CO_2 enrichment. The fan is set to turn on and vent out used CO_2 (depleted air) just before new CO_2-rich air is injected.

Pests, Fungi and Diseases

Insects, mites and maggots slither into garden rooms, eating, reproducing and destroying your garden. Outdoors, they live everywhere they can. Indoors, they live anywhere you let them. Fungi are present in the air at all times. They may be introduced by an infected plant or from air containing fungus spores. Fungi will settle down and grow if climatic conditions are right. Pests, fungi and diseases can be prevented, but if allowed to grow unchecked, extreme control measures are often necessary to eradicate them.

Prevention

Cleanliness is the key to insect and fungus prevention. The garden room should be totally enclosed, so the environment can be controlled easily. Keep the floor clean. Keep all debris off soil surface. Do not use mulch. Insects and fungi like nice hideaway homes found in dirty, dank corners and under dead decaying leaves or rotting mulch. Gardeners and their tools often transport many microscopic pests, diseases and fungi that could ultimately destroy the garden. This does not mean gardeners and their tools have to be *hospital* clean every time they enter a garden room, even though that would be nice. It does mean normal and regular sanitary precautions must be taken. Gardeners that wear clean clothes and use clean tools reduce problems immensely. A separate set of indoor tools is easy to keep clean. Pests, diseases and fungi intrinsically ride from plant to plant on dirty tools. Disinfect tools by dipping in rubbing alcohol or washing with soap and hot water after using them on each diseased plant. Another quick way to sterilize pruners is with a hand-held torch. A quick heating with the torch will sterilize metal tools immediately.

Personal cleanliness is fundamental to prevent pests and diseases. Wash your hands before touching foliage and after handling diseased plants. Smart gardeners do not walk around the buggy outdoor garden, and visit the indoor garden; they do it vice versa. Think before entering the indoor garden and possi-

bly contaminating it. Did you walk across a lawn covered with
rust fungi or pet the dog that just came in from the garden
outside? Did you just fondle your spider mite infested split leaf
philodendron in the living room? Avoid such problems by
washing your hands, and changing shirt, pants and shoes
before entering an indoor garden.

Once potting soil or soilless mix has been used, throw it out.
Some gardeners brag about using the same old potting soil
over and over. Unknowingly, this savings is repaid with a
diminished harvest. Used soil may harbor harmful pests and
diseases that have developed immunity to sprays. Starting new
crops in new potting soil will cost more up front, but will eliminate many potential problems. Used soil makes excellent outdoor garden soil. But remember that white perlite and other
soil additives can become unsightly in the garden.

Once potting soil is used, it loses much of the "fluff" in the
texture. Compaction becomes a problem. Roots penetrate
compacted soil slowly, and there is little room for oxygen,
which restricts nutrient uptake. Used potting soil is depleted
of nutrients. A plant with a slow-start is a perfect target for disease and worst of all, it will yield less!

Companion planting helps discourage insects outdoors.
Indoors pests have nowhere to go and companion planting is
not viable in many garden rooms.

 Super Size Secret: *Always plant about 10 percent more plants
than you plan to harvest. If one in 10 plants becomes infected
or sickly, remove it from the garden. Removing entire plants is
the easiest way to isolate and control most pest and disease
problems.*

Plant insect and fungus resistant varieties of plants. Always
check for disease resistance when buying seeds.

Keep plants healthy and growing fast at all times. Disease
attacks sickly plants first. Strong plants tend to grow faster
than pests and diseases can spread.

Forced air circulation makes life miserable for pests and diseases. Pests hate wind. Fungal spores have little time to settle
in a breeze and grow poorly on wind-dried soil, stems and
leaves.

Super Size Secret: *Preventing pests and diseases is much easi-er and more productive than eliminating an infestation.*

Ventilation changes the humidity of a room quickly. In fact, a vent fan attached to a humidistat is often the most effective form of humidity control. Mold is often a problem in garden rooms that do not have ventilation and exhaust fans. Upon entering such an enclosed room, the moist humid air is over-powering. The environment can be so humid that roots actual-ly grow from plant stems. When a vent fan that sucks out moist stale air is installed, the humidity drops from nearly 100 per-cent to around 50 percent. The mold problem also disappears, and flower and vegetable production increase.

Indoor horticulturists that practice all of the preventative measures have fewer problems with pests and diseases. It is much easier to prevent a disease from getting started than it is to wipe out an infestation. If pests and diseases are left unchecked, they could devastate the garden in a few short weeks.

Control

Sometimes, even when all preventative measures are taken, pests and diseases still slink in and set up housekeeping. First they establish a base on a weak, susceptible plant. Once set up, they launch an all-out assault on the rest of the garden. They move out in all directions from the infested base, taking over more and more space until they have conquered the entire garden. An infestation can happen in a matter of days. Most insects lay thousands of eggs in short periods of time. These eggs hatch and grow into mature adults within a few weeks. For example, if 100 microscopic munchers each laid 1,000 eggs, and these eggs grew into adults two weeks later. Two weeks later the 100,000 young adults would lay 1,000 eggs each. By the end of the month, there would be 100,000,000 pests attacking the infested garden. Imagine how many there would be in another two weeks!

Sprays often kill adults only. In general, sprays should be applied soon after eggs hatch so young adults are caught in their weakest stage of life. Very lightweight (low viscosity) hor-ticultural oil spray works well alone or as an additive to help kill larvae and eggs.

The availability of some sprays can be seasonal, especially in more rural areas. Garden sections of stores are changed for the winter, but the stock is sometimes kept in a storage room. Look for bargains on sprays at season end sales. Today, there are many hydroponic stores that carry pest and disease controls all year round.

Insect Control

Indoor gardeners have many options to control insects and fungi. Prevention and cleanliness are at the top of the "control" list. There is a logical progression to pest and disease control. It is outlined in the chart below. Notice it starts with cleanliness.

 Rule of Thumb: Follow the logical progression for disease and pest control.

Logical Progression of Insect Control

1. Prevention
   a. cleanliness
   b. use "new" soil
   c. one "indoor" set of tools
   d. disease resistant plants
   e. healthy plants
   f. climate control
   g. no animals
   h. companion planting
      (if possible)

2. Manual Removal
   a. fingers
   b. sponges

3. Organic Sprays

4. Natural Predators

5. Chemicals

Manual removal is just what the name implies: smashing all pests and their eggs in sight between the thumb and forefinger or between two sponges.

I like natural organic sprays such as pyrethrum and neem, and use harsh chemicals only as a last resort. Any spray, no matter how benign, always seems to slow plant growth a little. When a plant is sprayed and covered with a filmy residue, stomata become clogged and stay plugged up until the spray wears off or is washed off. Stronger sprays are often more phytotoxic, burning foliage. Spray plants as little as possible and avoid spraying for two weeks before harvest. Read all labels thoroughly before use.

Use only contact sprays that are approved for edible plants. Avoid spraying seedlings and tender unrooted cuttings. Wait until cuttings are rooted and seedlings are at least a month old before spraying. For spider mites, make sure you spray the underside of all the leaves affected.

Homemade sprays rely heavily on soap, garlic, peppers and oil mixed with water in a blender.

Sprays and Traps
Chemical fungicides, insecticides and miticides

A black light trap will keeps pesky flying insects in check.

Do not use chemical fungicides, fungistats, insecticides or miticides on plants that are destined for human consumption. Most contact sprays that do not enter the plant system are approved for edible fruits and vegetables. However, there are numerous ways to control fungi, diseases, and pests without resorting to chemicals. Below is a chart of common chemicals, their trade names and the insects they control.

 Warning! Do not use Systemic products.

Do not apply these substances to edible plants:

Generic Name	Purpose	Enter System
Griseofulvin	fungicide	systemic
Streptomycin	bactericide	systemic
Carbaryl	fungicide	systemic
Tetracycline (Terramycin®)	bactericide	semi synthetic
Nitrates	foliar fertilizers	systemic
Avid	insecticide	not truly systemic, actually translaminar
Pentac	miticide	systemic
Temik	everything – ide	systemic

Neem	insecticide	systemic
Funginex	fungicide	systemic
Vitavax	fungicide	systemic
Orthene	insecticide	systemic

NOTE: This list is not all-inclusive. The basic rule is to not use systemic products.

EPA pesticide acute toxicity classification

Class	*LD_{50} to kill Rat Oral (mg kg^{-1})	LD_{50} to kill Rat Dermal (mg kg^{-1})	LD_{50} to kill Rat Inhaled (mg kg^{-1})	Eye Effects	Skin Effects
I	50 or less	200 or less	0.2 or less Most severe	corrosive opacity not reversible	corrosive
II	50-500	200-2000	0.2-2.0	corneal opacity reversible within 7 days, irritation persisting for 7 days	severe irritation at 72 hours
III	500-5000	2000-20,000	2.0-20	no corneal opacity, irritation reversible within 7 days	moderate irritation at 72 hours
IV	> 5000	> 20, 000	> 20	no irritation Least severe	mild irritation at 72 hours

*LD_{50} is the lethal dose it takes to kill 50 percent the one kilogram (2.20 pound) rats in the study group.
> = greater than
< = less than

Natural Remedy Chart

Generic name Active ingredient	Form	Trade Name	Toxicity Precautions EPA Class
Bacillus species	G, D, WP	*Bt*, DiPel, M-Trak, Mattch, Javelin, etc.	IV
Copper sulfate	D, WP	Brsicop	III
Copper sulfate/lime	D, WP	Bordeaux mixture	III
Diatomaceous earth	D	Celite	IV

Neem	O, EL	Neem, Bioneem	IV
Nicotine sulfate	L, D	Black LeaF 40	II
Oil, dormant horti.	O	Sunspray	IV
Pyrethrins	A, L, WP	Many trade names	III, IV
Quassia	WP	Bitterwood	IV
Rotenone	D, WP, EC	Derris, Cubé	II, III
Ryania	D, WP	Dyan 50	IV
Sabadilla	D	Red Devil	IV
Soap, insecticidal	L	M-Pede, Safer's	IV
Sodium bicarbonate	P	Baking soda	IV
Sodium hypochlorite	L	Bleach	II, III
Sulfur	D, WP	Cosan	V

Legend
A = Aerosol
D = Dust
EL = Emulsifiable Liquid
L = Liquid
G = Granular
WP = Wettable Powder
O = Oil
P = Powder

Abamectin
Ingredients: abamectin, derivatives include *emamectin* and *milbemectin*. Does not bioaccumulate. Used extensively on hops, abamectin is not truly systemic. It is absorbed from the exterior of foliage to other leaf parts, especially young leaves in the process of *translaminar activity*.

Controls: Russet and spider mites, fire ants, leafminers and nematodes.

Mixing: Dilute in water. Mix one-quarter teaspoon per gallon. Use a wetting agent.

Application: Spray. Works best when temperature is above 70 degrees F. Repeat applications every 7 – 10 days.

Persistence: One day.

Forms: Liquid.

Toxicity: Toxic to mammals, fish and honeybees in high concentrations. Sucking insects are subject to control while beneficials are not hurt.

Safety: Wear gloves, mask and safety glasses.

Bacillus thuringiensis (Bt) and other Bacillus species

Ingredients: *Bacillus thuringiensis (Bt)*, is the best known of several bacteria that are fatal to caterpillars, larva and maggots.

Caterpillars, larvae and maggots eat *Bt* bacteria, applied as a spray, dust or granules. Inject liquid *Bt* into stalks to kill borers. Shortly after ingestion, their appetite is ruined and they stop eating. Within a few days they shrivel up and die. Cabbage loopers, cabbageworms, corn earworms, cutworms, gypsy moth larvae and hornworms are controlled. Commercial *Bt* products do not reproduce within insect bodies, so several applications may be necessary to control an infestation. Microbial *Bt* bacteria are nontoxic to animals (humans), beneficial insects and plants, however, some people do develop an allergic reaction. Commercial *Bt* products do not contain living *Bt* bacteria. But the *Bt* toxin is extremely perishable. Keep within prescribed temperature ranges and apply according to directions. Most effective on young caterpillars, larvae and maggots, apply as soon as they are spotted.

Get the most out of *Bt* applications by adding a UV inhibitor, spreader/sticker and a feeding stimulant such as Entice®, Konsume® or Pheast®. *Bt* is completely broken down by UV light in one to three days.

B thuringiensis var. *kurstaki* (*Btk*), introduced on the market in the early 1960s, is the most popular *Bt*. Toxic to many moth and caterpillar larvae, including most of the species that feed on flowers and vegetables. Sold under many trade names: DiPel®, BioBit®, Javelin®, etc. *Btk* is also available in a microencapsulated form: M-Trak®, Mattch®, etc. The encapsulation extends the effective life on foliage to more than a week.

B. thuringiensis var. *aizawai* (*Bta*) is effective against hard to kill budworms, borers and armyworms and pests that have built up a resistance to *Btk*.

B. thuringiensis var. *israelensis* (*Bt-i*) is effective against the larvae of mosquitoes, black flies and fungus gnats. Look for Gnatrol®, Vectobac® and Bacrimos®. All are lethal to larvae. Adults do not feed on plants and are not affected. Fungus gnats can cause root problems including rot. Use *Bti* to get rid of them as soon as they are identified.

B. thuringiensis var. *morrisoni* is a new strain of *Bt* under development for insect larva with a high pH in their guts.

B. thuringiensis var. *san diego* (*Btsd*) targets the larvae of Colorado potato beetles and elm beetle adults and other leaf beetles.

B. thuringiensis var. *tenebrionis* (*Btt*) is lethal to Colorado potato beetle larvae.

B. cereus helps control damping off and root-knot fungi. It flourishes in water-saturated mediums and promotes beneficial fungus that attacks the diseases.

B. subtilis is a soil dwelling bacterium that curbs *Fusarium, Pythium* and *Rhizoctonia,* the causes of damping-off. It is commercially available under the brand names: Epic®, Kodiac®, Rhizo-Plus®, Serenade®, etc. Soak seeds and apply as a soil drench.

B. popilliae colonizes larvae (grubs) bodies that consume it, causing them to turn milky white before dying. It is often called "milky spore disease." It is most effective against Japanese beetle grubs.

Baking soda
Ingredients: Sodium bicarbonate.
Controls: Powdery mildew.
Caution! Baking soda kills fungus by changing the pH of foliage surface. It functions as a fungistat, not as a fungicide that eradicates the organisms.
Mixing: Saturate in water.
Application: Spray or dust foliage.
Persistence: One to three days.
Forms: Powder.
Toxicity: None to mammals, fish, beneficials.
Safety: Wear a mask to avoid inhaling dust.

Bleach, laundry
Ingredients: Sodium hypochlorite.
Controls: Numerous bacteria and fungi.
Caution! Avoid skin contact and inhalation. Concentrate burns skin and stains clothes.

Mixing: Dilute to a 5 or 10 percent solution with water.

Application: Use as a disinfectant on containers, walls, tools, etc.

Persistence: Evaporates with little residual in a couple of days.

Forms: Liquid.

Toxicity: Toxic to humans if swallowed or gets in eyes. Toxic to fish, beneficials.

Safety: Wear a mask and gloves when handling concentrate. Avoid skin contact and respiration. Do not mix with ammonia! Deadly fumes result!

Bordeaux mixture

Ingredients: Water, sulfur, copper (copper sulfate) and lime (calcium hydroxide).

Controls: Most often used as a foliar fungicide, also controls bacteria and fends off other insects.

Caution! Phytotoxic when applied to tender seedlings or foliage in cool, humid conditions.

Mixing: Apply immediately after preparing.

Application: Agitate the mixture often while spraying so ingredients do not settle out.

Persistence: Until it is washed from foliage.

Forms: Powder, liquid, etc.

Toxicity: Not toxic to humans and animals, but somewhat toxic to honeybees and very toxic to fish.

Safety: Wear a mask, gloves and long sleeves.

Boric acid

Ingredients: Available in the form of borax hand soap and Boric acid powder.

Controls: Lethal as a contact or stomach poison to kill earwigs, roaches, crickets and ants.

Caution! Phytotoxic when applied to foliage.

Mixing: Mix borax soap in equal parts with powdered sugar to make toxic bait.

Application: Set bait out on soil near base of plants.

Persistence: Avoid getting bait wet as it disperses rapidly.

Forms: Powder.

Toxicity: Not toxic to honeybees and birds.

Safety: Avoid breathing dust.

Bug Bombs

Ingredients: Often bug bombs are packed with very strong insecticides and miticides including synthetic pyrethrins that exterminate every pest in the room. They were developed to kill fleas, roaches and their eggs that hide in furniture and in carpets.

Controls: According to most bug bomb labels, they kill everything in the room!

Caution! Use only as a last resort and follow label instructions to the letter.

Mixing: None.

Application: Place the bug bomb in the empty room on a piece of newspaper. Turn it on. Then leave the room. Follow directions to the letter!

Persistence: Low residual, but persistence is limited to a day or two.

Forms: Aerosol.

Toxicity: Read label for details.

Safety: Wear a mask, gloves and cover exposed skin and hair.

Copper

Ingredients: The compounds – copper sulfate, copper oxychloride, cupric hydroxide and cuprous oxide – are common forms of fixed copper used as a fungicide and are less phytotoxic than unfixed (pure) copper.

Controls: Gray mold, foliar fungus, anthracnose, blights, mildews and a number of bacterial diseases.

Caution! Easy to over-apply and burn foliage or create a copper excess in plant.

Mixing: Apply immediately after preparing.

Application: Agitate the mixture often while spraying so ingredients do not settle out. Preferred temperature range for application is 65 – 85 degrees F.

Persistence: Two weeks or longer indoors if not washed off.

Forms: Powder and liquid.

Toxicity: Toxic to fish, not toxic to birds, bees or mammals.

Safety: Wear a mask, gloves and cover exposed skin and hair.

Diatomaceous Earth

Ingredients: Naturally occurring DE includes fossilized silica shell-remains of the tiny one-celled or colonial creatures called diatoms. It also contains some trace minerals in a chelated (available) form.

Controls: Although not registered as a pesticide or fungicide, DE abrades the waxy coating on pest shells and skin – including aphids and slugs, causing body fluids to leak out. Once ingested, the razor-sharp particles rip tiny holes in pest guts causing death.

Caution! Do not use swimming pool diatomaceous earth. Chemically treated and heated, it contains crystalline silica that is very hazardous if inhaled. The body is unable to dissolve the crystalline form of silica, which causes chronic irritation, called silicosis.

Mixing: No mixing required. Dust as a powder, or encircle slug-damaged plants to use as a barrier.

Application: Apply as a spray to infestations of pest insects.

Persistence: Stays on foliage for a few days or until washed off.

Forms: Powder.

Toxicity: Earthworms, animals, humans and birds can digest diatomaceous earth with no ill effects. Avoid contact with skin and eyes. Do not breathe the dust.

Safety: Wear a protective mask and goggles when handling this fine powder to guard against respiratory and eye irritations.

Homemade Pest and Disease Sprays

Ingredients: A strong, hot taste, smelly odor, and a desiccating powder or liquid are the main ingredients in home-brewed pesticide and fungicide potions. See next page.

Controls: Home made sprays discourage and control pests including aphids, thrips, spider mites, scale and many others.

Caution! Be careful when testing a new spray. Apply it to a single plant and wait for a few days to learn the outcome before applying to all plants.

Mixing: Make spray concentrates by mixing repellent substances with a little water in a blender. The resulting slurry concentrate is strained through a nylon stocking or fine cheesecloth before being diluted with water for application.

Application: Spray foliage until it drips from both sides of leaves.

Persistence: A few days.

Forms: Liquid.

Toxicity: Usually not toxic to humans in dosages lethal to pests.

Safety: Wear a mask, gloves and cover skin and hair. Avoid contact with eyes, nose, lips and ears.

Recipes and Controls

Alcohol: Use isopropyl (rubbing). Add to sprays to dry out pests.

Bleach: Use a 5 percent solution as a general disinfectant.

Cinnamon: Dilute cinnamon oil with water. Use just a few drops per pint as pesticide.

Citrus: Citrus oils make great ingredients that kill insects dead.

Garlic: Use a garlic press to squeeze garlic juice into mix. Use liberal amounts.

Horseradish: Stinky stuff! Add as you would garlic. Best to use fresh root.

Hot pepper: Dilute Tabasco®, or any store-bought concentrate in water.

Hydrated lime: Saturate in water to form a fungicide.

Mint: Mint oil drives insects away. Dilute in water and several drops per pint.

Oil, vegetable: This is mainly fatty acids and glycerides. Mix with rubbing alcohol to emulsify in water. Great stuff!

Oregano: Grind up fresh herb and use as a repellent. Mix with water.

Soap: I like Ivory® or Castille® soap. Use as an insecticide and wetting agent. Mix with water.

Tobacco: Mix tobacco with hot water to extract the poisonous alkaloid. Do not boil. Dilute concentrate with water.

Cooking or heating preparations can destroy active ingredients. To draw out ingredients, mince plant and soak in mineral oil for a couple of days. Add this oil to the water including a little detergent or soap to emulsify (suspend) the oil droplets in water. Biodegradable detergents and soaps are good wetting/sticking agents for these preparations. Soap dissolves best if a teaspoon of alcohol is also added to each quart of mix.

Chrysanthemum, marigold and nasturtium blossoms; pennyroyal, garlic, chive, onion, hot pepper, insect juice (target insects mixed in a blender), horseradish, mints, oregano, tomato and tobacco residues all will repel many insects including aphids, caterpillars, mites and whiteflies.

Spray made from pests ground up in a blender and emulsified in water will reputedly repel related pests. Best used on large pests! Do not include insects mixed in a blender with other ingredients besides water. The insecticidal qualities in the dead bug parts will degrade quickly if combined with other things. Mixes that include tobacco may kill these pests if it is strong enough. These mixes can vary in proportions, but *always* filter the blended slurry before mixing with water for the final spray. Straining avoids clogging spray nozzles and plumbing.

Recipe 1. Mix three tablespoons each of isopropyl alcohol, lemon juice, garlic juice, horseradish juice, Ivory® liquid, and a few drops of Tabasco®, mint and cinnamon oil. Mix all of the ingredients in a small bowl into a slurry. Dilute the slurry at the rate of one teaspoon per pint of water and mix in a blender. Potent mix!

Recipe 2. Place one teaspoon of hot pepper or Tabasco® sauce and four cloves of garlic in a blender with a pint of water and liquefy. Strain through a nylon stocking or cheese cloth before using in the sprayer.

Recipe 3. A mix of one-eighth to one-quarter cup of hydrated lime combined with a quart of water makes an effective insect and mite spray. Mix a non-detergent soap with lime. The soap acts as both a sticking agent and insecticide. Lime can be phytotoxic to plants in large doses. Always try the spray on a test plant and wait a few days to check for adverse effects to the plant before applying to similar plants.

Recipe 4. Liquid laundry bleach (sodium hypochlorite) is a good fungicide for non-plant surfaces. Mix as a five or ten percent solution. It is an eye and skin irritant, so wear gloves and goggles when using it. Mix 1 part bleach to 9 parts water for a 5 percent solution. Mix 1 part bleach to four parts water for a 10 percent solution. Use this solution as a general disinfectant for garden room equipment, tools and plant wounds. The bleach solution breaks down rapidly and therefore has little if any residual effect.

Neem

Ingredients: Relatively new in the US, neem has been used for medicine and pest control for more than four centuries in India and Southeast Asia. Extracted from the Indian neem tree (*Azadirachta indica*) or the chinaberry tree (*Melia azedarach*). Neem is an antifeedant and disrupts insect life cycles. The trees are known as the "village pharmacy" because they supply cures for humans and animals as well as safely control for countless pests and fungi. Neem powder is made from leaves. The active ingredient, azadirachtin, confuses growth hormones and pests never mature into adults to produce more young. It is most effective against young insects, and is available in various concentrations.

Controls: Most effective against caterpillars and other immature insects, including larvae of whiteflies, fungus gnats, mealybugs and leafminers.

Caution! Neem is not as effective against spider mites as neem oil.

Mixing: Often mixed with vegetable (canola) oil. Mix just before using in water with a pH below 7 and use a spreader/sticker. Agitate constantly while using to keep emulsified. Throw out excess.

Application: Use as soil drench or add to nutrient solution. This allows neem to enter plant tissue and become systemic. Used as a spray, neem becomes a contact spray and an antifeedant when eaten by pest. Performs best in rooms with 60 percent plus humidity.

Persistence: Contact neem stays on foliage for up to a month or until it is washed off. Stays in plant system up to a month when absorbed via roots.

Forms: Emulsifiable concentrate.

Toxicity: Not toxic to honeybees, fish and earthworms. Not toxic to beneficial insects in normal concentrations that kill target insects.

Safety: Irritates eyes. Wear a mask and gloves.

Neem Oil

Ingredients: Purified extract from neem seeds. Buy only cold-pressed oil that is stronger and contains all the natural ingredients. Do not use heat-processed neem oil. Cold-pressed oil also contains azadirachtin, the active ingredient in neem. Brand names include: Neemguard®, Triact® and

Einstein Oil®. NOTE: Einstein Oil® is my favorite and works the best of all brands tested.

Controls: Effective against spider mites, fungus gnats and aphids. It is also a fungistat against powdery mildew and rust.

Note: Neem oil is very effective against spider mites.

Mixing: Mix just before using in water with a pH below 7 and use a spreader/sticker. Agitate constantly while using to keep emulsified. Throw out excess.

Application: Spray on foliage, especially under leaves where mites live. Apply every few days so hatching larvae will eat it immediately. Spray heavily, so mites have little choice but to eat it. Avoid spraying the last few days before harvest. Some gardeners report a foul taste when applied just before harvest.

Persistence: Contact neem stays on foliage for up to a month or until it is washed off. Stays in plant system up to a month when absorbed via roots.

Forms: Emulsifiable concentrate.

Toxicity: Toxicity to beneficial insects has been reported. Not toxic to humans.

Safety: Irritates eyes. Wear a mask and gloves.

Neem products have numerous other applications. For more information check out the Neem Foundation, http://www.neemfoundation.org and the Neem Association, http://hometown.aol.com/neemassoc, and www.einsteinoil.com, or the book *Neem: India's Miraculous Healing Plant,* by Ellen Norten, $9.95, ISBN: 0-89281-837-9.

Nicotine and Tobacco Sprays

Ingredients: Nicotine is a non-persistent pesticide derived from tobacco (*Nicotiana tabacum*). It is a stomach poison, contact poison and respiratory poison. This very poisonous compound affects the neuromuscular system, causing pests to go into convulsions and die. Nicotine sulfate is the most common form.

Caution! Do not swallow any of this vile poison, avoid skin contact. Do not use around nightshade family (eggplant, tomatoes, peppers and potatoes) because they may contract Tobacco Mosaic Virus (TMV) from exposure to tobacco-based substances.

Controls: Sucking and chewing insects.

Mixing: Use a spreader/sticker.

Application: Seldom phytotoxic when used as directed. Combine with insecticidal soap to increase killing ability.

Persistence: One week to ten days.

Forms: Liquid.

Toxicity: Although naturally derived, nicotine is very toxic to most insects including beneficials, honeybees, fish and humans if concentrate is ingested (or built-up over years to develop lung cancer and other cancers in humans).

Safety: Use a mask and gloves avoid skin and eye contact.

Oil, horticultural

Ingredients: Often underrated and overlooked as an insecticide and miticide, horticultural oil is very popular in greenhouses and regaining popularity among indoor gardeners. Similar to medicinal mineral oil, horticultural oils are made from animal (fish) oils, plant seed oils, and petroleum oils refined by removing most of the portion that is toxic to plants. Lighter weight oil (viscosity 60 – 70) is less phytotoxic. Vegetable oil is also horticultural oil.

Controls: Virtually invisible horticultural oil kills slow moving and immobile sucking insects, spider mites and their eggs by smothering and suffocation, as well as generally impairing their life cycles.

Caution! Do not use lubricating oil such as 3 in 1 or motor oil!!!

Mixing: Mix three quarters teaspoon of oil spray (no more than a 1 percent solution) per quart of water. More than a few drops could burn tender growing shoots.

Application: Spray foliage entirely, including undersides of leaf surfaces. Apply oil sprays up until two weeks before harvest. Repeat applications as needed, usually 3 applications, one every 5 to 10 days will put insects and mites in check. Lightweight oil residue evaporates into the air in a short time.

Persistence: Disappears in one to three days under normal growing conditions.

Forms: Liquid.

Toxicity: Safe non-poisonous and non-polluting insecticide. Can become phytotoxic if too heavy (viscosity) or applied too heavily or when temperatures are below 70 degrees F or very humid (this slows evaporation, increasing phytotoxicity).

Safety: Wear a mask and gloves.

Oil, vegetable

Ingredients: fatty acids and glycerides.

Controls: Lightweight vegetable oil kills slow moving and immobile sucking insects, spider mites and their eggs by smothering and suffocating, as well as generally interrupting their life cycles.

Caution! Vegetable oil does not kill as well as horticultural oil.

Mixing: Mix two drops of oil spray (no more than a 1 percent solution) per quart of water.

Application: Spray foliage entirely, including under leaf surfaces. Stop spraying two weeks before harvest.

Persistence: Several days.

Forms: Liquid.

Toxicity: Not toxic to mammals and fish.

Safety: Wear a mask and gloves.

Pyrethrum

Ingredients: Pyrethrum, the best-known botanical pesticide, is extracted from the flowers of the pyrethrum chrysanthemum (*Chrysanthemum coccineum* and *C. cinerariifolium*). Pyrethrins (pyrethrins, cinerins and jasmolins) are the active ingredients in natural pyrethrum and kill insects on contact. Pyrethrum is often combined with rotenone or ryania to ensure effectiveness. Aerosol forms contain synergists. See "Application" below.

Controls: A broad-spectrum contact pesticide, pyrethrum kills aphids, whiteflies, spider mites and insects, including beneficials. It is very effective to control flying insects, but they must receive a killing "knock down" dose, or they may revive and buzz off.

Caution! Do not mix with sulfur, lime, copper or soaps; the high pH of these substances renders it ineffective. Wash these substances off foliage with plain water (pH below 7) before applying pyrethrum.

Mixing: Mix in water with a pH below 7 and use a spreader/sticker.

Application: Spot spray infested plants. Aerosol sprays are most effective, especially on spider mites, but can burn foliage (spray is ice cold when it exits the nozzle) if applied closer than one foot. Aerosol sprays contain a synergist, piperonyl butoxide (PBO) or MGK 264, both toxic to people. Pyrethrum dissipates within a few hours in the presence of air and HID light and sunlight. Overcome this limitation by applying just before turning off the lights and turn off the circulation and vent fans for the night. One manufacturer, Whidmere, offers encapsulated pyrethrum in aerosol form called Exclude®. As the spray fogs out of the nozzle, a bubble forms around each droplet of pyrethrum mist. The outside coating keeps the pyrethrum intact and extends its life for several days. When a pest prances by, touching the bubble, it bursts, releasing the pyrethrum. Liquid and wettable pyrethrum applied with a pump-type sprayer is difficult to apply under leaves where spider mites live.

Persistence: Effective several hours after application when the lights are on; longer when applied after "lights out" and fan turned off.

Forms: Wettable powder, dust, liquid, granular bait and aerosol.

Toxicity: Not toxic to animals and humans when eaten, but becomes toxic to people when inhaled. It is toxic to fish and beneficials.

Safety: Wear a mask and protective clothing when applying sprays or breathing in any form of pyrethrum, especially aerosols. Aerosols contain toxic PBO and MGK 464, possible carcinogens, and are easy to inhale.

Synthetic Pyrethroids

Ingredients: Synthetic pyrethroids, such as permethrin and cypermethrin, act as broad-spectrum, non-selective contact insecticides and miticides. There are more than 30 synthetic pyrethroids available in different formulations. Deltamethrin is available as a sticky paint that is used as a trap when applied to stems and colored objects. Other pyrethroids include: allethrin, cyflutrin, fenpropathin, phenothrin, sumithrin, resmitherin and tefluthrin.

Controls: Aphids, whiteflies, thrips, beetles, cockroaches, caterpillars and spider mites. NOTE: Many insects and mites are resistant to pyrethroids.

 Caution! Non-selective pyrethroids kill all insects and mites including beneficials and bees.

Mixing: Follow directions on container.

Application: Follow directions on container. See "Application" under Pyrethrum above.

Persistence: Breaks down in one to three days. Newer pyrethroids such as Permethrin stay active the longest.

Forms: Powder, liquid, aerosol.

Toxicity: Toxic to all insects and bugs. It is somewhat toxic to mammals.

Safety: Wear a mask and protective clothing when applying sprays or breathing in any form of pyrethrum, especially aerosols. Aerosols contain toxic PBO and MGK 464, possible carcinogens, and are easy to inhale.

Quassia

Ingredients: Made from a subtropical South American tree (*Quassia amara*) and the tree-of-heaven (*Ailanthus altissima*).

Controls: Soft bodied insects including aphids, leaf miners and some caterpillars.

Mixing: Available in the form of bark, wood chips and shavings. Soak 6 ounces of chips per gallon of water for 24 hours, afterward boil for two hours. Add a phosphorus-based soap to increase effectiveness. Strain and cool before spraying.

Application: Spray on foliage until saturated.

Persistence: Two – five days on the surface of plants.

Forms: Bark, wood chips and shavings.

Toxicity: Safe for mammals and possibly beneficials.

Safety: Wear a mask and gloves.

Rotenone

Ingredients: An extract of roots of several plants including *Derris* species, *Lonchocarpus* species and *Tephrosia* species, this poison is a non-selective contact insecticide stomach poison and slow-acting nerve poison.

Controls: Non-selective control of beetles, caterpillars, flies, mosquitoes, thrips, weevils and beneficial insects, but death is slow. According to one source, target insects can consume up to 30 times their lethal dose before dying!

 Caution! Kills beneficials. *New evidence indicates rotenone may be toxic to people and may cause Parkinson's disease. Use only as a last resort!*

Mixing: Follow directions on the package.

Application: Follow directions on the package.

Persistence: Breaks down in three to ten days.

Forms: Powder, wettable powder, liquid.

Toxicity: To mammals is undetermined. Chronic exposure may cause Parkinson's disease. It is toxic to birds, fish and beneficials.

Safety: Wear a mask, gloves and cover exposed skin and hair. Avoid skin contact.

Ryania

Ingredients: This contact alkaloid stomach poison is made from stems and roots of the tropical shrub *Ryania speciosa.*

Controls: Toxic to aphids, thrips, European corn borers, flea beetles leaf rollers and many caterpillars. Once pests consume ryania, they stop feeding immediately and die within 24 hours.

Caution! Somewhat toxic to beneficials and mammals!

Mixing: Follow directions on package.

Application: Follow directions on package. Apply as dust.

Persistence: Two weeks or longer.

Forms: Powder, wettable powder.

Toxicity: Toxic to mammals, birds, fish and beneficials.

Safety: Wear a mask, gloves, safety glasses and cover exposed skin and hair. Avoid skin contact.

Sabadilla

Ingredients: This alkaloid pesticide is made from the seeds of a tropical lily, *Schoenocaulon officinale*, native to Central and South America, and a European hellebore (*Veratrum album*).

Controls: A contact and stomach poison, this centuries-old poison controls aphids, beetles, cabbage loopers, chinch bugs, grasshoppers and squash bugs.

Caution! Very toxic to honeybees and moderately toxic to mammals!

Mixing: Follow directions on package.

Application: Most potent when applied at 75 – 80 degrees F. Follow directions on package.

Persistence: Two or three days.

Forms: Powder, liquid.

Toxicity: Somewhat toxic to mammals, toxic to honeybees.

Safety: Wear a mask, gloves, safety goggles and cover exposed skin and hair. Avoid skin, eye, ear and nose contact. Irritates eyes and nose.

Seaweed

Ingredients: Numerous elements including nutrients, bacteria and hormones.

Controls: Suspended particles in seaweed impair and even kill insects and spider mites by causing lesions. The particles cut and penetrate the soft-bodied pest insects and mites causing their body fluids to leak out.

Mixing: Dilute as per instructions for soil application.

Application: Spray on foliage, especially under leaves where mites live.

Persistence: Up to two weeks when spreader/sticker is used.

Forms: Powder and liquid.

Toxicity: Not toxic to mammals, birds and fish. Non-selective, kills beneficials.

Safety: Wear a mask and gloves.

Soap, insecticidal

Ingredients: Mild contact insecticides made from fatty acids of animals and plants. A variety of soaps are available: phosphorus-salt based liquid concentrate. Soft soaps, such as Ivory® liquid dish soap, Castille® soap and Murphy's Oil® soap, are biodegradable and kill insects in a similar manner to commercial insecticidal soaps, but they are not as potent or effective.

Controls: Soft-bodied insects such as aphids, mealy insects, spider mites, thrips and whiteflies by penetrating and clogging body membranes.

Caution! Do not use detergent soaps because they may be caustic.

Mixing: Add a few capfuls of soap to a quart of water to make a spray. Ivory® or Castille® soap can also be used as a spreader-sticker to mix with other sprays. The soaps help the spray stick to the foliage better.

Application: Spray at the first appearance of insect pests. Follow directions on commercial preparations. Spray homemade mixes every 4 – 5 days.

Persistence: Soft soaps will last only for about a day before dissipating.

Forms: Liquid.

Toxicity: These soaps are safe for bees, animals and humans.

Safety: Wear a mask and gloves.

Sulfur

Ingredients: Sulfur. Mixed with lime, sulfur is more toxic to insects but more phytotoxic to plants.

Controls: Centuries old fungicide, effective against rusts and powdery mildew.

Caution! Do not apply in temperatures above 90 degrees F and less than 50 percent humidity, it will burn foliage.

Mixing: Follow directions on package.

Application: Apply in light concentration. It is phytotoxic, especially during hot (90 degrees F), arid weather.

Persistence: It stays on foliage until washed off.

Forms: Powder.

Toxicity: Not toxic to honeybees, birds and fish.

Safety: Wear a mask, gloves safety goggles and cover exposed skin and hair. Avoid skin, eye, ear and nose contact. Irritates eyes, lungs and skin.

Traps

Ingredients: Sticky traps, such as Tanglefoot™ resins, can be smeared on attractive yellow or red cards to simulate ripe fruit. When the pests land on the "fruit" they are stuck forever!

Controls: Contains spider mites and non-flying insects within the bounds of the barriers. Monitor fungus gnat populations and help control thrips. Other insects get stuck haphazardly to the sticky stuff.

Black light traps catch egg-laying moths and other flying insects, most of which are not plant pests. Light and fan traps attract many insects including beneficials and their use may do more harm than good.

Sex lure traps: Exude specific insect pheromones (sexual scents) of females that are ready to mate. These traps are most effective to monitor insect populations for large farms. Sex lure traps are extremely uncommon indoors.

 Warning: Do not touch sticky substance, it is difficult to remove!

Mixing: Follow directions on container. Smear on desired objects.

Application: Smear Tanglefoot™ around the edges of pots, base of stems and at the end of drying lines to form an impenetrable barrier/trap against mites and insects. This simple precaution helps keep mites isolated. However, resourceful spider mites can spin a line of silk and wind pitches can carry up the silk and the mite. The marauding mites ride the air currents created by fans from plant to plant!

Persistence: Until it is wiped off or completely fouled with insect bodies.

Forms: Sticky thick paint.

Toxicity: Not toxic to mammals or insects. Trapped insects and mites starve to death.

Safety: Wear gloves.

Water

Ingredients: A cold jet of water, preferably with a pH between 6 and 7, blasts insects, spider mites and their eggs off leaves and often kills them. Hot water vapor, steam, also works as a sterilant.

Controls: A cold jet of water is an excellent first wave of attack against spider mites, aphids and other sucking insects. Steam controls spider mites, insects and diseases on pots, growing medium, and other garden room surfaces.

Caution! Avoid spraying fully formed buds with water. Standing water in or on buds promotes gray mold. Do not apply hot steam to foliage.

Mixing: None.

Application: Spray leaf undersides with a jet of cold water to knock off sucking spider mites and aphids. Apply water as a mist or spray when predatory mites are resident. The extra humid conditions impair pest mite lifecycles and promote predatory mite health. Rent a wallpaper steamer. Get it cooking and direct a jet of steam at all garden room cracks and surfaces.

Persistence: None.

Forms: Liquid, steam vapor.

Toxicity: Not toxic to mammals, fish, beneficials.

Safety: Do not spray strong jet of water in eyes, up nose or into other body orifices.

Biological Controls

Predators and Parasites

Predator and parasite availability and supply has changed substantially over the last 10 years. Today many more predators and parasites are available to home gardeners than ever before. Shipping, care, cost and application of each predator or parasite is very specific and should be provided in detail by the supplier.

For more information about predators, check out the following web pages:

www.naturescontrol.com, www.koppert.nl/english, www.entomology.wisc.edu/mbcn/mbcn.html.

By definition, a predator must eat more than one victim before adulthood. Predators have chewing mouthparts, such as ladybugs (ladybird beetles), and praying mantises or piercing-sucking mouthparts, such as lacewing larvae. Chewing predators eat their prey whole while the piercing-sucking type suck the fluids from their prey's body.

Parasites consume a single individual host before adulthood. Adult parasitoids typically place single eggs into many hosts. The eggs hatch into larvae that eat the host insect from the inside out. They save the vital organs for dessert! Most often, the larvae pupate inside the host's body and emerge as adults.

Parasites, unlike predators, hunt until the prey is almost eliminated. Predators choose to be surrounded by prey. When prey population starts to diminish a little, predators move on to find a nice fat infestation. They never truly eradicate the pests. This is why predators are best for preventative control and are slow to stop an infestation.

The rate at which the predators and parasites keep the infestation in check is directly proportionate to the amount of predators. The more predators and parasites, the sooner they will get infestations into check. Predators and parasites out-breed their victims, reproducing faster than pests are able to keep up.

One of the best places in the country to buy predatory and parasitoid insects is from Natures Control, Medford, OR. Check out their very informative web site at www.naturescontrol.com. This supplier gives advice and supplies specific care and release instructions. Natures Control has a good predator and parasite supply and can ship year round. Predators and parasites are shipped special delivery and may arrive after the daily mail delivery. Make sure to pick them up as soon as they arrive. Do not let predators sit inside a mailbox in the hot sun. It could easily reach 120 degrees or more!

When predators and parasites are introduced into a garden, there must be special precautions taken to ensure their well-being. Stop spraying all toxic chemicals at least two weeks before introducing the predators. Pyrethrum and insecticidal soaps can be applied up to a few days before, providing any residue is washed off with fresh water. Do not spray after releasing predators and parasites.

Predators and parasites survive best in gardens that are not sterilized between plantings. Gardens with perpetual harvests are ideal for predators.

Most of the predators and parasites that do well in an indoor HID garden cannot fly. Insects that can fly often head straight for the lamp. Ladybugs are the best example. If 500 ladybugs are released on Monday, by Friday, only a few die-hards would be left. The rest would have popped off the lamp. If using flying predators or parasitoids, release when it is dark. They will live longer.

Predators are most often very small and must be introduced to each plant separately. Introducing predators to a garden and plants takes a little time and patience. Predators also have very specific climatic requirements. Pay attention to the predators needs and maintain them for best results.

Super Size Secret: Seclude the garden room. Screen off all entrances and exits. Nylon stockings make good inexpensive screening.

Spider Mites and Insects

Spider Mites
Identify: The spider mite is the most common pest found on indoor plants and causes the most problems. Spider mites have eight legs and are classified as spiders rather than insects, which have six legs. Find microscopic spider mites on leaf undersides, sucking away life-giving fluids. To an untrained naked eye, they are hard to spot; spider mites appear as tiny specks on leaf undersides. However, their telltale signs of feeding, yellowish-white spots (stippling) on the tops of leaves are easy to see. Careful inspection reveals tiny spider webs (easily seen when misted with water) on stems and under leaves as infestations progress. A magnifying glass or low-power microscope (10 – 30X) helps to identify the yellow, white, two spotted, brown, or red mites and their translucent eggs. Indoors the most common is the two-spotted spider mite. After a single mating, females are fertilized for life and reproduce about 75 percent female and 25 percent male eggs. Females lay about 100 eggs.

Damage: Mites, suck life-giving sap from plants, causing overall vigor loss and stunting. Leaves are pocked with suck hole marks and yellow from failure to produce chlorophyll. They lose partial to full function. Leaves yellow and drop. Once a plant is overrun with spider mites, the infestation progresses rapidly. Severe cases cause plant death.

Control: Cleanliness! This is the most important first step to spider mite control. Keep the garden room and tools spotless and disinfected. Mother plants often have spider mites. Spray mothers regularly with miticides, including once three days before taking cuttings. Once mite infestations get out of control and miticides work poorly, the entire garden room will have to be cleaned out and disinfected with a pesticide and 5 percent bleach solution. Steam disinfection is also possible, but it is too difficult in most situations.

Cultural and physical: Spider mites thrive in a dry, 70 – 80 degrees F, climate and reproduce every five days in temperatures above 80 degrees. Create a hostile environment by lowering the temperature to 60 degrees and spray foliage, especially under leaves, with a jet of cold water. Spraying literally blasts them off the leaves, as well as increases humidity. Their reproductive cycle will be slowed, and you will have a chance to kill them before they do much damage. Manual removal works for small populations. Smash all mites in sight between the thumb and index finger, or wash leaves individually with two sponges. Make sure to not infect other plants with contaminated hands or sponges.

Prune leaves with more than 50 percent damage, remove and throw away, making sure insects and eggs do not reenter the garden. If mites have attacked only one or two plants, isolate the infected plants and treat them separately. Take care when removing foliage, not to spread mites to other plants. Severely damaged plants should be carefully removed from the garden and destroyed.

Smear a layer of Tanglefoot™ around the lips of containers and at the base of stems to create barriers spider mites cannot cross. This will help isolate them to specific plants. Note: smear a layer of Tanglefoot™ at each end of drying lines, if drying flowers to contain spider mites. Once foliage is dead, mites try to migrate down drying lines to find live foliage with fresh flowing sap.

Biological: *Neoseiulus (Amblyseius) californicus* and *Mesoseiulus* (*phytoseiulus*) *longipes,* are the two most common and effective predators. *Phytoseiulus persimilis, Neoseiulus (Amblyseius) fallacius, Galendromus (Metaseiulus) occidentalis, Galendromus* (*Typhlodromus*) *pyri* predators are also available commercially.

When properly applied and reared, predatory spider mites work very well. However, if using them in a 12/12 day/night photoperiod, mites may go dormant and become useless. There are many things to consider when using the predators. First, predators can eat only a limited number of mites a day. The average predator can eat 20 eggs or 5 adults daily. As soon as the predator's source of food is gone, some mites die of starvation, others survive on other insects or pollen. Check with suppliers for release instructions of specific species. A general dosage of 20 predators per plant is a good place to start. Predatory mites have a difficult time traveling from plant to plant, so setting them out on each plant is necessary. Temperature and humidity levels are important to control so predators thrive. Both must be at the proper level to give the predators the best possible chance. When spider mites have infested a garden, the predatory mites cannot eat them fast enough to solve the problem. Predatory mites work best when there are only a few spider mites. Introduce predators as soon as spider mites are seen on vegetative growth, and release them every month thereafter. This gives predators a chance to keep up with mites. Before releasing predators, rinse all plants thoroughly to ensure all toxic spray residues from insecticides and fungicides are gone.

The fungus, *Hirsutella thompsonii* (trade name Mycar®) kills spider mites.

Sprays: Homemade sprays often lack the strength to kill infestations, but work as a deterrent, repelling mites. Popular homemade sprays include: Dr. Bronner's soap, garlic, hot pepper, citrus oil and liquid seaweed combinations. If these sprays do not deter spider mites after 4 – 5 applications, switch to a stronger spray such as Neem oil, pyrethrum, horticultural oil, or nicotine sulfate and cinnamaldehyde.

Insecticidal soap does a fair job of controlling mites. Usually two or three applications at 5 – 10 day intervals will do the trick.

Horticultural oil smothers eggs and can be mixed with pyrethrum and homemade sprays to improve extermination.

Spider Mites

Spider mites are easy to see
with a 30x to 50x magnifying glass.
Look for them on leaf undersides.

Wage biological warfare by
releasing predators.
Here a spider mite predator
is attacking and eating a
spider mite.

Spider mite predators are
difficult to distinguish from
the bad spider mites.

Enlarged drawing below
is of a spider mite
showing eight legs
and its translucent eggs.

Whiteflies Thrips & Mealybugs

Photos courtesy
Albuquerque Hydroponics,
Albuquerque, NM

Thrips do progressively more damage to leaf.

Thrip damaged leaf tip.

Swarms of whiteflies congregate on leaf undersides. They flutter away when disturbed.

Mealybugs can infest a stem relatively discretely. Before you know it, a colony can take over branch unions.

Photos courtesy
Nature's Control
www.naturescontrol.com

Left: Thrip and thrip nymph.

Whitefly parasites, *Encarsia formosa*, lay an egg inside whitefly pupae. The egg hatches out; the *Encarsia formosa* eats the whitefly from the inside out.

Thrip nymphs blend into the foliage.

Aphids

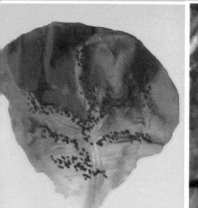

Aphid eggs on lettuce leaf above. Aphids can fill lettuce leaves virtually overnight.

ABOVE: Greatly magnified aphids rasp foliage and suck life-giving plant juices.

BELOW: This aphid parasite, *Aphidoletes matricariae*, lays its eggs inside aphids.

Seemingly slow-moving aphid predator *Aphidoletes aphidimyza*, hatches from its cocoon into a voracious aphid-eating machine.

Green lacewing adults lay eggs that turn into alligator-like larvae with ravenous appetites for aphids and a host of other insects.

Green lacewing larvae, *Chrysopa rufilabris*, patrol foliage for aphids and other prey.

Beneficial Insects

Ladybugs, *Hippodamia convergens,* is one of the most well-known beneficials. Indoors they are attracted to the light and burn out prematurely.

Pirate bugs, *Orius insidiosis,* are relentless spider mite, thrip and whitefly predators.

Parasitic *thrichogama* (species) wasps lay their eggs in more than 200 species of caterpillars

Mealybug predator, *Cryptolaemus montrouzieri,* look like tiny black ladybugs.

The praying mantis, *Tenodera sinensis,* eat any and all insects that cross its path!

This fly parasite, *Aphidoletes matricariae,* is emerging from its leathery shell.

Photos courtesy
Nature's Control
www.naturescontrol.com

Diseases of the Cucumber

Anthracnose on leaves appears as small spots that quickly enlarge and darken. The yellowish margin often grows and merges with others. Stems start to mold and darken. REMEDY: Remove and destroy affected foliage. Dust with sulfur. PREVENTION: Always use sterile growing medium. Good ventilation.

Basal stem rot attacks just above the soil line. Leaves wilt and eventually plants die. REMEDY: Dust with sulfur if damage is not terminal. Mulch with coco peat. remove and destroy severely affected growing medium and foliage. PREVENTION: Do not apply excessive water on or near the base of the stem.

Blotch is similar to Anthracnose, but spots are smaller and the disease doesn't spread to the stem. REMEDY: Destroy affected foliage and severely affected plants. PREVENTION: Use only sterile growing medium.

Cucumber Mosaic Virus, a widespread and serious disease, causes yellow and dark green blotches on leaves. Leaf surface wrinkles and distorts. Plants crumple when virus is advanced. REMEDY: None. Remove and destroy plant. Wash tools and hands. PREVENTION: Control vectors.

Powdery mildew covers foliage with dusty white mold. Promoted by dry soil and humid air. REMEDY: Spray with fungicide or baking soda. PREVENTION: Maintain moist soil and keep humidity low.

Stem rot causes a yellow circle that turns brown. Stems and fruit are also affected. REMEDY: Destroy all diseased plants. Do not wet foliage. PREVENTION: Use sterile growing medium.

Sun/HID burn causes brown papery foliage. Triggered by excessive heat from lamp or sunlight. REMEDY: None. PREVENTION: Move light further away. Shade foliage from hot sunlight.

Diseases and Pests

Verticillium Wilt first causes lower leaves to yellow then progresses up plant. Leaves later become dry and wilt. REMEDY: Maintain high humidity and warm temperatures. PREVENTION: Use only sterile growing medium.

Bolting makes the plant "run to seed." Caused by restraining fast growth. Sloppy transplanting, overcrowding and dry soil are common causes. REMEDY: None.

No Hearts are often caused by lack of nutrients, but can also be caused by lack of light, insect infestations, crowding and lack of water.

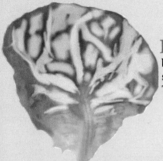

Downy Mildew causes older leaves to yellow between veins and whitish mold to form on leaf undersides. REMEDY: Remove affected foliage. PREVENTION: Good ventilation and do not over-water.

Slugs and Snails love lettuce, especially when young and tender. Look for tell-tale slime trails. REMEDY: Handpick or control with slug/snail bait. PREVENTION: Keep garden clean.

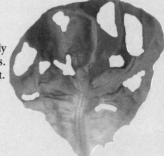

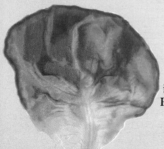

Tip Burn is most commonly caused by sudden increase in growroom temperatures. REMEDY: None. PREVENTION: lower grow room temperature.

aphids.

Damage: Aphids suck the life-giving sap from foliage causing leaves to wilt and yellow. When infestation mounts, you may notice sticky honeydew excreted by aphids. They prefer to attack weak, stressed plants. Some species prefer succulent new growth, and other aphids like older foliage or even flower buds. Look for them under leaves, huddled around branch nodes and growing tips. This pest transports (vectors) bacteria, fungi and viruses. Aphids vector more viruses than any other source. Destructive, sooty mold also grows on honeydew. Any aphid control must also control ants, if they are present.

Control: Manually remove small numbers. Spot spray small infestations. Control ants. Introduce predators if problem is persistent.

Cultural and physical: Manual removal is easy and works well to kill them. When affixed to foliage, sucking out fluid, aphids are unable to move and easy to crush with fingers or sponges dipped in an insecticidal solution.

Biological: Lacewings (*chrysoperla* species) are the most effective available predators for aphids. Release 1 to 20 lacewings per plant, depending on infestation level, as soon as aphids appear. Repeat every month. Eggs take a few days to hatch into larvae that exterminate aphids. *Aphidoletes aphidimyza* (gall-midge) is available under the trade name, Aphidend. *Aphidius matricariae,* (parasitic wasp) available commercially as Aphidpar.

Ladybugs also work well to exterminate aphids. Adults are easily obtained at many retail nurseries during the summer months. The only drawback to ladybugs is their attraction to the HID lamp. Release about 50 ladybugs per plant. At least half of them will fly directly into the HID, hit the hot bulb and buzz to their death. Within 1 or 2 weeks all the ladybugs will fall victim to the lamp, requiring frequent replenishment.

Verticillium lecanii (fungus) available under the trade name of Vertalec® is very aphid specific and effective.

Control ants by mixing borax hand soap or borax powder with powdered sugar. Ants eat the sweet mix and borax kills them. They excrete sweet borax mix in the nest, which other ants eat and die.

Sprays: Homemade and insecticidal soap sprays are very effective. Apply 2 or 3 times at 5 – 10 day intervals. Pyrethrum (aerosol) applied 2 – 3 times at 5 – 10 day intervals.

Bees and Wasps

Identify: Bees and wasps that sting are usually from a half inch to more than an inch long. Most have yellow stripes around their bodies, others have none. They are attracted to the garden indoors, especially when the weather cools outdoors, and they move inside.

Damage: They cause no damage to plants but can become a nuisance in garden rooms and hurt when they sting.

Control: Occasionally a problem indoors, bees and wasps are most efficiently controlled with sprays.

Cultural and physical: They enter garden rooms through vents and cracks – attracted by the growing plants – a valuable commodity in the middle of a cold winter! Screen all entrances to the room. Install more circulation fans to make flying difficult. Wasp traps, sweet flypaper and Tanglefoot™ also impair these pests. These pests are also attracted to the hot HID, fly into it and die.

Biological: Unnecessary.

Sprays: Pyrethrum is recommended. Stuff small nests into a wide-mouthed jar (do it at night when the wasps are quiet) and place the jar in a freezer for a few hours. Use Sevin (Carbaryl) only if there is a problem with a wasp nest.

Warning! Do not smash wasps like yellow jackets. Their crushed body releases a "death pheromone" that brings others from thousands of feet away, and the new arrivals are mad as hell!

Beetle Borers

Identify: Larvae from several boring beetles tunnel or bore into stems and roots. Look for their entry hole and dead growth on either side of the entry hole along the main stem, often accompanied by sawdust and discoloration. Borers are more common outdoors than indoors.

Damage: Tunnels inside the stem and roots curtail fluid flow, causing plant parts to wilt. If borer damages the main stem severely, fluid flow to the entire plant could stop, causing death.

Control: Seldom a problem indoors, borers often cause so much damage on a particular stem that it has to be removed and destroyed.

Cultural and physical: Handpick all beetle grubs.

Biological: Several mixes of beneficial nematodes control these borers in soil.

Sprays: *Bacillus popilliae* is specific to beetles or rotenone individually injected into stems.

Caterpillars and Loopers

Identify: From a half inch to four inches long, caterpillars and loopers are cylindrical with feet, often green, but can be virtually any color from white to black. Caterpillars have sets of feet the entire length of the body, while loopers have two sets of feet at either end of the body. Loopers place their front feet forward, arch their body upward in the middle, and pull their rear sets of legs forward. Some have stripes and spots and other designs that provide camouflage. Seldom a problem indoors, caterpillars and loopers are in a life stage between a larva and a flying moth or butterfly and are most common when prevalent outdoors. One way to check for caterpillars and loopers is to spray one plant with pyrethrum aerosol spray and shake it. The spray has a quick knockout effect and most caterpillars will fall from the plant.

Damage: These munching critters chew and eat pieces of foliage and leave tale-tell bites in leaves. Some caterpillars will roll themselves inside leaves. An infestation of caterpillars or leafhoppers will damage foliage, slow growth, eventually defoliate plants, stunt and kill a plant.

Control: Can become a problem indoors, especially on tomatoes.

Cultural and physical: Manually remove.

Biological: *Trichogramma* wasps, spined soldier bug (*Podisus maculiventris*) Podibug®.

Sprays: Homemade spray (repellent, hot pepper, garlic), *Bt*, pyrethrum and rotenone are recommended.

Leafhoppers

Identify: Leafhoppers include many small, one-eighth inch long, wedge-shaped insects that are usually green, white or yellow. Many species have minute stripes on wings and bodies. Their wings peak like roof rafters when not in use.
Leafhoppers suck plant sap for food and exude sticky honeydew as a by-product. Spittlebug (leafhopper) larvae, wrap themselves in foliage and envelop themselves in a saliva-like liquid (plant sap).

Damage: Stippling (spotting) similar to that caused by spider mites and thrips on foliage. Leaves and plants loose vigor, and in severe cases, death could result.

Control: Occasionally a problem indoors on tomatoes.

Cultural and physical: Cleanliness! Black light traps are attractive to potato beetles.

Biological: The fungus (*Metarhizium anisopliae*) is commercially available under the trade name, Metaquino®.

Sprays: Pyrethrum, rotenone, sabadilla.

Leafminers

Identify: Adult leafminer flies lay eggs that hatch into one-eighth inch long green or black maggots. You seldom see the maggots before you see the leaf damage they create when they tunnel through leaf tissue. Leafminers are more common in greenhouses and outdoors than indoors.

Damage: The tiny maggots burrow between leaf surfaces, leaving a tell-tale whitish tunnel outline. The damage usually occurs on or in young supple growth. It is seldom fatal, unless left unchecked. Damage causes plant growth to slow, and if left unchecked, flowering is prolonged and buds are small. In rare cases damage is fatal. Wound damage encourages disease.

Control: These pests cause little problem to indoor plants. The most efficient and effective control is to remove and dispose of damaged foliage, which includes the rogue maggot. Or use the cultural and physical control listed below.

Cultural and physical: Smash the little maggot trapped within the leaf with your fingers. If the infestation is severe, smash all larvae possible and remove severely infested leaves. Compost or burn infested leaves. Install yellow sticky traps to capture adults.

Biological: Branchid Wasp (*Dacnusa sibirica*), chalcid wasp (*Diglyphus isaea*), parasitic wasp (*Opius pallipes*).

Sprays: Repel with neem oil and pyrethrum sprays. Maggots are protected within tunnels and sprays are often ineffective. Water plants with a 0.4 percent solution of neem. This solution works fast and stays on plants for about four weeks after application.

Fungus Gnats

Identify: Maggots (larvae) grow to 4-5 mm long and have translucent bodies with black heads. Winged adult gnats are gray to black, 2-4 mm long, with long legs. Look for them around the base of plants in soil and soilless gardens. They love the moist dank environments in rockwool and the environment created in NFT-type hydroponic gardens. Adult females lay about 200 eggs every week to 10 days.

Damage: Infest growing medium and roots near the surface. They eat fine root hairs and scar larger roots, causing plants to loose vigor and foliage pales. Root wounds invite wilt fungi like *Fusarium* or *Pythium*, especially if plants are nutrient-stressed and growing in soggy conditions. Maggots prefer to consume dead or decaying soggy plant material; they also eat green algae growing in soggy conditions. Adults and larvae can get out of control quickly, especially in hydroponic systems with very moist growing mediums.

Control: The easiest way to control these pests is with *Bacillus thuringiensis* var. *israelensis* (*Bt-i*), sold under the trade names Vectobac®, Gnatrol® and Bactimos®. This strain of *Bt* controls the maggots. Unfortunately, it is available only in large one-gallon containers, and difficult to find at garden centers. Check hydroponic stores.

Cultural and physical: Do not over-water and keep ambient humidity low. Do not let growing medium remain soggy. Cover growing medium so green algae won't grow. Yellow sticky traps placed horizontally 1 – 2 inches over growing medium catches adults.

Biological: The aforementioned, *Bti* works best. Alternatives include the predatory soil mite (*Hypoaspis* (Geolaelaps) *miles*) and the nematode (*Steinernema feltiae*).

Sprays: Apply neem or insecticidal soap as a soil drench.

Mealybugs and Scales
Mealybugs

Identify: Somewhat common indoors, these 2 – 7 millimeter, oblong, waxy-white insects move very little, mature slowly and live in colonies that are usually located at stem joints. Like aphids, mealy bugs excrete sticky honeydew.

Scales: Identify: As uncommon indoors as mealy bugs, scale looks and acts similar to mealy bugs, but is usually more round than oblong. Scales may be white, yellow, brown, gray or black. Their hard protective shell is 2 – 4 millimeters across. Mealybugs rarely or never move. Check for them around stem joints, where they live in colonies. Scales sometimes excrete sticky honeydew.

Damage: These pests suck sap from plants, which causes growth to slow. They also exude sticky honeydew as a by-product of their diet of plant sap that encourages sooty mold and draws ants that eat the honeydew.

Control: These pests present little problem to indoor gardeners. The easiest and most efficient control is listed under "Cultural and physical" below. Biological controls are seldom necessary.

Cultural and physical: Manual removal is somewhat tedious, but very effective. Wet a Q-Tip in rubbing alcohol and wash mealybugs or scale away. A small knife, fingernails or tweezers may also be necessary to scrape and pluck the tightly affixed mealybugs and scales after they are Q-Tipped with alcohol.

Biological: There are numerous species of mealybugs and scales. Each has natural predators, including species of ladybeetles (ladybugs), parasitic and predatory wasps. There are so many species of each that it would be exhaustive to list them here.

Sprays: Homemade sprays that contain rubbing alcohol, nicotine, and soaps all kill these pests. Insecticidal soap, pyrethrum and neem oil are all recommended.

Nematodes

Identify: Of the hundreds and thousands of species of microscopic nematodes (sometimes big ones are called eelworms) a few are destructive to plants. Most often nematodes attack roots and are found in the soil. However, a few nematodes attack stems and foliage. Root nematodes can be seen in and around roots with the help of a 30x microscope. Often gardeners just diagnose the damage caused by destructive nematodes rather than actually seeing them.

Damage: Slow growth, leaf chlorosis, wilting several hours during daylight hours from lack of fluid flow. Symptoms can be difficult to discern from nitrogen deficiency. Root damage is often severe by the time they are examined. Root knot nematodes are one of the worst. They cause roots to swell with galls. Other nematodes scrape and cut roots, which is compounded by fungal attacks. Roots turn soft and mushy.

Control: Seldom a problem if using sterilized or clean new soil.

Cultural and physical: Cleanliness! Use new sterilized potting soil or soilless mix to exclude nematodes entrance. Nematodes rarely cause problems indoors, in clean garden rooms.

Biological: French marigolds (*Tagetes patula*) repel soil nematodes, fungus (*Myrothecium verrucaria*, trade name DeTera ES®)

Sprays: Neem used as a soil drench.

Thrips

Identify: More common in greenhouses than indoors, these tiny, winged, fast moving little critters are hard to see, but not hard to spot. From 1 – 1.5 millimeters long, thrips can be different colors, including white, gray and dark colors, often with petite stripes. Check for them under leaves by shaking parts of the plant. If there are many thrips present, they choose to jump and run rather than fly to safety. But often you will see them as a herd of specks thundering across foliage. Females make holes in soft plant tissue where they deposit eggs that are virtually invisible to the naked eye. Winged thrips migrate from infested plants to the entire garden easily.

Damage: Thrips scrape tissue from leaves and buds, afterward sucking out the plant juices for food. Stipples, whitish/yellowish specks, appear on top of leaves. Chlorophyll production diminishes and leaves become brittle. You will also see black specks of thrip feces and little thrips. Many times thrips feed inside flower buds or wrap up and distort leaves.

Control: Thrips are generally easy to control with cultural and physical means before they become established.

Cultural and physical: Cleanliness! Blue or pink sticky traps,

misting plants with water impairs travel. Manual removal works
OK if only a few thrips are present, but they are hard to catch.
Thrips can be very vexing to control once they get established.

Biological: Predatory mites (*Amblyseius cucumeris* and
*Amblyseius barkeri, Neoseiulus cucumeris, Iphiseius degenerans,
Neoseiulus barkeri, Euseius hibisci*), parasitic wasps (*Thripobis semi-
luteus, Ceranisus menes, Goetheana shakespearei*). Pirate bugs (*Orius*
species). The fungus *Verticillium lecanii* is effective.

Sprays: Homemade sprays (tobacco/nicotine base),
pyrethrum, synthetic pyrethrum, insecticidal soap. Apply 2 – 4
times at 5 – 10 day intervals. Apply at 5 – 10 day intervals.

Whiteflies

Identify: The easiest way to check for the little buggers is to
grab a limb and shake it. If there are any whiteflies, they will
fly from under leaves. Whiteflies look like a small, white moth
about one millimeter long. Adult whiteflies have wings. They
usually appear near the top of the weakest plant first. They will
move downward on the plant or fly off to infest another plant.
Eggs are also found on leaf underside where they are connected with a small hook.

Damage: Whiteflies, like mites, may cause white speckles
(stipples) on the tops of leaves. Loss of chlorophyll production
and plant vigor diminishes as infestation progresses.

Control: Whiteflies are difficult to remove manually, they fly.
Adults are attracted to the color yellow. To build a whitefly
trap similar to flypaper, cover a bright-yellow object with a
sticky substance like Tanglefoot™. Place the traps on the tops
of the pots among the plants. Traps work very well. When
they are full of insects, toss them out.

Biological: The wasp *Encarisa formosa* is the most effective
whitefly parasite. The small wasps only attack whiteflies, they
do not sting people! All toxic sprays must be washed completely off before introducing parasites and predators. Since the
Encarsia formosa is a parasite, about one-eighth inch long smaller than the white fly, it takes them much longer to control or
even keep the whitefly population in check. The parasitic wasp
lays an egg in the whitefly larva, which hatches and eats the
larva alive from the inside out. Death is slow. If you use them,
set them out at the rate of 2 or more parasites per plant as
soon as the first whitefly is detected. Repeat every two to four

weeks throughout the life of the plants.

The fungus *Verticillium lecanii* (AKA *Cephalosporium lecanii*), trade name Mycatal®, is also very effective in whitefly control.

Sprays: easily eradicated with natural sprays. Before spraying, remove any leaves that have been more than 50 percent damaged and cure with heat or burn infested foliage. Homemade sprays applied at 5 – 10 day intervals work well. Insecticidal soap applied at 5 – 10 day intervals. Pyrethrum (aerosol) applied at 5 – 10 day intervals does it.

Fungi and Diseases

Fungi are very primitive plants and do not produce chlorophyll, the substance that gives higher plants their green color. Fungi reproduce by spreading tiny microscopic spores rather than seeds. Countless fungal spores are present in the air at all times. When these microscopic airborne spores find the proper conditions, they will settle, take hold and start growing. Some fungi, such as bud-rotting gray mold (*Botrytis*), are so prolific that they can spread through an entire garden room in a matter of days! If your garden room is located near a swamp, *Botrytis* spores are omnipresent in the environment. In such an environment, plants contract gray mold quickly and are often reduced to a wisp of powdery foliage in short order. Too often, the easiest solution is to move to an area far away from swamps. Unsterile, soggy soil, coupled with humid stagnant air, provides the environment most fungi need to thrive. Although there are many different types of fungi, they are usually prevented with similar methods.

 Rule of Thumb: *To control a fungus, it should be identified so that a specific fungicide can be applied.*

Prevention

Prevention is the first step and the true key to fungus control. The section, "Setting up the Garden Room," instructs gardeners to remove anything – cloth curtains, clothes and other debris – that might attract, harbor and spread fungi. Cover carpet with white Visqueen® plastic. If mold should surface on the walls, spray with fungicide; wash walls with a 5 percent bleach solution, Pinesol® (made from natural pine oil) and apply paint that contains a fungus-inhibiting agent. Specially designed paints for damp conditions contain a fungicide and are attracted to moisture. When applied to a damp cracked basement wall, the paint is drawn into the moist crack. Remove all mold from the walls and wash with bleach solution before painting with fungus-resistant paint.

Cleanliness and climate control are the keys to preventing fungi. Few clean, well-ventilated garden rooms have problems with fungi. In contrast, every dingy, dank, ill-kept indoor garden will have fungal problems and yield substandard flowers and vegetables.

Install a vent fan(s) large enough to remove moist air quickly and keep humidity at 50 percent or less. A vent fan is the easiest and least expensive humidity control device available. Gas CO_2 generators produce humidity-increasing water vapor as a by-product. Dehumidifiers are relatively inexpensive, readily available at discount stores and do a good job of keeping humidity under control in enclosed garden rooms. Dehumidifiers draw extra electricity and the condensed water must be removed daily. Wood, coal and electric heat all dry and dehumidify the air. Most air conditioners can be set to a specific humidity level. If the garden room(s) have a central heating/air conditioning vent, the vent can be opened to control temperature and lower humidity. Aiming an oscillating table fan at an HID lamp a few feet away will dissipate its heat and lower humidity in the entire room.

Control

Prevent fungi by controlling all the factors contributing to its growth – remove hiding places, keep room clean, lower humidity to 50 percent and keep the air well circulated. If prevention proves inadequate and fungi appear, advanced control measures are necessary. Carefully remove and destroy dead leaves. Wash your hands after handling diseased foliage. If the problem attacks one or a few plants, isolate and treat them separately. Remember, fungi can spread like wildfire, if the conditions are right. If they get a good start, even after all preventative measures are taken, do not hesitate to take extreme control methods including spraying the entire garden with the proper fungicide.

Logical Progression of Fungus Control

Prevention:
a) cleanliness
b) low humidity
c) ventilation

Removal

Copper, lime sulfur sprays

Specific fungicide

Gray Mold *(Botrytis)*

Identify: The most common fungus that attacks indoor plants, gray mold flourishes in moist temperate climates common to many garden rooms. Botrytis damage is compounded by humid (above 50 percent) climates. Starting within flowers and difficult to see at the onset. Grayish-, whitish to bluish-green in color, Botrytis appears hair-like, similar to laundry lint, in moist climates. As the disease progresses foliage turns somewhat slimy. Damage can also appear as dark-brownish spots on flowers in less humid environments. Dry to the touch, Botrytis' affected area often crumbles if rubbed. Gray mold attacks countless other crops and airborne spores are present virtually everywhere. While most commonly found attacking dense, swelling flower buds, it also attacks stems, leaves, seeds, causes damping-off and decomposes dry stored produce. Also transmitted via seeds.

Damage: Flower buds are quickly reduced to slime in cool humid conditions or powder in warm dry rooms. Botrytis can destroy an entire garden in 7 – 10 days if left unchecked. Stem damage, where Botrytis starts on stems and not flower buds, is less common indoors. First, stems turn yellow, and cankerous growths develop. The damage causes growth above wound to wilt and can cause stems to fold over. Transported by air, contaminated hands, and tools, gray mold spreads very quickly indoors, infecting an entire garden room in less than a week when conditions are right.

Control: Minimize Botrytis attack incidence with low humidity (50 percent or less), and ample air circulation and ventilation. Grow plants that do not produce heavy, tightly packed flowers, and which provide a perfect place for this fungus to flourish. Cool (below 70 degrees) moist climates with humidity above 50 percent are perfect for rampant gray mold growth. Remove dead leaf stems (petioles) from stalks when removing damaged leaves to avoid Botrytis outbreaks, often harbored on dead rotting foliage. Increase ventilation and keep the garden room clean! Use fresh sterile growing medium when planting.

Cultural and physical: As soon as Botrytis symptoms appear, use alcohol-sterilized pruners to remove Botrytis-infected buds at least one inch below the infected area. Some gardeners amputate 2 – 4 inches below damage to ensure removal. Do not let the bud or anything that touched it contaminate other flowers and foliage. Remove from the garden and destroy. Wash your hands and tools after removing. Increase temperature to 80 degrees and lower humidity to below 50 percent. Excessive nitrogen and phosphorus levels make foliage tender so Botrytis can get a foothold. Make sure pH is around 6 to facilitate calcium uptake. Low light levels also encourage weak growth and gray mold attack. Avoid heavy crowding of plants and keep the light levels bright. Botrytis needs UV light to complete its life cycle. Without UV light it cannot live. Some plant varieties seldom fall victim to gray mold.

Biological: Spray plants with Gliocladium roseum and Trichoderma species. Prevent damping-off with a soil application of Gliocladium and Trichoderma species. You could also experiment with the yeasts Pichia guilliermondii and Candida oleophila or the bacterium Pseudomonas syringae.

Sprays: Bordeaux mixture keeps early stages of Botrytis in check as long as it is present on the foliage. But spraying buds near harvest time is not advised. Seeds are protected from Botrytis with a coating of Captan.

Damping-off

Identify: This fungal condition, sometimes called *Pythium* wilt, is often found in soil and growing mediums. It prevents newly sprouted seeds from emerging, attacks seedlings, causing them to rot at the soil line, yellows foliage and rots older plants at soil line, and occasionally attacks rooting cuttings at the soil line. It is caused by different fungal species, including *Botrytis*, *Pythium* and *Fusarium*. Once initiated, damping off is fatal. At the onset of damping-off, the stem looses girth at the soil line, weakens, then grows dark and finally fluid circulation is cut, killing the seedling or cutting.

Control: Damping-off is caused by a combination of the following: (1) fungi already present in an unsterile rooting medium, (2) over-watering, maintaining soggy growing medium (3) excessive humidity. The disease can be avoided by controlling soil moisture. Over-watering is the biggest cause of damping-off and the key to prevention. Careful daily scrutiny of soil will ensure the proper amount of moisture is available to seeds or cut-tings. Start seeds and root cuttings in fast draining, sterile, coarse sand,

Damping off is most often caused by over-watering, causing seedlings to rot at the soil line.

rockwool, Oasis™, or Jiffy™ cubes, which are difficult to over-water. Do not place a humidity tent over sprouted seedlings. A tent can lead to excessive humidity and damping-off. Cuttings are less susceptible to damping-off and love a humidi-ty tent to promote rooting. Keep germination temperatures between 70 – 85 degrees. Damping off is inhibited by bright light; grow seedlings under the HID rather than fluorescent bulbs. Keep fertilization to a minimum during the first couple of weeks of growth. Germinate seeds between clean, fresh paper towels and move seeds to soil once sprouted. Do not plant seeds too deep, cover with soil the depth of the seed. Use fresh, sterile growing medium and clean pots to guard against harmful fungus in the soil.

Biological: Apply Polygangron® (*Pythium oligandrum*) gran-ules to soil and seed. Bak Pak®, Intercept®, are applied to soil and Deny® or Dagger® (forms of the bacterium *Burkholderia cepacia*) put on seed. Epic®, Kodiac®, Quantum 4000®, Rhizo-

Plus®, System 3®, Seranade® also suppress many causes of damping-off.

Chemical: Dust seeds with Captan®. Avoid benomyl fungicide soil drench because it kills beneficial organisms.

Downy Mildew

Identify: Sometimes called false mildew, downy mildew affects vegetative and flowering plants. It appears as yellowish spots on top of leaves creating pale patches. Grayish mycelium spawn is on leaf undersides, opposite the pale patches. Downy mildew can spread very quickly, causing a lack of vigor and slow growth; leaves yellow, die back and drop. The disease is in the plant's system and grows outward. It is often fatal. Spreads quickly and can wipe out a garden.

Control: Cleanliness! Use sterile growing medium. Remove and destroy affected plants, not just foliage.

Biological: Apply Serenade® (*Bacillus subtilis*). Bordeaux mixture is also somewhat effective.

Blight

Identify: Blight is a general term that describes many plant diseases. Caused by fungi, most often a few weeks before harvest. Signs of blight include dark blotchy spots on foliage, slow growth, sudden yellowing, wilting and plant death. Most blights spread quickly through large areas of plants.

Control: Cleanliness! Use fresh sterile growing media. Avoid excess nitrogen fertilization. Avoid blights by keeping plants healthy with the proper nutrient balance and good drainage to prevent nutrient buildup.

Biological: Use Seranade® (*Bacillus subtilis*) against Brown Blight. Use Binab®, Bio-Fungus®, RootShield®, Supresivit®, Trichopel® (*Trichoderma harzianum*), or SoilGuard® (*Trichoderma virens*). Use a Bordeaux mixture to stop fungal blights. Stopping blights in advanced stages is difficult; the best solution is to remove diseased plants and destroy them.

Foliar Spots and Fungi

Identify: Leaf and stem fungi, including leaf spot, attack foliage; brown, gray, black, yellow to white spots or blotches develop on leaves and stems. Leaves and stems discolor and develop spots that impair plant fluid flow and other life processes. Spots expand over leaves causing them to yellow and drop. Growth is slowed, harvest prolonged and in severe cases, death could result. Leaf spot is the symptomatic name given to many diseases. The diseases can be caused by bacterium, fungi and nematodes. Spots or lesions caused by fungi often develop different colors as fruiting bodies grow. Leaf spots are often caused by cold water that was sprayed on plants under a hot HID. Temperature stress causes the spots that often develop into a disease.

Control: Cleanliness! Use fresh sterile growing medium when planting. Move HIDs away from the garden canopy about 30 minutes before spraying, so plants won't be too hot. Do not spray within four hours of turning the lights off. Excess moisture sets on foliage and fosters fungal growth. Do not wet foliage when watering. Avoid over-watering. Lower garden room humidity to 50 percent or less. Check the humidity, both day and night. Employ dry heat to raise the nighttime temperature to 5 – 10 degrees below the daytime levels and keep humidity more constant. Allow adequate spacing between plants to provide air circulation. Remove damaged foliage. Avoid excessive nitrogen application.

Biological: Bordeaux mixture may help keep leaf spots in check, but it is often phytotoxic when applied regularly indoors.

Sprays: Bordeaux mixture.

Fusarium Wilt

Identify: Fusarium starts as small spots on older lower leaves. Leaf chlorosis appears swiftly. Leaf tips may curl before wilting and drying to a crisp suddenly. Portions of the plant or the entire plant wilt. The entire process happens so fast that yellow, dead leaves dangle from branches. This disease starts in the plants xylem, the base of the fluid transport system. Plants wilt when the fungi plug the fluid flow in plant tissue. Cut one of the main stems in two and look for the tale-tell reddish-brown color.

Control: Cleanliness! Use fresh clean growing medium. Avoid nitrogen over-fertilization.

Biological: Mycostop® (*Streptomyces griseoviridis*), or Deny®, or Dagger® (*Burkholderia cepacia*) and *Trichoderma*.

Sprays: Treat seeds with chemical fungicides to eradicate the seed-borne infection. Chemical fungicides are not effective on foliage.

Green Algae

Identify: Slimy green algae need nutrients, light, and a moist surface to grow. These algae are found growing on moist rockwool and other growing mediums exposed to light. They cause little damage, but attract fungus gnats and other critters that damage roots. Once roots have lesions and abrasions, diseases enter easily.

Control: Cover moist rockwool and growing mediums to exclude light. Run an algaecide in the nutrient solution or water with an algaecide.

Powdery Mildew

Identify: First indication of infection is small sores (spots) on the top of leaves. Spots progresses to a fine pale gray–white powdery coating on growing shoots, leaves and stems. Powdery mildew is limited to the upper surface of foliage. Growth slows, leaves yellow and plants die as the disease advances. Occasionally fatal indoors, this disease is at its worst when roots dry out and foliage is moist. Plants are infected for weeks before they show the first symptoms.

Control: Cleanliness!! Prevent this mildew by avoiding cool, damp, humid, dim garden rooms. Low light levels and stale air mitigate this disease. Increase air circulation, ventilation and make sure light intensity is high. Space containers far enough apart, so air freely flows in between plants. Allow foliage to dry before turning off lights. Remove and destroy foliage more than 50 percent infected. Avoid excess nitrogen.

Biological control: Apply Serenade® (*Bacillus subtilis*) or spray with a saturation mix of baking soda and water.

Sprays: Bordeaux mixture may keep this mold in check. A saturation baking soda spray dries to a fine powder on leaf. The baking soda changes the surface pH of the leaf to 7 and powdery mildew cannot grow.

Root Rot

Identify: Root rot fungi cause roots to turn from a healthy white to light or dark brown. As the rot progresses, roots turn darker and darker brown. Leaf chlorosis is soon followed by wilting of older leaves the entire plant. Growth slows. When severe, rot progresses up to the base of the plant stock turning it dark. Root rot is most common when roots are deprived of oxygen and stand in un-aerated water. Soil pests that cut, suck and chew roots create openings for rotting diseases to enter. Inspect roots for discoloration and signs of pest damage with a 10x magnifying glass. Root hairs disappear and roots can look "jellified", slimy and shiny.

Control: Cleanliness! Use fresh sterile growing medium. Make sure calcium levels are adequate and do not over-fertilize with nitrogen. Keep pH above 6.5 in soil and about 6.0 in hydroponic mediums to lower disease occurrence. Control any insects, fungi, bacteria, etc., that eat roots.

Biological: Binab®, Bio-Fungus®, RootShield®, Supresivit®, Trichopel® (*Trichoderma harzianum*), or SoilGuard® (*Trichoderma virens*).

Sprays: Not effective.

Pythium Wilt/Rot
Identify: See "Damping-off."

Sooty Mold
Identify: Black sooty mold is a surface fungus that grows on sticky honeydew excreted by aphids, mealybugs, scale, white-flies, etc. Sooty mold is only a problem on indoor plants when honeydew is present. Sooty mold restricts plant development, slows growth and diminishes harvest

Control: Remove insects that excrete honeydew. Once honeydew is controlled, mold dies. Wash honeydew and mold off with a biodegradable soapy solution. Rinse soapy water off a few hours after applying.

Verticillium Wilt
Identify: Lower leaves develop chlorotic yellowing on margins and between veins before turning dingy brown. Plants wilt during the day and recoup when the light goes off. Wilt soon overcomes parts of the plant or the entire plant. Cut the stem in two and look for the tale-tell brownish xylem tissue. The fungus blocks the flow of plant fluids causing wilting.

Control: Cleanliness! Use fresh sterile soil with good drainage. Use amonical nitrogen as a source of nitrogen. Do not over-fertilize.

Biological: Bio-Fungus® (*Trichoderma species*), Rhizo-Plus® (*Bacillus subtilis*).

Sprays: No chemical spray is effective.

Viruses

Identify: Viruses are still a mystery. They act like living organisms in some instances and nonliving chemicals in other cases. Viruses are spread by insect, mite, plant, animal and human vectors. Aphids and whiteflies are the worst. Infected tools also transport viruses from one plant to another. Typical symptoms of viral infection are sickly growth and low yields. Viral diseases destroy a plant's fluid conduit system, which often cause leaf spots and mottling. Once a plant gets a virus, there's little you can do.

Control: Cleanliness! Always use fresh sterile growing medium. Disinfect tools before cutting foliage on different plants. Destroy all plants infected with virus.

Biological: None.

Sprays: No chemical sprays are effective against viruses.

Computer-Controlled Growing

Computer greenhouse controllers are now within the financial reach of most gardeners. My favorite controller interfaces with Microsoft Windows and costs less than $1,000. The computer-controlled garden room controller is attached to probes that are deposited strategically around the garden. The probes measure everything – water, temperature, humidity, CO_2, nutrient levels, moisture levels, etc. You can use the data gathered to monitor and optimize every facet of growth and harvest bumper crops!

Monitoring and controlling temperature, CO_2, humidity levels and EC minute by minute is what a computer setup is all about.

A computer control system looks like other home computers. Hook the computer to a greenhouse controller box, and you have the beginnings of a completely automated system. Old systems could control only the air or the nutrient solution. Now controllers monitor and direct every last function in the garden room. The information recorded by the controller is easy to read and apply to grow better crops.

Remote electrodes or probes that collect information on temperature, humidity, CO_2, etc., are located in each growth chamber. These electrodes send information to the controller attached to a PC where Windows-friendly software translates and compiles the data into a report. The software sends instructions to the hard-wired control devices – vent and intake fans, humidifiers, dehumidifiers, heaters and coolers – that adjust climate conditions round the clock.

Pencil-size and smaller probes measure temperature, humidity, CO_2, pH and EC. This information is routed back to the controller and computer. Windows friendly software interprets the information and makes it available in graphs, statically or other report forms. You can keep the entire history of your garden room on one of these programs.

Computer software tracks and records all information. When you look at temperature, humidity and CO_2 in relation to time, you can see how they interact. For example, when humidity increases, the vent fan is turned on. Often, during a short time the humidity rises and the vent fan does not come on. This "stress time" slows growth.

Small gardeners who want to hang up a single 400-watt lamp don't need to install a major computer system. Power packed little boxes that support various twinkling lights, meters and 120-volt outlets control gardens and connect to an RS-232 computer port. The control box has outlets for vent and circulation fans, cooling equipment, pumps, CO_2 burners, pH and EC controllers and humidifiers. You can set the parameters you desire and the software-driven microprocessor relays your commands.

Check out the Green Air Products Controller, Model GHC-3. It monitors and controls nutrients automatically with direct connect pH and conductivity probes that provide input to operate injectors or metering pumps. Connect this unit to your PC to display set points and real-time graphs on your terminal. You can make adjustments manually at the GHC-3 controller or with the keyboard on your PC computer screen. Record all the data – temperature, humidity, pH, EC, etc., with your PC, save it to disk and analyze it later. Operating interface software for Windows 95 makes setup and control as easy as picking a tomato. For information on this controller and others see www.greenair.com.

If you are working with an automated system, the operations should be verified as correct with the independent measurements.

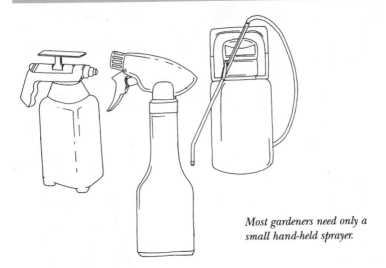

*Most gardeners need only a
small hand-held sprayer.*

About Spraying

Use only contact sprays approved for edible fruits and vegetables. Do not use TOXIC SYSTEMIC CHEMICALS! Read the entire label on all sprays. The toxic or active life of the spray is listed on the label. Wait twice as long as the label recommends, and thoroughly wash any foliage before ingesting it. Toxic life is many times longer indoors because sunlight and other natural forces are not able to break down chemicals.

Use a clean accurate measuring cup or spoon. Measure quantities carefully!

Mix pesticides and fungicides just before using them and safely dispose of unused spray. Mix fertilizer and use for several weeks.

Mix wettable powders and soluble crystals in a little hot water to make sure they get dissolved before adding the correct amount of tepid water.

Organic and natural based sprays are also toxic and should be used sparingly.

Use chemical sprays with extreme care (if at all) in enclosed areas; they are more potent indoors than outdoors in the open air.

Sprays are beneficial if not overdone. Every time a plant is sprayed the stomata are clogged and growth slows. Rinse leaves on both sides with plain water 24 – 48 hours until it

drips from leaves after spraying. Avoid sprays that leave a residual during the weeks before harvesting vegetables. Spraying
increases chances of gray (bud) mold on dense foliage and
flowers.

Phytotoxicity is the injury to plants caused by sprays.
Symptoms include burned leaves, slow growth or sudden wilt.
Spray a test plant and wait a few days to see if spray is phytotoxic. Water plants before spraying. Phytotoxicity is diminished
when more liquid is in the foliage tissues.

Use a facemask when spraying, especially if using an
aerosol/fogger.

Spray early in the day so ingredients absorb and foliage dries.
Spray two hours or less before lights turn off. This can cause
foliar fungus if water sets on the leaves too long in darkness.

Spray entire plants, both sides of the leaves, stems, soil and
pot. Be careful with new tender growing shoots, they are easily
burned by harsh sprays. Test some plants first. If damage
occurs, use one-half strength.

A one or two quart pump-up spray bottle with a removable
nozzle that is easy to clean is ideal. Keep a paper clip handy to
ream out clogged debris in nozzle.

A 1 – 2 gallon sprayer costs lest than $50 and works well for
large gardens. An application wand and nozzle attached to a
flexible hose makes spraying under leaves, where insects live,
easy. Plastic containers do not corrode or rust.

Electric foggers work well for large jobs. The spray is
metered out a nozzle under high pressure, which creates a fine
penetrating fog.

Wash sprayer and nozzle thoroughly after each use. Using
the same bottle for fertilizers and insecticides is OK. Do not
mix insecticides and fungicides together or with anything else.
Mixing chemicals could cause a reaction that lessens their
effectiveness.

 Warning! *Raise HID lamp out of the way, so mist
from spray will not touch the bulb. Temperature
stress, resulting from relatively cold water hitting the
hot bulb, may cause it to shatter. This could not only
scare you, it could burn eyes and skin. If the bulb
breaks, turn off the system immediately – unplug!*

Stages of Growth

Section
Two

Gardening
Indoors

In nature plants go through three separate stages of growth. The seedling stage lasts about a month. During the first growth stage, the seed germinates or sprouts, establishes a root system, grows a stem and a few leaves. In the second stage – vegetative growth – the plant produces much bushy leafy green growth and a supporting root system. Vegetative growth lasts from a few days to more than a year. Flowers form during the last stage of growth. If pollinated, flowers develop seeds. When fertilized with male pollen, female flower buds develop seeds.

Indoors when we create the entire climate – temperature, air humidity and flow, growing medium conditions, nutrient availability and artificial light – we can control the entire life cycle of any plant. For example, tomatoes flower and set fruit when the temperature is between 55 and 85 degrees. Lettuce grows best when the temperature is below 80 degrees. Tropical plants, such as peppers, thrive in high humidity conditions. Poinsettias, Christmas cactus and chrysanthemums bloom when given 12 hours of light and 12 hours of darkness.

Seeds and Seedlings

Check the Internet or your favorite garden magazine for seed catalog offers.

A seed contains all the genetic characteristics of a plant. Seeds are the result of sexual propagation and contain genes from both parents. Most plants, hermaphrodites, bear both male and female flowers on the same plant. Most other plants have distinct male and female plants. The genes within a seed dictate a plant's size, disease and pest resistance, root, stem, leaf and flower production and many other traits. The genetic makeup of a seed is the single, most important factor dictating how well the plant will grow under HID lamps.

Rule of Thumb: *Start with good seeds and reap a good harvest.*

Super Size Secret: *Start with great seeds and reap a bumper crop!*

Seeds

Careful seed selection can make the difference between a successful garden and complete failure. Certain seed varieties are better adapted to grow under certain conditions than others. For example, the early-maturing, cold-tolerant 'Oregon Spring' tomato grows in cool weather, setting flowers and fruit well before the larger beefsteak varieties. If you live in a cool region with a short growing season, selecting 'Oregon Spring' rather than a late-maturing beefsteak variety such as 'Brandywine' will make a fruitful harvest almost certain. If you love broccoli but live in a warm climate, planting heat-tolerant 'Premium Crop,' rather than 'Green Valiant,' will prolong the harvest.

Many vegetable seed varieties available today are developed for modern agriculture. They are bred for qualities such as long shelf life, uniformity, disease resistance and the ability to withstand mechanical harvesting with little damage. Taste is usually the last quality considered. Eating carefully selected varieties with superior taste, rather than tough vegetables that were developed for mechanized handling, is one of the rewards of indoor gardening.

Open-pollinated seeds, also referred to as heirloom seed varieties, are the products of parents, selected at random by nature. You can produce these seeds yourself and save them to sow the following year. They will produce plants very similar to their parents. Some open-pollinated seeds are very popular today, such as the 'Kentucky Wonder' pole bean. But since the advent of hybrids, many varieties have become difficult to find, even extinct. Several groups have been organized to preserve the heirloom varieties. The Seed Savers Exchange, RR 3, Box 239, Decorah, IA 52101 is the largest.

The introduction of hybrid or F^1 hybrid seed has revolutionized modern agriculture and gardening. Hybrid seed is the product of crossing true breeding parents that have desirable characteristics. The resulting seed is known as an F^1 hybrid. The F^1 hybrid has *hybrid vigor*, the ability to grow stronger and faster than the parents. The greater the vigor, the more obstacles, such as pests and diseases, it can overcome to produce a better plant. Hybrids are usually uniform in shape and size and become ripe at the same time. Even though the seeds are often more expensive, they are an excellent value. Carefully selecting hybrid seed for such qualities as taste, disease and pest resistance, cold and heat tolerance, and conditions that prevail both indoors and outdoors in your climate will help make your garden a success.

Today, modern seed production has largely replaced the older method of open field pollination. But this technology also has disadvantages. The growing of one variety on a very large scale can be dangerous. With no genetic diversification, if attacked by pests or diseases it can be wiped out. Diversify, grow more than one variety, and it will help overcome unchecked diseases and pests.

When selecting seed, you may notice some of them carry the label "All America Selection" or "AAS Winner". Seed varieties that were chosen as AAS winners have demonstrated superior growth characteristics in a wide variety of climates across America. AAS winners are easy to spot on seed racks and a good choice for indoor gardens.

Some seed is treated with a fungicide to prevent such diseases as damping-off, a disease that causes seedlings to rot at the soil line. Typically, the fungicide is color-coded and some seed companies state in their catalog or on the seed packet that it is treated. Some seed is available with a coating of fungicide. The most common fungicide in use is Captan (Carbaryl), known to be carcinogenic. At least one major seed producer is using naturally occurring diatomaceous earth to protect seed.

Typically, a gardener buys seeds from a reputable company. Once germinated, the seeds are carefully planted and grown to adults. For example, if 100 seeds are planted, some will be weak and grow poorly, others may fall victim to insect or fungal attacks, and a percentage will grow into strong adults.

A simple picture of a seed reveals an embryo, containing the genes and a supply of food wrapped in a protective outer coating. Soft, pale or green seeds are usually immature and should be avoided. Immature seeds germinate poorly and often produce sickly plants. Fresh, dry, mature seeds less than a year old sprout quickly and grow robust plants. Seeds a year or older take longer to sprout and have a lower rate of germination. Store seeds in a cool, dark, dry place, like a freezer. Some seeds will remain viable for five years or longer. Dried corn kernels can last hundreds of years.

Germination

Seeds need only water, heat and air to germinate. They sprout without light in a wide range of temperatures. Properly nurtured most seeds germinate in 2 – 7 days, in temperatures from 70 – 90 degrees F. Temperatures above 90 degrees F impair germination. At germination, the outside protective shell of the seed splits and a tiny, white sprout pops out. This sprout is the taproot. Cotyledon or seed leaves emerge from within the shell as they push upward in search of light.

Popular germination techniques:

Soak seeds overnight in a cup of water. Make sure seeds get good and wet so that growth is activated. Do not let seeds soak more than 24 hours, or they might get too wet, suffer oxygen depravation and rot. Once soaked, seeds are ready to be placed between moist paper towels to sprout, planted in a starter cube or fine, light soilless mix.

In a warm location (70 – 90 degrees F) place seeds in a moist paper towel or cheesecloth, making sure they are in darkness. Set the moist cloth or paper towel at an angle or in a vertical position (so tap root grows down) on a grate (for drainage) on a dinner plate.

Water the cloth daily, keeping it moist, letting excess water drain away freely. The cloth will retain enough moisture to germinate the seed in a few days. The seed contains an adequate food supply for germination, but watering with a mild fertilizer mix will hasten growth. If living in a humid climate, water with a mild 2 percent bleach or fungicide solution to prevent fungus. Once seeds have sprouted and the white sprout is visible, carefully pick up the fragile sprouts and plant them. Take care not to expose the tender rootlet to prolonged intense light or air. Cover the germinated seed in one quarter to one-half inch of fine planting medium with the white sprout tip (the root) pointing down.

Sow (direct seed) or move the sprout into a shallow planter, one to five-gallon pot, peat pellet or rooting cube. Keep the planting medium evenly moist. Use a spoon to contain the root ball when transplanting. Peat pellets or root cubes may be transplanted in 2 – 3 weeks or when the roots show through the sides. Plant cube and all to prevent root disturbance.

Fertilize with a dilute fertilizer solution usually one half strength (500-600 PPM).

To construct a moisture tent over the seedling container, place a baggie or piece of cellophane over the seeded soil. The cover will keep the humidity high and temperature elevated. Seeds usually need only one initial watering when under a humidity tent. Remove the cover as soon as the first sprout appears. Leaving the tent on will lead to damping-off and other problems.

Place planted seeds under the HID lamp while germinating to add dry heat. The heat dries soil, which requires more frequent watering. Place a heat pad or soil heating cables below growing medium to expedite germination. Most seeds germinate and sprout quickest when the soil temperature is between 75 – 80 degrees F, and the air temperature is at 70 degrees.

 Rule of Thumb: *Maintain the growing medium temperature between 75 – 80 degrees F, day and night to root cuttings fast.*

 Super Size Secret: *Keep the temperature of the rooting medium at 78 – 80 degrees and ambient air temperature 6 – 8 degrees cooler than the rooting medium, day and night. Root growth increases dramatically.*

 Warning! *Internodes will stretch if temperatures exceed 85 degrees F for long. The temperature must stay below 95 degrees F through flowering.*

Seedlings emerging from peat pots first develop seed (cotyledon) leaves before growing first set of "true leaves".

Over-watering is the biggest obstacle some gardeners face when germinating seeds and growing seedlings. Keep the soil uniformly moist, not waterlogged. Setting root cubes or planting flats up on a grate allows good drainage. A shallow flat or planter with a heat pad underneath may require daily watering, while a deep, one gallon pot will need watering every 3 days or more. A well-watered flat of rockwool cubes needs water every 3 – 5 days when sprouting seeds. When the surface is dry (one-eighth inch deep) it is time to water. Remember, there are few roots to absorb the water early in life, and they are very delicate.

Seedlings

When a seed sprouts, the white taproot emerges and soon afterward the cotyledon or seed or seedling leaves appear. The seed leaves spread out as the stem elongates. Within a few days the first true leaves appear, and the little plant is now officially a seedling. This growth stage lasts about three to six weeks. During seedling growth, a root system grows rapidly while green growth above ground is slow. Water and heat are critical at this point of development. The new fragile root system is very small and requires a small but constant supply of water and warmth. Too much water will drown roots, which often leads to root rot and damping-off. Lack of water will cause the infant root system to dry up. As the seedlings mature, some will grow faster, stronger and appear healthy in general. A little heat now will help nurture small seedlings to a strong start. Other seeds will sprout slowly and be weak and leggy. Sickly, weak plants should be thinned out and attention focused on the strong survivors. Seedlings should be big enough to thin the third to fifth week of growth. Thinning out seedlings is very difficult for gardeners, who have nurtured seeds into seedlings.

Seedlings need at least 16 hours of light daily. They require lower levels of light now and grow well under a fluorescent tubes for the first 2 – 3 weeks. After that, they need brighter light to grow well.

The seedling stage is over when rapid foliage growth starts. Rapid growth above ground is the beginning of the vegetative growth stage. Plants need more room to grow and are often transplanted into a larger container.

Buying Seedlings

Purchasing flower and vegetable starts at a tip-top retail nursery takes little skill. Purchasing from some discount outlets can be somewhat risky if the staff is not familiar with the care of seedlings.

Buy seedlings that are kept in good growing conditions. Do not buy seedlings that are kept in a sunny location. The small amount of soil around the roots in small plastic pots/packs can heat up "cooking" the roots. The temperature is more constant in a shade house, which also protects the tender plants from other climate extremes. The root system is the most important part of the seedling. Select plants that have good color and are of uniform size.

The best seedlings to transplant have a root system that holds the soil together and have just begun to reach the outside of the soil in the small container.

If only root-bound plants are available, soak the soil with water before planting. Remove any matted roots, then gently separate the remaining roots just before planting so that they will penetrate the soil better and not be inclined to bunch-up.

You may prefer to buy seedlings with root systems that are not fully developed and hold them at home in a partially shady location a week or two before transplanting. This way you can watch their progress as they gradually get used to their new environment.

Pull plants apart gently when transplanting from flats. Take care not to squeeze roots and crush tender root hairs.

Vegetative Growth

   Once a strong root system is established and foliage growth increases rapidly, seedlings enter the vegetative growth stage. When chlorophyll production is full speed ahead, a vegetative plant will produce as much green, leafy foliage as light, CO_2, nutrients and water permit. Properly maintained, many plants will grow from 0.5 – 2 inches per day. A plant stunted now could take weeks to resume normal growth. A strong, unrestricted root system is essential to supply much needed water and nutrients. Unrestricted vegetative growth is the key to a healthy harvest. During vegetative growth, the plant's nutrient and water intake changes. Transpiration is carried on at a more rapid rate, requiring more water. High levels of nitrogen are needed. Potassium, phosphorus, calcium, magnesium, sulfur and trace elements are used at much faster rates. The larger a plant gets and the bigger the root system, the faster the soil will dry out. Strong lateral branches that will later support flower buds develop.

 Super Size Secret: *Unrestricted, rapid vegetative growth is the key to a healthy harvest.*

   Vegetative growth is best maintained with 18 hours of HID light and 6 hours of darkness. Some gardeners keep the light on 24 hours a day claiming growth is faster, but I believe the extra hours of light are wasted. I have read that a point of diminishing returns is reached after 18 hours and the light losses effectiveness. Many annual plants will remain in the vegetative growth stage a year or longer - theoretically forever - as long as an 18 hour photoperiod is maintained.
   Some plants such as Christmas cactus, Chinese (Napa) cabbages, chrysanthemums, etc., are photoperiodic-reactive and flowering can be controlled with the light cycle. This allows indoor horticulturists to control vegetative and flowering growth. You can have garden fresh Napa cabbage and Christmas cactus

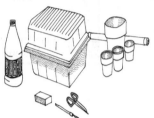

flowers in July just by turning the light cycle to an even 12 hours of light and 12 hours of darkness.

Cuttings, transplanting, pruning and bending are all initiated when plants are in the vegetative growth stage.

Cuttings

Get all supplies ready before starting to make cuttings.

Plants can be reproduced (propagated) sexually or asexually. Seeds are the product of sexual propagation; cuttings are the result of asexual or vegetative propagation. In its simplest form, taking a clipping is cutting a growing branch tip and rooting it. Taking a branch with 4 or 5 leaves on it, use an Exacto-knife or razor blade to cut it at a 45 – 60-degree angle, then trim one or two leaves off just above the cut location. Most people have taken cuttings or "slips" from houseplants, such as philodendrons, ivy or coleus and rooted them in water or sand.

Making cuttings or taking clones is the most efficient and productive means of propagating many plants. Technically, cloning is taking one cell of a plant and promoting its growth into a plant.

Once a plant is two months old or older, you are ready to practice the simple, yet incredibly productive art and science of cloning. If the climate is poor, the plant will develop poorly and be stunted. If the garden room is well maintained with a perfect climate, strong healthy plants will be harvested.

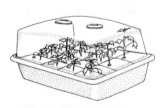

A humidity dome speeds rooting.

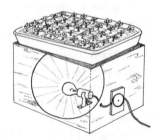

An incandescent light bulb attached to a rheostat provides exacting control of bottom heat.

Parent or "Mother" Plants

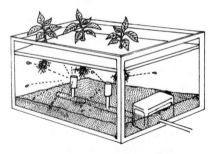

Any plant can be the parent or "mother" of a cutting garden, no matter how old. The parent can be grown from seed or be a cutting of a cutting. In fact, you can make cuttings of cuttings 20 times or more! That is, cuttings (C-1), are taken from the original parent grown from seed. These vegetative plants give cuttings (C-2), which are taken from the first cuttings (C-l). Then, cuttings (C-3) are taken from the second cuttings (C-2). This same growing technique is still going on with cuttings of cuttings well past (C-20), and there is seldom any breakdown in the vigor of the cuttings! The important thing to remember when taking cuttings from a parent is to never let it get sick and weak. All cuttings will have the same genetic characteristics as the parent plant. Select the best for cuttings!

Strong parents produce strong healthy cuttings. Start new parents from seed every year. Cuttings have a better chance of being strong and healthy when parents are not stressed.

Exact Genetic Replica

A cutting is an exact genetic replica of the parent plant. A plant will reproduce 100 percent exact genetic replica. When grown in the exact same environment, cuttings, from the same parent look alike. But the same cuttings subjected to distinct environments in different garden rooms, often look different. For example, a cutting that is under-fertilized and grown in a low-humidity environment will look different than a perfectly fertilized sibling grown in a humid environment. However, mutations can occur, and environmental stress can cause an occasional freak plant. Although rare, some can revert to hermaphrodites (change sex or have both male and female flowers)

A month old cutting from a six-month old parent is not really one month old; it is six months old, just like the parent.

This phenomenon is not totally understood, but valid. Remember the first animal clone, Dolly the sheep? She was reproduced asexually from the DNA retrieved from mammary glands of a sheep, hence the name Dolly (Parton)! The cells were nurtured, divided and grew into a sheep. One thing happened they did not expect, the cells retained their chronological age, the same age as the "mother" or "DNA donor."

Light intensity is much greater, since the cuttings do not have a chance to get too tall. Remember, the closer the light is to the entire plant and garden, the faster they grow. Lower branches, heavily shaded by upper branches and leaves, will grow slow and spindly.

Because a cutting of any age is larger than a plant grown from seed, the root system is small and compact, making cuttings well suited for containers. By the time the root system is inhibited by the container, it is time for harvest. A five- or six-month old plant, grown from seed, is easily pot-bound and stunted. This compounds any insect or nutrient disorder.

The stronger a plant and the faster it grows, the less chance it has of being affected by diseases or insects. A spider mite infestation, developed in the fifth or sixth month of a sexually propagated (seed) crop, may have to suffer through many applications until the infestation is arrested. The garden room cannot be totally cleaned and fumigated until the plants have completed flowering or producing vegetables and harvested.

All plants may be removed for a couple of days in order to fumigate the room or paint it with antiseptic whitewash. The plants are sick to begin with and moving injures them. When returned to the garden room, they will take a long time to resume normal growth. On the other hand, cuttings are not in the garden room as long, the infestations have less time to launch an all-out attack or build immunity to sprays.

Healthy cuttings taken from a proven, disease-resistant parent is the route to a bountiful harvest. An insect infestation that gets out of hand among small cuttings is easily stopped. The small cuttings are removed with little or no damage; the garden room is then fumigated. Plants grown in pots are much easier to move around than plants grown in large hydroponic system beds.

Experiments are more easily controlled with cuttings. Since

cuttings are all the same, different stimuli - fertilizer, light, bending, etc. - introduced on selected groups of cuttings can lead to a true comparative analysis.

Cuttings have some negative points. The parent plant will produce cuttings just like itself. If the parent is not disease-resistant or produces poorly, cuttings also share these weaknesses. An insect or fungus infestation, left unchecked, could wipe out an entire crop of cuttings.

Taking cuttings from three or four different parents will help ensure a healthy garden. Clean garden rooms rarely have insect or disease problems. Infestations are also promoted by continued use of an ineffective spray used to kill insects or fungi.

Taking cuttings is simple and easy. A consistent 100 percent survival rate may be achieved by following the simple procedures outlined in this book. The parent plant can be grown from seed or propagated by cutting. It should be at least two months old and possess all the characteristics you find desirable.

Cuttings can be taken from just about any plant, regardless of age or growth stage. Cuttings taken in the vegetative stage root quickly and grow fast. Cuttings taken from flowering plants may root a little slower.

Getting Ready

Most any plant can be propagated as a cutting, regardless of age or growth stage. For best results take cuttings from parent plants at least two months old. If cuttings are made before parent plants are two months old, they may develop unevenly and grow slowly. Cuttings taken from flowering plants root more slowly but are not recommended.

Becoming a cutting is the most traumatic incident plants experience. Cuttings go through an incredible transformation when they change from a severed growing tip to a rooted plant. Their entire chemistry changes; the stem that once grew leaves must now grow roots in order to survive.

Cuttings develop a dense system of roots quickly when stems have a high carbohydrate and low nitrogen concentration. Build carbohydrate levels by leaching the growing medium with copious quantities of water to flush out nutrients. The growing medium must drain very well to withstand heavy leaching without becoming waterlogged. Reverse foliar feeding will leach nutrients from leaves, especially nitrogen. To reverse foliar feeding, fill a sprayer with clean tepid water and mist the parent heavily every morning for three or four days to help wash nutrients from leaves. Older leaves may turn light green; growth slows as nitrogen is used and carbohydrates build. Carbohydrate content is highest in lower, older, more mature branches. A rigid branch that folds over quickly when bent is a good sign of high carbohydrate content.

While rooting, cuttings require a minimum of nitrogen and increased levels of phosphorus to promote root growth. A high phosphorus "bloom" formula can be used. Sprays should be avoided during rooting as they compound plant stress. By following directions and with a little experience, most gardeners achieve a consistent 100 percent survival rate of their cuttings. Taking off the bottom leaves from a cutting, slitting the stem for an inch or two and trimming off one-half of the remaining leaf tips lowers transpiration and encourages root formation.

Rooting Hormones

Root inducing hormones speed plant processes. When the stem of a cutting develops roots, it must transform from producing green stem cells to manufacturing undifferentiated cells and finally fabricate root cells. Rooting hormones hasten growth of undifferentiated cells. Once undifferentiated, cells quickly transform into root cells. Three substances that stimulate undifferentiated growth include: napthalenaecetic acid (NAA), indolebutyric acid (IBA) and 2,4-dichlorophenoxyacetic acid (2,4 DPA). Commercial rooting hormones contain one, two or all of the above synthetic ingredients and often include a fungicide to help prevent damping-off.

They are available in a liquid, gel or powder form. Liquid and gel types are the most versatile, penetrate stems evenly and are consistent. Powdered rooting hormones adhere inconsistently to stems, penetrate poorly, spur uneven root growth and yield a lower survival rate.

Some gardeners soak their cuttings in a diluted hormonal

solution for twenty-four hours. Generally these solutions contain between 20 and 200 PPM IBA or NAA. Results using this method vary. During the twenty-four hour soaking period, environmental conditions such as temperature, light and humidity affect the ability of a cutting to absorb the root promoter.

More concentrated solutions of IBA and NAA, 500 – 20,000 PPM, can be used for the quick dip method. Because of the high concentrations of synthetic hormones, cuttings, which are dipped for only 5 – 20 seconds, uniformly absorb the compound. To determine the rooting hormone concentration in PPM, multiply the percentage listed by the manufacturer by 10,000. For example, a product with 0.9% IBA contains 9,000 PPM IBA.

Synthetic rooting hormones sold in powder form are a mixture of talc and IBA and/or NAA. Powder rooting hormones are less expensive than their liquid and gel counterparts. To use, roll the moistened end of your cutting in the powder. Apply a thick, even coat. Like liquid rooting hormones, powders can become contaminated, so do not dip directly into the original packaging. Pour a small amount into a separate container. Tap or scrape excess powder off the cutting, because it can hinder rooting and growth. Make a hole bigger than the stem in the rooting medium. If the hole is too small the rooting powder gets scraped off upon insertion. Seal the top of hole around the cutting with a pinch of rockwool or perlite/peat. A pair of tweezers will help you with the task.

Clonex® was the first cloning gel in America. It has a blend of 7 vitamins, 11 minerals, 2 anti-microbial agents and 3,000 PPM concentration of rooting hormones. The gel seals the tissues of the cutting upon contact and reduces the chance of infection and embolisms to nil.

Dip-N-Grow® contains IBA, NAA, anti-bacterial and anti-fungal agents. Dip-N-Grow tends to be less expensive than its competitors, averaging a penny per 100 cuttings.

Earth Juice Catalyst® is an organic product derived from oat bran, kelp, molasses, vitamin B complexes, amino acids, hormones and low levels of nutrients.

Hormex is an IBA based powder, which is available in six different strengths, ranging from 1000 PPM to 45,000 PPM.

Hormodin® is a powder available in three strengths: 1000, 3000 and 8000 PPM. Its main active ingredient is IBA.

Maxicrop liquid seaweed manufactured by Maxicrop, does not use either IBA or NAA. Gardeners have found it to be an excellent natural root stimulator. Soak cuttings overnight in a solution of 2 ounces Maxicrop to one gallon of water. After planting, continue watering with this solution.

Nitrozyme® is an extract from a seaweed-like plant (*Ascophylum Nodosum*) and contains numerous hormones including cytokinins, auxins, enzymes, giberellins and ethylenes. Spray Nitrozyme on parent plants two weeks before taking cuttings.

NutriRoot® rooting gel can be used for micropropagation, tissue culture, stem and leaf cuttings for hardwood and softwood stock. Consists of a balanced blend of trace elements, sugars, vitamins, minerals and growth regulating hormones.

Olivia's Cloning Solution® and Olivia's Cloning Gel are very popular cloning solutions available in liquid and gel form. Gardeners report a very high success rate.

PowerThrive® contains kelp, Vitamin B^1, cytokinin, and many other growth stimulants, hormones and nutrients.

Rhizopon AA® (Rhizopon B.V.) is the worlds largest company devoted exclusively to research and manufacture of rooting products. Available in powder and water-soluble tablets in strengths from 500 to 20,000 PPM.

Rootech Cloning Gel from Tecknaflora is a wonderful product! Cuttings grow roots fast, plus it guards against shock and embolisms. IBA is at the rate of 0.55 percent grams per liter and packed with vitamins and an exact blend of nutrients.

StimRoot® is a root inducing liquid hormone containing both IBA and NAA.

Wilson's Roots® is a rooting hormone containing IBA, NNA, 5-ethoxy-3-trichlormethyl-1,2,4-thiadiazole and a fungicide. It is available in both powder and gel form.

Vita Grow Ready to use liquid concentrate, solution using IBA NAA. Many customers say, "You could root a popcycle stick."

Warning! Some of these products are not recommended for use with edible plants. Read the label carefully before deciding to use a product.

An all-natural root inducing substance is willow (tree) water. The substance in all willow trees that promotes rooting is unknown, but repeated experiments have proven that willow water promotes about 20 percent more roots than plain water. It contains some sort of aspirin-like substance. This willow water is mixed with commercial rooting hormones for phenomenal results.

To make willow water rooting compound, find any willow tree and remove some of this years branches that are about one and one-half inches in diameter. Remove the leaves and cut the branches in lengths of one-inch each. Place one-inch willow sticks on end, so a lot of them fit in a water glass or quart jar. Fill the jar with water and let it soak 24 hours. After soaking, pour off the willow water, and use for rooting hormone. Soak the cuttings in the willow water for 24 hours, then plant in rooting medium. If using a commercial liquid rooting hormone, substitute the willow water in place of regular water in the mix.

Trichoderma is contained in several commercial products. The bacterium causes roots to grow and absorb nutrients better. It is great stuff and should be used by every gardener in the world.

Cuttings root faster when the growing medium is a few degrees warmer than the ambient air temperature. A warmer substrate increases underground chemical activity and lower air temperature slows transpiration. For best results, keep the rooting medium at 75 – 80 degrees F. and the air 5 degrees cooler. Misting cuttings with water also cools foliage and slows transpiration to help traumatized cuttings retain moisture unavailable from nonexistent roots.

Rule of Thumb: Try 5 – 10 practice cuttings before making a serious cloning.

Super Size Secret: *give rooting cuttings air temperature of 70 degrees F and soil temperature of 75 degrees F for fastest strongest rooting.*

 Warning! *If air becomes trapped in the stem an embolism can form and cause the cutting to die. Gels seal cuttings immediately after they have been cut, which reduces embolisms, shock and infection. To guard against the risk of embolisms, dip cuttings quickly after cutting to prevent air from getting trapped in the hollow stem. Completely eliminate the threat of an embolism by taking cuttings under water. Embolisms are difficult to detect. Affected plants may die within a week or look healthy for a month or two but suddenly fall over, rotted at the soil line.*

Cloning: Step-by-Step

Step One: Choose a mother plant that is at least two months old and at least 24 inches tall. Some varieties give great cuttings even when pumped up with hydroponics and fertilizer to grow fast. If a variety is difficult to propagate with cuttings, leach the soil daily with two gallons of water for each gallon of soil every morning for a week before taking cuttings. Drainage must be good. Or mist leaves heavily with plain water every morning. Both practices help wash out nitrogen. Do not add fertilizer.

Step Two: Older branch tips root easiest. With a sharp blade, make a 45-degree cut across firm, healthy one-eighth to one quarter-inch-wide branches, 2 – 4 inches long. Take care not to smash the end of the stem when making the cut. Trim off two or three sets of leaves and growth nodes, so the stem can fit in the soil. There should be at least two sets of leaves above the soil line and one or two sets of trimmed nodes below ground. When cutting, make the slice halfway between the sets of nodes. Immediately place the cut end in fresh, tepid water to keep an air bubble from lodging in the hole in the center of the stem. Store cuttings in water while making more cuttings. Dip immediately in cloning gel or solution.

Step Three: Rockwool or Oasis™ root cubes cost a little

more than soilless mixes, but are very convenient and easy to maintain and transplant. Fill small containers or nursery flats with coarse, washed sand, fine vermiculite, soilless mix or if nothing else is available, fine potting soil. Saturate the substrate with tepid water. Use an unsharpened pencil or chop stick to make a hole in the rooting medium a little larger than the stem. The hole should bottom out about one-half inch from the bottom of the container to allow for root growth.

Step Four: Use a rooting hormone and mix, if necessary, just before using. For liquids, use the proper dilution ratio for softwood, semi-hardwood or hardwood cuttings. Swirl each cutting in the hormone solution for 5 – 10 seconds. Place the cuttings in the hole in the rooting medium. Pack rooting medium gently around the stem. Gel and powder root hormones require no mixing. Dip stems in gels as per instructions or roll the stem in the powder. When planting, take special care to keep a solid layer of hormone gel or powder around the stem when gently packing soil into place.

Step Five: Lightly water with a mild transplanting solution containing vitamin B[1] until the surface is evenly moist. Water as needed.

Step Six: Cuttings root fastest with 18 – 24 hours of fluorescent light. If cuttings must be placed under a HID, set them on the perimeter of the garden so they receive less intense light, shade them with a cloth or screen, white plastic bag or newspaper.

Step Seven: Cuttings root fastest when humidity levels are 95 and 100 percent the first two days and gradually reduced to 85 percent over the next week. A humidity tent will keep humidity above 90 percent. Construct the tent out of plastic bags, plastic film or glass. Remember to leave a breezeway so little cuttings can breathe. If practical, mist cuttings several times a day as an alternative to the humidity tent. Remove any rotting foliage.

Step Eight: Air temperature should stay about 5 degrees cooler than the 75 – 80-degree F rooting medium. Put cuttings in a warm place to increase air temperature, and use a heat pad, heating cables, or an incandescent light bulb below rooting cuttings.

Step Nine: Some cuttings may wilt but regain rigidity in a few days. Cuttings should look close to normal by the end of the week. Cuttings still wilted after 7 days may root so slowly that they never catch up with others. Consider culling out cuttings that root slowly.

Step Ten: In one to three weeks, cuttings should be rooted. Signals they have rooted include yellow leaf tips and roots growing out drain holes and cuttings will start vertical growth. To check for root growth in flats or pots, carefully remove the root ball and cutting to see if it has good root development. For best results, do not transplant cuttings until a dense root system is growing out the sides and bottom of rooting cubes.

Transplanting

When plants are too big for their container, they must be transplanted to continue rapid growth. Inhibited, cramped root systems grow sickly stunted plants. Signs of rootbound plants include slow, sickly growth and branches develop with more distance between limbs. Severely rootbound plants tend to grow straight up with few branches that stretch beyond the sides of the pot. To check for rootbound symptoms, remove a plant from its pot to see if roots are deeply matted on the bottom or surrounding the sides of the pot.

When growing plants that reach full maturity in two or three months, there is little need for containers larger than three gallons. If cultivating crops of flowers and vegetables that grow for more than two or three months, larger pots are necessary.

Transplant into the same type of growing medium, so a water pressure differential does not develop between the different mediums and slow root growth. Starting seeds and cuttings in root cubes or peat pots makes them easy to transplant. Just set the cube or peat pot in a hole in the growing medium and make sure growing medium is in firm contact. Remember to keep root cubes and soil wet after transplanting into soil or soilless mix. The difference in water holding capacity can cause roots to stop growing beyond the cube. In hydroponics, rockwool starter cubes with seedlings or cuttings can be transplanted directly into a gravel gravity-flow system.

Transplanting is the second most traumatic experience after taking cuttings. It requires special attention and manual dexterity. Tiny root hairs are very delicate and may easily be destroyed by light, air or clumsy hands. Roots grow in dark-

ness, in a rigid secure environment.
When roots are taken out of contact
with the soil for long, they dry up and
die.

Transplanting should disturb the root
system as little as possible. Water helps
the soil pack around roots and keeps
them from drying out. Roots need to
be in constant contact with moist soil,
so they can supply water and food to
the plant. Water the plants thoroughly
just before transplanting.

*Dip rooted cuttings into
a miticidal solution
before transplanting and
before moving into the
flowering room.*

After transplanting, photosynthesis
and chlorophyll production are slowed,
so is water and nutrient absorption via
roots. Transplant late in the day, so
transplants will have all night to recover. Transplants need subdued light to keep foliage growing at the same rate roots are
able to supply water and nutrients. Give new transplants filtered, less intense light for a couple of days. If there is a fluorescent lamp handy, move transplants under it for a couple of
days before moving them back under the HID.

Ideally plants should be as healthy as possible before being
traumatized by transplanting. But, transplanting a sick, root-
bound plant to a bigger container has cured more than one
ailing plant. Once transplanted, plants require low levels of
nitrogen and potassium and increased quantities of phosphorus. Use a hydroponic "bloom" formula for a week. Any product containing *Trichoderma* bacteria or Vitamin B[1] will help ease
transplant shock. Plants need a few days to settle-in and re-
establish a solid flow of fluids from the roots through the plant.
When transplanted carefully and roots are disturbed little,
there will be no signs of transplant shock or wilt.

Dip entire transplants in a bucket of miticide as soon as they
have resumed growth. A quick dip in a bucket of miticide will
protect them from these evil critters!

Transplanting
Step-by-Step

In this example, we will use a one-month-old cutting started in a 2-inch container of soilless mix and transplant it into a 3-gallon pot.

Step One: Water cutting with half-strength Vitamin B[1], two days before transplanting.

Step Two: Fill the 3-gallon container with rich potting soil or soilless mix to within 2 inches of the top.

Step Three: Water growing medium with a weak hydroponic fertilizer solution until saturated and it drains freely out the bottom.

Step Four: Carefully roll the 2-inch pot between your hands to break soil away from the sides of the pot. Place your hand over the top of container with the stem

Roots showing through a rooting cube means they are ready to transplant.

Transplant a cutting in a rooting cube into the pre-cut hole in a rock-wool cube.

Carefully rinse soil from roots with cold water before transplanting into soilless medium, only if necessary.

between your fingers; turn it upside down and let root ball slip out of pot into your hand. Take special care at this point to keep the root ball in one integral piece.

Step Five: Carefully place the root ball in the prepared hole in the 3-gallon container. Make sure all roots are growing down.

Step Six: Backfill around the root ball. Gently, but firmly, place soil into contact with root ball.

Step Seven: Water with half-strength fertilizer containing *Trichoderma* bacteria or Vitamin B[1]. Soil should be saturated, not waterlogged and drain freely.

Snip confining plastic mesh from peat pots before transplanting.

Step Eight: Place new transplants on the perimeter of the HID garden or under a screen to subdue light for a couple of days. Once transplants look strong a day or two later, move them under full light.

Step Nine: Fertilize soilless mixes after transplanting with a complete hydroponic fertilizer that contains soluble chelated nutrients. New potting soil usually supplies enough nutrients for a couple of weeks before supplemental fertilization is necessary.

Step Ten: See chart on "Minimum Container Size."

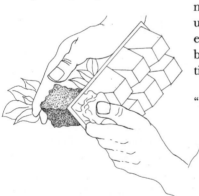

Roots showing through a rooting cube means they are ready to transplant.

Pruning and Bending

Bending and pruning alter the basic growth pattern of a plant. These modifications affect physical shape, liquid

Roots showing through a rooting cube means they are ready to transplant.

flow and growth hormones. The effects of pruning are much
stronger than the more subdued consequences of bending.
When a branch is pruned off, two branches will grow from the
nodes just below the cut. This does not mean the plant will
grow twice as much. A plant can only grow so fast. A quick
branch amputation is not going to make it grow faster or add
more foliage. But it will make for a bushier plant. This may be
desirable indoors in hydroponics because of limited ceiling
height. Indoor gardens are being pushed to the limit and
trimming or cutting branches will slow growth. Plants must
grow every day to produce well.

 Warning! *Pruning does not make plants produce a
heavier yield.*

Bending is similar to pruning; it alters the flow of hormones.
Bending effectively neutralizes the effect of the growth-inhibit-
ing hormone. Bending is much easier on plants than pruning.

To bend, lean a branch in the desired direction and tie it in place. Branches can take a lot of bending before they fold over or break. Even if a branch folds, tie it in place, it will heal itself. Young supple branches take bending much better than old stiff ones. Bending branches horizontally will encourage foliage and flowers to grow vertically towards the light. Each flower will be more full and vibrant, because they all receive more light. A wooden planter box with a lattice trellis alongside makes a great anchor to tie bent plants to.

This plant was pruned to four central branches that produced four large branches.

Wire ties, like the kind used to close bread sacks, can be purchased at the nursery. Wire ties are either pre-cut or cut by the gardener to length. Plastic coated electronic and telephone cable wire also works well and cost nothing. They are fastened with a simple twist and stay rigid, leaving the stem breathing room. But if applied too tight around a stem, the liquids cannot flow and death could result.

When bending, be gentle, even though most plants can take much abuse. Sometimes a crotch will separate or a branch will fold over, cutting off fluid flow. These mishaps are easily fixed with a small wooden splint, and snugly secured with wire ties or duct tape to support the split and broken stem. Wrap and secure a sponge around a broken stem and keep moist until it heals.

Gardeners also combine bending and pruning. It is easy to prune too much, but it is hard to over bend.

Pruning will make a plant grow bushier. Lower branches develop more rapidly when the terminal bud is removed. Removing the terminal bud alters the concentration of growth inhibiting hormones. These hormones - auxins - prevent the lateral buds from growing very fast. The further a branch is from hormones at the plant tip, the less effect the auxins have.

Most successful gardeners do not prune at all. Short low profile gardens require no pruning to increase light to bottom
leaves or to alter the profile of the garden. This method is the
easiest and probably the most productive.

Always use clean instruments when pruning. A single-edge
razor blade, Exacto-knife, a sharp pair of pruners or a pair of
scissors all work well. Do not use indoor pruners on anything
but the indoor garden. Pruners used outdoors have everything
from spider mites to dog dung on them. If outdoor clippers
must be used, use rubbing alcohol to sterilize them before use.

**There are a few basic techniques to pruning indoor plants,
including:**

Remove spindly lower branches that receive little light.
Pruning lower branches concentrates auxins in upper branches
which forces growth upwards. Cut lower branches off cleanly
at the stem so no stub is left to rot and attract pests and diseases.

Not pruning has several advantages. Floral hormones are
allowed to concentrate in tips of branches causing flowers and
fruit to grow stronger. Unpruned plants are crammed into a
small area. Crowded plants have less space to bush out lateral-
ly and tend to grow more upright. Little cuttings are packed
tightly together. Each one of the plants is taking up the minimum amount of space for the minimum amount of time to
produce the maximum harvest. Light is much more intense
and the entire plant grows stronger.

Pinching back tops (branch tips) diffuses floral hormones
and makes plants bushier. To pinch back a branch tip, simply
snip off the last set or two of leaves. When the main stem is
pinched back, side and lower growth is forced. When all the
tops are pinched back, it forces lower growth on the plant.
Continual pinching back, as when taking cuttings from a parent, causes many more little branches to form below the
pruned tips, and it eventually transforms plants into a hedge-
like shape.

Remove all but the four main branches. The meristem (central stem) is removed just above the four lowest (main) branches. Removing the central leader concentrates the floral hormones in the four remaining branches. Fewer branches are

stronger and bear more dense heavy flowers. Remove the stem above the four main branches; do not remove leaves on the main branches. Select plants with 3 sets of branch nodes, about 6 weeks old, and pinch or prune out the last set of nodes so that the two remaining sets of branches remain.

Pruning all the branches or removing more than 20 percent of the foliage in a short time frame stresses plants too much and diminishes harvest. But if taking cuttings, some gardeners effectively prune a parent down to stubby branches and let her recuperate for a month or longer.

Pruning too much over time often alters hormonal concentrations, causing spindly growth. This is often the case with parent plants that provide too many cuttings. The parent must rest and gain girth, because small spindly branches root poorly.

Avoid (heavy) pruning a month before flowering. Since pruning diffuses floral hormones, flowering is retarded. If heavily pruned shortly before flowers and fruit set, maturation is delayed for a week or longer. Sometimes it takes a month or longer for hormones to build up to pre-pruning concentrations.

 Super Size Secret: Do not remove healthy green shade leaves! Remove only dead leaves or if more than 50 percent damaged. Healthy leaves produce food and hormones for the rest of the plant, including roots!

Leave leaves alone! Leaf removal is not pruning, it is hacking up a healthy plant. Ill-informed gardeners believe that removing large shade leaves makes plants more productive, because it supplies more light to smaller leaves and growing tips. Wrong! This is bad gardening! Plants need all of their leaves to produce the maximum amount of chlorophyll and food. Removing leaves slows chlorophyll production, stresses a plant, and stunts growth. Stress is a growth inhibitor. Remove only dead leaves or leaves that are more than 50 percent damaged.

Stress

Plants grow best and produce the strongest, most robust flowers and fruit when given a stable environment. Stressed plants produce less than unstressed plants. Stress-induced trauma, including withholding water, photoperiod fluctuation, low light intensity, ultraviolet light, nutrient toxicities and deficiencies, cold and hot soil and ambient temperatures and mutilation, or any overt applications of growth hormones such as B^9 hormone, gibberellins, cytokinins, abscisic acid, ethylene, colchicene (polyploid inducer), etc., cause more trouble than they are worth.

Removing large green shade leaves allow more light to shine on smaller leaves, but it also causes growth to slow. The more leaves that are removed, the more severe the stunting and lower the harvest volume. Remove only leaves that are more than half damaged by pests or diseases. Often, partially yellow leaves green up once stress is eliminated. Removing spindly and dimly lit lower branches stresses plants much less than removing leaves, and actually speeds growth of upper foliage.

Withholding water impairs growth and diminishes leaf, stem, flower and fruit production. Water stress slows or stops cuttings from rooting. If cuttings have too many leaves and are to busy transpiring, root growth is very slow. Conversely, water-logged rooting mediums harbor no air, and rooting is also slowed to a crawl.

Flowering

In order for a plant to complete its annual lifecycle successfully, it must first flower. Dioecious plants are either male (pollen producing) or female (ovule producing). Hermaphrodite plants are bisexual, with both male and female flowers on the same plant. Most plants fall into the latter category. When dioecious plants turn hermaphrodite, any resulting seeds are usually female.

When a plant is fertilized, one of the many tiny grains of pollen from the male (staminate) flower pod lands on a pistil of the female (pistilate) flower. Each calyx harbors an ovule and a set of pistils. Actual fertilization takes place when the grain of male pollen slides down the pistil and unites with the female ovule, deep within the calyx. Once fertilization takes place, a seed will form within the calyx or seed bract. Seeds are the result of this sexual propagation and contain genetic characteristics of both parents.

Long-day Plants

In nature, annual plants' lifecycle comes to an end in the fall, after the long, hot, days of summer. The long nights and short days of autumn signal long-day plants to start the flowering stage. Growth patterns and chemistry change. Stems elongate, flower formation is rapid at first then slows. All this causes new nutrient needs. Attention is now focused on flower and fruit production, rather than on leafy vegetative growth. Production of chlorophyll, requiring much nitrogen, slows. Phosphorus uptake increases to promote floral formation. Light needs change as well. During autumn, in most climates, the sun takes on a slightly reddish appearance, emitting a light that is a more red than white. The harvest sun phenomenon is not fully understood. However, experiments have proved that by increasing the amount of red light during flowering, floral hormones are stimulated and flower yield increases substantially. Switch from halide to HP sodium lamps.

During summer, sunlight moves through only one or two atmospheres of air. Blue sky (sky color) is dominant. In the fall, the sun is low in the horizon and light goes through four to five atmospheres of air, blocking out much of the blue light. This is also why sunrises and sunsets are red.

Indoors, flowering may be induced in short-day plants just as it is in nature, by shortening the photoperiod from 18 to 12 hours. Once the days are changed to 12 hours, flowers should be clearly visible within one to three weeks. In fact, some gardeners have two garden rooms: a vegetative garden room with one metal halide that supplies 18 hours of light. The other room for growing short-day plants that has both a halide and HP sodium that is on for 12 hours a day.

Using this combination of rooms and lamps, the electricity bill remains relatively low and the horticulturist has the luxury of having both summer and fall every day of the year!

The harvest sun is simulated one of three ways: (1) Adding an HP sodium lamp to a garden room already containing a metal halide. This more than doubles the available light, especially in the red end of the spectrum. The halide maintains blues in the spectrum necessary for continued chlorophyll production. (2) Replacing the halide with a HP sodium. This increases the reds, but cuts the blues. A result of this practice has been more yellowing of vegetative leaves, due to lack of chlorophyll production and more stem elongation than if the halide were present. (3) Adding or changing to a phosphor-coated halide. Not only are these halides easier on the eyes, their coating makes them produce a little bit more red in their spectrum, thus promoting flowering.

Water needs of a flowering plant are somewhat less than in the vegetative stage. Adequate water during flowering is important to carry on the plant's chemistry. Withholding water to stress a plant will actually stunt growth and the yield will be less.

Hermaphrodites

A hermaphrodite is a plant that has both male and female flowers on the same plant. The majority of plants fall into this category.

Indoors, the outdoor environment is manufactured and the normal life cycle of any plant can be altered. Creating summer in December, taking cuttings, prolonging the life cycle and leaching the soil – all the wonderful things we are able to do indoors, mixes up even the strongest plant somewhat. When this stress is coupled with weak seeds, the outcome is uncertain. High humidity, over-pruning and old age seem to promote hermaphrodites more than other environmental factors. In short, if a plant starts to go sour, and you do not know the reason why, it could be because it was stressed too much.

Seed Crops

Seed crops are harvested when the seeds are mature. Often seeds may actually split open their containing calyx or seedpod. The flower grows many ready, receptive calyxes until pollination occurs. Seeds are normally mature within six to eight weeks. Watch out for fungus that might attack the weakening flower and cache of ripe seeds.

When seeds are mature, remove them from the pods and store them in a cool, dry place. The seeds are viable and ready for planting as soon as they are harvested, but they may grow sickly plants. Let the seeds dry out a few months before planting. Dry seeds will produce much healthier plants, and the germination rate will be higher.

Extending Growing Seasons

About Extending Growing Seasons

Outdoors, the easiest and most economical ways to extend growing seasons are to add warmth and shelter to protect plants from cold weather and high winds. Modern materials have greatly expanded the products available for protecting plants from early and late cold during spring and fall. These new products, in addition to traditional ones, such as cloches and improvised ones, allow gardeners to grow vegetables earlier and longer than the weather would suggest.

In addition, these products make it possible to be able to grow desirable plants in climates that are one or more zones farther north than the plants would grow if unprotected.

You can also lengthen the growing season by finding the microclimates on your property where the soil warms up and stays warm longer. Some mini-environments occur because of orientation to the sun, plus protection from wind. Other warm sites occur near buildings that are not very weather-tight. Warm microclimates occur next to brick, stone and mortar walls and fences which, by holding heat, buffer the surrounding climate and help prevent the very damaging freeze-thaw cycles so common in the Midwest and other parts of the country.

Dark walls will absorb and hold more heat than light-colored walls, another factor that may affect nearby growing conditions. Dark soil absorbs more heat than light-colored soil, which is another factor to take into account when trying to extend growing seasons for useful and ornamental plants.

A body of water such as a lake, pond, or small creek will also moderate the air temperature. If your garden is near water, the winter temperature will be higher and the summer temperature cooler than the more distant surrounding area.

*Covering garden beds
with floating row covers such
as Reemay™ will keep them warmer..*

If untimely, hard frosts threaten tender
plants, an old-fashioned trick to avoid
plant injury is to turn sprinklers or misters
on the plants. This will work for tender
trees and shrubs as well as smaller plants.
One year, we saw tuberous begonias that
were covered with thick ice after being
sprinkled to avoid frost damage. When the
sun came out, they were beautiful in a
strange and sparkling way. When the ice
melted, the plants were as healthy as
before the frost hit.

*The Wall –O–Water
will hold plants down
to below 20 degrees F.
The trick is, when
water freezes, it releas-
es energy to heat the
plant inside!*

Low spots will be colder than sites with a higher elevation.
Cold air sinks. That's why an ideal site for an orchard is on a
slope. Cold air flows down the slope providing good air circulation to the orchard trees while avoiding the frosty air that flows
down and lingers to the bottom of the slope.

If you have a cold-sensitive shrub, small tree or smaller plant
outdoors when early or late frost threatens, put a sheet or blan-
ket over the plant and rig a low-wattage electric light bulb
under the covering. Make sure the bulb is not near the fabric,
which might catch on fire. The bulb under the cover will keep
the temperature 10 to 15 degrees above the ambient temperature in the rest of the garden.

Dark plastic mulches, which also shade weeds and prevent
moisture loss, are an inexpensive way to increase the temperature of the soil 5 to 15 degrees on sunny days. As plants grow,
the leaves shade the dark soil, gradually stopping the warming
affect. Clear plastic is more efficient in warming the soil than
black.

Placing dark rocks strategically is a simple way to moderate
temperature in small areas of the garden. You can create your

own mini-environments with these rocks, which will absorb and hold heat over a long period, and slowly release it in the immediate vicinity.

In the Northwest where the winters are cloudy, you need to maximize available light. Greenhouses need to be glass or very clear plastic to transmit light well. Gardeners in southern climates with more intense sunlight can use less expensive plastic or double-walled greenhouses that do not transmit as much light.

Cool weather plants need the opposite kind of shelter. You must protect them from too much heat and sun in order to extend their growing season. If you shade these plants, including lettuce and cabbage family members, from afternoon sun when the hot season arrives, you can extend their harvest time and keep them from bolting. Thick organic mulches help hold moisture and keep the soil cool.

Covers, Tunnels & Cloches

Covering plants with row tunnels, cloches and covers will protect them from extreme cold and freezes. They make it easy to plant earlier in the spring and have harvests far into the fall.

Spun fiber coverings, including the brands Agronet™ and Reemay™, will protect plants from late and early frosts if set over young plants and anchored around the perimeter with soil or rocks. Plants will support the light spun-fiber row covers and no superstructure is needed.

When using flexible row covers, you may need to buy the large staples that are available for securing row covers and plastic mulches in place. Or you can make your own from old coat hangers by cutting off the two curved ends. Staples that are one-inch wide and four to six inches long are handy.

Row covers can be made of clear corrugated fiberglass that is bent into an arch and secured in the garden. The size of this kind of row cover is limited only by the size of the fiberglass panels.

There are commercial row covers that combine polypropylene with hoops to make season extenders that will protect garden crops down to temperatures as low as 25 degrees F. These come in sizes large enough to use on dwarf fruit trees and mature tomato vines. They also come in smaller sizes for pepper plants, eggplants and rose bushes.

A milk container with no lid or bottom is a great cloche. It protects tender plants and the hole in the top serves as a vent on hot days.

Cloches made of plastic, glass or wet-strength waxed paper, protect individual plants. Plastic milk jugs with the bottoms cut out make the simplest of cloches. And who does not remember rose fanciers who used Mason jars to protect small rose cuttings that they started in their garden beds.

There are commercial cloches in all sizes. Typical are the cone-shaped caps made of rigid, transparent plastic or wet-strength waxed paper that are easy to use and will stack conveniently.

The water-filled teepee known as Wall-O-Water is a season extender for protecting plants from cold at night and shielding them from excess heat during the day. They are ideal for extending the season for individual plants and, although most often used during spring months, also have potential for extending the fall season. Each water teepee holds three gallons of water and will last from three to five years if given proper care.

During the day, the water absorbs the heat of the sun and moderates the temperature inside the teepee. When night falls and the air becomes colder than the water in the teepee, the water slowly releases its heat. If the water begins to freeze, it will release more heat. These teepees will protect plants down to 10 degrees F. Each one can release as much as 900,000 calories according to the product literature.

Cold Frames

A cold frame is a rectangular plastic- or glass-topped container that is placed on the ground to protect plants from climatic extremes. The heat inside is provided by sunlight. A cold frame will slow soil-moisture evaporation, warm both soil and air and also protect plants from pests.

A cold frame will extend the spring season by six weeks to two months. If you plant tomatoes in a cold frame two months earlier than recommended, you will have fresh fruit up to six weeks earlier than your neighbors. This big jump on the growing season may be possible in mild climates such as the Pacific Northwest, but not in more rigorous climates like the Upper Midwest.

Cold frame lean-to with glass across the front will keep spring starts warm.

Open a cold frame or simple greenhouse during the heat of the day to provide cooling and air circulation. Fancier cold frames have wax-filled vents that operate automatically. When the heat rises in the frame, the wax expands, opening the vent. When the temperature cools, the wax contracts closing the vent.

Cold frames come in many forms, the simplest of which is old window sashes laid over a rectangle of straw bales. This simple cold frame is as effective as more expensive ones.

Half or three-quarter-inch galvanized metal conduit pipe bent into

Covered garden bed stays warmer in spring and still has open ends for ventilation.

an arc makes a great superstructure for a cold frame. Many local hardware stores or electrical supply companies will bend the pipe for you or loan you the pipe bender for a day to bend it yourself. Half-inch schedule 40 PVC irrigation pipe also works well and can simply be bent by hand.

A piece of plastic is simply stretched over the dome-shaped conduit or PVC pipe. It is held in place with clamps so that it can be easily removed on warm days or completely covered at night. The ends are easy to open to form a breezy tunnel on warm days.

PolyWeave™, made of 8-mil polyethylene reinforced with woven nylon mesh is a typical new plastic fabric. It transmits up to 90 percent sunlight, can be sewn or taped and has a life span of up to five years.

Greenhouses

A multipurpose solar greenhouse attached to the home can be used to grow plants and will also help heat and humidify the home. It is a nice place for afternoon tea or happy hour, and it is a bright and cheery spot for a winter picnic.

Conventional greenhouses do not retain heat well. As a result, at night or on cloudy days, they are expensive to heat. To solve this problem, one grower in Portland, Oregon heats his greenhouse with compost. He stacks organic matter up on the sides of the greenhouse to a height of about five feet, both inside and out. As the piles decompose they give off heat, which keeps the greenhouse warm.

Greenhouses are made of many materials and can function in many climatic conditions, if you're willing to foot the bill. The most economical way to use a greenhouse is as a large cold frame. Use it to extend growing seasons. But if you live in a cold climate and want to grow exotic tropicals, be prepared for high heating bills. In sunny regions, solar heat can help reduce heating costs.

Solar grow frames hold their heat by using insulation. Solar frames also benefit from insulation and, in larger units, heat-retaining materials such as drums filled with water to serve as thermal mass.

Commercial growers use greenhouses in hot climates to shade plants and keep them cooler than the ambient air. Shade cloth and whitewash are the two classic ways to shade greenhouses in the summer. Home greenhouses can be shaded in summer in the same ways, or you can plant deciduous trees, which will provide shade in the summer and allow the sun through their branches during cold months.

If you plan to add a greenhouse room onto your home, consult with experts and talk to someone who already has this kind of an addition. Double- or even triple-glazed coverings on greenhouses, although expensive, will be effective in cutting utility costs.

Before investing time, money and energy to build a greenhouse, analyze the project carefully on paper. List what you want to use the greenhouse for, and be very specific and figure in the square footage that you would need. Study the possible sites for a greenhouse and list the pluses and minuses of each.

Then and only then, you are ready to begin discussing the project with an expert or developing plans to do it yourself.

It may be that you want a simple freestanding work area with a potting bench where you can start plants from seed and grow them into transplants. If that is the case, you could probably have a temporary plastic cover such as a tent over the area during the late winter and early spring months. This, combined with heating cables and a heater in case of unseasonable freezes, might be all you need.

Protection From The Elements

Windbreaks protect plants from heat and water loss. They also can increase the average temperature from 1 to 5 degrees on the downwind side of the windbreak.

Traditional windbreaks - in the prairies and plains where prevailing winds are strong and constant - are poplars and other fast-growing deciduous trees, combined with tall evergreens such as Norway spruce. The evergreens are staggered along the windward side of the windbreak, with the deciduous trees arranged in random rows on the lee side.

Windbreaks for homes and home gardens need not be on such a heroic scale. They can include smaller trees and shrubs. They can also function as sound and sight barriers. Irregular rows of tall plants also can protect outdoor living areas from summer sun, often a very important function.

The best wind-breaking hedges are not orchard trees and bushes, but woody plants chosen for their foliage and growth pattern as wind buffers. The flowers and fruit of edibles are damaged by high winds. There are a few exceptions, such as carob, mulberry, olive and nut trees.

Arbors, Shade, & Lath Houses

Arbors, shade houses and lath houses are excellent ways to protect people and plants from too much heat and sun. A shade structure can be used over both the patio and garden beds, especially when the vegetable varieties are chosen for their ornamental appeal and arranged in an artistic way.

Arbors and pergolas, ornamental structures built to support plants and create pathways and sitting areas in the garden, are classic solutions to providing shade in an attractive way. They are ideal for grape vines, too.

Arbors and pergolas are well suited for climbing roses and clematis. They are also interesting challenges for growing vining vegetables, squashes, cucumbers, beans and peas. Once the vines are growing well, use the shade inside or on the north side for growing shade-loving plants. Leaf lettuce will do better in the shade during the hot months and make a beautiful border plant.

Create a shade house by attaching shade cloth to a frame. Use it for a picnic area or to provide protection for potted plants during the intense heat of summer. Shade cloth is a synthetic material available in a range of sun-blocking ability. Homeowners and gardeners are just beginning to discover the many uses for shade cloth. It can be found in most horticultural supply stores.

A lath house built from thin, narrow strips of wood can provide 25 percent shade, 50 percent shade or more, depending on how close you place the laths. Lath houses can be simple, stark structures to fulfill a practical function only, or they can be built with aesthetics in mind so that they are handsome as well as utilitarian.

Plant
Selection
Guide

African violets, begonias and impatiens all bloom constantly
under lights. Begonias of all types, ferns, oxalis, geraniums,
annuals, small shrubs and trees such as jasmine, gardenia,
crape myrtle, dwarf lantana and dwarf pomegranate, citrus
and figs all grow well under HIDs.

Cacti and succulents: jade, miniature crassulas, Christmas, Easter
and Thanksgiving cactus etc., are probably the easiest to care
for under lights. They require a minimum of care and infre-
quent watering, but lots of light.

African Violets: parent plants and cuttings of this short-day plant
are given 18 hours of light a day at a level of 6,000 mWm².
Flowering is induced with a short 12 to 14-hour photoperiod.

Azalea cuttings propagated under a light level of 6,000 mWm², 18
hours a day, grow fast and uniform. Flowers are effectively
forced by supplying 3,000 mWm² for 16 hours a day.

Begonias: Supplemental lighting promotes cuttings to form on
the varieties 'Rieger', 'Elatior' and 'Lorraine' when natural
light is lacking. A light level of 6,000 mWm² is the norm. Use
6,000 mWm² 18 hours a day to nurture young seedlings and to
speed flowering. Rooting is stimulated in begonia cuttings by
artificial light.

Bromeliads: A light level of 6,000 mWm² 18 hours a day is used to
promote stronger growth and the development of seedlings
and young plants. On larger bromeliads, supplemental lighting is normally used to help stimulate floral formation.
A light level of 4,500 mWm² for 24 hours a day is used to stimulate flowering. Many times other flower-inducing means are
combined with lighting to hasten blooming.

Cacti: In winter when the days are short, cacti greatly benefit
from intense supplemental light. A lighting level of 9,000
mWm² for 18 hours a day will produce phenomenal results in

seedlings, cuttings and adult cacti. Some varieties of cactus respond more favorably to 24 hours of light.

Calceolaria: Early flowering is achieved by applying supplemental lighting (3,000 mWm^2) for 24 hours a day from bud induction until flowering. Maintain the temperature between 60 and 65 degrees for maximum productivity.

Carnations: are propagated very successfully from cuttings and using supplemental light. Side shoots from cut flowers make excellent cuttings. Cuttings are taken and given 16 hours of light (6,000 mWm^2). Excessive flowering may occur if more than 16 hours of light per day is permitted. The carnation is a long-day plant. It is possible to light it 24 hours a day to grow more and more profuse flowers. However, after 18 hours of light a day, the extra light produces a minimum of growth.

Chrysanthemums: are one of the most responsive flowers to supplemental light in all stages of life. In winter parent plants are given 9,000 mWm^2, 20 hours a day. Given lighting during the first month of vegetative growth increases bud count and foliage production. Being a short-day plant, the chrysanthemum requires 20 hours of light a day during the first month of vegetative growth and 12 hours of light (4,500 mWm^2) and 12 hours of uninterrupted darkness to flower properly.

Cucumber: seedlings grow exceptionally well under HID lights. Give young seedlings a light level of 4500 mWm^2 for the first 10 days of growth for 24 hours a day. After this, shorten the photoperiod to 16 hours per day and increase the light level to 6000 mWm^2.

Cyclamen: seedlings given supplemental lighting (6,000 mWm^2) have more uniform growth and less damping off. The young plants are given 18 hours of light a day.

Geraniums and pelargoniums: propagated by seed or from cuttings greatly benefit from supplemental light. Parent plants are given 18 hours of light at a level of 6,000 mWm^2 to increase cutting production. The cuttings are given less light but for the same 18 hours a day. Geraniums are a short-day plant and flower with shorter days or colder temperatures. F^1 hybrid seed-propagated geraniums can be given 24 hours of light a day at a level of 6,000 mWm^2 from the beginning of life. These F[1] hybrids do not need short days for flower induction.

Gloxinas: are given a light level of 6000 mWm[2] 18 hours a day to enhance growth and development of seedlings and young plants. Give potted gloxinas a light level of 4500 mWm2 to promote large healthy flowers.

Kalanchoe: parent plants are given 18 hours of light a day to prevent flowering of this long-day plant. Normally propagated vegetatively, cuttings are given 18 to 24 hours of light at a level of 6,000 mWm[2]. Induce flowering by giving plants 12 hours of light and 12 hours of darkness.

Lettuce: is lighted at a level of 6000 mWm[2] during its entire life. If given a higher level of light, lettuce might bolt.

Orchids: The blooms and overall growth of many varieties of orchids are greatly enhanced by supplemental lighting during the winter. See section below on light requirements of orchids.

Roses: love light. Miniature roses grow incredibly well under HID light. Levels of 6,000 mWm[2], 24 hours per day will greatly increase flower yield, size and quality. Supplemental carbon dioxide really boosts growth of these super-productive roses.

Snapdragons: are a favorite fall and early spring flower. There are two genetically different types of snapdragons, short-day, referred to as Group I or II or "winter flowering," and long-day, referred to as Group III or IV or "summer flowering." When setting this plant out for early spring blooms, give seedlings supplementary lighting at a level of 9,000 mWm[2] so that a day length of 16 hours is reached. This will speed flowering by about four weeks. Even better results can be achieved by giving long-day plants 24 hours of light (4,500 mWm[2]) throughout their life. Short day snapdragons should receive short 12-hour days after they are about two months old for maximum blooming potential.

Tomatoes, peppers and eggplants flourish under HID light. The more light these plants are given the bigger they grow and the more fruit they produce. Give plants 9000 mWm[2] as soon the first true leaves appear and maintain the light level throughout their entire life.

Orchid Culture Under Lights

Light requirements for orchids fall into three categories.

High: 3000 foot-candles or more, which is equivalent to the amount of light available to plants growing in the middle of a sunny field.

Medium: 1500-3000 foot-candles, which is similar to the amount of light received by lightly shaded plants.

Low: under 1500 foot-candles, for plants that grow deep beneath the canopy of the forest.

Temperature requirements are divided into three groups:

Warm: (70 to 75 degrees F., 21 to 24 degrees C) day, (60 to 65 degrees F, 15 to 18 degrees 0 C) night similar to the climate of a seacoast or swampy lowland.

Medium: (65 to 70 degrees F, 18 to 21 degrees C) day, (55 to 60 degrees F, 13 to 15 degrees C) night similar to rolling forests and fields.

Cool: (60 to 65 degrees F, 15 to 18 degrees C) day, (50 to 55 degrees F, 10 to 13 degrees C) night similar to high mountainous regions.

Orchids can be referred to as being high light, cool-air plants. The Cymbidium is a good example of this type of orchid. The Phalaenopsis genus is a low-light, warm-air orchid.

All plants may be divided into two groups: species and hybrid. Hybridization often eliminates many of the natural limitations imposed by the original climatic requirements of an orchid. For example, if you breed a high light, warm-air species with a medium-light, medium-temperature species, the result is a hybrid that grows well in either category.

For growing requirements of specific plants, flowers and herbs, consult garden books and encyclopedias or get on the worldwide web if you have a computer. Good reference books include: The *Wise Garden Encyclopedia*, by Grosset and Dunlap Publishing (ISBN: 0-448-01997-3), *New Encyclopedia of Herbs and Their Uses* by Herbal Society of America and *Exotic House Plants* by Graf, Published by Roehrs Co., (ISBN: 0-9112266-10-0).

Troubleshooting

This simple, troubleshooting chart will solve most of the cultivation problems encountered indoors. One word of caution, this troubleshooting chart assumes the garden room is clean.

Cuttings are relatively easy to root. Success rate depends on the proper combination of heat, humidity, light, rooting hormone and growing medium aeration and moisture. The more precise the combination, the faster and stronger roots grow.

Vegetative growth is when problems begin to show. Often these problems continue through flowering. Remedy problems before they progress. If allowed to persist, through flowering and fruiting, yield is diminished substantially.

Flowering and fruiting are the last stage in life. Problems must be solved in the first two weeks (at the absolute latest 3 weeks) of flowering, or yields decrease in relation to the severity of the problems.

Note: Keep growing area super clean to help prevent problems. If you notice insects or fungus on foliage, remove them and check them against color photos and drawings in this book. If photos or drawings do not appear in this book, cross-reference with the Troubleshooting Chart. Look for specific causes, including nutrient deficiencies, toxicities and cultural problems.

Troubleshooting Chart

Growth Stage	Cause	Quick Fix
Seeds and Seedlings		
Seeds do not germinate	Damping off Bad seed	Buy new seed, start over Get your money back!
	Root maggots	Drench soil with neem or horticultural oil
Seed germinates, seedling has signs of pests eating/sucking foliage	Spider mites (stippled leaves) Aphids (exude honeydew)	Spray neem oil or pyrethrum Spray pyrethrum, insecticidal soap or nicotine sulfate
Seedling stem at base dark or sickly growth, suddenly falls over or suddenly wilts	Damping off Damping off or a wilt disease Too much or too little moisture	drench soil with metalaxyl or buy new seeds uncommon in clones correct accordingly
Seedling leaves have yellow, gray, black and/or dark green (fungus-like) spots	Blight or anthracnose	remove growing plants and growing medium
Cuttings		
Wilt and die	lack of moisture	add humidity dome, mist 4-6 times daily
Wilt and die	medium too wet	drain medium, do not water, no standing water in tray
Won't root	medium too dry or too wet	see "Wilt and die" above
	inconsistent rooting hormone	change to liquid or gel rooting hormone
Vegetative stage		
Leggy, weak plants	lack of light	add lamp, change reflector, move lamp closer to plants
Leggy weak plants	lack of ventilation, soil too wet soil too dry toxic nutrient buildup	add vent fan irrigate less irrigate more leach grow medium* change nutrient solution

Stunted stubby plants	insect damage, rotten roots toxic nutrient buildup	spray pyrethrum** irrigate less leach grow medium*
Burned leaf tips Purple stems & burned leaf spots	toxic nutrient buildup - could be one of many different nutrients	leach medium* weekly lower nutrient dose & leach medium* weekly
Leaf spots, margins burned, discolored leaves, pale leaves	nutrient toxicity	leach medium*, change nutrient solution, change fertilizer, refer to specific nutrient problems
Small whitish spots on leaves	spider mite damage	spray pyrethrum**, neem oil
Insect damage - chewed leaves, insects/eggs visible on plants - check under leaves with 20X loop.	whiteflies, aphids, scale, caterpillars, larva, etc.	spray pyrethrum** or neem oil
Fungus or mold on foliage or soil	high humidity (above 60%) high temp. (above 80 F)	add vent fan add vent fan Spray soil with 5% bleach solution and wash off next day. Spray foliage with 10 % baking soda solution
Severe sudden wilting of plant	fusarium or verticillium wilt lack of water roots in water	remove plant and growing medium and destroy irrigate plant submerge

Flowering

Slow growth and small buds	over-fertilized, water/light/air stressed, cooked or rotten roots	leach* grow medium add big/more vent fans Keep grow medium evenly moist. The closer to harvest less can be done. Must remedy 3-6 weeks before harvest for results
Older leaf discoloration and dieback	nitrogen, potassium, phosphorus or zinc deficiency	see specific nutrient for solution
New leaf discoloration and dieback	one of the secondary or trace elements	see specific nutrient for solution

| Dead grayish spots in buds | bud mold (Botrytis) | remove entire bud one inch below damage, drop the humidity |
| Pungent odors from grow room | ripening bud smells much more than early bud | install ozone generator in large rooms. Use "Ona" or "Odor Killer" in small rooms |

*Leach or flush growing medium with mild (quarter-strength) nutrient solution. Flush with at least three times the volume of nutrient solution per gallon of medium.

**Spray at 5-day intervals for 15 days. Use aerosol pyrethrum and spray under leaves. If problem persists, switch to neem oil and alternate with pyrethrum.

Checklist

A checklist adds necessary routine and stability to an indoor garden schedule. This weekly checklist consists of a few things that must be done every week to ensure a successful garden.

Savvy gardeners read and consider each and every point on the checklist weekly. They mark each point with a check when finished with it.

Gardeners should spend at least 10 minutes per day, per lamp to have a productive garden. This is enough time to complete all the stuff in the weekly checklist. Much of gardening is simply watching and paying attention. It takes time to have a decent and productive garden. If using CO_2 enrichment or hydroponics, allow up to 20 minutes per day for maintenance.

Weekly Checklist
Check the following to see if they function properly:
Air ventilation
Air circulation
Humidity – 40-50 percent
Temperature: day – 70 – 75: night: 55 – 60
Soil moisture (dry pockets) water as needed
Cultivate soil surface
Check pH
Rotate (turn) plants
Check for spider mites under leaves
Check for fungi
Check for nutrient deficiencies
Regular fertilization schedule
Check HID system for excessive dangerous heat at
    plug-in, timer, ballast and near ceiling
Cleanup!
Cleanup!
Cleanup!
Check walls and ceiling for mold
Move lamp up, 12 – 36 inches above plants

Conversion Charts and Tables

Appendix: Carbon Dioxide Facts and Figures

Molecular weight = 44 grams/mole
Sublimes (solid to gas) at 78.5 degrees C at 1 atmosphere: air
density = 1.2928 grams/liter (i.e. at equal temperatures and pressures carbon dioxide is heavier than air and CO_2 will fall to the
bottom of an air/ CO_2 mixture.

To calculate a new volume, if only previous volume, temperature,
and pressure are known use the formula:

$$V2 =: \frac{T2}{P2} \quad X \quad :\frac{P1}{T1} \quad X \quad V1$$

Where V2 = new volume in liters
V1 = old volume in liters
P1 = old pressure in atmospheres
P2 = new pressure in atmospheres
T1 = old temperature in degrees Kelvin
T2 = new temperature in degrees Kelvin

If the weight of gas is known use:

$$\text{Volume (liters)} = \frac{\text{Weight } CO_2 \text{ X } 0.08205 \text{ X temp. (degrees K)}}{44 \text{ X pressure in atmospheres}}$$

(K = Kelvin, absolute temperature)

(weight of CO_2 measured in grams)
Example:
Weight CO_2 = 5 kgs = 5000 grams
Pressure = 14.7 PSI = 1 atmosphere
Temperature = 25 degrees C = 25 + 273 = 298 degrees K

The volume of gas will be
$$5000 \times 0.08205 \times 298$$

$$44 \times 1 \qquad = 2{,}778 \text{ liters}$$
$$\qquad\qquad\qquad = 2.778 \text{ cubic meters}$$

Special thanks to Robin Moseby for this Appendix
Physical properties of Propane:

Formula	C_3H_8
Boiling point	-440 F
Specific gravity of gas (air = 1)	1.50
Specific Gravity of liquid @ 60 deg. F. (water = 1)	0.504
Latent heat vaporization total/bal.	773.0
Pounds per gallon of liquid @ 60 deg. F	4.23
Gallons per pound of liquid @ 60 deg. F.	0.236
BTU per cubic foot of gas @ 60 deg. F.	2488
BTU per lb. of gas	21548
BTU per gallon of gas @ 60 deg. F.	90502
Lower limit of flammability (% of gas)	2.15
Upper limit of flammability (% of gas)	9.60
Cubic feet of gas per gallon of liquid	36.38
Octane number	100+

Combustion Data:

Cubic feet of air to burn 1 gal. of propane	873.6
Cubic feet of CO_2 per gal. of Propane burned	109.2
Cubic feet of nitrogen per gal. of propane burned	688
Pounds of CO_2 per gal. of propane burned	12.7
Pounds of nitrogen per gal. of propane burned	51.2
Pounds of water vapor per gal. of propane burned	6.8
1 pound of propane produces in KWH	6.3
BTU's per KW hour	3412
BTU input per boiler horsepower	45,000
1 MCF of natural gas	1,000,000 BTU
	(11 gal. propane)
Therm	100,000 BTU
	(1.1 gal. propane)

BTU Content	Per Gal.	Per Lb.	LP Gas Properties	Propane
Propane	91,300	21,600	BTU pr cubic ft.	2,516
Fuel oil	135,435	16,200	Pounds per gallon	4.24
Liquefied Nat Gas	86,000	23,200	Cubic ft. per gallon	36.39
Soft coal	———	14,000	Cubic ft. per pound	8.58
			Specific gravity of vapor	1.52

1 Therm	100,000 BTU	**Specific gravity of liquid**	**0.509**
1 Cu. ft. Nat. Gas	1,000 BTU	Vapor pressure (psig) 00F	23.5
1 Lb. steam	970 BTU	Vapor pressure (psig) 700 F	109
1 Kilowatt	3,413 BTU	Vapor pressure (psig) 1000 F	172

Appendix: Calculations for Metric Users

1 cubic meter = 1m X 1m X 1m = 1,000 liters

Fans are rated at liters per minute or liters per second

Measure room length, width and height in meters
e.g. 3m X 3m x 2.4m = 21.6 cubic meters

Buy a fan that will clear the garden room volume of air in 1 to 5 minutes. Run the fan for twice the time to theoretically clear the garden room of air.

Work out the amount of CO_2 gas to add:
e.g. want 1,500 PPM: ambient is 350 PPM:
need to add 1,500: 350 = 1,150 PPM

Garden room size in cubic meters X PPM of CO_2 add = liters 1,000

Most garden rooms probably have a 20 percent leakage factor which has to be added to the CO_2 gas required.

For our garden room 21.6 cubic meters and 1,500 PPM of CO_2 we need to add
21.4 X 1,150 = 24.61 liters X 1.2 = 29.53 liters 1,000

Set the flow meter to 6 liters per minute and run the gas for 5 minutes.

Leave the gas enriched air for 20 minutes and then exhaust the air from the garden room and start the cycle again.

A short-range timer, programmable down to 1 minute and up to 54 cycles per day: with two of these one can set up a reliable CO_2 injection system: one timer working the inlet and exhaust fans and the other working the solenoid. This can make a simple mechanism for CO_2 enrichment.

Metric Conversion Chart: Approximations

When You Know	Multiply by	To Find Length
millimeters	0.04	inches
centimeters	0.39	inches
meters	3.28	feet
kilometers	0.62	miles
inches	25.40	millimeters
inches	2.54	centimeters
feet	30.48	centimeters
yards	0.91	meters
miles	1.666	kilometers

Area

square centimeters	0.16	square inches
square meters	1.20	square yards
square kilometers	0.39	square miles
hectares	2.47	acres
square inches	6.45	square centimeters
square feet	0.09	square meters
square yards	0.84	square meters
square miles	2.60	square kilometers
acres	0.40	hectares

Volume

milliliters	0.20	teaspoons
milliliters	0.60	tablespoons
milliliters	0.03	fluid ounces
liters	4.23	cups
liters	2.12	pints
liters	1.06	quarts
liters	0.26	gallons
cubic meters	35.32	cubic feet
cubic meters	1.35	cubic yards
teaspoons	4.93	milliliters
tablespoons	14.78	milliliters
fluid ounces	29.57	milliliters
cups	0.24	liters
pints	0.47	liters
quarts	0.95	liters
gallons	3.790	liters

Mass and Weight

grams	0.035	ounce
kilograms	2.21	pounds
ounces	28.35	grams
pounds	0.45	kilograms

1 inch (in.) = 25.4 millimeters (mm)
1 foot (12 in.) = 0.3048 meters (m)
1 yard (3 ft) = 0.9144 meters
1 mile = 1.60937 kilometers
1 square inch = 645 square millimeters
1 square foot = 0.0929 square meters
1 square yard = 0.8361 square meters
1 square mile = 2.59 square kilometers

Liquid Measure Conversion
1 pint (UK) = 0.56824 liters
1 pint dry (US) = 0.55059 liters
1 pint liquid (US) = 0.47316 liters
1 gallon (UK) (8 pints) = 4.5459 liters
1 gallon dry (US) = 4.4047 liters
1 pint liquid (US) = 3.7853 liters

1 ounce = 28.3495 grams
1 pound (16 ounces) = 0.453592 kilograms

1 gram = 15.4325 grains
1 kilogram = 2.2046223 pounds

1 millimeter = 0.03937014 inches (UK)
1 millimeter = 0.03937 inches (US)
1 centimeter = 0.3937014 inches (UK)
1 centimeter = 0.3937 inches (US)
1 meter = 3.280845 feet (UK)
1 meter = 3.280833 feet (US)
1 kilometer = 0.6213722 miles

Celsius to Fahrenheit
Degrees Celsius = (degrees Fahrenheit − 32) x 5/9
Degrees Fahrenheit = (degrees Celsius x 9/5) +32

Light Conversion
1 foot-candle = 10.76 = lux
1 lux = 0.09293
   Lux = 1 lumen/square meters

Glossary

This Glossary contains many very simple and some not so simple words in the context of their usage in this book. Many examples are given to promote good indoor horticultural practices.

Alternating Current (AC): An electric current that reverses its direction at regularly occurring intervals. Homes have AC.

Acid: A sour substance, an acid or sour soil has a low pH.

Adobe: Heavy clay soil, not suitable for container gardening.

Aeration: Supplying soil and roots with air or oxygen. Aeroponics: Growing plants by misting roots suspended in air

Aggregate: Medium, usually gravel, that is all nearly the same size and used for the inert hydroponic medium.

Alkaline: Refers to soil with a high pH; any pH over 7 is considered alkaline.

All-purpose (General-purpose) fertilizer: A balanced blend of N-P-K; all purpose fertilizer is used by most growers in the vegetative growth stage.

Amendment: Changing soil texture by adding organic or mineral substances.

Ampere (amp): The unit used to measure the strength of an electric current: A 20-amp circuit is overloaded when drawing more than 17 amps.

Annual: A plant that normally completes its entire life cycle in one year or less, marigolds and tomatoes are examples of plants grown as annuals.

Arc: Luminous discharge of electricity (light) between two electrodes.

Arc tube: A quartz container for luminous gases also houses the arc in HID lights.

Auxin: Classification of plant hormones; auxins are responsible for foliage and root elongation.

Bacteria: Very small, one-celled organisms that have no chlorophyll.

Beneficial insect: A good insect that eats bad flower and vegetable-munching insects.

Biodegradable: Able to decompose or break down through natural bacterial action, substances made of organic matter are
biodegradable.

Bleach: Ordinary laundry bleach is used in a mild water solution
as a soil fungicide.

Bolt: Term used to describe a plant that has gone to seed prematurely.

Bonsai: A very short or dwarfed plant.

Breaker box: Electrical circuit box having on/off switches rather
than fuses.

Breathe: Roots draw in or breathe oxygen, stomata draw in or
breathe carbon dioxide.

Bud blight: A withering condition that attacks flower buds.

Buffering: The ability of a substance to reduce shock and cushion against pH fluctuations. Many fertilizers contain buffering
agents.

Bulb: (1) The outer glass envelope or jacket that protects the arc
tube of an HID lamp and blocks UV light, (2) Clove or bulb of
garlic.

Calyx: The pod harboring female ovule and two protruding pistils, seed pod.

Carbon dioxide (CO_2): A colorless, odorless, tasteless gas in the
air necessary for plant life.

Carbohydrate: Neutral compound of carbon, hydrogen and oxygen. Sugar, starch and cellulose are carbohydrates.

Caustic: Capable of destroying, killing or eating away by chemical activity

Cell: The base structural unit that plants are made of, cells contain a nucleus, membrane and chloroplasts.

Cellulose: A complex carbohydrate that stiffens a plant; tough
stems contain stiff cellulose

CFM: Cubic feet per minute.

Chelate: combining nutrients in an atomic ring that is easy for
plants to absorb.

Chlorophyll: The green photosynthetic matter of plants.
Chlorophyll is found in the chloroplasts of a cell.

Chlorine: Chemical used to purify water.

Chloroplast: Containing chlorophyll.

Chlorosis: The condition of a sick plant with yellowing leaves
due to inadequate formation of chlorophyll Chlorosis is caused

by a nutrient deficiency, usually iron or imbalanced pH.

Circuit: A circular route traveled by electricity.

Clay: Soil made of very fine organic and mineral particles, clay is not suitable for container gardening.

Climate: The average condition of the weather in a garden room or outdoors.

Color spectrum: The band of colors (measured in nm) emitted by a light source.

Color tracer: A coloring agent that is added to many commercial fertilizers, so the horticulturist knows there is fertilizer in the solution. Peters has a blue color tracer.

Compaction: Soil condition that results from tightly packed soil; compacted soil allows for only marginal aeration and root penetration.

Companion planting: Planting garlic, marigolds, etc., along with other plants to discourage insect infestations.

Compost: A mixture of decayed organic matter, high in nutrients, compost must be at least one year old. When too young, decomposition uses nitrogen after sufficient decomposition, compost releases nitrogen.

Core: The transformer in the ballast is referred to as a core in HID lighting systems.

Cotyledon: Seed leaves, first leaves that appear on a plant.

Cross-pollinate: Pollinate two plants having different ancestry.

Cubic foot: volume measurement in feet: Width times length times height equals cubic feet.

Cutting: (1) Growing tip cut from a parent plant for asexual propagation (2) Cutting

Damping-off: Fungus disease that attacks young seedlings and cuttings causing stem to rot at base; over-watering is the main cause of damping-off.

Direct Current (DC): An electric current that flows in only one direction.

Deplete: Exhaust soil of nutrients, making in infertile: Once a soil is used it is depleted

Desiccate: Cause to dry up. Safer's Insecticidal Soap desiccates its victims.

Detergent: Liquid soap concentrate used as a: (1) wetting agent for sprays and water (2) pesticide. Note: Detergent must be totally organic to be safe for plants.

Dioecious: Having distinct male and female flowers.

Dome: The part of the HID outer bulb opposite the neck and threads.

Dome support: The spring-like brackets that mount the arc tube within the outer envelope.

Drainage: Way to empty soil of excess water: with good drainage, Water passes through soil evenly, promoting plant growth. With bad drainage water stands in soil, drowning roots.

Dripline: A line around a plant directly under its outermost branch tips: Roots seldom grow beyond the drip-line.

Drip system: A very efficient watering system that employs a main hose with small water emitters. Water is metered out of the emitters, one drop at a time.

Dry ice: A cold, white substance formed when carbon dioxide is compressed and cooled; dry ice changes into CO_2 gas at room temperatures.

Dry well: Drain hole, filled with rocks.

Electrode: A conductor used to establish electrical arc or contact with non-metallic part of circuit.

Elongate: Grow in length.

Envelope: Outer protective bulb or jacket of a lamp.

Equinox: The point at which the sun crosses the equator and day and night are each 12 hours long; the equinox occurs twice a year, in spring and fall.

Extension cord: Extra electrical cord that must be 14-gauge or larger (i.e. 12- or 10-gauge).

Feed: Fertilize.

Female: Pistilate, ovule, seed-producing.

Fertigate: To fertilize and irrigate at the same time.

Fertilizer burn: Over-fertilization: First leaf tips burn (turn brown) then leaves curl.

Fixture: Electrical fitting used to hold electric components.

Flat: Shallow (three-inch) deep container, often 18 by 24 or 10 x 20 inches with good drainage, used to start seedlings or cuttings.

Flat white: Very reflective, whitest white paint available. Magnesium or titanium white, semi-gloss is a favorite.

Fluorescent lamp: Electric lamp using a tube coated with fluorescent material, which has low lumen and heat output; a fluorescent lamp is excellent for rooting cuttings.

Foliage: The leaves or more generally, the green part of a plant.

Foliar feeding: Misting fertilizer solution which is absorbed by the foliage.

Fritted: Fused or embedded in glass or in semi-soluble material like calcium carbonate. Fritted trace elements (FTE) are long-lasting and do not leach out easily.

Fungicide: A product that destroys or inhibits fungus.

Fungistat: A product that inhibits fungus keeping it in check.

Fungus: A lower plant lacking chlorophyll which may attack green plants; mold, rust, mildew and mushrooms are fungi.

Fuse: Electrical safety device consisting of a metal that MELTS and interrupts the circuit when circuit is overloaded.

Fuse box: Box containing fuses that control electric circuits.

GPM: Gallons per minute

General purpose fertilizer: See: ALL-PURPOSE FERTILIZER.

Gene: Part of a chromosome that influences the development of a plant; genes are inherited through sexual propagation.

Genetic make-up: The genes inherited from parent plants; genetic make-up is the most important factor dictating vigor.

Halide: Binary compound of a (halogens) with an electropositive element(s).

Halogen: Any of the elements fluorine, chlorine, bromine, iodine and astatine existing in a free state; halogens are in the arc tube of a halide lamp.

Hermaphrodite: One plant having both male and female flowers; the breeding of hermaphrodite is hard to control.

Hertz (Hz): A unit of a frequency that cycles one time each second: A home with a 60 hertz AC current cycles 60 times per second.

HID: High Intensity Discharge.

Honeydew: A sticky, honey-like substance secreted onto foliage by aphids, scale and mealy bugs.

Hood: reflective cover of a HID lamp; a large, white HOOD is very reflective.

HOR: The abbreviation stamped on some HID bulbs meaning they may be burned in a horizontal position.

Horizontal: Parallel to the horizon, ground or floor.

Hormone: Chemical substance that controls the growth and development of a plant. Root-inducing hormones help cuttings root.

Hose bib: Water outlet containing an on/off valve.

Humidity (relative): Ratio between the amount of moisture in the air and the greatest amount of moisture the air could hold at the same temperature.

Humus: Dark, fertile, partially decomposed plant or animal matter; humus forms the organic portion of the soil.

Hybrid: An offspring from two plants of different breeds, variety or genetic make-up.

Hydrated lime: Instantly soluble lime, used to raise or sweeten soil.

Hydrogen: Light, colorless, odorless gas; hydrogen combines with OXYGEN to form water.

Hygrometer: Instrument for measuring relative humidity in the atmosphere. A hygrometer will save time, frustration and money.

Inbred: (True breed) offspring of plants of the same breed or ancestry.

Inert: Chemically non-reactive; inert growing mediums make it easy to control the chemistry of the nutrient solution.

Intensity: The magnitude of light energy per unit; intensity diminishes the farther away from the source.

Jacket: Protective outer bulb or envelope of lamp.

Jiffy 7 pellet: Compressed peat moss wrapped in an expandable plastic casing. When moistened, a Jiffy 7 pellet expands into a small pot that is used to start seeds or cuttings.

Kilowatt-hour: Measure of electricity used per hour; a 1000-watt HID uses one kilowatt in one hour.

Lacewing: Beneficial insect that preys on aphids.

Leach: Dissolve or wash out soluble components of soil by heavy watering.

Leader: See MERISTEM.

Leaf curl: Leaf malformation due to over-watering, over fertilization, lack of magnesium, insect or fungus damage or negative tropism.

Leaflet: Small immature leaf.

Leggy: Abnormally tall, with sparse foliage; leggyness of a plant is usually caused by lack of light.

Life cycle: A series of growth stages through which plant must pass in its natural lifetime; the stages for an annual plant are seed, seedling, vegetative and floral.

Light mover: A device that moves a lamp back and forth or in a circle across the ceiling of a garden room to provide more even distribution of light.

Lime: Used in the form of DOLOMITE or HYDRATED LIME to raise and stabilize soil pH.

Litmus paper: Chemically sensitive paper used for testing pH.

Loam: Organic soil mixture of crumbly clay, silt and sand.

Lumen: Measurement of light output: One lumen is equal to the amount of light emitted by one candle that falls on one square foot of surface located one foot away from one candle.

Macro-nutrient: One or all of the primary nutrients N-P-K or the secondary nutrients magnesium and calcium.

Mean: Average throughout life; HIDs are rated in mean lumens.

Meristem: Tip of plant growth, branch tip.

Micro- nutrients: Also referred to as TRACE ELEMENTS, including S, Fe, Mn, B, Mo, Zn and Cu.

Millimeter: Thousandth of a meter approximately 04. inch.

Moisture meter: An electronic device that measures the exact moisture content of soil at any given point.

Monochromatic: Producing only one color; LP sodium lamps are monochromatic.

Mulch: A protective covering of organic compost, old leaves, etc.; indoors, mulch keeps soil too moist and possible fungus could result.

Nanometer: .000001 meter, nm is used as a scale to measure electromagnetic wave lengths of light; color and light spectrums are expressed in nanometers (nm).

Necrosis: Localized death of a plant part.

Neck: Tubular glass end of the HID bulb, attached to the threads.

Nutrient: Plant food, essential elements N-P-K, secondary and trace elements fundamental to plant life.

Ohm's Power Law: A law that expresses the strength of an electric current; Volts times Amperes equals watts.

Organic: Made of, or derived from or related to living organisms. In agriculture organic means "natural". In chemistry, organic means "a molecule or substance that contains carbon".

Outbred: See hybrid.

Overload: Load to excess: A 20-amp circuit drawing 17 amps is overloaded.

Ovule: A plant's egg found within the calyx, it contains all the female genes; when fertilized, an ovule will grow into a seed.

Oxygen: Tasteless, colorless element, necessary in soil to sustain plant life as well as animal life.

Parasite: Organism that lives on or in another host organism; fungus is a parasite.

Peat: Partially decomposed vegetation (usually moss) with slow decay due to extreme moisture and cold.

Perennial: A plant, such as a tree or shrub, that completes its life cycle over several years.

pH: A scale from 1 to 14 that measures the acid-to-alkaline balance a growing medium (or anything); in general plants grow best in a range of 5.5 to 6.8 pH.

pH tester: Electronic instrument or chemical used to find where soil or water is on the pH scale.

Photometrics: The study of light, especially color.

Phosphor coating: Internal bulb coating that diffuses light and is responsible for various color outputs.

Photoperiod: The relationship between the length of light and dark in a 24-hour period.

Photosynthesis: The building of chemical compounds (carbohydrates) from light energy, water and carbon dioxide.

Phototropism: The specific movement of a plant part toward a light source.

Pigment: The substance in paint or anything that absorbs light, producing (reflecting) the same color as the pigment.

Pollen: Fine, yellow, dust-like micro-spores containing male genes.

Pod seed: A dry calyx containing a mature or maturing seed.

Pot-bound: Bound, stifled or inhibited from normal growth, by the confines of a container; root system becomes pot-bound.

Power surge: Interruption or change in intensity of electricity.

Primary nutrients: N-P-K.

Propagate: (1) Sexual: produce a seed by breeding different male and a female flowers (2) Asexual: to produce a plant by taking cuttings.

Prune: Alter the shape and growth pattern of a plant by cutting stems and shoots. A fruit that gives you diarrhea.

PVC pipe: Plastic (polyvinyl chloride) pipe that is easy to work with, readily available and used to pipe water into a garden room or make a watering wand.

Pyrethrum: Natural insecticide made from the blossoms of various chrysanthemums; Raids' Pyrethrum is the most effective natural spider mite exterminator.

Rejuvenate: Restore youth; a mature plant, having completed its life cycle (flowering), may be stimulated by a new 18 hour photoperiod, to rejuvenate or produce new vegetative growth.

Root-bound: See POT BOUND.

Salt: Crystalline compound that results from improper pH or toxic buildup of fertilizer. Salt will burn plants, preventing them from absorbing nutrients. Mineral salts-nutrients used to supply elements in hydroponic formulas.

Secondary nutrients: Calcium (Ca) and magnesium (Mg).

Short circuit: Condition that results when wires cross and form. a circuit. A short circuit will blow fuses.

Socket: Threaded, wired holder for a bulb.

Soluble: Able to be dissolved in water.

Spore: Seed-like offspring of a fungus.

Sprout: (1) A recently germinated seed (2) Small new growth of leaf or stem.

Square feet (sq. ft.): Length (in feet) times width equals square feet.

Stamen: Male, pollen-producing.

Starch: Complex carbohydrate: Starch is manufactured and stored food.

Sterilize: Make sterile (super-clean) by removing dirt, germs and bacteria.

Stroboscopic effect: A quick pulsating or flashing of a lamp.

Stress: A physical or chemical factor that causes extra exertion by plants; a stressed plant will not grow as well as a non-stressed plant.

Stomata: Small mouth-like or nose-like openings (pores) on leaf underside, responsible for transpiration and many other life functions; the millions of stomata, must be kept very clean to function properly.

Sugar: Food product of a plant. Carbohydrates that contain hydrocarbon chain.

Super-bloom: A common name for fertilizer high in phosphorus that promotes flower formation and growth

Synthesis: Production of a substance, such as chlorophyll, by uniting light energy and elements or chemical compounds.

Sump: Reservoir or receptacle that serves as a drain or holder for hydroponic nutrient solutions.

Tap root: The main or primary root that grows from the seed; lateral roots will branch off the tap root.

Teflon tape: Tape that is extremely useful to help seal all kinds of pipe joints. I like Teflon tape better than putty.

Tepid: Warm 70 to 80 degrees F (21 to 27 degrees C); always use tepid water around plants to facilitate chemical processes and ease shock.

Terminal bud: Bud at the growing end of the main stem.

Thin: cull or weed out weak, slow growing seedlings.

Toxic life: The amount of time a pesticide or fungicide remains active.

Transformer: A devise in the ballast that transforms electric power from one voltage to another.

Transpire: Give off water vapor and by-products via the stomata and carbon dioxide intake at the leaves.

Trellis: Frame of small boards (lattice) that trains or supports plants.

True breed: See INBRED.

Tungsten: A heavy, hard metal with a high melting point which conducts electricity well; tungsten is used for a filament in tungsten halogen and incandescent lamps.

Ultraviolet: Light with very short wave lengths, out of the visible spectrum, past the blue-violet.

Variety: Strain, phenotype (see strain).

Vent: Opening such as a window or door that allows the circulation of fresh air.

Ventilation: Circulation of fresh air, fundamental to healthy indoor garden. An exhaust fan creates excellent ventilation.

Vertical: Up and down perpendicular to the horizontal.

Wetting agent: compound that reduces the droplet size and lowers the surface tension of the water, making it wetter. Liquid concentrate dish soap is a good wetting agent if it is biodegradable.

Wick: Part of a passive hydroponic system using a wick suspended in the nutrient solution, the nutrients pass up the wick and are absorbed by the medium and roots.

Index

Gardening Indoors